Voices of the English Reformation

Voices of the English Reformation

A Sourcebook

Edited by
JOHN N. KING

PENN

University of Pennsylvania Press

Philadelphia

Publication of this volume was supported by a grant from
The Ohio State University.

10   9   8   7   6   5   4   3   2   1

Published by
University of Pennsylvania Press
Philadelphia, Pennsylvania 19104-4011

Library of Congress Cataloging-in-Publication Data

Voices of the English Reformation : a sourcebook / edited by John N. King.
    p.   cm.
    ISBN 0-8122-3794-3 (cloth : alk. paper)—ISBN 0-8122-1877-9 (pbk. : alk. paper)
    Includes bibliographical references (p.) and index.
    1. Reformation—England—Sources. 2. England—Church history—16th century—
Sources. 3. England—Church history—17th century—Sources. I. King, John N., 1945–
BR375 .V7   2004
274.2′06—dc22   2004052002

In honor of Barbara Kiefer Lewalski

Contents

Illustrations

Maps

Figures

Note on Texts

This collection aims to recover literary and extraliterary texts of the English Reformation, which have been unduly neglected for a variety of historiographical and cultural reasons (see Introduction). Edited from the original publications, each text is modernized in order to render it accessible to present-day readers. Contractions, abbreviations, and special symbols are expanded. Square brackets indicate conjectural reconstruction or editorial additions. Roman numerals are spelled out. Titles may be abridged. Commas replace virgules, and punctuation may be very lightly altered for the sake of sense. Capitalization and italics in early printed books are ignored unless they are essential to the sense of passages. Notes provide translations of nonbiblical quotations only when they are lacking in the original publications. They contain citations for biblical quotations. Unless otherwise noted, London is the place of publication in pre-1900 book titles, and reference is to first editions.

The introductions and explanatory notes contain essential information and definitions of isolated archaic word usages. The Glossary contains definitions of archaic words that occur twice or more. Introductions to the specific texts refer the reader to textual sources, modern editions, and recommended secondary scholarship that is typically listed in the Select Bibliography.

This book incorporates two kinds of annotation. Notes in conventional numerical order contain word meanings and factual information supplied by the editor. A small number of alphabetized notes at the conclusion of individual selections contain transcriptions of marginal glosses (place indicators and text references are omitted) printed in the original sources. Cross-references are keyed to the Contents of this book. The Appendix summarizes information about important figures and events.

Abbreviations

FQ   Edmund Spenser. *The Faerie Queene*. Edited by A. C. Hamilton et al. 2nd ed. London: Longman, 2001.

STC   *A Short-Title Catalogue of Books Printed in England, Scotland, and Ireland, and of English Books Printed Abroad, 1475–1640*, compiled by A. W. Pollard and G. R. Redgrave; 2nd ed. revised and enlarged by W. A. Jackson, F. S. Ferguson, and Katharine F. Pantzer. 3 vols. London: Bibliographical Society, 1976–91.

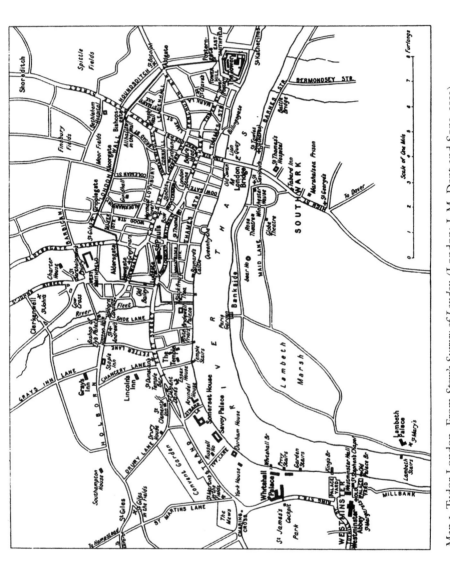

Map 1. Tudor London. From *Stow's Survey of London* (London: J. M. Dent and Sons, 1912).

Map 2. England. Adapted from an outline map provided by the Geography Department of Brigham Young University.

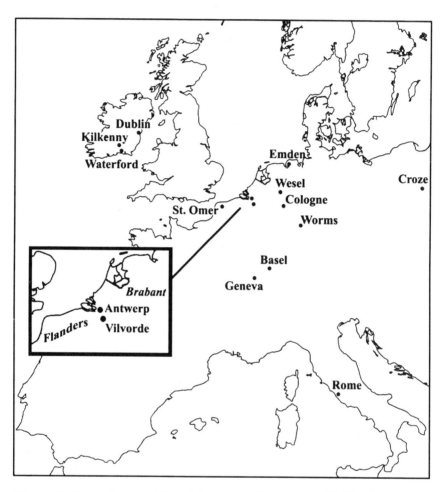

Map 3. Northwest Europe. Adapted from an outline map provided by the
Geography Department of Brigham Young University.

INTRODUCTION

Voices of the English Reformation juxtaposes utterances by Protestants and Roman Catholics, laypeople and clerics, women and men, commoners and queens. This selection of verse, drama, and fictional and nonfictional prose spans the different phases of the English Reformation, which revolutionized sixteenth- and seventeenth-century religious, intellectual, and social life. Many of these texts are here edited for the first time, and virtually all of them are inaccessible in standard collections. The selections include a large body of highly readable satires, allegories, martyrologies, and personal narratives that give rise to questions concerning subjectivity, conscience and consciousness, the status of women, gender conflict, canon formation, resistance to unjust authority, and related issues of pressing concern. No comparable collection serves the needs of students of British literature or scholars concerned with cross-disciplinary connections among the literature, history, politics, and religion of early modern England.[1]

William Tyndale's initial attempt to publish his translation of the New Testament (1525) and the death of Queen Elizabeth I (1603) define the chronological limits of this book. Tyndale espoused the appeal lodged by Erasmus in *Paraclesis*, the introduction to his 1516 Greek edition of the New Testament, for translation of the Bible into vernacular languages so that "even the lowliest women" could understand the scriptures for themselves. Erasmus advocated the popular dissemination and understanding of biblical texts: "Would that, as a result, the farmer sing some portion of them at the plow, the weaver hum some parts of them to the movement of his shuttle, the traveler lighten the weariness of the journey with stories of this kind."[2] Tyndale's translation exerted a seminal influence upon gospeling poets who celebrated the sagacity of artisans and plowmen during the reigns of Henry VIII and Edward VI, in addition to evangelical writers active later in the sixteenth century.

Despite the accusation that "Luther hatched the egg that Erasmus laid," the Dutch scholar never separated from the Church of Rome. Tyndale followed Erasmus in the humanistic return *ad fontes* ("to the sources"), but his translation presupposes distinctively Protestant tenets, most notably the Lutheran principle of *sola scriptura* ("scripture alone"). Under the influence of Luther, Tyndale led the way in attacking Roman Catholic belief in the doctrine of transubstantiation, auricular confession, clerical celibacy, and "unwritten traditions" added during centuries of Christian tradition. In addition to insisting on the grounding of worship upon scriptural sources, Tyndale's biblical prefaces, annotations, and tracts follow the Epistles of St. Paul in assuming the doctrines of justification by faith alone, unmerited election, and irresistible grace. These principles gave rise to a Protestant paradigm of salvation. It propounded that the divine gift of grace overcame the innate depravity of humanity by leading elect individuals to recognize a divine calling (vocation) by means of a conversion experience, repentance (as opposed to penitence), adoption by God, sanctification, and glorification after death.[3]

Until recent years, teacher-scholars have given inadequate notice to the literature and culture of the different phases of the English Reformation. The renewal of interest in religion as a formative component of early modern literature and culture affords an occasion for exploring this crucial but neglected field, thereby challenging standard, but outdated, categories that organize existing anthologies and concepts of periodicity that underlie them. Bridging the late medieval and early modern eras, *Voices of the English Reformation* demonstrates important continuities while also illustrating historical and cultural disruptions that distinguish these times. By satisfying demand for texts written by or containing the voices of long-forgotten women, satirists, and apocalyptic poets, this collection suggests avenues for expanding the early modern canon both by calling attention to important but little-known works and by illuminating unfamiliar contexts for well-known medieval and early modern texts such as *Piers Plowman* and *The Faerie Queene*. This book should enable both students and specialists to comprehend how literary and extraliterary texts of different phases of the English Reformation helped to spawn masterworks by William Shakespeare, Christopher Marlowe, Edmund Spenser, and Sir Philip Sidney.

By providing access to eloquent, humorous, or homely voices of sixteenth-century English men and women, this collection demonstrates how the literary Renaissance under Queen Elizabeth I absorbed struggles to redefine self and society in religious terms. Texts in the present collection range from satirical dialogues in which canny lay people bluntly mock the mystifying ignorance of pompous clerics to scenes from morality plays in which bawdy allegorical Vices symbolic of the old religion entrap unwary youths, despite the counsel of ministerial Virtues. Protestant satirists employed verbal violence, scurrility, and bawdy innuendo in order to attack religious "error," on the ground that what is truly unseemly is blasphemy and unbelief rather than indecorous language. Their employment of sharp-edged wit to mock clerical extravagance and religious formalism contradicts the stock view of early Protestants as humorless opponents of fiction and drama. This book also offers a generous selection of edifying and entertaining stories from *Acts and Monuments of These Latter and Perilous Days*, which John Foxe compiled in four increasingly massive editions published between 1563 and 1583. Foxe's compendium remains inaccessible to all but dedicated specialists, even though it was one of the most widely read and influential English books of the Elizabethan age. Citations will refer to it hereafter as the *Book of Martyrs*, the popular title in use from the beginning.

Resurgence of interest in religion and literature has spread beyond Protestant writings to the challenge posed by the Roman Catholic opposition. This collection thus acknowledges the intensity, integrity, and importance of a religious opposition whose defeat was by no means certain through the end of the Elizabethan age. It therefore includes Catholic texts, both early and late, which have been neglected by generations of scholars who view the English Reformation in terms of "triumph" over superstitious ignorance. This inclusion enables a view of early modern England as a diverse religious culture in which dissent was present, albeit problematic.

This book encourages consideration of gender issues and the superimposition of patriarchal values on writings by, for, and about women. The assertion by both low-born and high-born Protestant women of their autonomous right to read and interpret the Bible represents a radical extension of the appeal lodged by William Tyndale. The ideal of feminine chastity went unchallenged, but Reformation women nevertheless questioned patriarchal expectations concerning their silence and obedience. During an age when few men, and even fewer women, could read, biblical study led figures ranging from Catherine Willoughby, a duchess dowager, to Anne Askew, a gentlewoman, and Alice Driver, a peasant, to challenge the clerical monopoly on scriptural interpretation and to oppose the doctrine of transubstantiation and the Roman-rite Mass on grounds that many churchmen condemned as heretical. Even Catherine Parr, who was queen consort to Henry VIII and one-time regent of England, Lady Jane Grey, who succeeded to the throne at the death of Edward VI, and Princess Elizabeth, who was heir apparent to Mary I, were not immune to conservative opposition to feminine interpretation of the Bible. Controversy existed concerning the nature of feminine piety and martyrdom, despite praise of the "true" piety of these women by John Bale and John Foxe. Indeed, Robert Parsons, a Jesuit pamphleteer, attempted to demolish the reputations of women such as Askew and Parr on grounds that they were unchaste dissidents whose loquacious resistance to the authority of fathers, husbands, or clerics led them into proselytizing and heresy.

By complementing existing collections of historical documents,[4] this book should enable historians to enhance their understanding of the impact of literature upon history. This collection is in tune with the searching re-evaluation of English Reformation history triggered by revisionist studies published during the last two decades.[5] This scholarship has questioned long-standing understanding of the English Reformation as a time when religious changes imposed from above during the reigns of Henry VIII, Edward VI, and Elizabeth I were met with broad popular acceptance.[6] The revisionists instead stress the haphazard course of multiple Reformations that took place during the Tudor era, which were grounded upon dynastic accidents. Few historians now deny that the effort to introduce genuinely Protestant theology and worship remained a minority movement that met resistance from recusants, nonconformists, and a Pelagian majority indifferent to predestinarian theology until the end of the sixteenth century.[7]

Although revisionist historians have rehabilitated the vitality and strength of late medieval Christianity and the effort to restore Roman Catholicism during the reign of Mary I, they offer inadequate acknowledgment of how the triumphalist "Whiggish" vision of the transformation of a corrupt ecclesiastical establishment is rooted in the historiographical revisionism of sixteenth-century Protestant propagandists, whose views attain their fullest expression in Foxe's *Book of Martyrs*. Recognition of the centrality of English Protestant book culture takes on great significance at the present moment, as revisionists interpret early English Protestantism as a relentlessly destructive, if not malevolent, force.[8] In focusing on the smashing of saints' images, shattering of stained-glass windows, dismantling of altars, and despoliation of shrines, these scholars maintain an embarrassing silence about the contribution of the printing press to the production of richly diverse print culture grounded upon William Tyndale's scriptural translations and geared to readers (and hearers) at all social levels. Attention to the multiple voices of sixteenth-century English Protestants *and* Catholics addresses the failure of revisionist historians to explain how the English Reformation transformed English politics and religion despite intense resistance at all social levels.[9]

Texts selected for *Voices of the English Reformation* are enmeshed in divergent developments in sixteenth-century English politics and religion. They begin with the introduction of Erasmian and Lutheran ideas that influenced William Tyndale. Although Henry VIII was anything but a Protestant, he undertook a bitter assault on papal authority when he initiated England's schism from the Church of Rome on dynastic grounds. Declaring himself Supreme Head of the Church of England, Henry retained the sacramental system of the late medieval church. Nevertheless, he did embark upon the Dissolution of the Monasteries and permitted reading of the English Bible under the auspices of his Protestant deputies, Thomas Cromwell, vicegerent for religious affairs, and Thomas Cranmer, archbishop of Canterbury. The Pilgrimage of Grace (1536), a popular rebellion against religious innovation, contributed to Cromwell's downfall and to a conservative reaction implemented by the Act of Six Articles (1539), a harsh penal statute detested by Protestants.

The introduction of genuinely Protestant theology and reduction of allowable sacraments to the two endorsed by Luther, baptism and the Lord's Supper, awaited Cranmer's introduction of an English order of worship under Edward VI. The political instability of the reign of the boy king, whose government was dominated by Protestant aristocrats, was compounded by controversies concerning ecclesiastical vestments and the nature of Christ's presence in the communion service. The importation of radical ideas of Continental theologians such as Ulrich Zwingli, who advocated memorialism, and Heinrich Bullinger inspired these disputes. When Edward died in 1553, Protestant lords resorted to placing Lady Jane Grey on the throne in order to perpetuate their regime, but this attempted coup d'état failed. Mary Tudor then became queen through popular acclamation and attempted to return England to Roman Catholicism. Had she lived longer and given birth to an heir, England might have remained a Catholic nation.

The long reign of Elizabeth I, who acceded the throne at the death of Mary, witnessed the implantation of an ambiguous fusion of Protestant theology and Catholic ritual. The institutionalization of consensual theology based upon the ideas of John Calvin and the Rhineland reformers did not represent a Protestant "triumph." Indeed, the Elizabethan Compromise met popular resistance from Roman Catholics, including recusants, church papists, and missionary priests who participated in the English Mission that began circa 1580. After the advent of Puritan protest against clerical vestments and retention of ceremonial ritual during the 1560s and 1570s, presbyterians began to advocate congregational autonomy in place of the official episcopalian government of the English church.

In offering opposing accounts of the Woman Clothed with the Sun and the Whore of Babylon from the Book of Revelation, the opening section of *Voices of the English Reformation*, "Bible Translation and Commentary," provides a case study of the ways in which interpretation of the Bible was contested during the Reformation as well as the importance of Biblical controversy to the literature of the period. Section One exemplifies the plain vernacular style of William Tyndale's New Testament and its impact upon later translations, both Protestant and Catholic. The wording of later English versions, not the least of which was the 1611 Authorized Version (the "King James Version"), assimilated significant portions of Tyndale's wording. *The Obedience of a Christian Man*, his major prose composition, adapts Erasmus's seminal appeal for translation of the Bible into the vernacular so that ordinary readers may understand it for themselves. Thomas More challenges this view in *The Confutation of Tyndale's Answer*, which insists on the church's mediatory role in biblical instruction. A diametrically opposed view is drawn from *The Image of Both Churches*, an influential commentary by John Bale, who interprets the Woman Clothed with the Sun and the Whore of Babylon as respective figures for the "poor persecuted church of Christ" versus the "proud painted church of the Pope" (Figure 2). The polemical ideas of this renegade friar undergo assimilation into annotations added by the Puritan editors of the Geneva Bible, an unauthorized version favored by Shakespeare, Spenser, Sidney, and Marlowe. Directly or indirectly, Bale's *Image* influenced poetry written by these poets in addition to that by Donne, Milton, and others. The Rheims New Testament produced by English Catholic exiles rejects Bale's interpretation in the course of establishing a Roman Catholic alternative to Protestant translations in the Tyndale tradition. In attacking Tyndale's translation, Robert Parsons, the Jesuit commentator, discusses the danger of falling into heresy through Bible reading without mediation by priests.

The section on "Selfhood and Obedience to Church and State" explores the impact of the vernacular Bible on Reformation selfhood and both individual and collective obedience to political and religious governance. It begins with a selection from Tyndale's *Obedience of a Christian Man* that responds to charges that early English Protestants were subversive enemies of the state. Tyndale articulates seminal views that subjects are obliged to obey monarchical authority and that the papacy lacks authority over temporal rulers. This section also includes a portion of Hugh Latimer's *Sermon on the Plowers*, an outstanding example of native plain style by the spiritual father of the English Reformation. This sermon assimilates the imagery of biblical pastoral and the plainspoken voice of the husbandman associated with *Piers Plowman* into a stirring call for religious and social reform. Latimer's patron, Thomas Cranmer, oversaw production of the *Book of Homilies*, a sermon collection authorized under Edward VI. In conjunction with the *Book of Common Prayer*, this text revolutionized services of the Church of England by introducing an English order of worship after a millennium of ecclesiastical Latin. Cranmer's eloquent prose style influenced the emergence of an "easy and plain" vernacular style that enabled the understanding, through reading or hearing, of both aristocrats and commoners. Miles Hogarde's *Displaying of Protestants* countered reformist ideology and defended the burning of Protestants as heretics during the reign of Mary I.

The 1580s witnessed challenges to the Elizabethan Reformation by Roman Catholic exiles. After Queen Elizabeth's renewal in modified form of the settlement of religion imposed under Edward VI, Robert Parsons defended the authority of the Roman Catholic Church and rejected the Protestant understanding of the operation of faith and works in the *Book of Homilies*. William Cecil's *Execution of Justice in England* harks back to Tyndale's *Obedience of a Christian Man* in demanding absolute obedience of subject to ruler. Cecil defends the execution of missionary priests not as heretics, but as traitors. In *A True, Sincere and Modest Defense of English Catholics*, William Allen mirrors Tyndale's doctrine of obedience in an eloquent rejection of Cecil's legalistic argument that Jesuits suffer painful deaths not as martyrs, but as traitors loyal to the pope as a foreign sovereign.

Examples of drama, poetry, and fiction in Section Three, "Allegories of the English Reformations," demonstrate the profound influence of English Bible translation upon Reformation literature. These selections bring to life confusions inherent in a world in which competing churches lodged apparently equal claims to spiritual authority and in which even concerned laypeople or theologians could readily fall into "error." John Bale's *Comedy Concerning Three Laws* is a moral interlude of the kind performed by the composer's itinerant dramatic troupe, which performed under the auspices of Thomas Cromwell. This play personifies conflict between Vices subservient to Antichrist and "godly" Virtues in order to allegorize Protestant belief in the doctrine of justification by faith alone and worship based upon the Bible, rather than upon "innovations" introduced during the course of Christian history. Robert Crowley's *Philargyrie of Great Britain* satirizes failures of the Henrician Reformation, notably the broken promise that wealth seized during the dissolution of the monasteries would undergo distribution to impoverished commoners. Richard Weaver's *Lusty Juventus* is an education-of-youth play based upon the theme of Jesus' Parable of the Prodigal Son. It exploits conventions and techniques of late medieval morality plays in order to allegorize Protestant theology of salvation imposed as official doctrine during Edward VI's reign. William Baldwin, who worked in the printing trade, constructs a fantastic world of talking cats in order to satirize the secret observance of Roman Catholic devotion in *Beware the Cat*. He later edited *A Mirror for Magistrates*, an influential collection of tragedies concerning the downfall of high-ranking individuals that molded Shakespeare's history plays. Miles Hogarde's *Assault of the Sacrament of the Altar* launches a counter-attack on Bale, Crowley, and their fellow believers. Written by an artisan poet active during the reign of Mary I, this text defends the Church of Rome and condones the burning of heretics whom Foxe's *Book of Martyrs* praises as "true" saints and martyrs.

A set of quasi-dramatic writings concerning the introduction of religious reforms are assembled under the heading of "Laity Versus Clergy:

Dialogue and Monologue." In Luke Shepherd's *John Bon and Master Parson*, the seemingly naive questions and affected humility of a skeptical rustic afford thin disguise for an agrarian radical who, in the manner of William Tyndale (see 6.5.A), mocks an unlearned priest incapable of defending religious orthodoxy. *Doctor Double Ale* caricatures clerical ignorance exemplified by a drunken curate who, in the manner of Chaucer's Pardoner, haunts an alehouse where he mumbles a ludicrous jumble of dimly remembered Latin liturgical phrases. Anticlericalism informs a Puritan critique of the Church of England under Elizabeth I in *A Pleasant Dialogue Between a Soldier of Berwick and an English Chaplain*, composed by Anthony Gilby, a contributor to the Geneva Bible. Gilby stages a debate between a shrewd layperson and a formalistic cleric in order to attack the Elizabethan retention of ritualistic practices associated with the Church of Rome. The vigorous dialogue in George Gifford's *Country Divinity* responds to conservative resistance that the Puritan curate encountered during his career as a parson at a rural parish. Gifford reverses the dynamic of earlier anticlericalism by assigning to a Puritan cleric the task of educating ignorant laypeople resistant to religious reform. Unlike Gifford's dialogue, which does not advocate separation from the Church of England, a pamphlet ascribed pseudonymously to Martin Marprelate, but probably written by Job Throckmorton, opposes the episcopal hierarchy of the state church. *Oh Read Over Dr. John Bridges, For It Is a Worthy Work* constitutes the opening blast of the Marprelate controversy. Recalling the raciness of anticlerical satires by John Bale and others, this highly ironic tract transfers attacks formerly directed at Roman Catholic prelates to Elizabethan bishops.

Competition between iconoclastic destruction and reconstruction of drama represents the focus of Section 5, "Theatrical Controversy." This opposition attests to Protestant uneasiness, indeed suspicion, of products of the literary imagination. The prologue to Lewis Wager's dramatic interlude, *The Life and Repentance of Mary Magdalene*, acknowledges that hostility to drama existed during the Edwardian Reformation. Despite long-lasting stereotypes that still stigmatize early Protestants as sullen opponents of drama, poetry, and the visual arts, a treatise by Martin Bucer, a German theologian who was a professor at Cambridge University during Edward VI's reign, contains an eloquent defense of drama. The gathering strength of resistance to poetry (i.e., fiction) midway through the reign of Elizabeth I inspired Sir Philip Sidney's *Defense of Poesy*, which asserts that secular fiction is a suitable companion to exalted forms of divine poetry such as the Psalms. Sidney responded to the views of Puritans such as Philip Stubbes, whose *Anatomy of Abuses* attacks drama on the grounds that it inspires idleness and sexual transgression.

Section 6, "Biography, Autobiography, and Martyrology," contains poignant personal narratives composed by Protestant and Catholic men and women. Anne Askew's *Latter Examination* is a moving autobiographical account of her interrogation, torture, trial, and condemnation to death as a heretic. *The Vocation of John Bale* is an animated autobiographical narrative concerning Bale's experience as a missionary bishop in Roman Catholic Ireland. Published after his flight into exile at the accession of Mary I, this text functions in certain respects as a precursor of the spiritual autobiographies that would later come into fashion in Puritan circles. *The Path of Obedience* by James Cancellar, a chaplain to Queen Mary, offers a sharp rebuttal to Bale's claim to status as a latter-day saint whose career resembles that of Saint Paul.

Askew's prison narrative accords with the redefinition of saint's life or martyrology by John Bale, its first editor, and John Foxe, who assimilated it with omissions and alterations but without Bale's commentary into the *Book of Martyrs*. Both Foxe and Bale rejected medieval representations of miracle-working saints as intermediaries between believers and Christ. These editors instead styled martyrology as narrative focused on believers whose testimonials of faith led to execution. Their view affords a marked contrast to that of William Roper, whose *Life of Sir Thomas More* adheres to older definitions of sainthood in idealizing his late father-in-law in the manner of a saint of old, such as Saint Anthony or Saint Jerome. He makes little mention of More's writings, in contrast to Bale and Foxe, who stress the written testimonials of Protestant martyrs. Needless to say, the sanctification of More by Roper and other biographers failed to convince Foxe, who portrays the onetime lord chancellor of England as a persecutor who abused heretics at his household at Chelsea.

In a martyrology central to the *Book of Martyrs*, Foxe's life of William Tyndale affords a pronounced alternative to Roman Catholic lives of Thomas More. By contrast to their rich descriptions of More's ironic wit, friendships, and family life, Tyndale's personal life remains enigmatic. Foxe and his sources idealize him as a guileless innocent who sacrificed family life, wealth, and well being because of his commitment to translation of the Bible into the vernacular. In addition to his English New Testament and partial translation of the Old Testament, Tyndale's *monuments* are his biblical prefaces and polemical tracts such as the *Obedience of a Christian Man*. The *Book of Martyrs* contains a host of other narratives, including a vivid account of the burning of Hugh Latimer, the aged preacher, and Nicholas Ridley, the bishop of London deposed at the outset of the reign of Mary I. Although it contributes to Protestant patriarchal discourse, an important subgroup among its many narratives is by or about women. Examples include both the examination and burning of Alice Driver, a peasant who outwits male interrogators in the manner of Anne Askew, and a romantic thriller about the escape from England of the Dowager Duchess of Suffolk. The experience of both women accords with the strict sense of *martyr*, a word that denotes an individual who testifies to religious faith to the point of death, if necessary.

Section 6 concludes with writings by recusants and Jesuit missionary priests, which reverse the picture of Roman Catholic "peril" represented in the *Book of Martyrs*. Poetry by Chidiock Tichborne, a member of the Babington Plot to assassinate Queen Elizabeth, reflects circumstances leading up to his delivery of a moving speech prior to his hanging, drawing, and quartering at Tyburn. The poignantly antithetical style of "Tichborne's Lament" affords a touching counterpoint to satirical verse by poets such as Luke Shepherd and Edmund Spenser. As a member of the English Mission initiated by Edmund Campion and Robert Parsons, Robert Southwell composed *An Epistle of Comfort*, an eloquent devotional classic, to inspire persecuted recusants to maintain religious faith. Poems by this Jesuit martyr complement Tichborne's lyrics at the same time that they rival well-known verse by John Donne and George Herbert. Robert Parsons, who directed the English Mission from abroad following Campion's execution by hanging, drawing, and quartering, published a host of pamphlets including *A Treatise of the Three Conversions of England*. It singles out Anne Askew and Catherine Parr for criticism as unruly women and surly heretics, in addition to initiating an attack on the historical accuracy of the *Book of Martyrs* that has endured into modern times.

Voices of the English Reformation concludes with "Queenly Pageantry and Texts," a section that brings to life a unique moment in the latter half of the sixteenth century when the religious convictions of Roman Catholic and Protestant queens altered the course of English and Scottish history. Pietistic writings by Lady Jane Grey, the "nine-day queen" condemned to death for her role in a coup d'état aimed at denying the throne of England to Mary I, were published as inflammatory Protestant propaganda. They include highly dramatic letters such as a remarkable document that she addressed to her sister, Lady Catherine, on the flyleaf of her Greek New Testament the night before she died. In addition to assimilating writings by Lady Jane into the *Book of Martyrs*, Foxe transcribes her last words prior to decapitation.

Descriptions of pageants at London and Edinburgh portray a competition over the representation of British queens by royal partisans and their religious opponents. It was customary for citizens to organize pageantry in celebration of late medieval and early modern rulers upon their formal entry into Northern European cities. Festivities involved elaborate tableaux vivants that featured allegorical scenes, emblazoning of verses or recitation of quasi-dramatic speeches, and musical performances.

Pageants for the entry into London of Mary I and her husband-to-be, Prince Philip of Spain, celebrated their Roman Catholic orthodoxy. An account by John Elder describes a tableau that praised Mary as the personification of *Veritas Temporis Filia* ("Truth, the Daughter of Time"), a figure symbolic of the restoration of "true" religion. Richard Mulcaster appears to have had this scene in mind in a scripted account of Queen Elizabeth's entry into London on the day before her coronation. When a girl costumed as Truth presented the young queen with an English Bible, Elizabeth represented herself as Truth, the Daughter of Time, by exclaiming "Time hath brought me hither." Reflecting the apocalyptic worldview of Bale's *Image of Both Churches*, pageants scripted by Mulcaster, who served as headmaster of Edmund Spenser's grammar school, afforded a reservoir for allegories that pervade book I of *The Faerie Queene* and other Elizabethan texts. The symbolism of this London entry then underwent inversion during the entry into Edinburgh of Mary, Queen of Scots. In a striking reversal of Elizabeth's self-dramatization as Truth, the Scottish queen rejected a Bible proffered by a boy costumed as an angel. Presbyterian citizens demonized Mary as a manifestation of the Whore of Babylon.

A set of documents in the *Book of Martyrs* bring this collection to a conclusion. The feminine coloration of the *Book of Martyrs* is apparent in Foxe's patriotic dedication of his collection to Elizabeth I as a divine agent who has restored England to peace and plenty after a period of bloodshed and famine. The "Miraculous Preservation of the Lady Elizabeth," a romanticized account of her escape from the headsman's ax when she was the heir apparent during the reign of her sister, Mary I, affords a foundational myth concerning Elizabeth as a Protestant heroine, whose providential deliverance constitutes a mark of divine favor. A tragicomic tale that Foxe added to the 1570 edition represents Bishop Stephen Gardiner as an éminence grise bent upon destroying the Protestant faction at court. He does so by exploiting a marital rift between Henry VIII and his sixth wife, Catherine Parr, in order to secure the king's assent to a plot that threatens to lead yet another queen consort to decapitation on the headsman's block.

Reading selections in *Voices of the English Reformation* can enrich our understanding of well-known canonical works by Spenser, Shakespeare, Sidney, Marlowe, and their contemporaries. For example, book I of *The Faerie Queene* embodies an apocalyptic worldview aligned with Bale's *Image of Both Churches*, annotations on Revelation in the Geneva Bible, and Foxe's *Book of Martyrs*. The conflict between Una and Duessa recalls Protestant interpretation of the Woman Clothed with the Sun and Whore of Babylon as types for the "true" and "false" churches. At the outset of Spenser's romantic epic, monklike Archimago, monstrous Error, who spews books and papers reminiscent of Catholic propaganda printed on secret presses or smuggled into England, and her swarming offspring bring to mind Jesuit missionaries such as Campion, Parsons, and Southwell. Archimago's identification as Hypocrisy recalls polemical personifications of this Vice in Bale's *Three Laws*, Weaver's *Lusty Juventus*, and Crowley's *Philargyrie of Great Britain*.

Early in his career, Spenser dedicated *The Shepheardes Calender* to Sir Philip Sidney, a militant Protestant who advocated English intervention on behalf of Dutch coreligionists under attack from the forces of Roman Catholic Spain. Among the satirical eclogues that consider resistance to the introduction of religious reforms, the May Eclogue features debate between Piers, an agrarian descendant of Piers Plowman, and a cleric named Palinode, who is sympathetic to Catholic practices. Not only does Piers recall the rustic speaker in Luke Shepherd's *John Bon and Master Parson*, but he resorts to an allegorical beast fable in order to attack threatening religious practices. The shepherd's use of foxes and wolves to represent the Roman Catholic "peril" recalls mid-century satire on Stephen Gardiner as a prelatical wolf (see Figure 14). Pastoral poems such as "May" enable readers to understand how religious satire by Spenser, the epic poet of Elizabethan England, represents not only a domestication of newly imported poetic modes, but a continuing negotiation with polemical concerns that preoccupied earlier generations of English Protestants. Successive versions of Sidney's *Arcadia*, his sprawling prose romance, are comparable to Spenser's satirical eclogues in their use of pastoral disguise to veil criticism of Queen Elizabeth's pacifism and apocalyptic fears associated with her proposed marriage to the heir apparent of the throne of France.

Parodic inversions in Christopher Marlowe's plays transfer Reformation motifs to the Elizabethan stage. When Tamburlaine treads on the back of Bajazeth as he usurps his throne, this "scourge of God" reenacts the conventional triumph of the papal Antichrist familiar from Foxe's *Book of Martyrs*. Even though scholars debate the degree to which the different versions of *Doctor Faustus* dramatize predestination as opposed to free will, the play's Vatican scene invokes iconoclastic attack on the papacy that pervades the *Book of Martyrs* and other polemical texts. In the play's closing scene, Faustus enacts a Protestant theological position when he speaks, without intercession by saints or the Virgin Mary, of the yawning breach between himself and heaven.

Despite Shakespeare's avoidance of overt theological argumentation, plays such as *Hamlet* and *Othello* dramatize controversial issues related to conscience, confession, free will, and purgatory. Parodies of monastic characters in *Measure for Measure* recall earlier allegorical satires. Indeed, Shakespeare often incorporates comic portrayals of both Catholic and Protestant clerics including Friar Lawrence and Friar John in *Romeo and Juliet*, Sir Oliver Mar-text in *As You Like It*, and Nathaniel in *Love's Labor's Lost*. Dramatization of worldly churchmen in *Henry V* and *Romeo and Juliet* accords with clerical satire familiar in the works by Bale, Foxe, Spenser, and others. The 1613 staging of *Henry VIII* reverts to apocalyptic fervor familiar from the *Book of Martyrs* when a speech delivered at the christening of Princess Elizabeth by Archbishop Cranmer foresees the completion of the Protestant Reformation during the infant's future reign. Cranmer's prophecy concerning Elizabeth as a Protestant heroine nurtured by Truth and counseled by "Holy and heavenly thoughts" evokes regal symbolism familiar from Mulcaster's *Queen's Majesty's Passage* and Foxe's *Book of Martyrs*.

The worlds of the English Reformation were circumscribed ones in which writers such as John Bale, John Foxe, and Robert Crowley not only knew each other, but attended college together, shared lodgings, or fled into exile in each other's company. Jesuit priests such as Edmund Campion, Robert Parsons, and Robert Southwell studied together at English seminaries established in foreign lands before risking their lives to minister to Catholic believers in their hostile homeland. *Voices of the English Reformation* contains texts filled with unforgettable images of little-known worlds familiar to Queen Elizabeth and her courtiers and to Shakespeare, Marlowe, Spenser, and their contemporaries. It juxtaposes narratives from the closed world of the royal court and the open world of London, a city of about one-half million residents filled with playhouses, printing houses, and book stalls. Both London and the countryside sheltered recusant households with secret chambers used to conceal Jesuit missionaries from priest hunters or hide printing presses that produced outlawed books written by Parsons, Southwell, and others. The sheltering world of Oxford and Cambridge shielded Continental scholars who engaged in theological discourse or defended the validity of poetry and drama in learned Latin treatises.

Texts in this collection go beyond the vernacular and Latinate worlds of the royal court, London, Oxford, Cambridge, and England as a whole, however, to include materials written in Scotland and Ireland. A letter from Edinburgh describes a rude welcome offered by citizens hostile to Mary, Queen of Scots. John Bale's autobiographical account of a year spent as a missionary bishop ventriloquizes the voices of Irish Catholics who resorted to murder and mayhem in order to resist his ill-conceived struggle to impose Protestant doctrine and worship in an alien and hostile land. Through texts in this collection, readers may travel to Rhineland printing houses and the cloistered world of seminaries at Rome, Douai, and Rheims, which instilled thoughts of martyrdom in the minds of English exiles who joined the Jesuit mission to the secret world of recusant England. Baldwin's *Beware the Cat* takes readers behind the closed doors of recusant households to witness illegal worship practices through the eyes of a stealthy cat.

Voices of the English Reformation also contains the deservedly famous dying words of Roman Catholic and Protestant martyrs. They include the quip uttered by Thomas More as he feebly ascended the headsman's scaffold at the Tower of London: "I pray you, Master Lieutenant, see me safe up and, for my coming down, let me shift for myself." John Foxe criticized More for frivolity, but he heroized William Tyndale for uttering a prayer for the conversion of Henry VIII only moments before the headsman garroted and burned him: "Lord, open the King of England's eyes." Hugh Latimer's final words to his fellow victim sounded a clarion call for ecclesiastical reform: "Be of good comfort, Master Ridley, and play the man. We shall this day light such a candle, by God's grace, in England, as I trust shall never be put out." Words uttered by Anne Askew, Lady Jane Grey, Chidiock Tichborne, and others as they lived and died were equally eloquent.

Notes

1. *The Penguin Book of Renaissance Verse, 1509–1659*, ed. David Norbrook and H. R. Woudhuysen (New York: Penguin, 1993), affords a complementary challenge to the restriction of the canon of early modern literature. It contains brief extracts of Reformation poetry.

2. Desiderius Erasmus, *Christian Humanism and the Reformation: Selected Writings*, ed. and trans. John C. Olin (New York: Harper, 1965), 97.

3. Barbara Kiefer Lewalski, *Protestant Poetics and the Seventeenth-Century Religious Lyric* (Princeton, N.J.: Princeton University Press, 1979), 15–19.

4. E.g., *Documents of the English Reformation*, ed. Gerald Bray (Minneapolis: Fortress Press, 1994), and *Religion and Society in Early Modern England: A Sourcebook*, ed. David Cressy and Lori Anne Ferrell (London: Routledge, 1996). These collections respectively contain a set of ecclesiastical injunctions and parliamentary acts that effected the construction of the Church of England, on the one hand, and selections from social documents, memoirs, parish records, and other historical sources, on the other.

5. E.g., J. J. Scarisbrick, *The Reformation and the English People* (Oxford: Blackwell, 1984); Eamon Duffy, *The Stripping of the Altars: Traditional Religion in England, 1400–1580* (New Haven, Conn.: Yale University Press, 1992); and Christopher Haigh, *The English Reformations: Religion, Politics, and Society Under the Tudors* (Oxford:

Clarendon Press, 1993). For a range of recent perspectives, see Peter Marshall, ed., *The Impact of the English Reformation, 1500–1640* (London: Arnold, 1997).

6. A. G. Dickens is the great modern exponent of this view in *The English Reformation*, 2nd ed., rev. (London: Batsford, 1989).

7. Patrick Collinson, *The Religion of Protestants: The Church in English Society, 1559–1625* (Oxford: Clarendon Press, 1982), 189–241, passim.

8. Duffy, *Stripping of the Altars*, 377–477; Haigh, *English Reformations*, 1–21, et seq.

9. For post-revisionist reassessments of the strength of early English Protestantism as a movement that proceeded with both government and popular support, see Peter Marshall and Alec Ryrie, eds., *The Beginnings of English Protestantism* (Cambridge: Cambridge University Press, 2002), esp. the historiographical overview at 1–7; and Ethan Shagan, *Popular Politics and the English Reformation* (Cambridge: Cambridge University Press, 2003).

BIBLE TRANSLATION AND COMMENTARY

1.1. Revelation 12:1–6: The Woman Clothed with the Sun; Revelation 17:3–6: The Whore of Babylon

A. William Tyndale, New Testament Translation (1525–26)

William Tyndale undertook the first printed translation of the Bible in the English language. Frustrated in his effort to obtain patronage in England, he migrated to Germany where he secured publication of his New Testament at Worms in 1526. Printing had begun at Cologne during the previous year, but local authorities soon stopped it. He heeded the humanistic call to return *ad fontes* ("to the sources") by working from Hebrew texts and Erasmus's Greek New Testament (1516), whose preface (*Paraclesis*) advocates that humble people, including plowmen and women, be allowed access to the Bible in their native language. Erasmus influenced Tyndale's employment of everyday colloquial diction, but the translator's inclusion of Lutheran propaganda into prefaces and notes antagonized English authorities. He also translated a considerable part of the Old Testament by the time he was burned alive as a heretic in 1536. Tyndale's diction provides the foundation for later Protestant translations including the Authorized Version of 1611 (the "King James Bible").

Miles Coverdale expanded Tyndale's translation in the Coverdale Bible (1535), the first complete Bible printed in the English language. Instead of following Tyndale in the return *ad fontes*, Coverdale based his version on Luther's German New Testament, the Vulgate Bible, and other Latin texts to complete the text left unfinished by Tyndale. Although the volume was printed in Antwerp without official authorization, the title page border crafted by Hans Holbein the Younger implied the existence of royal consent by portraying Henry VIII in the act of handing the Bible to bishops kneeling before him (see Figure 1). Coverdale later used the "Matthew" Bible (John Rogers's edition of translations by Tyndale and Coverdale) as the basis for the Great Bible (1539), an officially licensed version produced under the patronage of Thomas Cromwell. Its publication without doctrinal notes and prefaces accorded with the government's caution concerning uncontrolled reading and interpretation of the Bible (see 6.1, 6.9, 7.5.C). See Tyndale's *Obedience of a Christian Man* (1.2.A and 2.1) and John Foxe's life of Tyndale (6.5.A).

SOURCE: *STC* 2825, 2X3ᵛ, 3A1ʳ⁻ᵛ.

EDITION: *The Bible in English* (online database).

REFERENCES: Booty; Daniell; Greenblatt; King 1982; Norton.

Revelation 12:1–6

And there appeared a great wonder in heaven: a woman clothed with the sun, and the moon under her feet, and upon her head a crown of twelve stars. And she was with child and cried travailing in birth and pained ready to be delivered. And there appeared another wonder in heaven, for behold a great red dragon having seven heads, and ten horns and crowns upon his heads, and his tail drew the third part of the stars, and cast them to the earth.

And the dragon stood before the woman which was ready to be delivered, for to devour her child as soon as it were born. And she brought forth a man child, which should rule all nations with a rod of iron. And her son was taken up unto God, and to his seat. And the woman fled into the wilderness, where she had a place prepared of God. . . .

Revelation 17:3–6

And he carried me a way into the wilderness in the spirit. And I saw a woman sit upon a rose colored beast full of names of blasphemy which had

Figure 1. *Henry VIII with the Sword and the Book*. Hans Holbein the Younger. Coverdale Bible (Antwerp, 1535), title page woodcut. By permission of the British Library. Kneeling bishops and nobles acknowledge the ecclesiastical supremacy of Henry VIII as an "English Pope." His bearing of the Bible and sword, which conflates the traditional regal figure of the sword of justice with "the sword of the spirit which is the word of God" (Ephesians 6:17), constitutes the definitive portrayal of English Protestant kingship. The flanking figure of Paul, the "Protestant saint" who symbolizes the New Testament, also bears the sword. Symbolic of his reputed authorship of the book of Psalms, King David plays upon the lyre in a representation of divine kingship and the Old Testament.

ten horns. And the woman was arrayed in purple and rose color, and decked with gold, precious stone, and pearls, and had a cup of gold in her hand, full of abominations and filthiness of her fornication. And in her forehead was a name written, a mystery: "Great Babylon the mother of whoredom and abominations of the earth." And I saw the wife drunk with the blood of saints, and with the blood of the witnesses of Jesus. And when I saw her, I wondered with great marvel.

B. John Bale, from
The Image of Both Churches (c. 1545)

John Bale's *The Image of Both Churches* (Antwerp, 1545?) was the first complete commentary on Revelation printed in the English language. Working from Tyndale's version, Bale modifies the Augustinian and Lutheran belief that "true" church has existed ever since the time of Adam and Eve. He views the papacy as the most recent manifestation of the "false" church headed by Antichrist. Bale denies the medieval interpretation of the Woman Clothed with the Sun (Rev. 12) as a figure for the Virgin Mary, associating her instead with the church descended from Christ. He sees the Whore of Babylon (Rev. 17) as a type for the Church of Rome (see Figure 2), whose clergy he associates with superstition, ostentatious vestments and processions, sexual transgression, empty ritualism, and erroneous belief in transubstantiation and the Mass. Bale is a vigorous word-smith, whose prose is notable for alliteration, ranting catalogs, and satirical epi-thets. His historical paradigm exerted considerable influence on later English Protestant literature, history, and hermeneutics, not least through its absorption into the marginal glosses of the Geneva Bible, Foxe's *Book of Martyrs*, and Spenser's *Faerie Queene*, in which Una and Duessa personify the "true" and "false" churches (book 1).

SOURCE: *STC* 1297, D5ᵛ–E4ʳ, R1ʳ–5ʳ.

REFERENCES: Bauckham; King 1982; McEachern.

Revelation 12:1–6

The Text

ᵃAnd there appeared a great wonder in heaven. ᵇA woman clothed with the sun, ᶜand the moon under her feet, ᵈand upon her head, a crown of twelve stars. ᵉAnd she was with child, ᶠand cried, travailing in birth, ᵍpained, ready to be delivered.

The Paraphrase

ᵃ *And there appeared (saith Saint John) a great token in heaven. For no wonder is this token here to be taken, as in other places of the scripture, but for a type or figure, containing under mystery great things.*

ᵇ *A woman was seen clothed with the sun. . . . Not Mary Christ's mother is this woman, though many hath so fantasied in their commentaries. But it is the true Christian church of whom Mary is a most notable member.*

This woman the church (as Solomon's Canticles speaketh) is fair, lovely, pleasant, sweet, wholesome, delectable, undefiled as the moon, excellent in clearness as the sun, and glorious as an army of men with their banners and streamers. This woman is beautifully decked with the shining sun of righteousness. None is of her that hath not done on Jesus Christ, being renewed in their hearts by faith. Her children are not they that persecuted God's word, no more than was Annas and Caiaphas, Joannes, and Alexander.[1]

        ^c *This woman seemed to have the moon under her feet. To the church or congregation of God are all other creatures subject. All movable things have the Lord subdued unto her. She is the right heir and inheritor of them through Christ, they with her to be delivered from the bondage of corruption and to serve in liberty.*

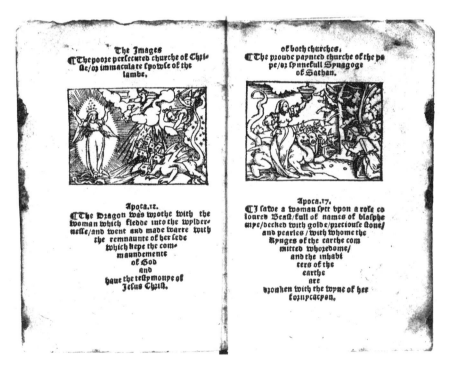

Figure 2. *The Images of Both Churches: The Woman Clothed with the Sun and the Whore of Babylon.* John Bale, *The Image of Both Churches* (Antwerp, c. 1545), woodcuts. By permission of the Bodleian Library. At the conclusion of Bale's commentary on the book of Revelation, two woodcuts represent the two women of Revelation as personifications of "The poor persecuted church of Christ, or immaculate spouse of the Lamb" (Rev. 12) and "The proud painted church of the Pope, or sinful synagogue [congregation] of Satan" (Rev. 17). These propagandistic images recur in Protestant attacks on the pope as Antichrist and the Church of Rome as the Whore of Babylon throughout the sixteenth and seventeenth centuries. Stories in Foxe's *Book of Martyrs* and Spenser's personification of Una and Duessa in book 1 of *The Faerie Queene* are notable examples of this typology.

[d] *Upon her head was also a crown of twelve stars, which betokeneth not only the Twelve Apostles declaring the glory of Christ's kingdom immediately after his death, but all other godly ministers of the word also, which have done the same ever since. Only reigneth the true Christian church by the word of God, by the sincere scriptures, by the doctrine of the Apostles, and neither superstitions nor ceremonies, neither by counsels nor customs, by doctors nor fathers, by miters nor rochets, by tippets nor hoods, by shaven crowns nor side gowns, by crosses nor cups, by bells nor torches, by shrines nor gilty[2] images, nor yet by twelve couples in a livery with golden chains and garded[3] coats. Her beauty consisteth only in faith, and in the observation of God's holy commandments. Her true ministers or preachers as very chosen stars, showeth forth his glory to the edification of other, and not their own pomp and magnificence.*

[e] *And she was as is the woman with child. She cried travailing in birth, and was pained as one ready to be delivered. With Christ is the church big when her members are in full faith. In the heart is he evermore conceived, and delivered forth such time as he is declared unto other. For this cause Christ called them his mother which had faith and thereupon did the will of his Father. Of faith in of the first promise that Christ should destroy the serpent, was he first conceived in Adam and Eve, and to grow forth in righteous Abel, in Seth, Enos, Enoch, Noah, Shem, Thare, Melchizedek, Abraham, and Lot. And as the promises waxed stronger (as in Abraham, Moses, David, and the Prophets) and the people of God more in number, so waxed the woman bigger and bigger, till the fullness of her time was come that she should be delivered. Which was such time as Christ appeared to the world, taught, and was conversant here among men. And this course have she kept ever since, and shall do to the latter day in them that believe. Thus have she had Christ in her womb since the beginning.*

[f] *And being full of his heavenly spirit, she had cried in the patriarchs and prophets, in the apostles and faithful ministers, as one travailing in birth. Her cry was the mighty and strong declaration of Christ's doctrine, the fervent zeal and desire of the glory of God, and of all men's health in Christ. She travaileth evermore a new like as did Paul, till Christ be fashioned in her Christian members. With all her strength, she laboreth that the promised seed may increase in the faith of all men.*

[g] *Finally she is pained with labors, dolors, blasphemies, troubles, and terrible persecutions, and never is delivered without them. Never is Christ earnestly received, till some of her members doth suffer. The constant spirit and invincible standing by the truth in them hath converted many. And like as the pained woman in all her agonies, is much comforted by the hope of a child, so are God's faithful witnesses, trusting that by their patient and glad sufferance Christ should be received and rightly fashioned in many. Yea, this causeth them to rejoice in all adversity, and little to esteem their pains.*

The Text

ⁱAnd there appeared another wonder in heaven, ʲfor behold a great red dragon, ᵏhaving seven heads, ˡand ten horns, ᵐand seven crowns upon his heads, ⁿand his tail drew the third part of the stars, ᵒand cast them to the earth.

The Paraphrase

ⁱ *After this (saith Saint John) appeared in heaven another token or marvel, all diverse from the first. The true church (which is God's kingdom) was never yet without contradiction, nor without the crafty assaults of enemies. Adam was not so soon created, but he was immediately assaulted of Satan. Christ entered not so soon the world, but he was by and by persecuted. The Devil goeth about like a roaring lion, seeking whom he may devour.*

ʲ *For behold there was seen a great red dragon, betokening the said Devil with his whole retinue, full of deceit, craft, malice, poison, pride, and fierceness, to enforce the poor weaklings to consent unto his falsehood. All red his body seemed, in token that they which are of him, are all full of cruelty, spite, and bloodshedding, afflicting the constant believers for withstanding his assaults. Seldom is he out of the earth, as witnesseth Job, but commonly in the company of men, impugning the faithful. And no power is able to match him, unless it cometh from above.*

ᵏ *The said dragon had seven heads, signifying all the crafty wiles, and subtle suggestions, that he hath practiced and used against Christ and his word under all the seven seals opening and the seven trumpets blowing.[4] Very easy it is to conjecture what manner of heads they were, marking other places of the scripture. A serpent's head should seem to be the first, considering that in the serpent he deceived our first parents with his venomed crafts. This head so maliciously poisoned man, that God repented him of his creation, and destroyed his whole kind in the Flood, eight persons only reserved. After the Flood had he the head of a calf for the second, in the signification of the shameful idolatry, and wicked worshippings that then begun in Nimrod, and so continued in the heathen. The third was the head of a lion, full of pride and oppression, expressed first in the cruel reign of the Assyrians and Chaldeans, and after in the proud bishops and priests. The fourth was a bear's head, full of ravin and cruelness, betokening the fierce kingdom of the Medes and Persians. Consequently his fifth head was like a leopard's head of many colors, full of fickleness and changeableness. And that was the unconstant reign of the Greek. His sixth was the head of a beast far unlike all other beasts, which signifieth the kingdom of the Romans with their monstrous laws more than needeth. The seventh is not unlike to a man's head, including all carnal wisdom, with all devilish policies and crafts, and this is the very papacy here in Europe, which is the general*

Antichrist of all the whole world almost, which hath already subdued and destroyed the Empire of Rome. For he is called the Apostate and man of sin. By this only head is the dragon named the envious man. The whole body followeth the heads. As the Devil is malicious, wicked, fierce, cruel tyrannical false, execrable, and deceitful, so are all his members. In the proudest of the flesh after him they walk in idolatry, hypocrisy, and all other filthiness. . . .

[l] The said dragon had also ten horns, or all subtle ways wherewith to impugn the feeble weak nature of man, or to provoke him evermore to rebel against God's commandments.

[m] Upon his seven heads he had seven crowns, signifying thereby that both he and his members hath not only possessed the aforenamed vices, but also they have over the world reigneth in them and yet do to this day. In pride, falsehood, malice, craft, cruelty, wickedness, and all other mischiefs triumph they yet.

[n] And his tail drew towards him the third part of the stars (and in conclusion) threw them down to the earth. By worldly promotion, lucre, favor, and other flattering fantasies, hath he tangled many learned men, and plucked them clean from Christ's true church, and from the life of the Gospel, so provoking them wholly to give themselves to the study of erroneous doctrine and lying prophecies, to seduce the worldly multitude and keep them in perpetual blindness.

[o] So that they are now cast in to the earth. They are become all carnal, filthy and ungodly in all their wisdom, study, and works, in all their counsels, preachings, and teachings. Now are they the wicked Apostles of Satan, no longer may they shine in the firmament.

The Text

[p]And the dragon stood before the woman, which was ready to be delivered, [q]for to devour her child as soon as it were born. [r]And she brought forth a manchild, [s]which should rule all nations with a rod of iron. [t]And her son was taken up unto God, and to his seat. [u]And the woman fled into the wilderness, where she had a place prepared of God. . . .

The Paraphrase

[p] Before the aforesaid travailing woman stood this dragon, ready to devour her child, so soon as it were born. Evermore is the Devil waiting his prey, whereas the Gospel is sincerely taught, least any thereby should become the children of God.

[q] He seeketh all crafts, policies, and engines,[5] to take the word from the heart, least they believing it should be saved. . . .

[r] Such a manchild (saith Saint John) brought this woman forth, as with an iron rod should rule all nations. Never is the true church idle, but conceiveth Christ at the Gospel preaching, retaineth him in faith and bringeth him forth in teaching

other the same. No woman child is he, impotent, weak and feeble, but a manchild, bringing with him always a strong, mighty, and invincible spirit, whereas he is unfeignedly received. For he is the mighty Lord that is valiant in battle.

ˢ *With the iron wand of his world invincible shall he govern his meek spirited flock, that none other laws shall they require. With the same also shall he subdue all power which are not of him, and drive them down to the bottom of hell. For by faith only in him is the victory over the world.*

ᵗ *This child was also taken up to God and unto his throne. Where as the Devil thought to devour him, and to wrap him up forever under death, he put him beside his purpose. Victoriously he arose up from death to life, he ascended unto heaven, and now sitteth upon the right hand of God the Father almighty. And whereas he is now, there shall his faithful followers and ministers be hereafter, for that is his, is also theirs, birth, life, resurrection, and ascension.*

ᵘ *The woman fled after this into the wilderness. What else doth the just people of God but flee the contagiousness, vanity, tumult, fornication, idolatry, and filthiness of this world? Seeking God in the solitary heart, and not in outward fantasies.*

Revelation 17:3–6

The Text

ᵃAnd I saw a woman sit upon ᵇa rose colored beast, ᶜfull of names of blasphemy, ᵈwhich had seven heads and ten horns. ᵉAnd the woman was arrayed, ᶠin purple and rose color, ᵍand decked with gold, precious stone, and pearls, ʰand had a cup of gold in her hand, ⁱfull of abominations, ʲand filthiness of her whoredom. ᵏAnd in her forehead was a name written, ˡa mystery: ᵐ "Great Babylon the mother of whoredom and abominations of the earth." ⁿAnd I saw the wife drunken with the blood of saints, and with the blood of the witnesses of Jesus. ᵒAnd when I saw her, ᵖI wondered with great marvel.

The Paraphrase

ᵃ *And I saw (saith Saint John) in mystery a woman (for a whore at the first blush seemeth only a woman) sitting upon a rose colored beast. This beast is the great Antichrist that was spoken of afore, or the beastly body of the Devil, comprehending in him popes, patriarchs, cardinals, legates, bishops, doctors, abbots, priors, priests and pardoners, monks, canons, friars, nuns, and so forth. Temporal governors also, as emperors, kings, princes, dukes, earls, lords, justices, deputies, judges, lawyers, mayors, bailiffs, constables, and so forth, learning their own duty offices as to minister rightly, to serve the abominations.*

ᵇ *All rose colored is this beast, in token of tyrannous murder and bloodshedding over those that will not agree to their devilishness.*

^c *Full of blasphemous names is this beast also, as your holiness, your grace, your lordship, your fatherhood, your mastership, your reverence, honor, highness, worship, magnificence, goodness, God's vicar, spiritual sire, ghostly father, physician of souls, defender of faith, head of the holy church, and so forth, besides the names of their properties, seats, and pageants, as procession, bishoping, aneling,[6] purgatory, pilgrimage, pardon, Mass, matins, evensong, placebo,[7] Candlemas Day, Palm Sunday, Ash Wednesday, Holy Rood Day, Saint Thomas' Day, and so forth.*

^d *This beast had seven heads and ten horns, signifying his universal crafts and suggestions to destroy the graces and gifts of the Holy Ghost, and also his falsely borrowed primacies and tyrannous authorities to withstand the commandments of God.*

^e *Upon this beast sitteth a woman. For what else advanceth or beareth out this malignant monster in their copes, crosses, oils, miters, robes, relics, ceremonies, vigils, holy days, blessings, censings, and foolings, but a wanton foolish and fantastical religion, a vainglorious pomp, and a shining pretence of holiness in superstition (calling it their holy church). She is said here to sit upon this bloody beast, as to be stayed, quieted, and saddled by them. Mark what labors and pains that crafty and wily Winchester[8] taketh with Bonner,[9] Tunstal,[10] and other of his faction, as her own sworn soldier to hold up this glorious whore in her old estate of Romish religion. Oh, he grunteth and groaneth, he sweateth and swelleth, he fretteth and belleth, he bloweth and panteth, he talketh and canteth, he stirreth and never ceaseth, to bring his matters to pass.*

^f *In token that this hypocritical church standeth in the murder of innocents, this woman is here gorgeously appareled in purple, as guilty of their deaths which hath been slain, and also in fresh scarlet as evermore fresh and ready to continue in the same bloodshedding. For if such terrible slaughter were not, the true Christian faith should increase, to the great diminishment of her glory.*

^g *She is in like case boarishingly[11] decked with gold, precious stone, and pearls, not only in her manifold kinds of ornaments, as is her copes, corporals, chasubles, tunicles, stools, fanoms, and miters,[12] but also in mystery of counterfeit godliness. Many outward brags maketh this painted church of Christ, of his Gospel, and of his apostles, signified by the gold, precious stone, and pearls, which is but a glittering color. For nothing mindeth the less than to follow them in conversation of living.*

^h *Moreover in her hand which is her exterior ministration, she hath a golden cup, full of abominations and filthiness of her execrable whoredom. This cup is the false religion that she daily ministereth, besides the chalice whom her merchants most damnably abuseth. And it containeth all doctrine of devils, all beastly errors and lies, all deceitful power, all glittering works of hypocrites, all crafty wisdom of the flesh, and subtle practices of man's wit, besides philosophy, logic, rhetoric, and sophistry. Yea, all prodigious kinds of idolatry, fornication, sodomy, and wickedness.*

Outwardly it seemeth gold, pretending the glory of God, the holy name of Christ, the sacred scriptures of the Bible, perpetual virginity of life, and all are but counterfeit colors and shadows of hypocrisy in the outward letter and name.

[i] *Full of abominations is the drink of the execrable faith of that Romish religion received of other, and full of filthiness also. For both retaineth the people thereof innumerable kinds of idol worshippings under the title of God's service, and also their shavelings of prodigious beastliness in lecherous living under the color of chastity. Here were much to be spoken of Saint Germain's evil, Saint Syth's keep, Saint Unromber's oats, Master John Shorn's boat, Saint Gertrude's rats, Saint Job for the poor, Saint Fiacre for the ague, Saint Apollonia for the toothache, Saint Gracian for lost thrift, Saint Walstone for good harvest, Saint Cornelius for the foul evil, and all other saints else almost.* [13]

[j] *Of the buggery boys also among prelates and priests, ghostly fathers and religious, might much be said here, were it not for infecting men's eyes, ears, and understandings. For all these noyful nocuments* [14] *are the holy fruits of the whoredom of that holy whorish church.*

[k] *In the forehead of this glittering whore, which is her outward show, is written a name, expressly declaring what she is. By her ungodly fruits is she known to the elect servants of God, having the light of the scriptures. In their conveyances appeareth she none other than a pestiferous whore, by the judgments of the same.*

[l] *A very mystery is this show to the infidels, a hidden secret, an unknown wonder. For they are so blinded with her fopperies and tangled with her toys, that they judge all that she doth holy, religious, and perfect. And all this suffereth God for their unbelief's sake, destroying nevertheless the wisdom of the wise and prudence of the prudent in his.*

[m] *Her very name agreeing to her fruits, is this: "Great Babylon, in mischief far above the city of the Chaldeans, and much more full of confusion." For she is the original mother, the cause, the beginning, the root, the spring, and the fountain of all spiritual fornications, and in a manner of all fleshly abominations also done upon the earth. This is to the faithful sort, as a written name of her, evident, clear open and manifest. But to the unfaithful it is only as a mystery, hidden, dark, obscure, and neglect. For so are the secrets that God openeth to babes, and hideth from wise.*

[n] *And I (saith Saint John) perceived it evidently in my fore understanding, that this woman the very wife of the Devil and of his beastly body (for the bishops are the husbands of their Romish churches) was all drunken in the bloody slaughter of saints, or earnest Christian believers and in the exceeding tyrannous murder of the faithful witnesses of Jesus or sincere preachers of his word. For neither of both she spareth. Besides all godly wisdom is she, and forgetful of herself, through this same bloody drunkenness, so great excess hath she taken.*

° *And when I perceived and saw her with all her adders' whelps so beastish (saith Saint John) with exceeding wonder I marveled. Not only that she was thus overset with blood drinking or outrageous murdering of innocents, but also of her exceeding great abominations.*

ᵖ *And most of all I wondered that the almighty God could with so much patience suffer her in such mischief.*

Notes

1. Acts 4:5–6.
2. With a pun on "guilty."
3. Ornamented.
4. Rev. 6:1–12:6.
5. Stratagems
6. Anointing.
7. The first antiphon for the Vespers for the Dead.
8. Stephen Gardiner (see Appendix).
9. See Appendix.
10. Cuthbert Tunstal, Bishop of London (1522–30), a religious conservative.
11. Sensually.
12. A catalog of ecclesiastical vestments.
13. A catalog of alleged cures effected by saints.
14. Annoying noxious things.

C. The Geneva Bible (1560)

Protestants who emigrated under Mary I constructed a translation very different from earlier versions of the English Bible. The editors of the Geneva Bible (1560), William Whittingham, Anthony Gilby (see 4.4), and Thomas Sampson, aimed to improve upon the philological scholarship of earlier versions. Published in relatively affordable quarto format, it contains a variety of aids to popular understanding. It is the first printed Bible to include verse divisions. The polemical annotations held out a special appeal to Puritan readers. Poets such as Shakespeare and Spenser, and even prelates such as Archbishop Matthew Parker, who oversaw production of the Bishops' Bible (1568), used the Geneva Bible.

SOURCE: *STC* 2093, 3G4ʳ.

EDITION: *The Bible in English* (online database).

Revelation 12:1–6

And there appeared a great wonder in heaven: a ᵃwoman clothed with the sun, and the ᵇmoon was under her feet, and upon her head a ᶜcrown of twelve stars. And she was with child, and ᵈcried travailing in birth, and was pained ready to be delivered. And there appeared another wonder in heaven: for behold, a great ᵉred dragon having ᶠseven heads, and ten horns, and seven crowns upon his heads. And his tail drew the ᵍthird part of the stars of heaven, and cast them to the earth. And the dragon stood before the woman, which was ready to be delivered, to devour her child, when she had brought it forth. ʰSo she brought forth a man child, which should rule all nations with a rod of iron, and her son was taken up unto God and to this throne. And the woman fled into ⁱwilderness, where she hath a place prepared of God, that they should feed her there a thousand, two hundred and threescore days. . . .

Marginal Glosses

ᵃ *In this third vision is declared how the church which is compassed about with Jesus Christ the son of righteousness is persecuted of Antichrist.*

ᵇ *The church treadeth under foot whatsoever is mutable, and inconstant, with all corrupt affections and such like.*

ᶜ *Which signify God and his word.*

ᵈ *The church ever with a most fervent desire longed that Christ should be born, and that the faithful might be regenerate by his power.*

ᵉ *The Devil, and all his power which burneth with fury and is red with the blood of the faithful.*

ᶠ *For he is prince of this world and almost hath universal government.*

ᵍ *By his flatteries and promises he gaineth unity of the excellent ministers and honorable persons, and bringeth them to destruction.*

h Which is Jesus Christ the firstborn among many brethren, who was born of the Virgin Mary as of a special member of the church.

i The church was removed from among the Jews to the Gentiles, which were as a barren wilderness, and so it is persecuted to and fro.

Revelation 17:3–6

Then there came ᵃone of the seven angels, which had the seven vials, and talked with me, saying unto me, "Come: I will show thee the damnation of the great ᵇwhore that sitteth upon many ᶜwaters. With whom have committed fornication the kings of the earth, and the inhabitants of the earth are drunken with the wine of her fornication." So he carried me away into the wilderness in the spirit, and I saw a woman sit upon a scarlet colored ᵈbeast, full of names of ᵉblasphemy, which had seven heads, and ten horns. And the ᶠwoman was arrayed in purple and scarlet, and gilded with gold, and precious stones and pearls, and had a cup of gold in her hand, full of ᵍabominations, and filthiness of her fornication. And in her forehead was a name written, ʰa mystery, "Great Babylon, the mother of whoredoms, and abominations of the earth." And I saw the woman drunken with the blood of saints, and with the blood of the martyrs of Jesus. . . .

Marginal Glosses

ᵃ *Which was Christ Jesus, who will take vengeance on this Romish harlot.*

ᵇ *Antichrist is compared to an harlot because he seduceth the world with his vain words, doctrines of lies, and outward appearance.*

ᶜ *Meaning, diverse nations and countries.*

ᵈ *The beast signifieth the ancient Rome; the woman that sitteth thereon, the new Rome which is the papistry, whose cruelty and bloodshedding is declared by scarlet.*

ᵉ *Full of idolatry, superstition and contempt of the true God.*

ᶠ *This woman is the Antichrist, that is, the Pope with the whole body of his filthy creatures, as is expounded, verse eighteen, whose beauty only standeth in outward pomp and impudence and craft like a strumpet.*

ᵍ *Of false doctrines and blasphemies.*

ʰ *Which no one can know to avoid but the elect. . . .*

D. The Rheims New Testament (1582)

The Rheims-Douai Bible represented a Roman Catholic alternative to earlier English translations. A group of exiles at the English College at Rheims produced the New Testament in 1582; publication of the Old Testament followed at Douai in 1609–10. Notable for its Latinate diction and technical vocabulary, this literal translation of the Vulgate version lacked the popular appeal of other English versions. Not only does the Rheims commentary identify the Woman Clothed with the Sun as a figure for the Catholic Church, but it also espouses an interpretation rejected by Protestants when it regards her as a representation of the Virgin Mary. The annotations identify Babylon with sinfulness in general and with the Roman Empire as a persecutor of early Christians. They insist that Protestant interpretation of the Whore of Babylon as a figure for the Church of Rome is heretical.

SOURCES: *STC* 2884, pp. 719–21.

EDITION: *The Bible in English* (on-line database).

Revelation 12:1–6

The great dragon (the Devil) watching the woman that brought forth a manchild, to devour it, God took away the child to himself, and fed the woman in the desert.

[a]And a great sign appeared in heaven: [b]a woman clothed with the sun, and the moon under her feet, and on her head a crown of twelve stars. And being with child, she cried also travailing, and is in anguish to be delivered. And there was seen another sign in heaven, and behold [c]a great red dragon having seven heads, and ten horns, and on his heads seven diamonds. And his tail drew [d]the third part of the stars of heaven, and cast them to the earth, and the dragon stood before the woman which was ready to be delivered, that when she should be delivered, he might [e]devour her son. And she brought forth a manchild, who was [f]to govern all nations in an iron rod. And her son was taken up to God and to his throne, [*]and the woman fled into the wilderness, where she had a place prepared of God, that there they might feed her a thousand two hundred sixty days.

Marginal Glosses

[a] *The third part. The dragon's incredulous and persecuting multitude, and Antichrist the chief head thereof.*

[b] *This is properly and principally spoken of the church, and by allusion, of our Blessed Lady also.*

[c] *The great Devil, Lucifer.*

[d] *The spirits that fall from their first state into apostasy with him and by his means.*

ᶜ *The Devil's endeavor against the Church's children, and specially our Blessed Lady's only son, the head of the rest.*

ᶠ *Psalm 2:9, Apocalypse 2:27.*

Annotation

The woman fled. This great persecution that the church shall flee from, is in the time of Antichrist, and shall endure but three years and a half. . . . In which time for all that, she shall not want our Lord's protection, nor true pastors, nor be so secret, but all faithful men shall know and follow her. Much less shall she decay, err in faith, or degenerate and follow Antichrist, as heretics do wickedly feign. As the Church Catholic now in England in this time of persecution, because it hath no public state of regiment nor open free exercise of holy functions, may be said to be fled into the desert, yet it is neither unknown to the faithful that follow it, nor the enemies that persecute it, as the hid company that the Protestants talk of, was for some worlds together, neither known to their friends nor foes, because there was indeed none such for many ages together. And this is true, if we take this flight for a very corporal retiring into wilderness. Where indeed it may be, and is of most expounded, to be a spiritual flight, by forsaking the joys and solaces of the world, and giving herself to contemplation and penance, during the time of persecution under Antichrist. And by enlarging the sense, it may also very well signify the desolation and affliction that the church suffereth and hath suffered from time to time in this wilderness of the world, by all the forerunners and ministers of Antichrist, tyrants and heretics.

Revelation 17:3–6

Chapter 17

And I saw a woman sitting upon a scarlet colored beast, full of names of blasphemy, having seven heads, and ten horns. And the woman was clothed round about with purple and scarlet, and gilded with gold, and precious stone, and pearls, having a golden cup in her hand, full of the abomination and filthiness of her fornication. *And in her forehead a name written, ‡Mystery: "Babylon the great, mother of the fornications and the abominations of the earth." And I saw the woman †drunken of the blood of the saints, and of the blood of the martyrs of Jesus. And I marveled when I had seen her, with great admiration.

Annotations

* *In the end of Saint Peter's first Epistle, where the Apostle dateth it at Babylon, which the ancient writers (as we there noted) affirm to be meant of Rome. The*

Protestants will not in any wise have it so, because they would not be driven to confess that Peter ever was at Rome. But here for that they think it maketh for their opinion, that the Pope is Antichrist, and Rome the seat and city of Antichrist, they will needs have Rome to be this Babylon, this great whore, and this purple harlot. For such fellows, in the exposition of holy scripture, be led only by their prejudicate opinions and heresies, to which they draw all things without all indifference and sincerity.

But Saint Augustine, Arethras,[1] and other writers, most commonly expound it, neither of Babylon itself a city of Chaldea or Egypt, nor of Rome, or any one city, which may be so called spiritually. . . . but of the general society of the impious, and of those that prefer the terrene kingdom and commodity of the world, before God and eternal felicity. . . . Now to apply that to the Roman church and apostolic see, either now or then, which was spoken only of the terrene state of that city, as it was the seat of the emperor, and not of Peter, when it did slay above thirty popes, Christ's vicars, one after another, and endeavored to destroy the whole church: that is most blasphemous and foolish.

The Church in Rome was one thing, and Babylon in Rome another thing. Peter sat in Rome. And Nero sat in Rome. But Peter, as in the Church of Rome; Nero, as in the Babylon of Rome. Which distinction the heretics might have learned by Saint Peter himself (Epistle 1, Chapter 5), writing thus: "The church saluteth you, that is in Babylon, coelect." So that the church and the very chosen church was in Rome, when Rome was Babylon. Whereby it is plain that, whether Babylon or the great whore do here signify Rome or no, yet it cannot signify the Church of Rome, which is now, and ever was, differing from the terrene empire of the same. And if, as in the beginning of the church, Nero and the rest of the persecuting emperors (which were figures of Antichrist) did principally sit in Rome, so also the great Antichrist shall have his seat there, as it may well be (though others think that Jerusalem rather shall be his principal city). Yet even then shall neither the Church of Rome nor the pope of Rome be Antichrist, but shall be persecuted by Antichrist, and driven out of Rome, if it be possible. For to Christ's vicar and the Roman Church he will bear as much good will as the Protestants now do, and he shall have more power to persecute him and the church, than they have. . . .

‡ *Saint Paul calleth this secret and close working of abomination, the mystery of iniquity (2 Thessalonians 2) and it is called a little after in this chapter, verse 7, the sacrament (or mystery) of the woman, and it is also the mark of reprobation and damnation.*

† *It is plain that this woman signifieth the whole corps of all the persecutors that have and shall shed so much blood of the just: of the prophets, apostles, and other martyrs from the beginning of the world to the end. The Protestants foolishly expound it of Rome, for that there they put heretics to death, and allow of their*

punishment in other countries. But their blood is not called the blood of saints, no more then the blood of thieves, mankillers, and other malefactors, for the shedding of which by order of justice, no commonwealth shall answer.

Note

1. Archbishop of Caesarea (d. c. 944)

1.2. Translation Theory
A. William Tyndale, from
The Obedience of a Christian Man (1528)

After Tyndale (c. 1495–1536) published his translation of the New Testament, he spent the rest of his life in Antwerp. Johannes Hoochstraten concealed his role as printer of his polemical prose with the pseudonymous colophon of "Marburg in the Land of Hesse, Hans Lufft." The actual Hans Lufft printed Luther's books at Wittenberg. *The Obedience of a Christian Man*, Tyndale's most important tract, defends the validity of English as a "mother tongue" suitable for scriptural translation because it is akin to the Hebrew of the Pentateuch, Koine Greek of the New Testament, and Latin of the Vulgate translation of the Bible, which were spoken by ordinary people when those texts came into existence. Affirming the Lutheran principle of *sola scriptura* ("scripture alone"), which insists upon the primacy of the Bible in spiritual affairs, Tyndale's forcefully plain and popular language attacks the Roman Catholic clergy as avaricious and hypocritical "jugglers" of scripture who fail to teach the laity and are ignorant of the Vulgate Bible and the liturgical Latin that they recite. In addition to attacking them for condoning wantonness and ribaldry that he associates with popular Robin Hood ballads, Tyndale rejects the fourfold method of literal, tropological, allegorical, and anagogical interpretation of the Bible. Late medieval Scholastic scholars employed this hermeneutic method to construct arcane readings of the Bible that Tyndale regards as mystifications of the literal sense, which he defines as the only valid textual level. For a section of this book that seems to have pleased Henry VIII, see 2.1. Also see John Foxe's life of Tyndale (6.5.A).

SOURCE: *STC* 24446, fol. 129–33.

EDITION: William Tyndale, *The Obedience of a Christian Man*, ed. David Daniell (London: Penguin, 2000).

REFERENCES: Daniell; Greenblatt.

[The following defense of translation of the Bible into the vernacular comes from Tyndale's prefatory epistle to the reader.]

That thou mayest perceive how that the scripture ought to be in the mother tongue and that the reasons which our spirits[1] make for the contrary are but sophistry and false wiles to fear thee from the light, that thou mightest follow them blindfold and be their captive to honor their ceremonies and to offer to their belly.

First, God gave the children of Israel a law by the hand of Moses in their mother tongue,[2] and all the prophets wrote in their mother tongue, and all the Psalms were in the mother tongue. And there was Christ but figured[3] and described in ceremonies, in riddles, in parables, and in dark prophecies. What is the cause that we may not have the Old Testament with the New also, which is the light of the Old, and wherein is openly declared before the eyes that there was darkly prophesied? I can imagine no cause verily except it be that we should not see the work of Antichrist and juggling of hypocrites. What should be the cause that we which walk in the broad day, should not see as well as they that walked in the night,[4] or that we should not see as well at noon, as they did in the twilight? . . .

They will say haply,[5] the scripture requireth a pure mind and a quiet mind. And therefore the layman because he is altogether encumbered with worldly business, cannot understand them. If that be the cause, then it is a plain case that our prelates understand not the scriptures themselves. For no layman is so tangled with worldly business as they are. The great things of the world are ministered by them. Neither do the laypeople any great thing, but at their assignment.

"If the scripture were in the mother tongue," they will say, "then would the laypeople understand it every man after his own ways." Wherefore serveth the curate, but to teach them the right way? Wherefore were the holy days made, but that the people should come and learn? Are ye not abominable schoolmasters, in that ye take so great wages, if ye will not teach? If ye would teach, how could ye do it so well, and with so great profit, as when the lay people have the scripture before them in their mother tongue? For then should they see, by the order of the text, whether thou jugglest or not. And then would they believe it, because it is the scripture of God, though thy living be never so abominable. Where now because your living and your preaching are so contrary, and because they grope out in every sermon your open and manifest lies, and smell your insatiable covetousness, they believe you not when you preach truth.[a] But alas, the curates themselves (for the most part) wot no more what the New or the Old Testament meaneth, than do the Turks. Neither know they of any more than that they read at Mass, matins, and evensong, which yet they understand not. Neither care they but even to mumble up so much every day (as the pie and popinjay[6] speak they wot not what) to fill their bellies withal. If they will not let the layman have the word of God in his mother tongue, yet let the priests have it, which for a great part of them do understand no Latin at all, but sing, and say, and patter all day, with the lips only, that which the heart understandeth not. . . .

Christ saith that there shall come false prophets[7] in his name and say that they themselves are Christ, that is, they shall so preach Christ that men must believe in them, in their holiness and things of their imagination without God's word: yea, and that against-Christ, or Antichrist[8] that shall come is nothing but such false prophets that shall juggle with the scripture and beguile the people with false interpretations as all the false prophets, scribes, and Pharisees did in the Old Testament. How shall I know whether ye are that against-Christ, or false prophets, or no, seeing ye will not let me see how ye allege the scriptures? Christ saith: "By their deeds ye shall know them."[9] . . .

The sermons which thou readest in the Acts of the Apostles and all that the apostles preached were no doubt preached in the mother tongue. Why then might they not be written in the mother tongue? As, if one of us preach a good sermon, why may it not be written? Saint Jerome also translated the Bible into his mother tongue.[10] Why may not we also? They will say it cannot be translated into our tongue, it is so rude. It is not so rude as they are false liars. For the Greek tongue agreeth more with the English than with the Latin. And the properties of the Hebrew tongue agreeth a thousand times more with the English than with the Latin. The manner of speaking is both one so that in a thousand places thou need not but to translate it into the English word for word; when thou must seek a compass[11] in the Latin and yet shalt have much work to translate it well-favorably, so that it has the same grace and sweetness, sense and pure understanding with it in the Latin, as it hath in the Hebrew. A thousand parts better may it be translated into the English than into the Latin. Yea, and except my memory fail me, and that I have forgotten what I read when I was a child thou shalt find in the English chronicle how that King Athelstan[12] caused the holy scripture to be translated into the tongue that was then in England,[13] and how the prelates exhorted him there unto.

Moreover, seeing that one of you ever preacheth contrary to another. And when two of you meet, the one disputeth and brawleth with the other, as it were two scolds. And for as much as one holdeth this doctor and another that, one followeth Duns [Scotus], another Saint Thomas [Aquinas], another Bonaventura, Alexander de Hales, Raymond, Lyre, Brygot, Dorbell, Holcott, Gorram, Trumbett, Hugo de Sancto Victore, De Monte Regio, De Nova Villa, De Media Villa,[14] and such like out of number.[b] So that if thou hadst but of every author one book, thou couldst not pile them up in any warehouse in London, and every author is one contrary unto another. In so great diversity of spirits how shall I know who lieth and who saith truth? Whereby shall I try them and judge them? Verily by God's word which only is true. But how shall I that do when you will not let me see the scripture?

"Nay," say they, "the scripture is so hard that thou couldst never understand it but by the doctors." That is, I must measure the meteyard[15] by the cloth. Here be twenty cloths of diverse lengths and diverse breadths. How shall I be sure of the length of the meteyard by them? I suppose rather I must be first sure of the length of the meteyard, and thereby measure and judge of the cloths. If I must first believe the doctor, then is the doctor first true, and the truth of the scripture dependeth on his truth. And so the truth of God springeth of the truth of man. Thus Antichrist turneth the roots of trees upwards. What is the cause that we damn some of Origen's works[16] and allow some? How know we that some is heresy and some not? By the scriptures I trow. How know we that Saint Augustine[17] (which is the best or one of the best that ever wrote upon the scripture) wrote many things amiss at the beginning, as many other doctors do? Verily by the scriptures,[c] as he himself well perceived afterward, when he looked more diligently upon them, and revoked many things again. He wrote of many things which he understood not when he was newly converted, ere he had thoroughly seen the scriptures and followed the opinions of Plato and the common persuasions of man's wisdom that were then famous. . . .

    Finally, that this threatening and forbidding the laypeople to read the scripture is not for love of your souls (which they care for as the fox does for the geese), is evident and clearer than the sun, in as much as they permit and suffer you to read Robin Hood,[18] and Bevis of Hampton,[19] Hercules, Hector, and Troilus,[20] with a thousand histories and fables of love and wantonness and of ribaldry as filthy as heart can think,[d] to corrupt the minds of youth withal, clean contrary to the doctrine of Christ and his apostles. For Paul (Ephesians 5) saith: "See that fornication and all uncleanness, or covetousness, be not once named among you, as it becometh saints: neither filthiness, neither foolish talking nor jesting which are not comely. For this ye know that no whoremonger, other unclean person, or covetous person (which is the worshipper of images) hath any inheritance in the kingdom of Christ and of God." And after, saith he: "Through such things comes the wrath of God upon the children of unbelief." Now seeing they permit you freely to read those things which corrupt your minds and rob you of the kingdom of God and Christ and bring the wrath of God upon you, how is this forbidding for love of your souls?

    A thousand reasons more might be made (as you may see in *Paraclesis Erasmi*[21] and in his preface to the *Paraphrase of Matthew*[22]) unto which they should be compelled to hold their peace or to give shameful answers. But I hope that these are sufficient unto them that thirst the truth. God for his mercy and truth shall well open them more, yea and other secrets of his Godly wisdom, if they be diligent to cry unto him, which grace grant God. . . .

    [Tyndale then provides an extended definition of a doctrine of obedience that requires different levels of the social hierarchy to accept leadership from familial and political superiors (e.g., children must obey parents, and subjects must obey ruler). He goes on to reject the application of fourfold interpretation of the Bible by Scholastic commentators.]

They divide the scripture into four senses, the literal, tropological, alle-gorical, and anagogical. The literal sense is become nothing at all. For the Pope hath taken it clean away and hath made it his possession. He hath partly locked it up with the false and counterfeited keys of his traditions, cer-emonies, and feigned lies and partly driveth me from it with violence of sword. For no man dare abide by the literal sense of the text, but under a protestation, "if it shall please the Pope." The tropological sense pertaineth to good manners (say they) and teacheth what we ought to do. The allegory is appropriate to faith, and the anagogical to hope and things above. Tropo-logical and anagogical are terms of their own feigning and altogether unnec-essary. For they are but allegories both two of them and this word allegory comprehendeth them both and is enough. For choplogical[23] is but an alle-gory of manners and anagogical an allegory of hope. And allegory is as much to say as strange speaking or borrowed speech. As when we say of a wanton child, "This sheep hath maggots in his tail, he must be anointed with birchen salve,"[24] which speech I borrow of the shepherds.

Thou shalt understand therefore that the scripture hath but one sense which is the literal sense. And that literal sense is the root and ground of all and the anchor that never faileth where unto if thou cleave thou canst never err or go out of the way. And if thou leave the literal sense, thou canst not but go out of the way. Never the later, the scripture useth proverbs, simili-tudes, riddles, or allegories, as all other speeches do, but that which the proverb, similitude, riddle, or allegory signifieth is ever the litera' sense which thou must seek out diligently. As in the English we borrow words and sentences of one thing and apply them unto another, and give them new sig-nifications. We say, "let the sea swell and rise as he will yet God hath ap-pointed how far he shall go": meaning that the tyrants shall not do what they would, but that only which God hath appointed them to do. "Look ere you leap," whose literal sense is, do nothing suddenly or without advisement. . . .

So in like manner the scripture borroweth words and sentences of all manner things, and maketh proverbs and similitudes or allegories. As Christ saith (Luke 4), "Physician, heal thyself." Whose interpretation is do that at home which thou dost in strange places, and that is the literal sense. So when I say, "Christ is a lamb,"[25] I mean not a lamb that beareth wool, but a meek and patient lamb which is beaten for other men's faults. Christ is a vine,[26] not that beareth grapes, but out of whose root the branches that believe, suck the spirit of life, and mercy, and grace, and power to be the sons of God and do his will. The similitudes of the gospel are allegories borrowed of worldly matters to express spiritual things. The Apocalypse, or Revelation of John are allegories whose literal sense is hard to find in many places.[27]

Beyond all this,[c] when we have found out the literal sense of the scripture by the process of the text or by a like text of another place. Then go we as the scripture borroweth similitudes of worldly things, even so we again borrow similitudes or allegories of the scripture and apply them to our purposes, which allegories are no sense of the scripture but free things besides the scripture and altogether in the liberty of the spirit. Which allegories I may not make at all the wild adventures; but must keep me within the compass of the faith and ever apply mine allegory to Christ and unto the faith. Take an example, thou hast the story of Peter how he smote off Malchus' ear and how Christ healed it again.[28] There hast thou in the plain text great learning, great fruit, and great edifying which I pass over because of tediousness. Then come I, when I preach of the law and the gospel, and borrow this example to express the nature of the law and of the gospel and to paint it unto thee before thine eyes. And of Peter and his sword make I the law and of Christ the gospel saying, "as Peter's sword cutteth off the ear, so doth the law. The law damneth, the law killeth, and mangleth the conscience."

There is no ear so righteous that can abide the hearing of the law. There is no deed so good but the law damneth it. But Christ, that is to say the gospel, the promises, and testament that God hath made in Christ healeth the ear and conscience which the law hath hurt. The gospel is life, mercy, and forgiveness freely, and altogether an healing plaster. And as Peter doth but hurt and make a wound where was none before, even so doth the law. For when we think that we are holy, and righteous, and full of good deeds if the law be preached aright, our righteousness and good deeds vanish away, as smoke in the wind and we are left damnable sinners only. And as thou seest how that Christ healeth not till Peter had wounded, and as an healing plaster helpeth not till the corsie[29] hath troubled the wound, even so the gospel helpeth not, but when the law hath wounded the conscience, and brought the sinner into the knowledge of his sin. This allegory proveth nothing, neither can do. For it is not the scripture, but an example or similitude borrowed from the scripture to declare a text or a conclusion of the scripture more expressly and to root it and grave it in the heart. For a similitude or an example doth print a thing much deeper in the wits of a man than doth a plain speaking, and leaveth behind him as it were a sting to prick him forward and to awake him withal. Moreover, if I could not prove with an open text that which the allegory doth express, then were the allegory a thing to be jested at and of no greater value than a tale of Robin Hood.[30] This allegory as touching his first part is proved by Paul in [the] third chapter of his epistle to the Romans where he saith, "the law causeth wrath;" and in the seventh chapter to the Romans, "when the law or commandment came, sin revived, and I became dead;" and in the second epistle to the Corinthians in the third chapter, the law is called "the minister of death and damnation," etc. And as concerning the second part, Paul saith to the Romans in the fifth chapter, "in that we are justified by faith we are at peace with God." And in the second epistle to the Corinthians in the third [chapter], the gospel is called "the ministration of justifying and of the spirit." And Galatians 4, "the spirit cometh by preaching of the faith," etc. Thus doth the literal sense prove the allegory and bear it, as the foundation beareth the house. And because that allegories prove nothing, therefore are they to be used soberly and seldom, and only where the text offereth thee an allegory.

And of this manner (as I above have done) doth Paul borrow a similitude, a figure or an allegory of Genesis to express the nature of the law and of the gospel, and by Hagar and her son declareth the property of the law and of her bond-children which will be justified by deeds; and by Sarah and her son declareth the property of the gospel and of her free children which are justified by faith,[31] and how the children of the law which believe in their works persecute the children of the gospel which believe in the mercy and truth of God and in the testament of his son Jesus our Lord. And likewise do we borrow likenesses or allegories of the scripture, as of Pharaoh and Herod and of the scribes and Pharisees, to express our miserable captivity and persecution under Antichrist the Pope.

The greatest cause of which captivity and the decay of the faith and this blindness wherein we now are, sprang first of allegories. For Origen and those of his time drew all the scripture unto allegories. Whose example they that came after followed so long, till at the last they forgot the order and process of the text, supposing that the scripture served but to feign allegories upon. Insomuch that twenty doctors expound one text twenty ways, as children make descant upon plain song. Then came our sophisters with their anagogical and choplogical sense, and with an antetheme[32] of half an inch, out of which some of them draw a third of nine days long. Yea, thou shall find enough that will preach Christ, and prove whatsoever point of the faith that thou wilt, as well out of a fable of Ovid or any other poet,[f] as out of Saint John's gospel or Paul's epistles. Yea, they are come unto such blindness that they not only say the literal sense profiteth not, but also that it is hurtful, and noisome, and killeth the soul. Which damnable doctrine they prove by a text of Paul (2 Corinthians 3) where he saith "the letter killeth, but the spirit giveth life." "Lo," say they, "the literal sense killeth and the spiritual sense giveth life." We must therefore, say they, seek out some choplogical sense. . . .

Marginal Glosses

   ᵃ Why the preachers are not believed when they say truth.

   ᵇ Contrary doctors.

   ᶜ The scripture is the trial of all doctrine and the right touchstone.

   ᵈ Read what thou wilt: yea and say what thou wilt save the truth.

   ᵉ The right use of allegories.

   ᶠ Poetry is as good divinity as the scripture to our schoolmen [i.e., Scholastics].

Notes

   1. Clergy.
   2. The Pentateuch.
   3. Rom. 5:14.
   4. Prior to Christ.
   5. Perchance.
   6. Magpie and parrot.
   7. Matt. 24:4–6.
   8. 1 John 2:18–27.
   9. Matt. 7:16.
   10. The Vulgate Bible.
   11. Guidance.
   12. King of the West Saxons, 925–39.
   13. An unknown translation into Old English.
   14. Scholastic theologians and philosophers.
   15. Measuring stick.
   16. Theologian (c. 185–254).
   17. Patristic theologian (354–430).
   18. Legendary hero familiar from ballads.
   19. A medieval romance.
   20. Mythological heroes.
   21. The introduction to Erasmus's Greek New Testament (1516), in which he appeals for translation of the Bible into the vernacular.
   22. A section of Erasmus's *Paraphrases on the New Testament.*
   23. Nonsensical, a coinage based on "chop logic."
   24. Beaten with switches.
   25. John 1: 29, 36.
   26. John 15:1
   27. Like Erasmus, Tyndale did not comment on Revelation.
   28. John 18:10.
   29. Corrosive.
   30. An untrue fable.
   31. Gal. 4:22–31.
   32. Preface to a sermon.

B. Thomas More, from *The Confutation*
of Tyndale's Answer (1532–33)

Sir Thomas More (1478–1535) and William Tyndale engaged in bitter controversy concerning the validity of Bible translation, the nature of the "true" church,
and the authority of the pope in religious and temporal affairs. Written in
response to Tyndale's *An Answer unto Sir Thomas More's Dialogue* (Antwerp,
1531), More's *Confutation* appeared in two parts, the first written while he was
lord chancellor (1532) and the second after he had resigned from that office
(1533). William Rastell, a printer who was More's nephew, printed both parts.

More's tract advocates the burning of Tyndale's translation of the New Testament on the ground that it contains Lutheran propaganda (see 1.1.A). More
cites Tyndale's translation of Greek words with polemical equivalents that substi-
tute inward *repentance* for *penitence* requiring priestly absolution and that deny
the authority of the Church of Rome (*congregation* instead of *church*) and its
priesthood (*senior* instead of *priest*), the doctrine of good works (*love* instead of
charity), and key Roman Catholic practices (*idols* and *witchcraft* instead of *images*
and *ceremonies*). More also attacks Tyndale's rejection of fourfold allegorical
interpretation of the Bible (see 1.2.A), citing Christ's use of parables and Saint
Paul's allegorical interpretation of Deuteronomy 25 by reference to providing
priests with a livelihood (1 Cor. 9).

SOURCE: *STC* 18079, M4ᵛ–N1ʳ; 18080, H1ᵛ–3ᵛ.

EDITION: More.

REFERENCES: Daniell; Greenblatt; Marius.

In the beginning of my dialogue I showed that Tyndale's translation of the
New Testament was well worthy to be burned, because it well showed in
itself that he had of an evil mind translated it in such manner of wise, as it
might serve him for a principal instrument, toward the setting forth of all
such heresies as he had learned of Luther, and intended to send over hither
and spread abroad within this realm, the truth of which my saying Tyndale
and his fellows have in such open fashion testified and declared themselves,
that I need for myself, in that point to use no further defense.

For every man well seeth that there was never English book of heresy
sent hither since (as there hath been many, some particularly against the
blessed sacrament of the altar . . . and some were against purgatory, and some
against almost altogether that good is in Christ's church, as are the books of
Tyndale himself, his wicked Mammon,[1] his obedience,[2] and diverse other) in
all these ever more one piece of their complaint hath been the burning of
Tyndale's testament. For surely first his false translation with their farther
false construction, they thought should be the bass and tenor whereupon
they would sing the trouble with much false descant. And therefore very hot

they take it, that the goodness of the king's grace with the lords of his honorable council and the clergy of the realm, have burned up their false pricked books. So was it now that among other tokens of Tyndale's evil intent in this translation, I showed as for example that he changed commonly this word *church* into this word *congregation*, and this word *priest*, into this word *senior*, and *charity* into *love*, and *grace* into *favor*, *confession* into *knowledge*, and *penitence* into *repentance*; with many words more which he changeth and useth daily, as in turning *idols* into *images*, and *anointing* into *smearing*, *consecrating* into *charming*, *sacraments* into *ceremonies*, and the *ceremonies* into *witchcraft*, and yet many more. . . .

Now cometh Tyndale and for answer thereof, and, to disprove all that I lay against him in the translating of diverse of these words, showeth that the Latin text and the Greek may be his excuse and defense. Forasmuch as the words in the Latin text and the Greek, do as he saith signify such things as he hath expressed in his English translation, by those English words that I find the fault in. But first to what purpose serveth all his defense? When he hath since himself, proved by his own other books, that he is an heretic, and that his heresies be such, as it must needs make it clear that, though another man translating the Testament and being good and faithful might have used happily those changes among, without evil meaning or any suspicion thereof. Yet he saith those changes so served for his heresies, must needs be, not suspected, but manifestly detected and perceived to have used them being such so many and so often, not of any chance or good intent, but of very plain purpose to give his heresies in the ears of unlearned men, some color of proof in the text of the New Testament. . . .

Now where he saith that the clergy useth to destroy the literal sense of the scripture with false fained allegories, this is falsely said of him. For the allegory neither destroyeth nor letteth the literal sense, but the literal sense standeth whole beside.

And where he saith that there is none allegory sense, as Luther and he say both, and that in more places than one, yet shall our old mark of old holy doctors and saints, mark him for an heretic again. For I am sure he shall not lightly find any of those old, but that he used allegories.

Luther and Tyndale would have all allegories and all other senses taken away, saving the literal sense alone. But God whose plenteous spirit indited the scripture, foresaw full well himself that many godly allegories holy men should by his inspiration at diverse times draw out thereof. And sometime he indited it, and our savior himself sometime spake his words in such wise, that the letter had none other sense than mysteries and allegories, as commonly all his parables be, of which he expounded some himself and some he expounded not, but hath left them to be expounded by holy doctors after his death, and some of them hath he helpen diverse to expound diversely, as his high wisdom saw that diverse good fruit should follow and ensue thereupon.

Sometime also though the literal sense be full good, yet doth God give the grace to some man to find out a further thing therein. Which sense God that indited the letter, did when he made it foresee, and more did set thereby than by the sense that immediately riseth upon the letter, which letter his high wisdom so tempered for the nonce, that such other sense might be perceived therein and drawn out thereof, by such as himself had determined to give the grace to find it.

And for example our Lord saith in the book of Deuteronomy, "Thou shall not bind the mouth of the ox as he goeth in the flower and thresheth the corn."[3] The very letter is of itself good, and teacheth men a certain reason and justice to deal well and justly, even with the very beasts that labor with them, and to abhor without good cause either to pine them or pain them. Now though this sentence be good, and the Jews were bounden by the letter of the law, to order themselves in that wise toward their oxen, seeing no further therein, nor some so far neither peradventure; yet did the Apostle[4] find out another secret sense therein, and that sense such as in respect thereof he set the other at naught, and showed that God meant thereby that the priest which laboreth spiritually in his office, must have his temporal living therefore. And to prove that the spirit of God intended this sense and understanding therein, he saith, "Careth God aught for the oxen,"[5] as though he would say nay. And yet indeed God careth and provideth for the living of every living thing. For it is written in the Psalm, that God giveth the meat to the beasts and to the young birds of the crows that call upon him.[6] And our savior saith himself, "Look ye upon the birds of the air, they neither sow nor spin, and yet your father that is in heaven feedeth them."[7]

And thus it appeareth that God careth for the feeding of all that ever he hath made.

But yet saw Saint Paul, that God so much cared for the priests' living, above that he careth for the oxen's living, that in respect of the tone compared with the other, God cared not for the ox at all, but would we should understand thereby, that we should in any wise provide that the priest which laboreth with us in spiritual business, should have of us his temporal living. And I ween Tyndale is even angry with Saint Paul for this exposition.

Now are there many other texts in the Old Law, which in likewise receive like exposition, by goodly and fruitful allegories, as in the old holy saints' books appeareth. All which will Tyndale here have wiped out in any wise and will have none allegories at all.

Notes

1. *The Parable of the Wicked Mammon.*
2. *The Obedience of a Christian Man* (see 1.2.A, 2.1).
3. Deut. 25:4.
4. Saint Paul.
5. 1 Cor. 9:9.
6. Ps. 145:15 (Vulg. Ps. 146:15).
7. Matt. 6:26.

C. Robert Parsons, from
A Temperate Ward-Word (1599)

Robert Parsons, or Persons, S.J. (1546–1610) resigned his fellowship at Balliol College, Oxford, and went abroad because of his Catholic leanings. A period of study at Louvain preceded his ordination as a Jesuit priest in 1578. Joining Edmund Campion as a pioneer member of the English Mission, he eluded capture by Elizabethan authorities for his missionary endeavors. A secret press that he established near London printed Catholic devotional texts and polemics including William Allen's *True, Sincere, and Modest Defense of English Catholics* (see 2.7). Parsons left England after Campion's apprehension in 1580. In addition to founding an English school at Eu, Normandy, which he later relocated at Saint-Omer, Parsons became rector of the English College at Rome and founded Jesuit seminaries at Valladolid and Seville. He traveled widely in support of a Roman Catholic invasion of England. Under his own name and a variety of pseudonyms including N. D. and John Doleman, he published a total of thirty-two books.

    A. Conincx published Parsons's *Temperate Ward-Word* (1599) at Antwerp in response to Sir Francis Hastings's attack on English Catholics in *A Watchword to All Religious, and True Hearted Englishmen* (1598). Parsons rightly rejects the claim that the Roman Catholic Church opposes translation of the Bible into English, but he does insist on the need for clerical licensing and supervision of vernacular readers because of the danger of misinterpretation. He cites Anne Askew (see 6.1) and Joan Bocher as examples of misinformed readers who fell into heresy because they interpreted the Bible without clerical intercession. Like More, Parsons rejects Tyndale's attack on allegorical interpretation of the Bible (see 1.2.A). See Parsons, *Christian Directory* (2.5) and *Treatise of the Three Conversions of England* (6.9).

SOURCE: *STC* 19415, pp. 13–17.

And here I must begin in this very place to tell him, that two manifest untruths, properly called lies (for that they are willful), are set down by him in the words alleged, and known to be such to very children and novices in the Catholic religion.

    The first, that it is holden for heresy, or ever was, to read upon the Bible or "Book of God" (as he calleth it) in what language soever, for even in vulgar tongues it is permitted to infinite laypeople in all Catholic countries, by license of the ordinary,[1] as all men know, and it cannot be denied.

    The other lie is, "that for this fault only men were called before the Romish clergy in England, and branded to the slaughter."

    These I say are apparent fictions; let the knight defend his honor in avowing them. It remaineth to me only to lay down what the Catholic

Church did ordain in this behalf, and what reasons she might have to restrain some of this man's "dim and glimmering" people from reading at their pleasure, upon vulgar[2] Bibles without license, or without the spectacles of competent learning and understanding requisite for to profit thereby; and how far this prohibition of the church stretched, and whether this may justly be accounted "bloody and savage proceedings" or rather prudent and provident circumspection for simple men's safety.

First then, most certain it is that no man or woman was ever forbidden to read any part of the holy scriptures in any of the three learned languages wherein they were written, to wit Hebrew, Greek, and Latin. And second, the restraint that was made of vulgar translations, as French, Dutch, and English and the like, was only that no such translation should be admitted or used, except it were first examined by learned men by order of the bishop and ordinary to see whether it were well and truly translated or no. And then such men and women of the laity were permitted to use the said translation approved, as should have license of the said ordinary, and be thought fit and able to profit, and not to take hurt or hindrance thereby; others had the same in effect and substance delivered unto them by sermons, books, and other means.

This was the order, let indifferent men judge and determine what cruelty or mercy, impiety or piety, might be herein. For first, no man will deny but if the translator did not put down truly and sincerely the words of scriptures in his vulgar translation, then the simple reader that cannot discern, should take man's word for God's word, which were great inconvenience, and for this cause only (if none other were) most necessary was it, that some order should be set down for examining of translations, whereby might be distinguished when God and when man speaketh in the scriptures. And secondly though it were certain that the words of scripture were set down truly in vulgar translations, yet if the same reader by ignorance did take out of the true words a false sense; then sucked he poison instead of wholesome doctrine. If then in a fair and pleasant garden, there should be this danger, not only that one herb taken for another might endanger a man's life, but the selfsame herb gathered and dressed in different sort, might be either poison or treacle, who would condemn the master of the garden, if he suffered not every one indifferently to gather herbs there, but such as either had skill of themselves to discern, or were directed by others how to gather and use those herbs to their help and health, and not to their hurt and destruction; and to the very same end was the prohibition that ignorant people should not read scriptures, but with leave and direction.

Who can deny but that Saint Paul talking of the scriptures as they were in the learned tongues (especially of the Old Testament) saith of them, *Litera occidit, spiritus autem vivificat*, the letter or literal sound doth oftentimes murder the reader, and the only spirit that is the internal true and spiritual meaning of the scriptures, doth give life.[3] And albeit Saint Augustine in his learned book *De spiritu et litera* doth extend these words of the apostle to a farther meaning also, yet he teacheth this too, and so do the rest of the ancient fathers, namely Saint Jerome *Ad Nepotianum*, handling the story of King David (3 Regum 1)[4] where the young virgin Abishag was sought out to heat him in his old age; Saint Jerome saith, that if we should follow *literam occidentem*, the murdering letter, it seemeth a jest and fable, but if we fly to the hidden spiritual sense and meaning, it is most holy.

But now let us ask of you Sir Knight, how will your unlearned readers those whom you call "dim and glimmering people," discern these things without a guide, such as the Catholic Church doth appoint for expounding the scriptures to simple people, by catechisms, sermons, homilies, teaching of pastors, and the like, without delivering the whole Bible into their hands, to be used or abused to their destruction.

Furthermore you cannot deny, but that the understanding of scriptures is a particular gift of God, reserved specially unto Christ, who had the key to open the book sealed with seven seals, as Saint John testifieth,[5] and to the same effect is it recorded in Saint Luke's Gospel[6] for a singular grace, bestowed by our Savior upon the church, *tunc apervit illas sensum, ut intelligerint scripturas*. Then after his resurrection did he open to them the sense, whereby they might understand scriptures of themselves. For ever before he had interpreted the same lightly unto them, as in the Gospels appeareth. He sent also Saint Philip the Apostle by commandment of his angel, to go and interpret a certain place of the prophet Isaiah, unto the great eunuch and treasurer of the queen of Ethiopia, when he would convert him.[7] And it is to be observed, that albeit Christ might have opened the sense of the scripture to himself immediately, yet would he send him a guide. Yea though the said eunuch were learned (as may appear by that being an Ethiopian read the prophet in Hebrew) and though he were also instructed in the Jew's religion (as it is proved by that the story recordeth that he came to adore in Jerusalem) yet all this notwithstanding, was he so far from the pride of our "peevish proud Protestant people" nowadays, which make no bones at any difficulty of scriptures, as when he was asked by Saint Philip, *Putasne intelligis, que legis?* Thinkest thou that thou understandest the scripture which thou readest? He answered, how can I understand it, except somebody do expound the same unto me? Which answer I believe many a good wife in London, that goeth up and down with her Bible under her arm, would be ashamed to give if she were asked whether she understood the whole Bible or no.

These then (Sir Knight) are the reasons why some of those, your "glimmering and enlightened people," were restrained by Catholic discipline to read upon ("God's Book" you call it) vulgar translations; not to bar them from light as you maliciously calumniate, but rather lest they being but half blind should become whole blind, that is to say mad and obstinate blind of ignorance, and unlearned blind; for such effects do ensue sometimes of the rash reading of this "Book of God," when thereof is engendered falsehood and heresy, that is, the doctrine of the Devil, for proof whereof, let us consider whether in a thousand years together in England, France, and Germany and other places of Christendom, while this prudent restraint of Catholic Church lasted, of not permitting all ignorant people to read scriptures at their pleasures, in vulgar languages, without an interpreter, there arose so many sects, heresies, and alterations about religion, as there have risen in fifty or threescore years, since this reading was left open to all; there is no comparison. And if we consider only England, the matter is evident, that more sects have sprung up of late by many degrees. Yea though we leave all other sects that are permitted, or winked at in England, and respect such only as have been punished openly by the magistrate, namely such persons as have been whipped or burned in London, Norfolk, and other places for heretics, in the time of her Majesty's reign that now is, for denying Christ himself or other points of the blessed Trinity, being altogether unlearned people, as our chronicles testify, of whom I ask, had they ever fallen into such errors and obstinacy, but only by reading scriptures in the vulgar language? Had ever William Hacket[8] dreamed himself to be Christ, or William Geoffrey[9] before him, but by this way? We see then the inconvenience.

In King Henry's time when Tyndale had translated and printed the New Testament in English at Cologne, and began to seek means to have them dispersed into England, the laws and King's commandment being then against it; there was a certain foul fustilings,[10] dishonest of her body with base fellows, as was openly reported, whose name was Joan Knell, alias Bocher,[11] if I forget not, who beginning to be a great reader of scriptures herself, became a principal instrument also in that time to divulge such Bibles as were sent, especially in the court, where she became known to certain women in authority; and to convey the books more safely, she used to bind them in strings under her apparel, and so to pass them into the court; but her nearest friendship was with Anne Askew,[12] whom King Henry afterward caused to be burned for denying the Real Presence in the sacrament of the altar.

But this other scripturian profited so well, as in the fifth year of King Edward's reign she was burned also by the Protestants of that time, for denying Christ to have taken flesh of the Virgin Mary. Who when she was condemned to die, spake very scornfully to the judges, and said: "It is a goodly matter to consider your ignorance; it is not long ago since you burned Anne Askew for a piece of bread, and yet came your selves soon after to believe and profess the same doctrine, for which you burned her; and now, forsooth, you will needs burn me for a piece of flesh, and in the end you will come to believe this also, when you have read the scriptures and understand them." And when she came to die in Smithfield and Doctor Story endeavored to convert her she scoffed at him, saying "He lied like, etc." and bade him "Go read scriptures."

And thus much may serve for the repelling those "clouds, mists, and darkness" which this "watch-word giver" will needs imagine to be among us, for that all cobblers do not clout scriptures in our commonwealth. . . .

How manifest a falsehood it is that reading of scriptures is forbidden to all laymen, is sufficiently showed by that which goeth before; for in any of the three learned tongues, any layman or woman may read them at their pleasure, and in vulgar translations also such as have license. And I think Sir Francis will not deny, that many of the laity understand Latin; how then, and with what face complaineth he so piteously or rather hypocritically, "that the sacred word of God which was given to be a lantern to our feet, etc." was forbidden to the lay sort?

Notes

1. Person in authority.
2. Vernacular.
3. 2 Cor. 3:6.
4. 1 Kings 1:2.
5. Rev. 5:5–7.
6. Luke 24:45.
7. Acts 8:27–38.
8. A Brownist believer in the complete autonomy of each church congregation, whose messianic delusions and plot against Elizabeth I led to execution for treason in 1591.
9. A religious visionary.
10. A ponderous, clumsy person, esp. a fat, slovenly woman.
11. Anabaptist who was burned alive for heresy in 1550.
12. See 6.1, 6.9.

SELFHOOD AND OBEDIENCE IN CHURCH AND STATE

2.1. William Tyndale, from
The Obedience of a Christian Man (1528)

Writing in response to accusations lodged by Thomas More and others that Protestants wished to overthrow the English monarchy, Tyndale responds that the New Testament promulgates a doctrine of obedience of inferior members of the social hierarchy to their superiors, including children to parents and servants to masters. Subjects therefore owe obedience to the King, who renders an account to God alone. In supporting royal supremacy over the Church of England, Tyndale rejects the authority of the Pope, whom he vilifies as the Antichrist of Rome. From this time onward, anti-popery would represent a distinctive feature of early modern English Protestant thinking. When Anne Boleyn shared her copy of *The Obedience of a Christian Man* with Henry VIII, according to Foxe's *Book of Martyrs*, he announced that "This is a book for me and all kings to read." For another selection from *The Obedience of a Christian Man*, see 1.2.A. Also see Tyndale's New Testament and John Foxe's life of Tyndale (1.1.A and 6.5.A).

SOURCE: *STC* 24446, fol. 29^r–31^r, 41^v–42^r, 44^v.

The Obedience of Subjects unto Kings, Princes, and Rulers

The thirteenth chapter of Paul (Romans): Let every soul submit himself unto the authority of the higher powers. There is no power but of God. The powers that be are ordained of God. Whosoever therefore resisteth the power resisteth the ordinance of God. They that resist, shall receive to themself damnation. For rulers are not to be feared for good works but for evil. Wilt thou be without fear of the power? Do well then and so shalt thou be praised of the same. For he is the minister of God, for thy wealth. But and if thou do evil, then fear. For he beareth not a sword for nought. For he is the minister of God, to take vengeance on them that do evil. Wherefore ye must needs obey not for fear of vengeance only, but also because of conscience. Even for this cause pay ye tribute. For they are God's ministers, serving for the same purpose. . . .

God therefore hath given laws unto all nations and in all lands hath put kings, governors, and rulers in his own stead, to rule the world through them. And hath commanded all causes to be brought before them, as thou readest (Exodus 22). In all cases (saith he) of injury or wrong, whether it be ox, ass, sheep, or vesture, or any lost thing which another challengeth, let the cause of both parties be brought unto the gods: whom the gods condemn the same shall pay double unto his neighbor. Mark, the judges are called gods in the scriptures because they are in God's room and execute the commandments of God. And in another place of the said chapter Moses chargeth saying: see that thou rail not on the gods neither speak evil of the ruler of thy people. Whosoever therefore resisteth them resisteth God (for they are in the room of God) and they that resist shall receive their damnation. . . .

Neither may the inferior person avenge himself upon the superior or violently resist him for whatsoever wrong it be. If he do he is condemned in the deed doing: inasmuch as he taketh upon him that which belongeth to God only which saith vengeance is mine and I will reward (Deuteronomy 32). And Christ saith (Matthew 26), all they that take the sword shall perish with the sword. Takest thou a sword to avenge thyself? So givest thou not room unto God to avenge thee but robbest him of his most high honor, in that thou wilt not let him be judge over thee.

If any man might have avenged himself upon his superior, that might David most righteously have done upon King Saul which so wrongfully persecuted David, even for no other cause, than that God had anointed him king and promised him the kingdom. Yet when God had delivered Saul into the hands of David, that he might have done what he would with him as thou seest in the first book of Kings the twenty-fourth chapter, how Saul came into the cave where David was. And David came to him secretly and cut off a piece of his garment. And as soon as he had done it his heart smote him because he had done so much unto his lord. And when his men encouraged him to flee him he answered, "The lord forbid it me, that I should lay my hand on him." Neither suffered he his men to hurt him.

Against the Pope's False Power

What good conscience can there be among our spirituality[1] to gather so great treasure together and with hypocrisy of their false learning to rob almost every man of house and lands, and yet not therewith content but with all craft and wiliness to purchase so great liberties and exemptions from all manner bearing with their brethren, seeking in Christ nothing but lucre? I pass over with silence how they teach princes in every land to lade new exactions and tyranny on their subjects more and more daily, neither for what purpose[a] they do it say I. God I trust shall shortly disclose their juggling and bring their falsehood to light and lay a medicine to them, to make their scabs break out. Nevertheless this I say, that they have robbed all realms, not of God's word only but also of all wealth and prosperity, and have driven peace out of all lands and withdrawn themselves from all obedience to princes and have separated themselves from the lay men, counting them viler than dogs, and have set up that great idol, the Whore of Babylon, Antichrist of Rome whom they call Pope, and have conspired against all commonwealths and have made them a several kingdom, wherein it is lawful unpunished to work all abomination. In every parish have they spies and in every great man's house and in every tavern and alehouse. And through confessions know they all secrets, so that no man may open his mouth to rebuke whatsoever they do, but that he shall be shortly made an heretic. In all councils is one of them, yea the most part and chief rulers of the councils are of them: But of their council is no man. . . .

Heads and governors are ordained of God[2] and are even the gift of God, whether they be good or bad. And whatsoever is done unto us by them, that doth God, be it good or bad. If they be evil why are they evil? Verily for our wickedness' sake are they evil. Because that when they were good we would not receive that goodness of the hand of God and be thankful, submitting ourselves unto his laws and ordinances, but abused the goodness of God unto our sensual and beastly lusts. Therefore doth God make his scourge of them and turn them unto wild beasts contrary to the nature of their names and offices, even into lions, bears, foxes and unclean swine, to avenge himself of our unnatural and blind unkindness and of our rebellious disobedience. . . .

Annotation

[a] What purpose even to flatter the princes that they may abuse their authority to slay whosoever believeth in Christ and to maintain the Pope.

Notes

1. Clergy.
2. 1 Peter 2:14.

2.2. *Book of Homilies* (1547)

Published near the outset of Edward VI's reign, *Certain Sermons, or Homilies, Appointed by the King's Majesty, to Be Declared and Read, by All Parsons, Vicars, or Curates, Every Sunday in their Churches* (commonly known as the *Book of Homilies*) represents the first cautious step toward an English Protestant church service. Mandatory reading of these sermons reflected the scarcity of educated ministers and enabled the government to control pulpit discourse. Produced by churchmen under the supervision of Archbishop Thomas Cranmer (see Appendix), this collection shifted the center of worship from celebration of the Mass to preaching and Bible instruction. By official order, every parish church was to acquire and employ the Great Bible, the *Book of Homilies*, and the *Book of Common Prayer*. Following the reign of Mary I, the Elizabethan regime restored use of the Edwardian service books with little revision.[1]

The "Homily of Faith" resorts to the Catholic Epistles attributed to James, Peter, and John, in asserting that although humanity depends wholly upon divine grace, "true" faith invariably produces good works. It denies antinomian belief that justification by faith exempts believers from works and laws. The "Homily of Good Works" relies on the Pauline Epistles in proclaiming that faith validates "true" works. This homily concludes with an iconoclastic attack on nonscriptural traditions such as pilgrimages, purchase of indulgences, and veneration of images and relics. The allegory in book 1, Canto 10 of Spenser's *Faerie Queene* corresponds to these homilies in subordinating Charissa (Charity or Works) to her elder and middle sisters, Fidelia (Faith) and Speranza (Hope).

SOURCE: *STC* 13640, F2ʳ–4ʳ, I3ʳ–K2ᵛ.

EDITION: Bond.

REFERENCES: Booty; King 1982.

A. From the "Homily of Faith"

The first entry unto God, good Christian people, is through faith, whereby, as it is declared in the last sermon, we be justified before God. And lest any man should be deceived, for lack of right understanding thereof, it is diligently to be noted that faith is taken in the Scripture two manner of ways.

There is one faith, which in Scripture is called a dead faith,[2] which bringeth forth no good works, but is idle, barren and unfruitful. And this faith, by the holy apostle Saint James, is compared to the faith of devils, which believe God to be true and just, and tremble for fear, yet they do nothing well, but all evil. And such a manner of faith have the wicked and naughty Christian people, which confess God, as Saint Paul sayeth, in their mouth, but deny him in their deeds, being abominable, and without the right faith, and to all good works reprovable.[3] And this faith is a persuasion and belief in man's heart, whereby he knoweth that there is a God, and assenteth unto all truth of God's most holy word contained in Holy Scripture. So that it consisteth only in believing of the Word of God that it is true. And this is not properly called faith. But as he that readeth Caesar's *Commentaries*, believing the same to be true, hath thereby a knowledge of Caesar's life and noble acts, because he believeth the history of Caesar. Yet it is not properly said that he believeth in Caesar, of whom he looketh for no help nor benefit. Even so, he that believeth that all that is spoken of God in the Bible is true, and yet liveth so ungodly that he cannot look to enjoy the promises and benefits of God, although it may be said, that such a man hath a faith and belief to the words of God, yet it is not properly said that he believeth in God, or hath such a faith and trust in God, whereby he may surely look for grace, mercy, and eternal life at God's hand, but rather for indignation and punishment, according to the merits of his wicked life. For as it is written in a book entitled to be of Didimus Alexandrinus, "forasmuch as faith without works is dead, it is not now faith, as a dead man is not a man." This dead faith, therefore, is not the sure and substantial faith which saveth sinners.

Another faith there is in Scripture which is not, as the foresaid faith, idle, unfruitful, and dead, but worketh by charity,[4] as Saint Paul declareth (Gal. 5). Which, as the other vain faith, is called a dead faith, so may this be called a quick or lively faith. And this is not only the common belief of the articles of our faith, but it is also a sure trust and confidence of the mercy of God through our lord Jesus Christ, and a steadfast hope of all good things to be received at God's hand. And that although we, through infirmity or temptation of our ghostly enemy, do fall from him by sin, yet if we return again unto him by true repentance, that he will forgive and forget our offences for his Son's sake our savior Jesus Christ, and will make us inheritors with him of his everlasting kingdom, and that in the meantime, until that kingdom come, he will be our protector and defender in all perils and dangers, whatsoever do chance; and that, though sometime he doth send us sharp adversity, yet that evermore he will be a loving Father unto us, correcting us for our sin, but not withdrawing his mercy finally from us, if we trust in him, and commit ourselves wholly unto him, hang only upon him, and call upon him, ready to obey and serve him. This is the true, lively, and unfeigned Christian faith, and is not in the mouth and outward profession only, but it liveth and stirreth inwardly in the heart. And this faith is not without hope and trust in God, nor without the love of God and of our neighbors, nor without the fear of God, nor without the desire to hear God's Word, and to follow the same in eschewing evil, and doing gladly all good works.

This faith, as Saint Paul describeth it, is the sure ground and foundation of the benefits which we ought to look for and trust to receive of God, a certificate[5] and sure expectation of them, although they yet sensibly appear not unto us.[6] And after he saith: "He that cometh to God must believe, both that he is, and that he is a merciful rewarder of well doers."[7] And nothing commendeth good men unto God so much as this assured faith and trust in him. Of this faith, three things are specially to be noted. First, that this faith doth not lie dead in the heart, but is lively and fruitful in bringing forth good works. Second, that without it, can no good works be done, that shall be acceptable and pleasant to God. Third, what manner of good works they be, that this faith doth bring forth.

For the first, as the light cannot be hid, but will show forth itself at one place or other, so a true faith cannot be kept secret, but when occasion is offered, it will break out and show itself by good works. And as the living body of a man ever exerciseth such things as belongeth to a natural and living body for nourishment and preservation of the same, as it hath need, opportunity, and occasion, even so the soul that hath a lively faith in it will be doing always some good work, which shall declare that it is living, and will not be unoccupied. Therefore, when men hear in the Scriptures so high commendations of faith, that it maketh us to please God, to live with God, and to be the children of God, if then they fantasize that they be set at liberty from doing all good works, and may live as they list, they trifle with God and deceive themselves. And it is a manifest token that they be far from having the true and lively faith, and also far from knowledge, what true faith meaneth. For the very sure and lively Christian faith is not only to believe all things of God, which are contained in Holy Scripture, but also is an earnest trust and confidence in God, that he doth regard us, and hath cure of us, as the father of the child whom he doth love, and that he will be merciful unto us for his only Son's sake, and that we have our savior Christ, our perpetual advocate and priest, in whose only merits, oblation,[8] and suffering we do trust that our offences be continually washed and purged, whensoever we, repenting truly, do return to him with our whole heart, steadfastly determining with ourselves, through his grace, to obey and serve him in keeping his commandments, and never to turn back again to sin. Such is the true faith that the Scripture doth so much commend, the which, when it seeth and considereth what God hath done for us, is also moved through continual assistance of the spirit of God, to serve and please him, to keep his favor, to fear his displeasure, to continue his obedient children, showing thankfulness again by observing his commandments, and that freely, for true love chiefly, and not for dread of punishment, or love of temporal reward, considering how clearly, without our deservings, we have received his mercy and pardon freely.

This true faith will show forth itself and cannot long be idle. For as it is written: "The just man doth live by his faith."[9] He neither sleepeth, nor is idle, when he should wake and be well occupied. And God by his prophet Jeremiah sayeth, that he is a happy and blessed man which hath faith and confidence in God. For he is like a tree set by the waterside, that spreadeth his roots abroad toward the moisture, and feareth not heat when it cometh; his leaf will be green, and will not cease to bring forth his fruit:[10] even so faithful men, putting away all fear of adversity, will show forth the fruit of their good works, as occasion is offered to do them.

B. From the "Homily of Good Works"

Thus have you heard how much the world from the beginning until Christ's time was ever ready to fall from the commandments of God, and to seek other means to honor and serve him, after a devotion imagined of their own heads, and how they extolled their own traditions, as high or above God's commandments. . . .

Which sects and religions had so many hypocritical works in their state of religion, as they arrogantly named it, that their lamps, as they said, ran always over, able to satisfy not only for their own sins, but also for all other their benefactors, brothers, and sisters of their religion, as most ungodly and craftily they had persuaded the multitude of ignorant people, keeping in diverse places, as it were, marts or markets of merits, being full of their holy relics, images, shrines, and works of supererogation,[11] ready to be sold. And all things which they had were called holy: holy cowls, holy girdles, holy pardoned beads, holy shoes, holy rules, and all full of holiness. And what thing can be more foolish, more superstitious, or ungodly, than that men, women, and children should wear a friar's coat to deliver them from agues or pestilence, or when they die, or when they be buried, cause it to be cast upon them in hope thereby to be saved.[12] Which superstition, although, thanks be to God, it hath been little used in this realm, yet in diverse other realms it hath been, and yet is used, both among many, both learned and unlearned. But to pass over the innumerable superstitiousness that hath been in strange apparel, in silence, in dormitory, in cloister, in chapter, in choice of meats, and in drinks, and in such like things, let us consider what enormities and abuses have been in the three chief principal points, which they called the three essentials of religion, that is to say, obedience, chastity, and willful poverty.

First, under pretense of obedience to their father in religion, which obedience they made themselves, they were exempted by their rules and canons from the obedience of their natural father and mother, and from the obedience of emperor and king, and all temporal power, whom of very duty by

God's laws they were bound to obey. And so the profession of their obedience not due was a renunciation of their due obedience. And how their profession of chastity was observed, it is more honesty to pass over in silence, and let the world judge of that which is well known than with unchaste words, by expressing of their unchaste life, to offend chaste and godly ears. And as for their willful poverty, it was such then, when in possessions, jewels, plate and riches they were equal or above merchants, gentlemen, barons, earls, and dukes, yet by this subtle sophistical term, *Proprium in communi*,[13] they deluded the world, persuading that notwithstanding all their possessions and riches, yet they observed their vow, and were in willful poverty. But for all their riches, they might neither help father nor mother, nor other that were indeed very needy and poor, without the license of their father abbot, prior, or warden. And yet they might take of every man, but they might not give aught to any man, no, not to them whom the laws of God bound them to help. And so through their traditions and rules the laws of God could bear no rule with them. And therefore of them might be most truly said, that which Christ spake unto the Pharisees: "You break the commandments of God by your traditions; you honor God with your lips, but your hearts be far from him."[14] And the longer prayers they used by day and by night, under pretense of such holiness, to get the favor of widows and other simple folks, that they might sing trentals[15] and service for their husbands and friends, and admit them into their suffrages, the more truly is verified of them the saying of Christ: "Woe be to you Scribes and Pharisees, hypocrites, for you devour widows' houses under color of long prayers; therefore your damnation shall be the greater. Woe be to you Scribes and Pharisees, hypocrites, for you go about by sea and by land to make more novices and new brethren, and when they be admitted of your sect, you make them the children of hell, worse than yourselves be."[16]

Honor be to God, who did put light in the heart of his faithful and true minister of most famous memory, King Henry VIII, and gave him the knowledge of his word, and an earnest affection to seek his glory, and to put away all such superstitious and pharisaical sect, by Antichrist invented, and set up against the true word of God and glory of his most blessed name, as he gave the like spirit unto the most noble and famous princes: Jehoshaphat, Josiah, and Hezekiah. God grant all us, the king's highness's faithful and true subjects, to feed of the sweet and savory bread of God's own word, and, as Christ commanded, to eschew all our pharisaical and papistical leaven of man's feigned religion. Which, although it were before God most abominable and contrary to God's commandments and Christ's pure religion, yet it was extolled to be a most godly life, and highest state of perfection. As though a man might be more godly and more perfect by keeping the rules, traditions, and professions of men than by keeping the holy commandments of God.

And briefly to pass over the ungodly and counterfeit religions, let us rehearse some other kinds of papistical superstitions and abuses, as of beads, of Lady Psalters[17] and rosaries, of Fifteen Oes,[18] of Saint Bernard's Verses,[19] of Saint Agatha's letters,[20] of purgatory, of masses satisfactory, of stations and jubilees,[21] of feigned relics, of hallowed beads, bells, bread, water, palms, candles, fire and such other,[22] of superstitious fastings, of fraternities,[23] of pardons, with such like merchandise, which were so esteemed and abused to the great prejudice of God's glory and commandments, that they were made most high and most holy things, whereby to attain to the eternal life, or remission of sin. Yea also, vain inventions, unfruitful ceremonies and ungodly laws. Decrees and councils of Rome were in such wise advanced that nothing was thought comparable in authority, wisdom, learning, and godliness unto them. So that the laws of Rome, as they said, were to be received of all men as the four Evangelists, to the which all laws of princes must give place. And the laws of God also partly were omitted and less esteemed, that the said laws, decrees and councils, with their traditions and ceremonies, might be more duly observed and had in greater reverence. Thus was the people, through ignorance, so blinded with the goodly show and appearance of those things that they thought the observing of them to be a more holiness, a more perfect service and honoring of God, and more pleasing to God than the keeping of God's commandments. Such hath been the corrupt inclination of man, ever superstitiously given to make new honoring of God, of his own head, and then to have more affection and devotion to observe that, than to search out God's holy commandments and to keep them. And furthermore, to take God's commandments for men's commandments, and men's commandments for God's commandments, yea, and for the highest and most perfect and holy of all God's commandments. And so was all confused that scant well learned men, and but a small number of them, knew, or at the least, would know, and durst affirm the truth, to separate God's commandments from the commandments of men: whereupon did grow much error, superstition, idolatry, vain religion, preposterous judgment, great contention, with all ungodly living.

Wherefore, as you have any zeal to the right and pure honoring of God, as you have any regard to your own souls, and to the life that is to come, which is both without pain and without end, apply yourselves chiefly above all things to read and to hear God's Word, mark diligently therein what his will is you shall do, and with all your endeavor, apply yourselves to follow the same. First you must have an assured faith in God, and give yourselves wholly unto him, love him in prosperity and adversity, and dread to offend him evermore. Then, for his sake, love all men, friends and foes, because they be his creation and image, and redeemed by Christ, as ye are. Cast in your minds,[24] how you may do good unto all men unto your powers, and hurt no man. Obey all your superiors and governors, serve your masters faithfully and diligently, as well in their absence as in their presence, not for dread of punishment only, but for conscience sake, knowing that you are bound so to do by God's commandments. Disobey not your fathers and mothers, but honor them, help them, and please them to your power. Oppress not, kill not, beat not, neither slander, nor hate any man; but love all men, speak well of all men, help and succor every man, as you may, yea, even your enemies that hate you, that speak evil of you, and that do hurt you. Take no man's goods, nor covet your neighbor's goods wrongfully, but content yourselves with that which ye get truly, and also bestow your own goods charitably, as need and case[25] requireth. Flee all idolatry, witchcraft, and perjury; commit no manner of adultery, fornication, nor other unchasteness in will nor in deed, with any other man's wife, widow, maid, or otherwise. And travailing continually during your life, thus in the observing the commandments of God, wherein consisteth the pure, principal, and direct honor of God, and which, wrought in faith, God hath ordained to be the right trade and pathway unto heaven, you shall not fail, as Christ hath promised, to come to that blessed and eternal life, where you shall live in glory and joy with God forever. To whom be laud, honor, and impery[26] forever and ever. Amen.

Notes

1. See Cressy and Ferrell, 2.
2. James 2:17,19.
3. Titus 1:16.
4. Gal. 5:6.
5. Definite.
6. Heb. 11:1.
7. Heb. 11:6.
8. Offering.
9. Heb. 2:4.
10. Jer. 17:7–8.
11. Works in excess of those strictly required.
12. People believed that wearing a friar's habit would confer protection against disease and damnation.
13. "Personal [property] in common."
14. Matt. 15:3.
15. Thirty-day cycles of Requiem Masses.

16. Matt. 23:14–15.

17. Rosaries whose 150 "Hail Marys" correspond to the Book of Psalms.

18. Cycle of fifteen prayers beginning with "O."

19. Psalms thought to confer immortality and knowledge of the day of one's death.

20. Letters blessed in the name of this martyr were said to be invulnerable to fire.

21. Occasions for the granting of indulgences.

22. A list of objects of veneration.

23. Religious communities.

24. Ponder.

25. Occasion.

26. Power.

2.3. Hugh Latimer, from
The Sermon on the Plowers (1548)

Hugh Latimer (c. 1485–1555) was the spiritual leader of the first generation of English Protestants. Having risen from humble birth to become bishop of Worcester, he resigned from office when his evangelical style of episcopal practice conflicted with Henry VIII's reaffirmation of Catholic theology and church polity during the late 1530s. He was imprisoned in the Tower of London in 1546 at a time when Queen Catherine Parr, whom he served as spiritual adviser, and her associates fell under suspicion during the Anne Askew affair (see 6.1, 7.5.C). Restored to favor during the reign of Edward VI, he became an influential royal counselor and court preacher (see Figure 3). Latimer's *Sermon on the Plowers* exemplifies the colloquial plainness, alliterative language, and anecdotal style for which his preaching gained renown. He delivered it in the Shrouds (a crypt) at Saint Paul's Cathedral in London in 1548 because rainfall interrupted delivery at Paul's Cross, an outdoor pulpit. Interpreting the Parable of the Sower (Luke 8) as an allegory concerning a humble preaching ministry dedicated to Bible instruction, Latimer identifies the husbandman with religious reform and the redress of social and political corruption in a long tradition associated with *Piers Plowman,* Tyndale's plowboy (see 6.5.A), and religious satires including Spenser's May Eclogue. John Day and William Seres printed a popular edition of this sermon under the auspices of Latimer's patroness, the Duchess of Suffolk.

SOURCE: *STC* 15291, A2ʳ–A6ʳ, B3ʳ–B4ʳ, C2ᵛ–C4ᵛ.

EDITION: *Selected Sermons of Hugh Latimer,* ed. Allan Chester (Charlottesville: University Press of Virginia for the Folger Shakespeare Library, 1968).

REFERENCES: Chester; King 1982.

All things which are written are written for our erudition and knowledge. All things that are written in God's book, in the Bible book, in the book of the Holy Scripture, are written to be our doctrine.[1]

I told you in my first sermon, honorable audience, that I purposed to declare unto you two things. The one, what seed should be sown in God's field, in God's plowland. And the other, who should be the sowers. That is to say, what doctrine is to be taught in Christ's church and congregation, and what men should be the teachers and preachers of it. The first part I have told you in the three sermons past, in which I have assayed to set forth my plow, to prove what I could do.

And now I shall tell you who be the plowers, for God's word is a seed to be sown in God's field, that is, the faithful congregation, and the preacher is the sower. And it is in the Gospel: *Exivit qui seminat seminare semen suum,* "He that soweth, the husbandman, the plowman went forth to sow his seed"[2] so that a preacher is resembled to a plowman, as it is in another place:

Nemo admota aratro manu, et a tergo respiciens, aptus est regno Dei, "No man that putteth his hand to the plow and looketh back is apt for the kingdom of God."[3] That is to say, let no preacher be negligent in doing his office. Albeit this is one of the places that hath been racked, as I told you of racking scriptures. And I have been one of them myself that hath racked it, I cry God mercy for it, and have been one of them that have believed and have expounded it against religious persons that would forsake their order which they had professed and would go out of their cloister, whereas indeed it

A defcription of Maifter Latimer, preaching before Kyng Edward the fyxt, in the preachyng place at *Weftminfter.*

K. Edward

M. Latimer

Figure 3. *Hugh Latimer Preaching Before Edward VI.* John Foxe, *Book of Martyrs* (1563), p. 1353, woodcut. By permission of The Ohio State University Libraries. Latimer's high standing as the most influential preacher during the reign of Edward VI may be noted in his delivery of sermons at the royal court. The young king listens at a casement window because a wooden pulpit was erected in the privy gardens when the Chapel Royal could not accommodate the throng of courtiers and other members of the congregation. Bibles in the hands of Latimer and the woman sitting on the steps typify the evangelical piety of this time. Figures of women and men reading from the Bible recur in other propagandistic pictures (see Figures 5, 10, and 16) as an endorsement of universal literacy so that humble individuals including women and children might read and understand the Bible in vernacular translation.

toucheth not monkery, nor maketh anything at all for any such matter, but it is directly spoken of diligent preaching of the word of God.

For preaching of the Gospel is one of God's plow works, and the preacher is one of God's plowmen. Ye may not be offended with my similitude, in that I compare preaching to the labor and work of plowing and the preacher to a plowman. Ye may not be offended with this my similitude, for I have been slandered of some persons for such things. It hath been said of me, "Oh, Latimer! Nay, as for him I will never believe him while I live, nor never trust him, for he likened our blessed Lady to a saffron bag." Where indeed I never used that similitude. But it was, as I have said unto you before now, according to that which Peter saw before in the spirit of prophecy and said that there should come afterward men: *per quos via veritatis maledictis afficeretur*, there should come fellows "by whom the way of truth should be ill spoken of and slandered."[4] But in case I had used this similitude, it had not been to be reproved, but might have been without reproach. For I might have said thus, as the saffron bag that hath been full of saffron, or hath had saffron in it, doth ever after savor and smell of the sweet saffron that it contained. So our blessed Lady, which conceived and bare Christ in her womb, did ever after resemble the manners and virtues of that precious babe which she bare. And what had our blessed Lady been the worse for this or what dishonor was this to our blessed Lady?

But as preachers must be ware and circumspect that they give not any just occasion to be slandered and ill spoken of by the hearers, so must not the auditors be offended without cause. For heaven is in the gospel likened to a mustard seed. It is compared also to a piece of leaven, as Christ saith, that at the last day he will come like a thief, and what dishonor is this to God? Or what derogation is this to heaven? Ye may not then, I say, be offended with my similitude, for because I liken preaching to a plowman's labor and a prelate to a plowman. But now you will ask me whom I call a prelate. A prelate is that man, whatsoever he be, that hath a flock to be taught of him, whosoever hath any spiritual charge in the faithful congregation, and whosoever he be that hath cure of soul.

And well may the preacher and the plowman be likened together. First, for their labor of all seasons of the year, for there is no time of the year in which the plowman hath not some special work to do, as in my country in Leicestershire the plowman hath a time to set forth and to assay his plow, and other times for other necessary works to be done. And then they also may be likened together for the diversity of works and variety of offices that they have to do. For as the plowman first setteth forth his plow, and then tilleth his land, and breaketh it in furrows, and sometime ridgeth it up again.

And at another time harroweth it and clotteth it, and sometime dungeth it and hedgeth it, diggeth it and weedeth it, purgeth it and maketh it clean. So the prelate, the preacher, hath many diverse offices to do. He hath first a busy work to bring his parishioners to a right faith, as Paul calleth it. And not to a swerving faith, but to a faith that embraceth Christ, and trusteth to his merits, a lively faith, a justifying faith, a faith that maketh a man righteous without respect of works, as ye have it very well declared and set forth in the Homily. He hath then a busy work, I say, to bring his flock to a right faith and then to confirm them in the same faith. Now casting them down with the law and with threatenings of God for sin. Now ridging them up again with the gospel and with the promises of God's favor. Now weeding them by telling them their faults and making them forsake sin. Now clotting them by breaking their stony hearts and by making them supplehearted, and making them to have hearts of flesh, that is, soft hearts and apt for doctrine to enter in. Now teaching to know God rightly and to know their duty to God and to their neighbors. Now exhorting them, when they know their duty, that they do it and be diligent in it. . . .

But now methinketh I hear one say unto me, "Wot you what you say? It is a work? It is a labor? How then hath it happened that we have had so many hundred years so many unpreaching prelates, lording loiterers, and idle ministers?" Ye would have me here to make answer and to show the cause thereof. Nay, this land is not for me to plow; it is too stony, too thorny, too hard for to plow. They have so many things that make for them, so many things to lay for themselves, that is not for my weak team to plow them. They have to lay for themselves long customs, ceremonies, and authority, placing in Parliament, and many things more. And I fear me this land is not yet ripe to be plowed. For as the saying is, it lacketh weathering, this gear lacketh weathering, at least way it is not for me to plow. For what shall I look for among thorns but pricking and scratching? What among stones but stumbling? What (I had almost said) among serpents but stinging? But this much I dare say, that since lording and loitering hath come up, preaching hath come down, contrary to the Apostles' times. For they preached and lorded not. And now they lord and preach not. For they that be lords will ill go to plow. It is no meet office for them. It is not seeming for their estate. Thus came up lording loiterers. Thus crept in unpreaching prelates, and so have they long continued. For how many unlearned prelates have we now at this day? And no marvel. For if the plowmen that now be were made lords, they would clean give over plowing, they would leave off their labor, and fall to lording outright, and let the plow stand. And then, both plows not walking, nothing should be in the commonweal but hunger. For ever since the prelates were made lords and nobles, the plow standeth, there is no work done; the people starve. They hawk, they hunt, they card, they dice, they pastime in their prelacies with gallant gentlemen, with their dancing minions, and with their fresh companions, so that plowing is set aside. And by the lording and loitering, preaching and plowing is clean gone. And thus if the plowmen of the country were as negligent in their office as prelates be, we should not long live, for lack of sustenance. And as it is necessary for to have this plowing for the sustentation of the body, so must we have also the other for the satisfaction of the soul, or else we cannot live long ghostly. For as the body wasteth and consumeth away for lack of bodily meat, so doth the soul pine away for default of ghostly meat. . . .

And now I would ask a strange question. Who is the most diligent bishop and prelate in all England, that passeth all the rest in doing his office? I can tell, for I know him who it is. I know him well. But now I think I see you listing and hearkening that I should name him. There is one that passeth all the other, and is the most diligent prelate and preacher in all England. And will ye know who it is? I will tell you. It is the Devil. He is the most diligent preacher of all other, he is never out of his diocese, he is never from his cure, ye shall never find him unoccupied, he is ever in his parish, he keepeth residence at all times, ye shall never find him out of the way, call for him when you will, he is ever at home. The diligentest preacher in all the realm, he is ever at his plow, no lording nor loitering can hinder him, he is ever applying his business, ye shall never find him idle I warrant you.

And his office is to hinder religion, to maintain superstition, to set up idolatry, to teach all kind of popery. He is ready as can be wished for to set forth his plow, to devise as many ways as can be to deface and obscure God's glory. Where the Devil is resident and hath his plow going, there away with books, and up with candles, away with Bibles and up with beads, away with the light of the gospel, and up with the light of the candles, yeah, at noondays. Where the Devil is resident, that he may prevail, up with all superstition and idolatry: censing, painting of images, candles, palms, ashes, holy water, and new service of men's inventing, as though man could invent a better way to honor God with than God himself hath appointed. Down with Christ's Cross, up with purgatory pickpurse, up with him, the popish purgatory, I mean. Away with clothing the naked, the poor and impotent, up with decking of images and gay garnishing of stocks and stones. Up with man's traditions and his laws, down with God's traditions and His most holy word. Down with the old honor due to God, and up with the new God's honor, let all things be done in Latin. There must be nothing but Latin, not as much as: *Memento, homo, quod cinis es, et in cineram reverteris*, "Remember, man, that thou art ashes, and into ashes thou shalt return."[5] Which be the words that the minister speaketh to the ignorant people when he giveth them ashes upon Ash Wednesday, but it must be spoken in Latin. God's word may in no wise be translated into English.

Notes

1. Rom. 15:4.
2. Luke 8:5.
3. Luke 9:62.
4. 2 Pet. 2:2.
5. Gen. 3:9.

2.4. Miles Hogarde, from
The Displaying of Protestants (1556)

Miles Hogarde, or Huggarde (fl. 1553–58), was an artisan who flourished as a controversialist during the reign of Mary I. Although this shoemaker-poet lacked formal education, he underwent self-instruction in theology and both classical and vernacular literature. His voice was the closest Roman Catholic counterpart to those of gospelers active during the reign of Edward VI (see 3.2–3, 4.1–2). Luke Shepherd mocked Hogarde, John Bale Latinized his name as Milo Porcarius ("Hoggish Miles"), and Robert Crowley ridiculed him with the sobriquet Hogherd. Foxe's *Book of Martyrs* records that Hogarde participated in the interrogation of Protestants accused of heresy by Edmund Bonner, Bishop of London. In addition to Hogarde's printed books, some of his writings are preserved in manuscript. Indeed, one of his poems remains extant only in the form in which Crowley printed it for purposes of refutation in *Confutation of the Misshapen Answer to the Ballad, Called the Abuse of the Blessed Sacrament* (1548).

Published by Robert Caly, *The Displaying of Protestants* (1556) reverses the dynamic of Bale's *Image of Both Churches* (see 1.1.B) by attacking Protestants as heretical adherents of a "false" church opposed to the Church of Rome. Hogarde refutes key Protestant positions by defending ecclesiastical control of religious doctrine and scriptural exposition and by asserting the authority of the pope on the basis of apostolic succession from Saint Peter as the first Bishop of Rome.

SOURCE: *STC* 13557, A3ᵛ–A4ʳ.

REFERENCES: King 1982; Joseph W. Martin, "Miles Hogarde: Artisan and Aspiring Author in Sixteenth-Century England," *Renaissance Quarterly* 34 (1981): 359–83.

Now forasmuch as I know that they which commonly do err, being reproved therefore, will immediately make as though they were ignorant what heresy is, and sometime will demand what heresy is, or who is an heretic. To whom, if answer be made according to the definition of learned men: It is any false or wrong opinion, which any man chooseth to himself to defend against the Catholic faith of the universal church. Truth indeed say they. But what meaneth the Catholic Church? Then answer is made. It is that congregation which wholly doth agree in one unity of faith and ministration of sacraments. Which answer when they likewise affirm: Then, proceed they to know whether it be known or unknown, and so forth. Doubtless, the Catholic faith is so known to the world, that neither heretic nor other miscreant can plead ignorance, to learn that truth which leadeth to salvation. For the church is like unto a castle[1] standing upon a hill, which cannot be hid, which hill is cut out of the hard rock, and exalted so high that it replenisheth the earth as the prophet Daniel saith.[2] It is resembled also by the psalmist to a tabernacle placed in the sun,[3] so shining throughout the world that it can by no cloud or tempest be obscured. It is also as Paul saith, the foundation and pillar of truth,[4] and cannot be deceived though her adversaries allege the contrary. Full well doth the late most famous Master Lodovicus Vives say,[5] "I do and will stand" (saith he) "to the true judgment of the church, although I saw to the contrary a most manifest reason. I may be deceived as I am diverse times, but the church in those things which tend to religion cannot be deceived."

Therefore the church being so manifestly known as it cannot be hidden, so replenished and garnished with truth, as it is the very foundation and pillar of truth, with what face or countenance can the adversaries thereof stand in contention therewith? Unless they be infected with Circe's cups or else by her enchantments transformed into the shape of swine,[6] as the company of Ulysses was, who had they followed Ulysses, they had not been allured by Circe, and then by her not turned into that swinish shape. But now these swinish adversaries will object, saying: "Sir those which you name heretics, we will prove to be the true congregation." And this is their proof: "We allege, preach, utter, or talk of nothing but scripture, which cannot deceive us, whereby we are the true church, and not you which call yourselves Catholics." Which reason seemeth to them so infallible that it cannot be avoided. But forasmuch as the knowledge of all truth, and overthrow of heresy, dependeth upon the authority of the church, both for the knowledge of the scriptures, and also for the exposition of the same, I purpose briefly to say somewhat therein. The head of the church is Christ, who by the apostles was preached to all nations, of whom also his doctrine was received, at least of so many as were converted to the faith. The converters of whom were the apostles, which in the beginning were the mystical body of Christ their head, who then being the church, exalted their voices in such sort, as it penetrated the whole earth, and their words extended to the ends of the world.[7] The succession of which apostles, have continued from time to time, in unity of the same faith, which faith is left unto the church as permanent forever, thereby to strengthen the weak, and to confound the proud, to establish the elect, and to overthrow all misbelievers and sects heretical.

Notes

1. Matt. 5:14.
2. Dan. 2:33.

3. Ps. 19:4.
4. 1 Tim. 3.
5. *De veritate fides christianae* 1.
6. *Odyssey* 10.
7. Ps. 19:4.

2.5. Robert Parsons, from
The Christian Directory (1582)

Robert Parsons (1546–1610) originally published the initial version of his *Christ-ian Directory* (also known as *The Book of Resolution* or *The Book of the Christian Exercise*) on his own printing press at Rouen in 1582. This devotional classic was a very popular pietistic work read by English Catholics *and* Protestants during the late sixteenth and early seventeenth centuries. Parsons initially expanded James Sancer's translation of Gaspar Loarte's Jesuit manual, *The Exercise of a Christian Life*. Many editions of an altered version of *The Christian Directory* by Edmund Bunny, a Protestant minister who deleted some passages and added a *Treatise Tending to Pacification* (1584), remained in print through the 1630s. Parsons attacked Bunny's appropriation of his work and responded with revised and expanded versions of this book, which went into five editions printed at Louvain, Rouen, and Saint-Omer between 1585 and 1633.

In defending the integrity of the Church of Rome as the Catholic (i.e., uni-versal) Church, the present selection opposes the religious settlement imposed under Elizabeth. It rejects the Protestant doctrine of faith alone by insisting on the primacy of charity and necessity of good works that flow from it. Parsons agrees with Thomas More in rejecting William Tyndale's translation of *agape* (ʾαγάπη) as *love* rather than *charity* (see 1.2.B). See the *Book of Homilies* (2.2), and Parsons's *Temperate Ward-Word* (1.2.C) and *Treatise of the Three Conversions of England* (6.9).

SOURCE: STC 19354.5, Cap.3.51–53, Cap.3.61–62, Cap. 3.64–65.

EDITION: *Robert Persons, S.J.: The Christian Directory (1582)*, ed. Victor Houliston. Studies in the History of Christian Thought 84 (Leiden: Brill, 1998).

The End Whereunto Man Was Created

For discerning of which kind of most pernicious people (as Saint Augustine and other holy Fathers do note) and for more perfect distinction between them and true Christians, the said apostles invented the name Catholic, and set down in their common Creed, that clause or article, I believe the holy Catholic Church. By which word Catholic (that signifieth universal) they gave to understand to all posterity, that whatsoever doctrine or opinion should be raised afterward among Christians, disagreeing from the general consent, doctrine, and tradition of the universal church, was to be reputed as error and heresy, and utterly to be rejected. And that the only anchor, stay, and security of a Christian man's mind in matters of belief for his salvation, was to be a Catholic; that is (as all ancient Fathers do interpret the same) one, who laying aside all particular opinions and imaginations, both of him-self and others, doth subject his judgment to the determination of Christ's universal, visible, and known church upon earth, embracing whatsoever that believeth, and abandoning whatsoever that Church rejecteth. . . .

The Gospel of Christ being once preached, and received uniformly over all the world, and churches of Christianity erected throughout all countries, provinces, and nations in the apostles' time, as hath been said: it is to be considered, that this universal church, body, or kingdom so gathered, founded, and established, was to continue visibly, not for one or two ages, but unto the world's end. For so it was foreshowed and promised most perspicuously by Daniel, when he foretold the four great monarchies that after him should ensue, adjoineth these evident words of the Church and kingdom of Christ: "In the days of these kingdoms, shall God raise up a celestial kingdom, which shall endure forever, without subversion; and that kingdom shall not be delivered over to any other people."[1] By which last words, as also by diverse promises of Christ himself in the Gospel, we are ascertained that the very same visible congregation, church, body, commonweal, government, and kingdom, which was established by the apostles in their time, shall endure and continue by succession of followers, unto the world's end: neither should it pass over, or be delivered to an other people; that is, no new teachers or later doctrines dissenting from the first, shall ever finally prevail against it. Which prophesy to have been fulfilled from that day unto this, is made evident and most apparent, by the records of all ages; wherein, albeit diverse errors and heresies have sprung up, and made great blustering and disturbance for a time: yet have they been repressed and beaten down again by the same church, and her visible pillars, pastors and doctors, in the end. . . .

Concerning Good Works

For that this wicked opinion of only faith,[2] was sprung up in the apostles's time, by ill understanding of Saint Paul, all the other apostolical epistles which ensue, of Saint Peter, Saint John, Saint James, and Saint Jude,[3] were directed principally to this end, to prove with all vehemency, that faith without good works is nothing worth. Even as indeed Saint Paul himself did not define every manner of faith, whereby we believe in God; but only meaneth that profitable and evangelical faith, which hath works annexed, proceeding of charity. And as for that faith, which is without works, and yet seemeth to these men to be sufficient for their salvation, he protecteth, that it is so unprofitable, as he doubteth not to say of himself: "If I should have all faith, in such sort, as I were able to move mountains, and yet had not charity, I were nothing."[4] By which charity (no doubt) good life is meant, for that, as in another place it is said: "Charity is the fulfilling of all the law."[5] . . .

For that a true faith doth not contradict in manners, the things which it professeth in words. For which cause, it was said of certain false Christians. . . . by Saint John: "That whosoever saith, he knoweth God, and he keepeth not his commandments, is a liar."[6] Which being so, we must examine the truth of our faith, by consideration of our life: for then, and not otherwise, are we true Christians, if we fulfil in works that whereof we have made promise in words: that is, in the day of our baptism, we promised to renounce the pomp of this world, together with all the works of iniquity; which promise, if we perform now after baptism, then are we true Christians, and may be joyful. . . . Wherefore, let no man trust that his faith may save him without good deeds, seeing that we know it is written expressly: "That faith without works is dead: and consequently, cannot be profitable, or save us from damnation."[7]

Notes

1. Dan. 8:23–24.
2. Protestant doctrine of faith alone.
3. The Catholic Epistles.
4. 1 Cor. 13:2.
5. Rom. 13:10.
6. 1 John 2:4.
7. James 2:17.

2.6. William Cecil, from
The Execution of Justice in England (1583)

Sir William Cecil, Lord Burghley (1520–98) wrote the official governmental response to the Roman Catholic Mission to England that began in 1580 under the leadership of Robert Parsons (see 1.2.C, 2.5, 6.9). English Protestants feared that missionaries trained at seminaries on the Continent and their lay adherents were engaged in plots to overthrow Elizabeth I. The Jesuit endorsement of equivocation and mental reservation as methods of argument heightened this anxiety. Royal proclamations declaring that Jesuits and seminarians were guilty of treason led to the hanging, drawing, and quartering of scores of missionary priests.

   Although it was published anonymously, Cecil wrote *The Execution of Justice in England for Maintenance of Public and Christian Peace, Without Any Persecution for Questions of Religion* (1583) in his capacity as Queen Elizabeth's chief minister. Asserting that the queen possesses divinely ordained authority to counter rebellion, it declares that execution represents just punishment of Catholic missionaries for treason rather than religious belief. It rejects dual allegiance to both the queen and the pope. This defense of the Elizabethan regime against charges of torture and persecution underwent translation into Latin, French, Dutch, and Italian for a continental readership. William Allen countered Cecil's arguments in *A True, Sincere, and Modest Defense of English Catholics* (see 2.7).

   SOURCE: *STC* 4902, A2ʳ⁻ᵛ, A3ʳ–A4ʳ, E2ᵛ–E3ʳ, E4ʳ⁻ᵛ.

   EDITION: Kingdon

   REFERENCE: Conyers Read, *Lord Burghley and Queen Elizabeth* (London: Jonathan Cape, 1960).

It hath been in all ages and in all countries a common usage of all offenders for the most part, both great and small, to make defense of their lewd and unlawful facts by untruths and by coloring and covering their deeds (were they never so vile) with pretenses of some other causes of contrary operations or effects: to the intent not only to avoid punishment or shame but to continue, uphold, and prosecute their wicked attempts to the full satisfaction of their disordered and malicious appetites. And though such hath been the use of all offenders, yet of none with more danger than of rebels and traitors to their lawful princes, kings, and countries. Of which sort of late years are specially to be noted certain persons, naturally born subjects in the realm of England and Ireland, who, having for some good time professed outwardly their obedience to their sovereign lady Queen Elizabeth, have nevertheless afterward been stirred up and seduced by wicked spirits, first in England sundry years past, and secondly and of later time in Ireland, to enter into open rebellion, taking arms and coming into the field against Her Majesty and her lieutenants, with their forces under banners displayed, inducing by

notable untruths many simple people to follow and assist them in their traitorous actions. And though it is very well known, that both their intentions
and manifest actions were bent, to have deposed the Queen's Majesty from
her crown, and to have traitorously set in her place some other whom they
liked, whereby if they had not been speedily resisted, they would have committed great bloodsheds and slaughters of Her Majesty's faithful subjects,
and ruined their native country. Yet by God's power given unto Her Majesty,
they were so speedily vanquished, as some few of them suffered by order of
law according to their deserts, many and the greatest part upon confession
of their faults were pardoned, the rest (but they not many) of the principal,
escaped into foreign countries, and there because in none or few places rebels
and traitors to their natural princes and countries dare for their treasons challenge at their first muster open comfort or succor, these notable traitors and
rebels have falsely informed many kings, princes and states, and specially the
Bishop of Rome, commonly called the pope (from whom they all had
secretly their first comfort to rebel), that the cause of their fleeing from their
countries was for the religion of Rome and for maintenance of the said
pope's authority. . . .

But notwithstanding the notorious evil and wicked lives of these and
others their confederates, void of all Christian religion, it liked the Bishop
of Rome, as in favor of their treasons, not to color their offenses as themselves openly pretend to do, for avoiding of common shame of the world,
but flatly to animate them to continue their former wicked purposes, that
is, to take arms against the lawful queen, to invade her realm with foreign
forces to pursue all her good subjects and their native countries with fire
and sword: for maintenance whereof there had some years before, at sundry
times, proceeded, in a thundering sort, bulls, excommunications, and other
public writings denouncing Her Majesty, being the lawful queen and God's
anointed servant, not to be the queen of the realm, charging and, upon pains
of excommunication, commanding all her subjects to depart from their natural allegiances, whereto by birth and by oath they were bound. Provoking
also and authorizing all persons of all degrees within both the realms to
rebel, and upon this anti-Christian warrant, being contrary to all the laws of
God and man, and nothing agreeable to a pastoral officer, not only all the
rabble of the foresaid traitors that were before fled, but also all other persons
that had forsaken their native countries, and being of diverse conditions and
qualities, some not able to live at home but in beggary, some discontented
for lack of preferments, which they gaped for unworthy in universities and
other places, some bankrupt merchants, some in a sort learned to con-
tentions, being not contented to learn to obey the laws of the land, have

many years running up and down from country to country, practiced some in one corner, some in another, some with seeking to gather forces and money for forces, some with instigation of princes by untruths to make war upon their natural country, some with inward practices to murder the greatest, some with seditious writings, and very many of late with public infamous libels, full of despiteful vile terms and poisoned lies, altogether to uphold the foresaid anti-Christian and tyrannous warrant of the pope's bull.[1] And yet also by some other means, to further these intentions, because they could not readily prevail by way of force, finding foreign prices of better consideration and not readily inclined to their wicked purposes, it was devised to erect by certain schools which they call seminaries, to nourish and bring up persons disposed naturally to sedition, to continue their race and trade and to become seedmen in their tillage of sedition, and them to send secretly into the Queen Majesty's realms of England and Ireland under secret masks, some of priesthood, some of other inferior orders, with titles of seminaries for some of the meaner sort, and of Jesuits for the stagers[2] and ranker sort and suchlike, but yet so warily they crept into the land, as none brought the marks of their priesthood with them, but in diverse corners of Her Majesty's dominions these seminaries or seedmen and Jesuits, bringing with them certain Romish trash, as of their hallowed wax, their Agnus Dei, many kind of beads, and suchlike, have as tillage men labored secretly to persuade the people to allow of the pope's foresaid bulls and warrants, and of his absolute authority over all princes and countries, and striking many with pricks of conscience to obey the same, whereby in process of small time, if this wicked and dangerous, traitorous and crafty course had not been by God's goodness espied and stayed, there had followed imminent danger of horrible uproars in the realms, and a manifest bloody destruction of great multitude of Christians. . . .

Now, therefore, it resteth to apply the facts of these late malefactors that are pretended to have offended but as scholars, or bookmen, or at the most but as persons that only in words and doctrine and not with armor did favor and help the rebels and the enemies. For which purpose let these persons be termed as they list: scholars, schoolmasters, bookmen, seminaries, priests, Jesuits, friars, beadmen, Romanists, pardoners, or what else you will, neither their titles, nor their apparel doth make them traitors, but their traitorous secret motions and practices: their persons make not the war, but their directions and counsels have set up the rebellions. The very causes final of these rebellions and wars have been to depose Her Majesty from her crown: the causes instrumental are these kind of seminaries and seedmen of sedition: the fruits and effects thereof are rebellion to shed the blood of all her faithful subjects. The rewards of the invaders (if they could prevail) should be the disinheriting of all the nobility, the clergy and the whole community, that would (as they are bound by the laws of God, by their birth, and oaths) defend their natural gracious queen, their native country, their wives, their children, their family, and their houses. And now examine these which you call your unarmed scholars and priests, wherefore they lived and were conversant in company of the principal rebels and traitors at Rome, and in other places, where it is proved that they were partakers of their conspiracies? Let it be answered why they came thus by stealth into the realm? Why they have wandered up and down in corners in disguised sort, changing their titles, names, and manner of apparel? Why they have enticed and sought to persuade by their secret false reasons the people to allow and believe all the actions and attempts whatsoever the Pope hath done or shall do to be lawful? Why they have reconciled and withdrawn so many people in corners from the laws of the realm to the obedience of the pope, a foreign potentate and open enemy, whom they know to have already declared the queen to be no lawful queen, to have maintained the known rebels and traitors, to have invaded Her Majesty's dominions with open war? . . .

Wherefore, with charity to conclude, if these rebels and traitors and their fautors[3] would yet take some remorse and compassion of their natural country, and would consider how vain their attempts have been so many years, and how many of their confederates are wasted by miseries and calamities, and would desist from their unnatural practices abroad; and if these seminaries, secret wanderers, and explorators in the dark would employ their travails in the works of light and doctrine, according to the usage of their schools, and content themselves with their profession and devotion; and that the remnant of the wicked flock of the seedmen of sedition would cease from their rebellious, false, and infamous railings and libelings; there is no doubt, by God's grace (Her Majesty being so much given to mercy and devoted to peace), but all color and occasion of shedding the blood of any more of her natural subjects of this land should utterly cease. Against whose malices, if they shall not desist, almighty God continue Her Majesty with his spirit and power long to reign and live in his fear, and to be able to vanquish them and all God's enemies, and her rebels and traitors both at home and abroad, and to maintain and preserve all her natural good loving subjects to the true service of the same almighty God according to his holy word and will.

Many other things might be remembered for defense of other Her Majesty's princely, honorable, and godly actions in sundry other things, wherein also these and the like seditious railers have of late time, without all shame, by feigned and false libels sought to discredit Her Majesty and her government. But at this time, these former causes and reasons alleged by way of advertisements are sufficient to justify Her Majesty's actions to the whole world in the cases remembered.

Notes

1. Pope Pius V excommunicated Elizabeth and encouraged English subjects to depose her by means of the bull *Regnans in excelsis* (1570).

2. Organizers.

3. Supporters.

2.7. William Allen, from
A True, Sincere, and Modest
Defense of English Catholics (1584)

William Allen (1532–94) was a scholar at Oxford University whose recusancy led him to emigrate to the Continent, where he founded the Jesuit seminary at Douai, which underwent later relocation at Rheims; he became Regius Professor of Divinity at the University of Douai and founded the English College at Rome. He inspired the English Mission that led to the death of missionary priests such as Edmund Campion and Robert Southwell (see 6.7–8). Pope Sixtus V elevated him to a cardinalate in 1587.

As the spiritual leader of the recusant community and head of the English colleges at Rheims and Rome, Allen wrote his *Defense of English Catholics* in response to William Cecil's *Execution of Justice in England* (see 2.6). Published in 1584 at a printing press operated by Robert Parsons (see 1.2.C, 2.5, 6.9) at Rouen, this tract defends missionary priests against the charge that they seek to depose Elizabeth I. It declares that their cause, rather than suffering, makes these victims "true" martyrs. With considerable eloquence, Allen rejects Cecil's assertion that English authorities prosecute Catholics and execute missionaries for treason rather than religious belief. Allen also defends the legality of the prosecution of Protestants as heretics under Mary I. A Latin translation published in the same year addressed Allen's arguments to a learned Continental readership. Thomas Bilson composed the official response to Allen's tract, *The True Difference Between Christian Subjection and Unchristian Rebellion* (1585).

SOURCE: *STC* 373, *2, *3ʳ, 34–36, 37, 38–39.
EDITION: Cecil and Allen.

The Preface to the Reader

Albeit the late pamphlet entitled *The Execution of Justice*,[1] put forth in diverse languages for defense or excuse of the violent proceeding against Catholics in England, and for accusation as well of them at home as of us their fellows in faith abroad, passing forth without privilege and name either of writer or printer (even thence where such matter is specially current, and might easily have been authorized), and moving indiscreet, odious, and dangerous disputes of estate, replenished with manifest untruths, open slanders of innocent persons, and namely with immodest malediction and seditious motions against the chief bishop, the prince of God's people; though (I say) it might rightly have been reputed an infamous libel, either to be condemned or with such freedom of speech refelled,[2] as that manner of writing doth deserve; yet considering the matter, meaning, and phrase thereof to be agreeable to the humor and liking of some in authority, and the book not only not suppressed (as diverse others of that argument, seeming over-simple to the wiser

Protestants, of late have been) but often printed, much recommended, diligently divulged, and sought to be privileged in foreign places, where for shame they durst not publicly allow it at home; yea, and in a manner thrust into the hands of strangers and therefore like to proceed (though in close sort) from authority: we are forced and, in truth, very well contented and glad it hath pleased God to give this occasion, or rather necessity, to yield (for the answer of the said book) our more particular account in the behalf of our Catholic brethren dead and alive, at home and in banishment. . . .

Secondly, we set forth these things for the memory and honor of such notable martyrs, as have testified the truth of the Catholic faith by their precious death. Which was an ancient canon and custom of the primitive Church, which appointed certain special persons of skill and learning to note the days of everyone's glorious confession and combat, that their memories might afterward be solemnly celebrated forever among Christians.

Thirdly, we do it to communicate our calamities with our brethren in faith, and the churches of other provinces standing free from this misery, both for their warning, and our comfort, and to excite in them Christian compassion toward us; that thereby and by their counsel and prayers, we may find mercy and relief at God's hand, by the example of the Oriental Churches afflicted by the Arians, which, as we may read in Saint Basil,[3] in their like distresses made their general complaints by often letters and messengers to the west Churches, standing more entire and void of that heresy and persecution.

Finally, we are forced to publish these things so particularly and diligently to defend the doings of the said holy confessors and their fellows in faith against the manifold slanders and calumniations of certain heretics or politiques, unjustly charging them with treason and other great trespasses against the commonwealth. . . .

The libeler by sophistical reasons and popular persuasion going about to make men think the English persecution to be nothing so violent as is divulged, nor anything comparable to the justice exercised toward the Protestants in the reign of the late Queen Mary, telleth of hundreds for our scores, as also of the qualities of them that then suffered, of their innocence in all matters of state, and treason, and suchlike.

To which we say briefly, clearly, and to the purpose that we measure not the matter by the number, nor by the severity of the punishment only or specially, but by the cause; by the order of justice in proceeding; by the laws of God and all Christian nations, and such other circumstances; whereby we can prove Queen Mary's doings to be commendable and most lawful; the other, toward us and our brethren, to be unjust and impious.

The difference is in these points: You profess to put none to death for religion; you have no laws to put any man to death for his faith; you have purposefully repealed by a special statute made in the first year and Parliament of this queen's reign, all former laws of the realm of burning heretics, which smelleth of something that I need not here express; you have provided at the same time that nothing shall be deemed or adjudged heresy but by your Parliament and Convocation; you have not yet set down by any new law what is heresy or who is an heretic; therefore you can neither adjudge of our doctrine as of heresy nor of us as of heretics; nor have you any new law left whereby to execute us; and so, to put any of us to death for religion is against justice, law, and your own profession and doctrine.

But nevertheless you do torment and punish us, both otherwise intolerably, and also by death most cruel; and that (as we have proved) for Agnus Deis, for ministering the holy sacraments, for our obedience to the See Apostolic, for persuading our friends to the Catholic faith, for our priesthood, for studying in the Society or colleges beyond the seas, and suchlike, which you have ridiculously made treason; but afterward (being ashamed of the foul absurdity) acknowledge them to be matters of religion and such as none shall die for. And therefore we most justly make our complaint to God and man that you do us plain violence and persecute us without all equity and order.

On the other side, Queen Mary against the Protestants executed only the old laws of our country and of all Christendom made for punishment of heretics, by the canons and determination of all popes, councils, churches, and ecclesiastical tribunals of the world, allowed also and authorized by the civil and imperial laws, and received by all kingdoms Christian besides; and who hath any cause justly to be grieved? Why should any man complain or think strange for executing the laws which are as ancient, as general, and as godly against heretics as they are for the punishment of traitors, murderers, or thieves? . . .

And we may marvel in what age or world those people were born, which the libeler noteth to have been burned in Queen Mary's time, having never heard (as he saith)[4] of any other religion, than that for which they suffered? For the sect which they pretended to die for was not extant in England above five or six years before in the short reign of King Edward the Sixth, or rather his Protector; for before that, in King Henry's days, the same profession was accounted heresy, and the professors thereof were burned for heretics, and that by public laws, no less than in the reign of Queen Mary. But the truth is, that because we Catholic Christian men do justly ground ourselves upon the former profession of our faith notoriously known to be, and to be called Catholic, these men apishly would imitate our phrase and argument in a thing as far differing as heaven and hell. . . .

It is not only the slaughter of many, and them specially the priests of God, which is most proper to heretical persecution, but the other infinite spoil of Catholic men's goods, honors, and liberty, by robbing them for receiving priests, hearing Mass, retaining Catholic schoolmasters, keeping Catholic servants, mulcting[5] them by twenty pounds a month (which by their cruel account they make thirteenscore a year) for not repairing to their damnable schismatical service. By which a number of ancient gentlemen fall to extremity, either of conscience, if for fear they obey, or of their undoing in the world, if they refuse; the taking of their dear children from them by force and placing them for their seduction with heretics (which violence cannot be done by the law of God to Jews themselves); the burning of our priests in the ears; the whipping and cutting of the ears of others; carrying some in their sacred vestments through the streets; putting our chaste virgins into infamous places appointed for strumpets; and other unspeakable villainies, not inferior to any of the said heathenous persecutions.

They have pined and smothered in their filthy prisons above thirty famous prelates; above forty excellent learned men; of nobles, gentlemen, and matrons a number; whose martyrdom is before God as glorious, as if they had by a speedy violent death been dispatched; every dungeon and filthy prison in England full of our priests and brethren; all provinces and princes Christianed witnesses of our banishment. In all this we yield them our bodies, goods, country, blood, and lives; and nothing will quench their hatred of our priesthood, faith, and profession. Thus in all causes we suffer, and yet they would not have us complain. They say all is sweet, clement, and merciful in this regiment.

Notes

1. See 2.6.
2. Refuted.
3. *Against Eunomius*, an anti-Arian treatise by a fourth-century bishop of Caesarea.
4. William Cecil.
5. Punishing with a fine.

3

ALLEGORIES OF THE ENGLISH REFORMATIONS: DRAMA, POETRY, AND FICTION

3.1. John Bale, from
A Comedy Concerning Three Laws
(1538, pub. c. 1548)

John Bale (1495–1563) was an extraordinarily forceful and prolific propagandist. After leaving the order of Carmelite friars, he led a troupe of itinerant players that performed his own propagandistic plays under the patronage of Thomas Cromwell (see Appendix). Bale composed *A Comedy Concerning Three Laws of Nature, Moses, and Christ Corrupted by the Sodomites, Pharisees, and Papists* in 1538, not long after the dissolution of the monasteries, but he waited until around 1548 to publish it in Wesel, a Rhineland port, during exile that followed his patron's downfall.

Applying conventions and devices of late medieval morality plays to Protestant purposes, Bale allegorizes conflict between the "true" and "false" churches (see 1.1.B–D) by means of personified Virtues and Vices. These dramatic parts double for performance by a troupe of five actors. The use of clerical vestments as costumes enforces Bale's attack on the Church of Rome: "Let Idolatry be decked like an old witch, Sodomy like a monk of all sects, Ambition like a bishop, Covetousness like a Pharisee or spiritual [i.e., canon] lawyer, False Doctrine like a popish doctor, and Hypocrisy like a grey [i.e., Franciscan] friar. The rest of the parts are easy enough to conjecture." A caesura divides each line of text into halves.

The following transcription of Act 4 dramatizes the alleged corruption of the "true" church, personified as the spouse of Gospel, by figures such as Infidelity and Hypocrisy. The satirical attack on practices and beliefs attributed to the Church of Rome, personified by these Vices, accords with the polemical view of the pre-Reformation articulated in writings such as Martin Luther's *Babylonian Captivity of the Church* and William Tyndale's *Obedience of a Christian Man* (see 2.1). In accordance with the convention of doubling dramatic roles, Bale himself may have played multiple parts such as those of God the Father and Infidelity, the leading Vice, who inherits the comic mannerisms and vulgar jesting of his medieval forebears. Roman Catholic practices under attack include clerical celibacy and veneration of religious images.

SOURCE: *STC* 1287, A1ʳ⁻ᵛ, D6ᵛ–E2ʳ, E2ʳ–E5ᵛ, E6ʳ–F2ᵛ. Names of characters and stage directions are translated into English (see Bale 1985–86 for the original text).

EDITION: Bale 1985–86.

REFERENCES: Happé; Kendall; King 1982; White 1993.

Cast of Characters

God the Father	Law of Nature
Law of Moses	Law of Christ,
Infidelity	or the Gospel
Idolatry	Sodomy
Ambition	Covetousness

Figure 4. *Portrait of John Bale*. Bale, *A Comedy Concerning Three Laws* (Wesel, c. 1548), woodcut frontispiece. By permission of the Bodleian Library. The New Testament in Bale's hand is a symbol of religious faith found in many Reformation texts. Other instances include the New Testaments carried by characters such as Lusty Juventus (see 3.2) and Fidelia at the House of Holiness in Book One of Spenser's *Faerie Queene*. Bale himself flourished a New Testament when he preached to resistant Irish Catholics at a market square in Kilkenny (see 6.2).

> False Doctrine   Hypocrisy
> Divine Punishment   Christian Faith
>   Bale the Prolocutor

Enter Bale the Prolocutor.[1]

> *Bale.* In each commonwealth   most high preeminence
> Is due unto laws,   for such commodity[2]
> As is had by them.   For, as Cicero giveth sentence,[3]
> Whereas[4] is no law,   can no good order be,
> In nature, in people,   in house, nor yet in city.   5
> The bodies above[5]   are underneath a law;
> Who could rule the world   were it not under awe? . . .
> Our Heavenly Maker,   man's living to direct,   15
> The laws of Nature,   of Bondage, and of Grace,
> Sent into this world,   with viciousness infect,
> In all righteousness   to walk before his face.
> But Infidelity   so worketh in every place,
> That under the heavens   nothing is pure and clean,   20
> So much the people   to his perverse ways lean.
>   The Law of Nature,   his filthy disposition
> Corrupteth with idols   and stinking Sodometry,[6]
> The Law of Moses   with Avarice and Ambition
> He also polluteth;   and ever continually   25
> Christ's Law he defileth   with cursed Hypocrisy
> And with False Doctrine,   as will appear in presence[7]
> To the edifying   of this Christian audience.
> Of Infidelity   God will himself revenge
> With plagues of water,   of wildfire, and of sword.[8]   30
> And of his people,   due homage he will challenge
> Ever to be known   for their God and good Lord,
> After that[9] he hath   those laws again restored
> To their first beauty,   committing them to faith.
> He is now in place;   mark therefore what he saith.   35

[A speech attributed to God follows.]

Exit.

Act 4 Begins.
Enter the Gospel.

Gospel. Unfaithfulness hath   corrupted every law
To the great decay   of Adam's posterity.
Were it not for me,   which now do hither draw,
All flesh would perish,   no man should saved be.   1290
I am Christ's Gospel   and infallible verity,
Such a power of God   as saveth all that believe,
No burden nor yoke,   that any man will grieve.

In the blood of Christ   I am a full forgiveness,
Where faith is grounded   with a sure confidence.   1295
I am such a grace,   and so high tidings of gladness
As raise the sinner   and pacify his conscience.
I am spirit and life;   I am necessary science.[10]
I require but love   for man's justification,
With a faith in Christ   for his health and salvation.   1300

Enter Infidelity.

Infidelity. God's benison[11] have ye!   It is joy of your life.
    I have heard of ye   and of my mistress, your wife.
Gospel. If thou heardst of me,   it was by the voice of God.
Infidelity. Nay, he that spake of ye   was selling of a cod
    In an oyster boat,   a little beyond Queenhithe;[12]   1305
    A northern man was he,   and besought ye to be blithe.
Gospel. If he spake of me,   he was some godly preacher.
Infidelity. Nay, sir, by the rood,[13]   nor yet a wholesome teacher.
Gospel. After what manner   did he speak of me? Tell!
Infidelity. He swore like a man,   by all the contents of the
                        Gospel,   1310
    He swore and better swore,   yea, he did swear and swear
                        again.
Gospel. That speaking is such   as procureth eternal pain.
    Will not the people   leave that most wicked folly?
    And it so damnable?   To hear it I am sorry.
    But what didst thou mean   when thou spakest of my
                        wife,   1315
Infidelity. Nothing; but I thought   it was joy of your life
    That ye were so good   to your neighbors as ye are.
Gospel. Why, how good am I?   Thy fantasy declare.
Infidelity. Ye ease[14] them among,   if it be as I hear;

When ye are abroad there is fine merry cheer. 1320
Gospel. As thou art, thou speakest after thy heart's abundance
For as the man is, such is his utterance.
My wife is the church, or Christian congregation,
Regenerate in spirit, doing no vile operation,
Both clean and holy, without either spot or wrinkle, 1325
The Lamb with his blood did her wash and besprinkle.
This is not the church of disguised hypocrites,
Of apish shavelings, or papistical sodomites.
Nor yet, as they call it, a temple of lime and stone,
But a livish[15] building grounded in faith alone, 1330
On the hard rock, Christ, which is the sure foundation.[16]
And of this church, some do reign in every nation
And in all countries, though their number be but small.
Infidelity. Their number is such as hath run over all;
The same Danes[17] are they men prophesy of plain[ly] 1335
Which should overrun this realm, yet once again.
Gospel. Which Danes speakest thou of? Thy meaning show more
clearly.

Infidelity. Don John, Don Robert, Don Thomas, and Don Harry,[18]
These same are those Danes that lay with other men's wives
And occupied their lands to the detriment of their lives. 1340
These are accounted a great part of the church,
For in God's service they honorably worch,[19]
Yelling and crying till their throats are full sore.
Gospel. That church was described of[20] Esau long afore:
"This people," saith God, "with their lips honor me";[21] 1345
In vain worship they, teaching men's fatuity.
Apparent is that church and open to the eyes;
Their worshippings are in outward ceremonies.
That counterfeit church standeth all by men's traditions,
Without the scriptures and without the heart's affections. 1350
My church is secret and evermore will be,
Adoring the Father in spirit and in verity.
By the Word of God this church is ruled only,
And doth not consist in outward ceremony.[22]
This congregation is the true church militant; 1355
Those counterfeit desards[23] are the very church malignant
To whom Christ will say, "I know none of your sort."[24]
Infidelity. Much are they to blame that their brethren so report.

Gospel. Such are no brethren,   but enemies to Christ's blood
    As put salvation   in shaven crown, miter, or hood.[25]   1360
Infidelity. I pray ye, how long   have your sweet spouse continued?
Gospel. Since the beginning,   and now is in Christ renewed.
    Adam had promise   of Christ's incarnation,
    So had Abraham   with his whole generation,
    Which was unto them   a preaching of the Gospel   1365
    Into salvation   and deliverance from hell.
Infidelity. By this time I hope   ye have a fair increase?
Gospel. She is not barren,   but beareth, and never cease.
    The Corinths' first epistle   hath this clear testimony:
    "In Christo Jesu   *per Evangelum vos genui.*   1370
    I have begot you   in Jesu Christ," saith Paul,
    "By the Gospel preaching   to the comfort of your soul."[26]
Infidelity. Then are ye a cuckold,   by the blessed holy mass?
    As I said afore,   so cometh it now to pass,
    For I am a prophet   by high inspiration led.   1375
    Now like I myself   much better than I did.
    Ye said that St. Paul   begat your wife with child!
Gospel. By misunderstanding   thou art ungraciously[27] beguiled.
    An only[28] minister   was Paul in that same doing;
    That he therein   did was by the Gospel preaching.   1380
    His mind is [for] the Gospel   to have done that operation,
    And this must thou hold   for no carnal generation.[29]
Infidelity. Marry, so they say,   ye fellows of the new learning[30]
    Forsake holy church,   and now fall fast to wiving.
Gospel. Nay, they forsake whoredom,   with other damnable
                          usage,   1385
    And live with their wives in   lawful marriage,
    Whiles the Pope's oiled swarm[31]   reign still in their old buggerage.[32]
Infidelity. Yea, poor married men   have very much ado;
    I count him wisest   that can take a snatch and to go.[33]
Gospel. Thou seemest one of them   that detesteth matrimony,   1390
    Which is afore God   a state both just and holy.
    Of such as thou art,   Saint Paul did prophesy
    By the Holy Ghost   that a certain company
    In the latter days   from the truth of God should fall,
    Attending to spirits   of error diabolical   1395
    Which in hypocrisy   will teach lies for advantage
    With marked consciences[34]   inhibiting marriage.

Thou appearest by thy fruits   to be Infidelity.
Infidelity. I am none other   but even the very he,
And hither now come I to commune the matter with ye.   1400
Gospel. Avoid![35] Cursed fiend,   and get thee out at the gates!
Infidelity. Nay, first will I serve ye,   as I lately served your mates;
And hence will I not [go],   for this place is for me.
Who should here remain   but Infidelity?
Gospel. Well then, for a time,   I must depart from hence.   1405
But this first will I say   before this audience:
Easier it will be,   concerning punishment
To Sodom and Gomor[36]   in the day of judgement,
Than to those cities   that resist the verity
At the suggestions   of Infidelity.   1410
That people will be   forever and ever lost,
For it is the great sin   against the Holy Ghost.
In the Old Law first,   the Father his mind expressed;
Then came his son, Christ,   and made it more manifest;
And now the Holy Ghost   is come to close up all—   1415
If he be not heard,   extreme damnation will fall.
No prayer remaineth,   nor expiation for sin,
To them that no profit   of[37] the Word of God will win.
Take good heed, therefore,   and say that ye have warning.

Exit.

Infidelity. God send your mother   of you to have a
    foundling![38]   1420
By the mass, I think   he is well out of the way.
Now will I contrive   the drift[39] of another play.
I must work such ways   [that] Christ's law may not continue.
In a while am I like   to have none else of my retinue.
Companions I want   to begin this tragedy: 1425
Namely, False Doctrine   and his brother Hypocrisy.
They will not be long,   I suppose now verily,
By cock's soul, methink,   I see such a company.
Hem, I say! Children,   will not my voice be heard?
As good is a beck   as is a *Dieu vous garde*.[40]   1430
By my honesty, welcome,   mine own companions both! . . .

False Doctrine and Hypocrisy enter.

False Doct. Gramercies,[41] by God, my old friend, Infidelity!

Hypocrisy. What, Brother Snip-Snap,[42] how goes the world with thee?

Infidelity. What, Friar Flip-Flap,[43] how say ye to Benedicite? 1435

Hypocrisy. Marry, nothing but well, for I cry now advantage.

Infidelity. At her purse[44] or arse, Tell me, good Friar Succage?[45]

Hypocrisy. By the mass, at both, for I am a great penitencer,[46]
And sit at the pardon. Tush! I am the Pope's own vicar;
If thou lackest a piece,[47] I know where thou mayst be sped[48] 1440
With choice of a score, and brought even to thy bed.

False Doct. Art thou not ashamed to talk so like a knave?

Hypocrisy. No, for it is such gear as the holiest of us will have;
Pope, cardinal, bishop, monk, canon, priest, and friar,
Not one of ye all but a woman will desire. 1445

False Doct. Our orders permit us not to have them in marriage.

Hypocrisy. No, but ye fetch them in by another carriage.
Ye do even as we do; we both are of one rate.

Infidelity. By the mass, I laugh to hear this whoreson prate.

False Doct. What fashion use ye? To us here, intimate. 1450

Hypocrisy. Ego distinguo[49] whether ye will have Lyons or Paris.

False Doct. Of them both to show, it will not be far amiss.

Hypocrisy. In Paris, we have the mantle of St. Louis[50]
Which women seek much for help of their barrenness.
For be it once laid upon a woman's belly, 1455
She go[es] thence with child; the miracles are seen there daily.
And besides all this, ye would marvel in confession
What our fathers do to assoil them of transgression.
Johan Thessecclius assoiled[51] a young woman once
Behind the high altar till she cried out of her bones. 1460
And as for Lyons, there is the length[52] of our Lord
In a great pillar. She that will with a cord
Be fast bound to it and take such chance as fall
Shall sure[ly] have [a] child, for within it is hollow all.
Tush! I could tell ye of much more wonder than this; 1465
In course to hear them I think ye would ye bless.

False Doct. As thou hast begun, go forward in it and tell.

Infidelity. Such a knave, I suppose, is not from hence to hell.

Hypocrisy. In our religion was an holy, popish patriarch
Which of all bawdry might be the great monarch; 1470

The nuns to confess, he went from place to place,
And two hundred of them he broached[53] in that space.
Many spices he eat, his courage to provoke;
Such a fellow was he as of that gear[54] had the stroke.
False Doct. Now, somewhat will I tell to confirm thy tale
withal. 1475
In King Ferdinand's time in Spain was a cardinal,
Petrus Mendoza was the very man that I mean.
Of lemans he had great number besides the queen.
One of his bastards was earl, another was duke,
Whom also he abused[55] and thought it no rebuke. 1480
Joannes Cremona, another good cardinal,
For reformation of the clergy spiritual[ly]
Came once into England to damn priests' matrimony,
And the next night after, was taken doing bitchery.[56]
Doctor Eckius[57] also, which fiercely came to dispute 1485
In Leipzig with Luther, minding there him to confute
For[58] marriage of priests, three children had that year.
By this may ye see that sometime[s] we make merry cheer.
Infidelity. Marry, that ye do, I shall bear ye record[59] now.
But how will ye answer for breaking of your vow? 1490
False Doct. We never break vow so long as we do not marry,
Though we in whoredom be never so bold and busy.
Infidelity. By your order, then, ye may walk much at large.[60]
What hast thou, Hypocrisy, to lay for thy discharge?[61]

[In lines 1496–1538, the Vices continue to discuss clerical abuses.]

False Doct. Then do they compare the papists unto dogs.
Infidelity. Marry, that they do, and to such swinish hogs 1540
As in swill and soss[62] are brought up all their life.
Such are the papists, they say, both man and wife.
They say of thee also that thou art a naughty knave;
By prowling and lying ye friars would all have.
Thine order, they say, is sprung even out of hell, 1545
And all this knowledge they have now of the Gospel.
Hypocrisy. Why, where is he now? I beseech thee heartily, tell.
Infidelity. By the mass, abroad, and I warrant ye, maketh revel.
I communed with him, and he did us despise;
Against him, therefore, somewhat must we devise. 1550

False Doct. Marry, that must we,   or else it will be wrong;
    He will sure[ly] destroy us   if we do suffer him long.
    Needs must we serve him   as we once served Christ.
Infidelity. Why, mad-brained whoresons,   how did ye handle Christ?
False Doct. As he preached here,   we followed from place to
                         place   1555

    To trap him in snare,   and his doctrine to deface.
    Then found we the means   to put him so to death,
    Lest he against us   should open any more breath.
    And we set four knights   to keep him down in his grave,[63]
    That he never more   our living should deprave.   1560
    And thus must we serve   the Gospel, no remedy,
    Else will he destroy   our living perpetually.
    Better one were lost   than we should perish all,[64]
    As Caiaphas once said in   counsel pharisaical.
Infidelity. By God; and well said!   When ye have him in his
                         grave,   1565
    Stamp him down till he shit   and serve him like a knave.
Hypocrisy. We must so order him   that he go no more at large. . . .
Infidelity. Yea, and let the pope,   as God's own vicar here,   1585
    In his hand three crosses   and three crowns on his head bear,
    His power betokening   in heaven, in earth, and in hell,
    That he may command   all kings to subdue the Gospel.
False Doct. Himself may do that,   he need command none other.
    Is not he the head   of the holy church, our mother?   1590
    May not he make saints   and devils at his own pleasure,
    Which hath in his hands   the keys and church's treasure,
    So well as he made   Saint Herman first a saint,
    And twenty years after,   of heresy him attaint?
    First he sent him to heaven   by his canonization,   1595
    And from thence to hell   by an excommunication.
    We read of Formosus,[65]   that after he was dead,
    One pope his fingers,   another cut off his head
    And threw his carcass   into the flood of Tiber,
    With the head and fingers,   as Platina[66] doth remember.   1600
    In token that he   is judge over quick and dead,
    And may damn and save by   his pardons under lead,
    Silvester the second[67]   to the devil himself once gave
    For that high office   that he might damn and save.
    He offered also   his stones to Satan, they say,   1605
    For priests' chastity,   and so went their marriage away.

Enter Gospel.

Hypocrisy. Here is one coming;   inquire what he intend.
Infidelity. Ha! It is the Gospel!   From him God us defend!

Exit secretly.

False Doct. Show me, brother mine,   who did thee hither send.
Gospel. The Father of Heaven   of his mere benevolence.   1610
    I desire, therefore,   to have free audience.
False Doct. Ye mind then to preach   afore this company?
Gospel. In the laws of God   would I instruct them gladly;
    For none other way   there is unto salvation
    But the word of God   in every generation,   1615
    That quickeneth, that saveth,   that bringeth unto heaven,
    As before his death   Christ taught the Apostle[s] eleven.
False Doct. Preach here, thou shalt not,   without the authority
    Of pope or bishop,   or of some[one] of their affinity.
Gospel. God's word never taketh   his authority of man.   1620
False Doct. Thou shalt not here preach,   do thou the best thou can.
Hypocrisy. God's blessing on your good heart,   it is spoken even like
                            a man.

    Ye know this day, sir,   we have a full holy feast
    And must go [in] procession   with the blessed Rood of Rest.[68]
    We have long matins,   long lauds, long hours, long prime, 1625
    Mass, evensong, compline,   and all must be done in time;
    Censing of the altars,   and casting of holy water,
    Holy bread-making   with other necessary matter.
Gospel. Have God commanded   any such things to be done?
False Doct. What is that to thee?   Go meddle thou with old
                  shoon.[69]   1630
    Canst thou say but they   are good significations?
Gospel. I say they are fruits   of your imaginations
    To bring in lucre   and darken God's high glory.
    Of you, God doth ask   no such vain beggary.[70]
    Christ never sent his[71]   to show significations,   1635
    But his living word   to all the Christian nations.
    Ye forsake the Lord   as Isa. doth [fore]tell,[72]
    And highly[73] blaspheme   the holy of Israel.
    In his first chapter   this horrible sentence is:
    "*Quis haec frustranea*   *quaesivit de manibus vestris*";[74]   1640

Who hath required   of you such sacrifice?
In vain offer you   that uncommanded service.
"Your incense to me   is great abomination;
I sore[ly] abhor it   and much detest your fashion.
When ye pray to me   I give ye none attendance,   1645
But avert my face,"   saith God, "and my countenance."[75]
By this ye may see   that the Lord doth not regard
Your mangy[76] muttering,   neither grant[s] it any reward.
No man willeth [Saint] Paul   to speak in the congregation
In a strange language   without interpretation.   1650
In your Latin hours   the flock do ye not consider,[77]
But declare yourselves   to be Romish altogether.
"Be not led about,"   saith Paul, "by any strange learning."[78]
What else is your doctrine   but a blind popish thing?
He testifieth also,   *"Non enim ut baptizarem*   1655
Misit me Christus,   *sed ut evangelizarem—*
Christ hath not me sent   that I should baptize," saith Paul,
"But to preach his word   to the comfort of man's soul."[79]
Lo, though baptism be   a thing very necessary,
Yet must it give place   to God's Word, no remedy.[80]   1660
Why then prefer ye   your draffish[81] ceremonies
To the Gospel preaching?   O, damnable injuries!
Hypocrisy. Why suffer ye him   to prattle here so long?
False Doct. Get thee hence shortly,   or with thee it will be wrong.

He [Infidelity] *enters.*

Infidelity. Peace be here, and God;   master doctor, by your
                                                                      leave,   1665
That I may declare   a pardon, here in my sleeve,
Of our Lady of Boston,   Ingham, and Saint John's Friary,
With the indulgence   of blessed Saint Anthony.[82]
False Doct. Well, take thy pleasure,   and do it hardly.[83]
Hypocrisy. Sir, he doth me wrong,   for this day it is my station   1670
To preach [to] my brotherhood   and gather my limitation.[84]
False Doct. Who first speak, first speed;   step forth and read thy
                                                                      pardon,
And when he hath done,   your course is father warden.[85]
Gospel. What course appoint ye   for preaching of the Gospel?

False Doct. I would thy Gospel and thou were both now in
hell. 1675

Gospel. Why, and shall this baggage put by the word of God?

False Doct. Thou wilt not be answered till thou feel a sharper rod.

Infidelity. Good Christian people, I am come hither verily
As a true proctor[86] of the House of Saint Anthony.
Of clean remission I have brought ye indulgence, 1680
A pena et culpa,[87] for all your sin and offense.
By the authority of Pope Leo and Pope Clement,
Pope Boniface, Pope Pius, Pope John and Pope Innocent.[88]
And here I bless ye with a wing of the Holy Ghost,
From thunder to save ye, and from spirits in every coast.[89] 1685
Lo, here is a bell to hang upon your hog,[90]
And save your cattle from the biting of a dog.
So many as will come to this holy fraternity,
Come pay your money, and ye shall have letters of me.

False Doct. Let me have a letter, for I will be a brother. 1690

Hypocrisy. Then give me a bell, for I will be another.

Gospel. O damnable leading of Babylonical sodomites!
Yourselves ye declare to be shameful hypocrites.
Lord, pity thy people, and take away these guides,
These scorners, these robbers, these cruel homicides. 1695
Such prophets are they as God did never send.
As Jeremiah saith, they damnable ways pretend.[91]
Woe, hypocrites, woe! For here ye trifle and mock
With Christian people, and the Kingdom of Heaven uplock.
Ye count it a game to lose that Christ hath bought 1700
With his precious blood, and here most dearly sought.
O, ye are wretches and pestilent Antichrists,
Ministers of Dagon,[92] and most deceitful papists.
Like ravenous wolves, poor widows ye devour;
By title of prayer, eternal damnation is your[s]. 1705
Your own dreams ye follow, but matter much more weighty
Ye do not esteem, as judgement, faith, and mercy.
Woe, Pharisees, woe! Ye make clean outwardly,
But inwards ye are full of covetousness and bawdry.
Painted tombs are ye, appearing right beautiful,[93] 1710
But within ye stink and have thoughts very shameful.
Ye slew the prophets, your doings yet bear witness.

How think ye to avoid	that point[94] of unrighteousness?	
Oh, raging serpents	and viperous generation,	
How can ye escape	the danger of damnation?[95]	1715
False Doct. Who made thee so bold	to meddle within my cure,[96]	
And teach new learning?	An heretic art thou sure[ly].	
If due search were made,	we should find thee, I think, no priest.	
Gospel. Yes, anointed of God,	but no popish Antichrist.	
False Doct. Let me see, where are	the letters of thy orders?	1720
Gospel. Where Christ his-self is,	and not in these same borders.	
No such priest am I	as is anointed with oil,	
But the Holy Ghost,	for I am none of this soil.[97]	
False Doct. Here I attach[98] thee	for a busy schismatic,	
And will thee accuse	for an heinous heretic.	1725
Lay hands upon him	and deprive him of this apparel.	

Hic veste spoliatum sordidioribus induunt.[99]

Lo, thus will I handle	all them that shall take thy quarrel.	
Hold; away with this gear,	and lay it forth, aside!	
Hypocrisy. Nay, tarry, brother mine,	for away shalt thou not slide.	
Gospel. I am not going;	why dost thou slander me?	1730
Infidelity. Burn him to ashes,	and show to him no pity.	
False Doct. Burnt shall he not be	if he will no more do so.	
Fellow, how sayst thou?	Wilt thou here abjure, or no?	
Gospel. I will neither abjure,	nor yet recant God's glory.	
False Doct. I offered thee reason,	and thereto thou wilt not apply.	1735
Well, get thee forward,	for thou shalt sure[ly] die.	
The temporal power	shall judge thee to the fire[100]	
At our accusement[101]	and holy religious desire.	
Gospel. Though you, for my sake,	imprison men cruelly,	
Famish them, stock them,	and them with faggots fry;	1740
Hurt me, ye shall not,	for I can never die,	
And they, for my sake,	shall live perpetually.	
False Doct. Here is a prating!	With a very vengeance, hence!	
Hypocrisy. This horrible heretic	now shall we well recompense.	

They exit with him.

Infidelity. Yea, burn him well, friar,   and let him no longer

reign.   1745

Lay on green faggots[102]   to put him to the more pain.

By the mass, I laugh   to see how this gear doth work.

He is like of them   to have no more grace than a Turk,

For such knaves they are   as a man shall not lightly find

And rake hell over.   Companions they are, to my mind.   1750

My business all   is now at a good conclusion,

That I have here brought   these three laws to confusion;

Now shall I be able   to live here peacably,

And make frolic cheer,   with "Hey! How! Friscajoly!"[103]

The Law of Nature   I cast first in a lepry[104]   1755

By the secret help   of Idolatry and Sodomy.

The Law of Moses   I made a cripple blind,

Avarice and Ambition   to help me were not behind.

And now, Christ's Law   I have burnt for heresy

By the help of False Doctrine   and my cousin, Hypocrisy.   1760

On these same three laws,   all other laws depend,

And cannot prevail   now these are at an end.

If Christian governors   do not these laws uphold,

Their civil ordinances   will soon be very cold.

Well, this valiant George[105]   hath made them all to stoop;   1765

Cheer now may I make,   and set cock on the hoop.[106]

Fill in all the pots   and bid me welcome, hostess,

And go call me hither   mine own sweet minion,[107] Bess!

Act 4 Ends.
Exeunt.

Notes

1. One who speaks for, an advocate, especially in a court of law.
2. Usefulness.
3. Opinion.
4. Wherever.
5. Heavenly bodies.
6. Sodomy.
7. Be presented before.
8. Gen. 6–8, 18–19; Lev. 26:17, 25.
9. After which.
10. Knowledge.
11. Blessing.

12. Dock on Thames River in London.

13. By the Cross (an oath).

14. Provide sexual pleasure.

15. living.

16. Eph. 2:20–22.

17. Pagan invaders of England.

18. Clerics whose identity is obscure.

19. Work.

20. By.

21. Isa. 29:13.

22. Gospel describes the "true" church as an invisible congregation of believers governed by the Bible and devoid of formalistic ritual.

23. Dicers.

24. Matt. 35:41.

25. Catholic tonsure and headgear.

26. 1 Cor. 4:15.

27. Erroneously.

28. Mere.

29. Physical reproduction.

30. Protestantism.

31. Anointed priests.

32. Sodomy.

33. Copulate swiftly and depart.

34. 1 Tim. 4:1–3.

35. Depart.

36. Gen. 19.

37. From.

38. Procreate with your mother.

39. Plot.

40. "God guard you."

41. Thank-you's.

42. Friar Thief.

43. Infidelity suggests that Hypocrisy have intercourse with False Doctrine.

44. Vagina.

45. One who sucks.

46. Confessor.

47. Sexual partner.

48. Helped.

49. "I distinguish."

50. A relic belonging to Louis IX (Saint Louis), king of France.

51. John of the Church (Happé); obscene wordplay on "absolved."

52. Phallic quibble.

53. Copulated with.

54. Apparatus (i.e., genitals).

55. Molested sexually.

56. Harlotry.

57. Johann Eck (1486–1543), theologian who disputed with Luther.

58. Against.
59. Pay attention to.
60. Friars who were not members of a specific house could move freely.
61. Justification.
62. Dog food.
63. Matt. 27:64–66.
64. Inversion of the Parable of the Lost Sheep (Luke 15:4–7).
65. Pope (891–896).
66. Bartolomeo Platina (Bartolomeo Sacchi), historian (1421–81).
67. Sylvester II, pope (c. 945–1003).
68. A famous crucifix.
69. Old shoes (i.e., worthless things).
70. Trash.
71. His disciples.
72. Isa. 1:4.
73. Rashly.
74. "Who hath required this at your hand?" (Isa. 1:12).
75. Isa. 1:12–15.
76. Despicable.
77. Liturgy incomprehensible to most congregants.
78. Eph. 4:14, Heb 13.9.
79. 1 Cor 1:17.
80. Inescapably.
81. Worthless.
82. Saint Anthony of Egypt, desert hermit (c. 251–356), founder of the first Christian monastery.
83. Steadfastly.
84. Area granted to a traveling friar in which to preach.
85. Supervisor of a Franciscan convent.
86. Supervisor.
87. "From pain and guilt."
88. This gallery of abusive popes probably refers to Leo X (1513–21), who tried to silence Luther; Clement VII (1523–34), who supported the Edict of Worms and denied Henry VIII's request for annulment of his marriage to Catherine of Aragon; Boniface IX (1389–1404), who began to market indulgences and other wares; Pius II (1458–64), who denied that ultimate authority rested with the councils of bishops; John XXIII (1410–15), the antipope who condemned writings by Wyclif; and Innocent III (1198–1216), who argued in favor of papal supremacy over temporal government.
89. From every direction.
90. Symbols of St. Anthony.
91. Intend.
92. Philistine idol.
93. Matt. 23:27.
94. Result.
95. Matt. 23:27
96. Priestly responsibility.
97. Place.

98. Arrest.

99. "Here having removed his apparel they put more shabby ones on him."

100. To be burned alive.

101. Accusation.

102. Unseasoned wood that burns slowly.

103. Song refrain.

104. Leprosy.

105. Saint George.

106. To engage in wild merriment.

107. Lover.

3.2. Richard Weaver, from
Lusty Juventus (c. 1550)

Richard Weaver (fl. 1547–53), a preacher about whose life virtually nothing is known, designed *Lusty Juventus* for performance by a troupe of four players (see also 3.1) before audiences of youths and apprentices who flocked to sermons and plays under Edward VI. Its allegorical combat for the soul of an erring Mankind figure recalls *Everyman*, but it praises Protestant belief in justification by faith and rejection of the doctrine of good works (see 2.4). The Virtues (Good Counsel, Knowledge, and God's Merciful Promises) personify ministerial instruction, Bible education, and divine grace. They speak in rhyme royal (ababbcc), an elevated meter suitable to catechetical speeches filled with scriptural quotations and allusions. Indeed, Juventus (i.e., Youth) carries the New Testament as a symbolic prop (see also 6.2). The Virtues double with antithetical Vices: the Devil, Hypocrisy (also disguised as Friendship), Abominable Living (also disguised as Unknown Honesty), and Fellowship. Harlotry associates the latter two characters with the Whore of Babylon, whom Protestants identified with the Church of Rome (see 1.1.B–C). Ribald comedy and obscene innuendo are traditional attributes of Vices. The Devil's status as a conjurer and the use of Hypocrisy to personify Roman Catholicism recall attacks on Catholic priests as necromancers and pitchmen of worthless trifles (see 2.1) that endure in figures such as the sorcerer, Archimago, in Spenser's *Faerie Queene*. Juventus's fall into despair represents anxiety concerning faith, just as his standing upright near the end of the play personifies "true" conversion and repentance as a gift of divine grace.

SOURCE: *STC* 25148, A2–A4ʳ, A4ʳ–B1ʳ, B1ᵛ–B2ʳ, B2ʳ–C3ᵛ, C3ᵛ–D2ʳ, D2ʳ–D2ᵛ, D4ʳ–D4ᵛ, D4ᵛ–E1ᵛ, E2ʳ–E2ʳ. Text missing from this edition is supplied in square brackets from the second edition of 1565 (*STC* 25149).

EDITION: Somerset.

REFERENCES: Bevington; King 1982; Paul Whitfield White 1993.

The Personages That Speak:
Messenger
Lusty Juventus
Good Counsel
Knowledge
Satan, the Devil
Hypocrisy
Fellowship
Abominable Living
God's Merciful Promises . . .

Here entereth Lusty Juventus, or Youth, singing as followeth.

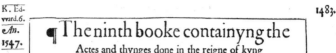

¶ The ninth booke containyng the
Actes and thynges done in the reigne of kyng
Edvvard the 6.
(*₊*)

King Edward the vj.

Figure 5. *Allegory of Edward VI's Reign*. John Foxe, *Acts and Monuments* (1570), p. 1483, woodcut. Courtesy of The Ohio State University Libraries. Representations of allegedly "true" and "false" worship fill this iconoclastic woodcut. The portrayal of Edward VI in the royal presence chamber emulates Holbein's picture of Henry VIII with the sword and the Book (see Figure 1). The upper register shows "The Papists packing away their paultry" aboard "The ship of the Romish church" and "The burning of Images." The destruction of papal "trinkets" and saints' images, like the one undergoing removal from the church wall, is a recurrent feature of writings by John Bale and other Protestants. The portrayal of "The Temple well purged" at the bottom incorporates central features of Protestant worship: preaching, Bible reading, and reduction of the seven sacraments of the Roman rite to Holy Communion and baptism.

Juventus. In a herber[1] green, asleep where as I lay
    The birds sang sweet in the midst of the day.
    I dreamed fast of mirth and play.
    In youth is pleasure, in youth is pleasure.   40

      Methought I walked still to and fro,
    And from her company I could not go,
    But when I waked it was not so,
    In youth is pleasure, in youth is pleasure.

      Therefore my heart is surely pight,[2]   45
    Of her alone to have a sight,
    Which is my joy and heart's delight,
    In youth is pleasure, in youth is pleasure. *Finis.*

Lusty Juventus, or Youth, he speaketh.

Juventus. What, how are they not here?
    I am disappointed, by the blessed mass,   50
    I had thought to have found them making good cheer,
    But now they are gone to some secret place.
    Well, seeing they are gone, I do not greatly pass,[3]
    Another time I will hold them as much,[4]
    Seeing they break promise, and keep not the touch.[5]   55

      What shall I do now to pass away the day?
    Is there any man here that will go to game?[6]
    At whatsoever he will play,
    To make one, I am ready to [do] the same.
    Youth full of pleasure is my proper name,   60
    To be alone is not my appety,[7]
    For of all things in the world I love merry company.

      Who knoweth where is e'er a minstrel?
    By the mass, I would fain go dance a fit;[8]
    My companions are at it, I know right well;   65
    They do not all this while in a corner sit.
    Against[9] another time they have taught me wit;
    I beshrew their hearts for serving me this;
    I will go seek them whether I hit or miss.

Here entereth Good Counsel, to whom Youth yet speaketh.

Juventus. Well I met, father, well I met.   70
    Did you hear any minstrels play,
    As you came hitherward upon your way?
    And if you did, I pray you wise[10] me thither,
    For I am going to seek them, and in faith I know not whether.
Good Counsel. Sir, I will ask you a question, by your favor: 75
    What would you with the minstrel do?
Juventus. Nothing but have a dance or two,
    To pass the time away in pleasure.
Good Counsel. If that be the matter, I promise you sure,
    I am the more sorrier that it should so be,   80
    For there is no such passing the time appointed in the scripture,
    Nor yet thereunto it doth not agree.
    I wish that ye would so use your liberty
    To walk as ye are bound to do,
    According to the vocation which God hath called you to.   85
Juventus. Why, sir, are you angry because I have spoken so?
    By the mass, it is alone for my appety.
Good Counsel. Show me your name, I pray you heartily,
    And then I will my mind express.
Juventus. My name is called Juventus, doubtless.   90
    Say what you will, I will give you the hearing.
Good Counsel. For as much as God hath created you of nothing,
    Unto his own likeness by spiritual illumination,
    It is unmeet that ye should lead your living
    Contrary to his godly determination.   95
    Saint Paul unto the Ephesians giveth good exhortation
    Saying, "Walk circumspectly, redeeming the time,"[11]
    That is, to spend it well and not to wickedness incline.
Juventus. No, no, hardly none of mine,
    If I would live so straight, you might count me a fool.   100
    Let them keep those rules which are doctors divine[12]
    And have been brought up all their days in school.
Good Counsel. Moses in the Law exhorteth his people,
    As in the book of Deuteronomy he doth plainly write
    That they should live obedient and thankful,   105
    For in effect these words he doth recite:

"All ye this day stand before the Lord's sight,
   Both princes, elders, and parents,
   Children, wives, young and old, therefore obey his commandments."[13]
Juventus. I am too young to understand his documents;   110
   Wherefore did all they stand before his presence?
Good Counsel. To enter with God peace and alliance,
   Promising that they would him honor, fear, and serve.
   All kind of people were bound in those covenants,[14]
   That from his law they should never swerve,   115
   For God useth no partiality.
Juventus. What, am I bound, as well as the clergy,
   To learn and follow his precepts and law?
Good Counsel. Yea, surely, or else God will withdraw
   His mercy from you, promised in his covenant;   120
   For except you live under his obedience and awe,
   How can you receive the benefits of his testament?
   For he that submitteth himself to be a servant,
   And his master's command will not fulfill nor regard,
   According as he hath done, is worthy his reward.   125
Juventus. It is as true a saying as ever I heard,
   Therefore your name I pray you now tell,
   For by my truth your communication I like wonders[15] well.
Good Counsel. My name is called Good Counsel.
Juventus. Good Counsel,   130
   Now in faith I cry you mercy.
   I am sorry that I have you thus offended,
   But I pray you bear with me patiently,
   And my misbehavior shall be amended,
   For I know my time I have rudely spended   135
   Following my own lust, being led by ignorance
   But now I hope of better knowledge through your acquaintance.
Good Counsel. I pray God guide you with his gracious assistance
   Unto the knowledge of his truth, your ignorance to undo,
   That you may be one of those numbered Christians   140
   Which followeth the Lamb whither he doth go;
   The Lamb, Jesus Christ, my meaning is so,
   By sure faith and confidence in his bitter death and Passion,
   The only price of our health and salvation.
Juventus. Sir, I thank you for your hearty oration,   145

And now I pray you show me your advisement,
How I may live in this my vocation
According to God's will and commandment.
Good Counsel. First of all, it is most expedient
    That you exercise yourself in continual prayer,   150
    That it might please the Lord omnipotent
    To send unto you his Holy Spirit and comforter,
    Which will lead you every day and hour
    Unto the knowledge of his word and verity,
    Wherein you may learn to live most Christianly.   155

He [Juventus] *kneeleth.*

Juventus. Oh Lord, grant me of thy infinite mercy
    The true knowledge of thy law and will,
    And illumine my heart with [thy] spirit continually,
    That I may be apt, thy holy precepts to fulfill.
    Strengthen me, that I may persevere still   160
    Thy commandments to obey,
    And then shall I never slip nor fall away.

He riseth.

Good Counsel. Full true be these words, which Christ himself did say:
    "He that seeketh shall surely find."[16]

Knowledge entereth.

Good Counsel. Behold, Youth, now rejoice we may,   165
    For I see Knowledge of God's Verity stand here behind.
    He is come now to satisfy your mind
    In those things which you will desire.
    Therefore together, let us approach him near.
Juventus. Ah, Good Counsel, now it doth appear   170
    That God never rejecteth the humble's petition.
Knowledge. Now the Lord bless you all with his heavenly benediction
    And with his fiery love your hearts inflame,
    That of his merciful promises you may have the fruition,
    The subtlety of the Devil utterly to defame.   175
    Now good Christian audience I will express my name,

The True Knowledge of God's Verity, this my name doth hight,
Whom God hath appointed to give the blind their sight. . . .

And Christ in the Gospel saith manifestly,
"Blessed is he which heareth the word of God and keepeth it,"[17]
That is, to believe his word and live accordingly,
Declaring the faith by the fruits of the spirit,
Whose fruits are these, as Saint Paul to the Galatians doth write: 205
"Love, joy, peace, long-suffering and faithfulness,
Meekness, goodness, temperance, and gentleness."[18]

Good Counsel. By these words which unto you he doth express,
He teacheth that you ought to have a steadfast faith,
Without the which it is impossible, doubtless,   210
To please God, as Saint Paul saith:
"Where faith is not, godly living decayeth,
For whatsoever is not of faith," saith St. Paul, "is sin,
But where a perfect faith is, there is good working."[19]

Juventus. It seemeth to me that this is your meaning,   215
That when I observe God's commandments and the works of charity,
They shall prevail unto me nothing,
Except I believe to be saved thereby.

Knowledge. No, no, you are deceived very blindly,
For faith in Christ's merits doth only justify   220
And make us righteous in God's sight.

Juventus. Why should I then in good works delight,
Seeing I shall not be saved by them?

Good Counsel. Because they are required of all Christian men,
As the necessary fruits of true repentance.   225

Knowledge. But the reward of the heavenly inheritance
Is given through faith, for Christ's deservings,
As Saint Paul declareth in the fourth chapter to the Romans:
"Therefore we ought not to work as hirelings,
Seeing Christ hath purged us once from all our wicked living.   230
Let us no more wallow therein,
But persevere like good branches, bearing fruit in him."

Juventus. Now I know whereabout you have been,
My elders never taught me so before.

Good Counsel. Though your elders were blind, doubt not you therefore,   235
For St. Peter saith, "Vain is the conversations[20]
Which ye receive by your elders' traditions."[21]

Juventus. I will gladly receive your godly admonitions,
    But yet I pray you show me the cause
    That they being men of great discretions   240
    Did not instruct me in God's laws
    According to his will and ordinance.
Knowledge. Because they themselves were wrapped in ignorance,
    Being deceived by false preachers.
Juventus. Oh Lord, deliver me from wicked teachers,   245
    That I be not deceived with their false doctrine.
Good Counsel. To God's word you must only incline,
    All other doctrine clean set apart. . . .
Juventus. I pray God give me grace so for to do,
    That unto his will I may be obedient.   275

[Good Counsel here presents a New Testament to Juventus.]

Good Counsel. Here you shall receive Christ's testament,
    To comfort your conscience when need shall require,
    To learn the contents thereof, see that you be diligent,
    The which all Christian men ought to desire.
    For it is the well, or fountain most clear,   280
    Out of the which doth spring sweet consolation
    To all those which thirst after eternal salvation.

Knowledge. Therein shall you find most wholesome preservation,
    Both in troubles, persecutions, sickness, and adversity,
    And a sure defense in the time of temptation   285
    Against whom the Devil cannot prevail with all his army.
    And if you persevere therein unfeignedly,
    It will set your heart at such quietness and rest
    Which can never be turned with storms nor tempest.

Good Counsel. With this thing you must never flatter nor jest,   290
    But steadfastly believe it every day and hour,
    And let your conversation openly protest
    That of your heart it is the most precious treasure.
    And then your godly example shall other men procure,
    To learn and exercise the same also.   295
    I pray God strengthen you so for to do.

Juventus. Now for this godly knowledge which you have brought me to,
    I beseech the living God to reward you again;
    From your company I will never depart nor go,
    So long as in this life I do remain.   300
    For in this book I see manifest and plain,
    That he that followeth his own lusts and imagination
    Keepeth the ready path to everlast[ing] damnation.

      And he that leadeth a godly conversation
    Shall be brought to such quietness, joy, and peace,   305
    Which in comparison passeth all worldly gloriation,[22]
    Which cannot endure, but shortly cease.
    Both the time and hour I may now bless
    That I met with you father Good Counsel
    To bring me to the knowledge of this heavenly gospel. . . .   310

Good Counsel. For this conversation[23] of Youth, the Lord's name be praised!
    Let us now depart for a season.   *Exit.*

Knowledge. To give God the glory it is convenient[24] and reason[able];   320
    If you will depart, I will not tarry.   *Exit.*

Juventus. And I will never forsake your company
    While I live in this world.   *Exit.*

Here entereth the Devil.

[*Devil*]. Oh, oh, all too late;
    I trow this gear will come to naught,   325
    For I perceive my power doth abate,
    For all the policy that ever I have wrought.
    Many and sundry ways I have sought
    To have the word of God deluded utterly;
    Oh, for sorrow, yet it will not be.   330

      I have done the best that I can,
    And my ministers also in every place,
    To root it clean from the heart of man;
    And yet for all that, it flourisheth apace.
    I am sore in dread to show my face,   335

My authority and works are so greatly despised,
My inventions, and all that ever I have devised.

    Oh, oh, full well I know the cause
That my estimation doth thus decay.
The old people would believe still in my laws,   340
But the younger sort lead them a contrary way.
They will not believe, they plainly say,
In old traditions and made by men,
But they will live as the scripture teacheth them.

    Out! I cry upon them; they do me open wrong   345
To bring up their children thus in knowledge;
For if they will not follow my ways when they are young,
It is hard turning them when they come to age.
I must needs find some means this matter to [as]suage;
I mean to turn their hearts from the scripture quite,   350
That in carnal pleasures they may have more delight.

    Well, I will go taste[25] to infect this Youth
Through the enticement of my son Hypocrisy,
And work some proper feat to stop his mouth.
That he may lead his life carnally,   355
I had never more need my matters to apply.
Oh, my child Hypocrisy, where art thou?
I charge thee of my blessing appear before me now.

Here entereth Hypocrisy.

Hypocrisy. "Oh, oh," quod he, keep again the sow!
    I come as fast as I can, I warrant you.   360
    Where is he that hath the sow to sell?
    I will give him money if I like her well;
    Whether it be sow or hog, I do not greatly care,
    For by my occupation I am a butcher.
Devil. Oh, my child, how dost thou fare?   365
Hypocrisy. Sancti, amen,[26] who have we there?
    By the mass, I will buy none of thy ware;
    Thou art a chapman[27] for the Devil.
Devil. What, my son, canst thou not tell

Who is here, and what I am? 370
I am thine own father, Satan.
Hypocrisy. Be you so, sir? I cry you have mercy then.
You may say I am homely and lack learning,
To liken my father's voice unto a sow's groaning,
But I pray you to show me the cause and why, 375
That you called me hither so hastily.
Devil. Ah, Hypocrisy, I am undone utterly.
Hypocrisy. Utterly undone, nay stop there hardly,[28]
For I myself do know the contrary
By daily experience. 380
Do not I reign yet abroad?
And as long as I am in the world,
You have some treasure and substance.

I suppose I have been the flower
In setting forth thy laws and power 385
Without any delay.
By the mass, if I had not been,
Thou hadst not been worth a Flander's pin[29]
At this present day.

The time were too long now to declare 390
How many and how great the number are
Which have deceived be[en],
And brought clean from God's law
Unto thy yoke and awe,
Through the enticement of me. 395

I have been busied, since the world began,
To graft thy laws in the heart of man,
Where they ought to be refused.
And I have so mingled God's commandments
With vain zeals and blind intents 400
That they be greatly abused.

I set up great idolatry,
With all kind of filth[y Sodomitry],[30]
To give [mankind a fall];
And I bro[ught up such superstition] 405

Under th[e name of holiness and religion],
That dec[eived almost all].

   As holy [cardinals, holy popes],[31]
Holy vest[ments, holy copes],
Holy hermits and friars,   410
Holy priests, holy bishops,
Holy monks, holy abbots,
Yea, and all obstinate liars.

   Holy pardons, holy beads,[32]
Holy saints, holy images,   415
With holy, holy blood,
Holy stocks,[33] holy stones,
Holy clouts,[34] holy bones,
Yea, and holy, holy wood.

   Holy skins, holy bulls,   420
Holy rochets, holy cowls,
Holy crutches and staves,
Holy hoods, holy caps,
Holy miters, holy hats,
A[nd] good holy, holy knaves.   425

   And holy days, holy fastings,
Holy twitching, holy tastings,
Holy visions and sights,
Holy wax, holy lead,
Holy water, holy bread,   430
To drive away spirits.

   Holy fire, holy palm,[35]
Holy oil, holy cream,[36]
And holy ashes also,
Holy broaches, holy rings,   435
[Holy] kneeling, holy censings,[37]
[And an hundred trim-trams[38] mo'].

   [Holy crosses, holy bells,
Holy relics, holy jewels,

Of mine own invention, 440
Holy candles, holy tapers,
Holy parchments, holy papers;
Had not you a holy son?]
Devil. All these things which thou hast done
My honor and laws hath maintained. 445
But now, oh alas, one thing is begun
By the which my kingdom is greatly decayed.
I shall lose all I am sore afraid.
Except thy help I know right plain,
I shall never be able to recover it again. 450

God's word is so greatly sprung up in Youth,
That he little regardeth my laws or me.
He telleth his parents that [it] is very truth,
That they of long time have deceived be.
He saith according to Christ's verity 455
All his doings he will order and frame,
Mortifying the flesh with[39] the lusts of the same.
Hypocrisy. Ah, sirrah, there beginneth the game.
What, is Juventus become so tame
To be a new gospeler? 460
Devil. As fast as I do make, he doth mar.
He hath followed so long in the steps of Good Counsel
That Knowledge and he together doth dwell,
For who is so busy in every place as Youth,
To read and declare the manifest truth? 465
But oh, Hypocrisy, if thou could stop his mouth,
Thou shouldest win my heart forever.
Hypocrisy. What would you have me do in the matter?
Show me therein your advisement.
Devil. I would have thee go incontinent, 470
And work some craft, feat, or policy,
To set Knowledge and him at controversy,
And his company thyself greatly use
That God's word he may clean abuse.
Hypocrisy. At your request, I will not refuse 475
To do that thing which in me doth lie;
Doubt ye not but I will excuse
Those things which he doth plainly deny.

And I will handle my matters so craftily
That ere he cometh to man's state,   480
God's word and his living shall be clean at the [de]bate.[40]
Devil. Thou shall have my blessing both early and late,
And because thou shalt at my counsel keep,
Thou shalt call thy name Friendship.
Hypocrisy. By the mass, it is a name full meet   485
For my proper and amiable person.
Devil. Oh, farewell, farewell, my son.
Speed thy business, for I must be gone.   *Exit.*
Hypocrisy. I warrant you, let me alone;
I will be with Juventus anon,   490
And that ere he be ware.
And iwis if he walk not straight,
I will use such a sleight
That shall trap him in a snare.

How shall I bring this gear to pass?   495
I can tell now, by the mass,
Without any more advisement:
I will infect him with wicked company,
Whose conversation shall be so fleshly,
Yea, able to overcome an innocent.   500

This wicked Fellowship
Shall him company keep
For awhile,
And then I will bring in
Abominable Living,   505
Him to beguile.

With words fair I will him [en]tice,
Telling him of a girl nice,[41]
Which shall him somewhat move.
Abominable Living though she be,   510
Yet he shall no other ways see,
But she is for to love.

She shall him procure
To live in pleasure,

After his own fantasy.   515
And my matter to frame,
I will call her a name:
Unknown Honesty.

    Thus will I convey
My matter, I say,   520
Somewhat handsomely,
That through wicked Fellowship
And false pretend[ed] Friendship,
Youth shall live carnally.

    Trudge, Hypocrisy, trudge,
Thou art a good drudge   525
To serve the Devil.
If thou shouldest lie and lurk
And not intend[42] thy work,
Thy master should do full evil.   530

Here entereth Youth, to whom Hypocrisy yet speaketh.

Hypocrisy. What, Master Youth,
    Well I met, by my truth,
    And whither away?
    You are the last man
    Which I talked on,   535
    I swear by this day.

    Methought by your face,
    Ere you came in place,
    It should be you.
    Therefore I did abide,   540
    Here in this tide,
    For your coming, this is true.
Juventus. For your gentleness, sir, most heartily I thank you;
    But yet you must hold me somewhat excused,
    For to my simple knowledge I never knew   545
    That you and I together were acquainted;
    But nevertheless, if you do it renew,
    Old acquaintance will soon be remembered.

Hypocrisy. Ah, now I see well Youth is feathered,
    And his crumbs he hath well gathered,   550
    Since I spake with him last.
    A poor man's tale cannot now be heard
    As in times past.

        I cry you mercy; I was somewhat bold
    Thinking that your mastership would   555
    Not have been so strange.[43]
    But now I perceive that promotion
    Causeth both man, manners, and fashion
    Greatly for to change.
Juventus. You are to blame thus me to challenge,   560
    For I think I am not he which you take me for.
Hypocrisy. Yes, I have known you ever since you were bore.
    Your age is yet under a score,
    Which I can well remember.
    Iwis, iwis you and I   565
    Many a time have been full merry
    When you were young and tender.
Juventus. Then pray you, let us reason no longer,
    But first show your nomination.[44]
Hypocrisy. Of my name to make declaration   570
    Without any dissimulation,
    I am called Friendship.
    Although I be simple and rude of fashion,
    Yet by lineage and generation
    I am nigh kin to your mastership.   575
Juventus. What, Friendship,
    I am glad to see that you be merry.
    By my truth, I had almost you forgot,
    By long absence brought out of memory.
Hypocrisy. By the mass, I love you so heartily,   580
    That there is none so welcome to my company.
    I pray you tell me, whither are you going?
Juventus. My intention is to go hear a preaching.
Hypocrisy. "A preaching," quod ha, ah, good little one,
    By Christ she will make you cry out of the winning,[45]   585
    If you follow her instructions so early in the morning.
Juventus. Full greatly I do abhor this your wicked saying,

For no doubt they increase much sin and vice;
    Therefore I pray you, show not your meaning,
    For I delight not in such foolish fantasies. 590
Hypocrisy. Surely, then you are the more unwise.
    You may have a sport amongst them now and then;
    Why should not you as well as other men?
Juventus. As for these filthy doings, I utterly detest them.
    I will hear no more of your wicked communication. 595
Hypocrisy. If I may be so bold by your deliberation,
    What will you do at a preaching?
Juventus. Learn some wholesome and godly teaching
    Of the true minister of Christ's gospel.
Hypocrisy. Tush, what he will say, I know right well. 600
    He will say that God is a good man,
    He can make him no better, and say the best he can.
Juventus. I know that, but what then?
    The more that God's word is preached and taught,
    The greater the occasion is to all Christian men 605
    To forsake their sinful livings, both wicked, vile, and naught[y],
    And to repent their former evils which they have wrought,
    Trusting by Christ's death to be redeemed.
    And he that this doth, shall never be deceived.
Hypocrisy. Well said, master doctor, well said. 610
    By the mass, we must have you into the pulpit.
    I pray you be remembered,[46] and cover your head,
    For indeed you have need to keep in your wit.
    Ah, sirrah, who would have thought it,
    That Youth had been such a well-learned man? 615
    Let me see your portas, gentle Sir John.
Juventus. No, it is not a book for you to look on.
    You ought not to jest with God's testament.
Hypocrisy. What, man, I pray you be content
    For I do nothing else but say my fantasy. 620
    But yet if you would do after my advisement,
    In that matter you should not be so busy.
    Was not your father as well-learned as ye?
    And if he had said then, as you have now done,
    Iwis he had been like to make a burn.[47] 625
Juventus. It were much better for me, then, to return
    From my faith in Christ and the profession of his word.

Hypocrisy. Whether is better a halter or a cord,[48]
    I cannot tell, I swear by God's mother.
    But I think you will have the one or the other.   630
    Will you lose all your friends' goodwill
    To continue in that opinion still?
    Was there not as well-learned men before as now?
    Yea, and better too, I may say to you.
    And they taught the younger sort of people   635
    By the elders to take an example.
    And if I did not love you as nature doth me bind,
    You should not know so much of my mind.
Juventus. Whether were I better be ignorant and blind
    And to be damned in Hell for infidelity,   640
    Or to learn godly knowledge, wherein I shall find
    The right pathway to eternal felicity?
Hypocrisy. Can you deny but it is your duty
    Unto your elders to be obedient?
Juventus. I grant I am bound to obey my parents   645
    In all things honest and lawful.
Hypocrisy. "Lawful," quod ha, ah fool, fool.
    Wilt thou set men to school
    When they be old?
    I may say to you secretly,   650
    The world was never merry
    Since children were so bold.

      Now every boy will be a teacher,
    The father a fool, and the child a preacher.
    This is a pretty gear;   655
    The foul presumption of youth
    Will turn shortly to great ruth,
    I fear, I fear, I fear.
Juventus. The sermon will be done ere I can come there.
    I care not greatly whether I go or no,   660
    And yet for my promise, by God I swear,
    There is no remedy but I must needs go.
    Of my companions there will be mo',
    And I promised them, by God's grace,
    To meet them there as the sermon was.   665
Hypocrisy. For once, breaking promise do not you pass;[49]

Make some excuse the matter to cease.
What have they to do?
And you and I were I wot where,
We would be as merry as there, 670
Yea, and merrier too.
Juventus. I would gladly in your company go;
But if my companions should chance to see,
They would report full evil by me.
And peradventure if I should it use, 675
My company they would clean refuse.
Hypocrisy. What, are those fellows so curious[50]
That yourself you cannot excuse?
I will teach you the matter to convey.
Do what your own lust and say as they say. 680
And if you be reproved with your own affinity,
Bid them pluck the beam out of their own eye.[51]

The old popish priests mock and despise,
And the ignorant people that believe their lies,
Call them papists, hypocrites, and clowns[52] of the plow. 685
Face out[53] the matter and then good enough,
Let your book at your girdle be tied,
Or else in your bosom that he[54] may be spied. . . .
Juventus. Now, by my truth, you are merrily disposed. 695
Let us go thither as you think best.
Hypocrisy. How say you, shall we go to breakfast?
Will you go to the pie feast,
Or, by the mass, if thou wilt be my guest,
It shall cost thee nothing. 700
I have a furney card[55] in a place
That will bear a turn besides the ace.

She purveys now apace
For my coming.
And if thou wilt ibere[56] as well as I, 705
We shall have merry company.
And I warrant thee if we have not a pie,
We shall have a pudding.[57]
Juventus. By the mass, that meat I love above all thing,
You may draw me about the town with a pudding. 710

Hypocrisy. Then you shall see my cunning.
  A poor shift for a living
  Amongst poor men used is.[58]

Here entereth Fellowship.

Hypocrisy. The kind heart of hers,
  Hath eased my purse   715
  Many a time ere this.
Fellowship. I marvel greatly where Friendship is;
  He promised to meet me here ere this time.
  I beshrew his heart that his promise doth miss,
  And then be ye sure it shall not be mine.   720
Hypocrisy. Yes, Fellowship,[59] that it shall be thine,
  For I have tarried here this hour or twain,
  And this honest gentleman in my company hath been
  To abide your coming; this thing is plain.
Fellowship. By the mass, if you chide I wilt be gone again, 725
  For in faith, Friendship, I may say to thee
  I love not to be there where chiders be.
Hypocrisy. No God it knoweth you are as full of honesty
  As a marrow bone is full of honey.
  But sirrah, I pray you bid this gentleman welcome, 730
  For he is desirous in your company to come.
  I tell you he is a man of the right making
  And one that hath excellent learning.
  At his girdle he hath such a book
  That the popish priests dare not on him look. 735
  This is a fellow for the nonce.
Fellowship. I love him the better, by dog's precious bones.[60]
  You are heartily welcome as I may say.
  I shall desire you of better acquaintance,
  That of your company be bold I may.   740
  You may be sure, if in me it lie,
  To do you pleasure you should it find,
  For by the mass, I love you, with both heart and mind.
Juventus. To say the same to you, your gentleness doth me bind,
  And I thank you heartily for your kindness. 745
Hypocrisy. Will you see this gentleman's fineness,

Your gentleness and your kindness?
I thank him and I thank you.
And I think if the truth were sought,
The one bad, and the other naught[y].   750
Never a good I make God a vow,
But yet Fellowship tell me one thing:
Did you see little Bess this morning?
"We should have our breakfast yesternight," she said,
But she hath forgotten it now, I am afraid.   755
Fellowship. Her promise shall be performed and paid,
For I spake with her since the time I rose,
And then she told me how the matter goes:
We must be with her between eight and nine,
And then her master and mistress will be at the preaching.   760
Juventus. I purposed myself there to have been,
But this man provoked me to the contrary
And told me that we should have merry company.
Fellowship. "Merry," quod ha, we cannot choose but be merry,
For there is such a girl where as we go,   765
Which will make us to be merry whether we will or no.
Hypocrisy. The ground is the better on the which she doth go,
For she will make better cheer with that little which she can get
Than many a one can with a great banquet of meat.
Juventus. To be in her company my heart is set;   770
Therefore I pray you let us be gone.
Fellowship. She will come for us herself anon,
For I told her before where we would stand
And then she said she would beck[61] us with her hand.
Juventus. Now, by the mass, I perceive she is a gallant;   775
What, will she take pains to come for us hither?
Hypocrisy. Yea, I warrant you, therefore you must be familiar with her
When she cometh in place.
You must her embrace
Somewhat handsomely,   780
Lest she think it danger[ous]
Because you are a stranger
To come in your company.
[*Juventus.*] Yea, by God's foot, that I will be busy
And I may say to you I can play the knave secretly.   785

[Enter Abominable Living.]

Abominable. Hem, come away quickly!
　　The back door is open; I dare not tarry.
　　Come Fellowship, come on away.
Hypocrisy. What, Unknown Honesty, a word, [I pray].
　　You shall not go yet, by God, I swear;　　　　　　　　　790
　　Here is none yet but your friends, you need not to fray,
　　Although this strange young gentleman be here.
Juventus. I trust in me she will think no danger,
　　For I love well the company of fair women.
Abominable. Who, you? Nay, you are such a holy man　　　795
　　That to touch one ye dare not be bold.
　　I think you would not kiss a young woman
　　If one would give you twenty pound in gold.
Juventus. Yes, by the mass, I would;
　　I could find in my heart to kiss you in your smock.[62]　　800
Abominable. My back is broad enough to bear away that mock,
　　For one hath told me many a time
　　That you have said you would use no such wanton's company as mine.
Juventus. By dog's precious wounds,[63] that was some whoreson villain.
　　I will never eat meat that shall do me good,　　　　　　805
　　Till I have cut his flesh, by gog's precious blood.[64]
　　Tell me, I pray you, who it was,
　　And I will trim the knave, by the blessed mass.
Abominable. Tush, as for that, do not you pass,
　　That which I told you was but for love.　　　　　　　810
Hypocrisy. She did nothing else but prove
　　Whether a li[tt]le thing would you move
　　To be angry and fret.
　　What, and if one had said so,
　　Let such trifling matters go　　　　　　　　　　　　815
　　And be good to men's flesh for all that.

Juventus he kisseth [Abominable Living].

Juventus. To kiss her since she came I had clean forgot;
　　You are welcome to my company.
Abominable. Sir, I thank you most heartily,
　　By your kindness it doth appear.　　　　　　　　　　820

Hypocrisy. What a hurly-burly is here,
    Smick-smack[65] and all this gear.
    You will to tick-tack[66] I fear,
    If you had time.
    Well, wanton, well,   825
    Iwis I can tell
    That such smock smell
    Will set your nose out of tune.
Abominable. What man, you need not to fume.
    Seeing he is come into my company now,   830
    He is as well welcome as the best of you;
    And if it lie in me to do him pleasure,
    He shall have it, you may be sure.
Fellowship. Then old acquaintance is clean out of favor.
    Lo, Friendship, this gear goeth with a sleight;   835
    He hath driven us twain out of conceit.
Hypocrisy. "Out of conceit," quod ha, no, no;
    I dare well say she thinketh not so.
    How say you Unknown Honesty?
    Do you not love Fellowship and me?   840
Abominable. Yea, by the mass, I love you all three;
    But yet indeed, if I should say the truth,
    Amongst all other welcome Master Youth.
Juventus. Full greatly I do delight to kiss your pleasant mouth.

He kisseth [Abominable Living].

    I am not able your kindness to recompense;   845
    I long to talk with you secretly, therefore let us go hence.
Abominable. I agree to that, for I would not for twenty pence
    That it were known where I have been.
Hypocrisy. What, and it were known, it is no deadly sin.
    As for my part, I do not greatly care
    So that they find not your proper buttocks bare.   850
Abominable. Now much fie upon you; how bawdy you are!
    I wot Friendship, it might have been spoken at twice.
    What think you for your saying that the people will surmise?
Juventus. Who dare be so bold us to despise?   855
    And if I may hear a knave speak one word,
    I will run through his cheeks with my sword.

Fellowship. This is an earnest fellow of God's word;
    See, I pray you, how he is disposed to fight.
Juventus. Why should I not, and if my cause be right?   860
    What and if a knave do me beguile,
    Shall I stand crouching like an owl?
    No, no, then you might count me a very cow[ard].
    I know what belongeth to God's law as well as you.
Abominable. Your wit therein greatly I do allow,   865
    For and if I were a man as you are,
    I would not stick to give a blow
    To teach other knaves to beware. . . .
Fellowship. Let us depart, and if that we shall;
    Come on, masters, we twain will go before.
Juventus. Nay, nay, my friend, stop there.
    It is not you that shall have her away;   875
    She shall go with me and if she go today.
Hypocrisy. She will go with none of you, I dare well say;
    She will go with me before you both.
Abominable. To forsake any of your company, I would be very loath;
    Therefore I will follow you all three.   880
Hypocrisy. Now I beshrew his heart, that to that will not agree.
    But yet because the time shall not seem very long,
    Or ere we depart, let us have a merry song.

They sing as followeth:

        Why should not Youth fulfill his own mind
    As the course of nature doth him bind?   885
    Is not everything ordained to do his kind?[67]
    Report me to you, report me to you.

        Do not the flowers spring fresh and gay,
    Pleasant and sweet in the month of May?
    And when their time cometh, they fade away.   890
    Report me to you, report me to you.

        Be not the trees in winter bare?
    Like unto their kind, such they are,
    And when they spring, their fruits declare.
    Report me to you, report me to you.   895

What should Youth do with the fruits of age,
But live in pleasure in his passage?
For when age cometh, his lusts will [as]suage.
Report me to you, report me to you.

Why should not Youth fulfill his own mind　　　　900
As the course of nature doth him bind?
[Is not everything ordained to do his kind?
Report me to you, report me to you.]

They go forth. Here entereth Good Counsel.

[*Good Counsel.*] Oh, merciful Lord, who can cease to lament
Or keep his heart from continual mourning,　　　　905
To see how Youth is fallen from thy word and testament
And wholly inclined to Abominable Living.
He liveth nothing according to his professing;
But alas, his life is to thy word abusion,[68]
Except[69] thy great mercy, to his utter confusion.　　　　910

Oh, where is now the godly conversation
Which should be among the professor[s] of thy word?
Or where may a man find now one faithful congregation
That is not infected with dissension or discord?
Or amongst whom are all vices utterly abhorred?　　　　915
Oh, where is the brotherly love between man and man?
We may lament the time our vice began. . . .

[*Juventus enters here.*]

To speak of pride, envy, and abominable oaths,
They are the common practices of Youth.　　　　1000
To a[d]vance your flesh, you cut and jag[70] your clothes,
And yet ye are a great gospeller in the mouth.
What shall I say for this blaspheming the truth?
I will show you what St. Paul doth declare
In his Epistle to the Hebrews, and the tenth chapter.　　　　1005

"For him," saith he, "Which doth willingly sin or consent
After he hath received the knowledge of the verity,

Remaineth no more sacrifice, but a fearful looking for judgement,
And a terrible fire, which shall consume the adversary."
And Christ saith that this blasphemy   1010
Shall never be pardoned nor forgiven
In this world, nor in the world to come.
Juventus. Alas, alas, what have I wrought and done?
Here in this place I will fall down desperate
To ask for mercy now I know it is too late.   1015

He lieth down.

      Alas, alas, that ever I was begat;
I would to God I had never been born.
All faithful men that behold this wretched state
May very justly laugh me to scorn.
They may say my time I have evil spent and worn,   1020
Thus in my first age to work my own destruction;
In the eternal pains is my part and portion.
Good Counsel. Why, Youth, art thou fallen into desperation?
What man, pluck up thine heart and rise.
Although thou see nothing now but thy condemnation,   1025
Yet it may please God again to open thy eyes.
Ah, wretched creature, what dost thou surmise?
Thinkest not that God's mercy doth exceed thy sin?
Remember his Merciful Promises and comfort thyself in him. . . .
Juventus. I would believe, if I might them hear,
With all my heart, power, and mind.
Good Counsel. The living God hath him hither assigned.   1045
Lo, where he cometh even hereby;

Here entereth God's Merciful Promises.

      Therefore mark his sayings diligently.
[*Promises.*] The Lord, by his Prophet Ezekiel, saith in this wise plainly,
As in the thirty-third chapter it doth appear,
"Be converted, oh ye children and turn unto me,   1050
And I shall remedy the cause of your departure."
And also he saith in the twenty-eighth chapter,
"I do not delight in a sinner's death,
But that he should convert and live," thus the Lord saith.

Juventus. Then must I give neither credit nor faith   1055
  Unto Saint Paul's saying which this man did allege?
Promises. Yes, you must credit them, according unto knowledge,
  For Saint Paul speaketh of those which resist the truth by violence,
  And so end their lives without repentance.
  Thus St. Augustine doth them define.   1060

      If unto the Lord's word you do your ears incline,
  And observe those things which he hath commanded,
  This sinful state in the which you have lain
  Shall be forgotten and never more remembered.
  And Christ himself in the gospel hath promised   1065
  That he which in him unfeignedly doth believe,
  Although he were dead, yet shall he live.
Juventus. These comfortable sayings doth me greatly move
  To arise from this wretched place.

He riseth.

Promises. For me, his mercy sake, thou shalt obtain his grace,   1070
  And not for thine own deserts, this must thou know.
  For my sake alone he shall receive solace,
  For my sake alone he will thee mercy show.
  Therefore to him as it is most due,
  Give most hearty thanks with heart unfeigned,   1075
  Whose name forevermore be praised.
Good Counsel. The Prodigal Son as in Luke we read,[71]
  Which in vicious living his goods doth waste,
  As soon as his living he had remembered,
  To confess his wretchedness he was not aghast.   1080
  Wherefore his father lovingly him embraced,
  And was right joyful, the text saith plain,
  Because his son was returned again.
Juventus. Oh, sinful flesh, thy pleasures are but vain.
  Now I find it true, as the scripture doth say,   1085
  Broad and pleasant is the path which leadeth unto pain,
  But unto eternal life full narrow is the way.[72]
  He that is not led by God's spirit surely goeth astray,
  And all that ever he doth shall be clean abhorred,
  Although he brag and boast never so much of God's word.   1090

Oh, subtle Satan, full deceitful is thy snare.
Who is able thy falsehood to disclose?
What is the man that thou dost favor or spare
And dost not tempt him, eternal joys to lose?
Not one in the world, surely I suppose;   1095
Therefore, happy is the man which doth truly wait,[73]
Always to refuse thy deceitful and crafty bait.

    When I had thought to live most Christianly
And followed the steps of Knowledge and Good Counsel,
Ere I was ware thou hadst deceived me   1100
And brought me into the path which leadeth unto Hell.
And of[74] an earnest professor of Christ's gospel,
Thou madest me an hypocrite, blind and pervert[ed],
And from virtue unto vice, ye hadst clean turned my heart. . . .

[Juventus turns to address the audience.]

    All you that be young, whom I do now represent,   1140
Set your delight, both day and night, on Christ's testament.
If pleasures you tickle, be not fickle and suddenly slide,
But in God's fear everywhere see that you abide.
In your tender age, seek for Knowledge, and after wisdom run,
And in your old age, teach your family to do as you have done.   1145
Your bodies subdue unto virtue; delight not in vanity.

    Say not "I am young, I shall live long," lest your days shortened be.
Do not incline to spend the time in wanton toys and nice,
For idleness doth increase much wickedness and vice.
Do not delay the time and say, "My end is not near,"   1150
For with short warning, the Lord's coming shall suddenly appear.
God give us grace his word to embrace and live thereafter,
That by the same, his holy name may be praised ever.
Good Counsel. Now let us make our supplications together
For the prosperous estate of our noble and virtuous king,[75]   1155
That in his godly proceedings he may still persevere,
Which seeketh the glory of God above all other thing.
Oh Lord, endue his heart with true understanding,
And give him a prosperous life, long over us to reign,
To govern and rule his people as a worthy ca[ptain].   1160

Juventus. Also, let us pray for all the nobility of this [realm],
    And namely for those whom his Grace has au[thorized]
    To maintain the public wealth over us and them,
    That they may see his gracious acts published,
    And that they, being truly admonished   1165
    By the complaint of them which are wrongfully oppressed,
    May seek a reformation and see it redressed.
Good Counsel. Then shall this land enjoy great quietness and rest,
    And give unto God most hearty thanks therefore,
    To whom be honor, praise, and glory forevermore.   1170

Notes

1. Orchard.
2. Set.
3. Care.
4. Treat them accordingly.
5. Promise.
6. Sport.
7. Appetite.
8. A spell.
9. In anticipation of.
10. Direct.
11. Eph. 5:15–16.
12. Doctors of divinity.
13. Deut. 29:10–11.
14. Old Testament.
15. Wondrous.
16. Matt. 7:7, Luke 11:9.
17. Luke 11:28.
18. Gal. 5:22–23.
19. Rom. 14:23.
20. Counsel.
21. 1 Peter 1:18.
22. Glorification.
23. Conversion.
24. Fitting.
25. Try.
26. "Holy, amen" (an oath).
27. Peddler.
28. Assuredly.
29. Worthless thing.
30. Sodomy.
31. 408–43: catalog of Roman Catholic offices, practices, and objects.
32. Rosary.

33. Idolatrous images.

34. Clothes.

35. Bearing of palms (a forbidden practice).

36. Holy oil.

37. Uses of incense.

38. Trifles.

39. Against.

40. At odds.

41. Coy.

42. Attend to.

43. Unfriendly.

44. Tell me your name.

45. Fail to profit.

46. Remember.

47. To have been burnt at the stake for heresy.

48. Hangman's noose or rope.

49. Scruple.

50. Meticulous.

51. Matt.7:3–4.

52. Peasants.

53. Brazen out.

54. It.

55. Marked card.

56. Wait.

57. A bawdy quibble.

58. 712–13: Poor men maintain themselves by deficient means.

59. Hypocrisy in disguise as Friendship.

60. God's precious bones (blasphemous oath).

61. Summon.

62. Undergarment (with a bawdy innuendo).

63. God's precious wounds (blasphemous oath).

64. God's precious blood (blasphemous oath).

65. Kissing.

66. A game played on a board with holes (with a punning reference to sexual intercourse).

67. Nature.

68. Perversion.

69. Without.

70. Decorate clothing with fashionable slashes.

71. Parable of the Prodigal Son (Luke 15:11–31)

72. Matt 7:14–15.

73. Watch.

74. From.

75. Edward VI.

3.3. Robert Crowley, from
Philargyrie of Great Britain (1551)

Robert Crowley (1518?–88) flourished as a Protestant controversialist during the reign of Edward VI. He modeled *Philargyrie* on *Piers Plowman*, the visionary allegory that he edited for its initial publication and interpreted as a prophecy of the English Reformation, which he regarded as a return to the "true" faith of Wyclif and other medieval clerics. Relying on alliteration and devices of medieval complaint and satire also used by John Skelton, Crowley versifies bluntly moralistic teachings in tailed rhyme, a popular minstrel form related to ballad measure that alternates iambic dimeter couplets with one trimeter line and rhymes aabccb.

Philargyrie ("lover of silver") personifies avarice as a despotic giant (see Figure 6) who governs at Nodnoll (an anagram for London) and appoints Vices named Hypocrisy and Philaute ("self-love") to serve in sequence as his chief minister. Their respective personification of Roman Catholic and Protestant doctrine affords an unmistakable metaphor for Henry VIII's ecclesiastical policy. In acquiring vast wealth and property, however, Hypocrisy is indistinguishable from Philaute, who represents the Protestant elite as a successor to Roman Catholic clergy in oppressing the commonwealth by means of abuses such as rack-renting and hoarding. Crowley follows Tyndale and social reformers such as Simon Fish and Henry Brinkelow in claiming that Henry VIII should have redistributed the property of dissolved monasteries to the poor rather than giving it to the aristocracy. Truth, the sole personified virtue, resolves this conflict by persuading the king, who resembles both Henry VIII and Edward VI, to restore order.

SOURCE: *STC* 6089.5, A3ʳ–A4ʳ, A7ʳ⁻ᵛ, A8ʳ⁻ᵛ, B4ʳ–B7ʳ, B8ᵛ, D4ᵛ–D5ᵛ, D6ʳ–D7ᵛ, D8ʳ⁻ᵛ.

EDITION: John N. King, "*Philargyrie of Great Britayne* by Robert Crowley," *English Literary Renaissance* 10 (1980): 46–75.

REFERENCES: King 1982; Norbrook.

Give ear awhile
And mark my style,   30
You that hath wit in store,
For with words bare
I will declare
Things done long time before.
   Sometime certain   35
Into Britain
A land full of plenty,
A giant great
Came to seek meat
Whose name was Philargyrie.   40

Figure 6. *The Great Giant Philargyrie*. Robert Crowley, *Philargyrie of Greate Britayne* (1551), title-page woodcut. By permission of the British Library. This portrayal of Philargyrie as a fur-clad Protestant aristocrat who uses a Bible to rake gold coins into a sack is an inversion of the royal emblem of the sword and the Book (see Figures 1 and 5). It introduces the analysis of the potential for misgovernment brought by the Protestant Reformation in Crowley's text, which satirizes the diversion to Henry VIII and newly appointed nobles of wealth confiscated during the dissolution of the monasteries and argues that an ideal king would care for the needy by overseeing equitable distribution of wealth according to Jesus' Parable of the Wise Steward (Matt. 24:45–51).

He was so strong
That none among
That brutish[1] nation
Darest take in hand
Him to withstand 45
In any station.
    That cursed lad
A free course had
That island overall,
Both vale and hill 50
Were at his will,
With towns both great and small.
    Then let he cry
That low and high,
That would to him resort, 55
Should still endure
In all his pleasure,
And live in play and sport.
    So that they would
Do as they should, 60
And honor him as god,
With bags of gold
In manifold
In number even or odd.
    "Come unto me 65
Whoso will," quoth he,
"There shall no law him bind,
I will him make
Free for to take
All things that he can find. 70
    Force and strong hand
By sea and land
Shall be his law and right,
He shall be bold
To take and hold 75
All things by force and might. . . ."

Philargyrie's Oration

        "You must me feed,
Aye, at my need,
With bags of most pure gold,
For I could eat
None other meat   225
Since I was two days old.
        A god am I
That cannot die
Wherefore I must be fed
With gold most pure
That will endure   230
And not with brittle bread.
        Bring, bring, bring, bring,
Always something,
And then you shall me please.
All that is sold   235
For ready gold
Doth my stomach much ease. . . ?"

How the People of Britain Became Subject to Philargyrie

        Then with one voice
All did rejoice   270
And clapped their hands apace,
And after that
They all fell flat
Prostrate before his face.
        Then rose they up   275
And in a cup
Of gold, they did him bring,
Mo' thousands than
Any man can
Well express by writing. . . .   280

[Philargyrie then appointed Hypocrisy to serve as his chief minister.]

How Philargyrie Committeth the Governance of All His Subjects to Hypocrisy

Full mildly than
This god began
And bade his men arise,
"Stand up," quoth he,
"For well I see   465
Thou art prudent and wise.
    Wherefore with me
Thou shalt chief be
I will work by thy rede,
And all that be   470
Subject to me
Thou shalt govern and lead."
    Then let he cry
That low and high
That would take him as king,   475
Should with all speed
Fulfill indeed
Hypocrisy's bidding.
    "For he is my wise²
And can devise   480
Ways to get gold and fee,
And make men fill
With right good will
Your bags to bring to me."
    Then all that were   485
Present to hear
That proclamation,
Showed them content
With full assent
And thus they said each one,   490
    "Hypocrisy
Is most worthy
To rule under our King,
For he can preach
And men so teach   495
That they will gladly bring."
    Then went there out
A full great rout
From Philargyrie's place,

And by and by 500
Hypocrisy
Began to preach apace.
    All manner men
Were ready then
To give even what he would, 505
They were so mad
They thought he had
Salvation to be sold.
    Then builded he
A great city 510
Nodnoll he did it name,
It was all one
With Babylon
If it were not the same.
    In that city 515
Then builded he
A temple to his god,
Setting therein
Of his own kin
An hundred knights and odd. 520
    The arch knight was
Bishop Caiaphas
Who rode with spear and shield,
Having his corse
Armed with force 525
To cause all men to yield.
    Then in each place
That pleasant was
He planted houses sure,
Of lime and stone 530
They were each one
Because they should endure.
    Bulwarks also
A thousand mo'
Than any man can tell, 535
To beat them down
That wear the crown
If they did once rebel.

So was the land
Whole in the hand   540
Of Philargyrie's men,
No wight was free
From them if he
Were worth poor shillings ten.
    But to color   545
His endeavor,
He did those places name
Houses for clerks,
And the bulwarks
Lodgings for blind and lame.[3]   550
    Then [ap]pointed he
That there should be
Leeches[4] of wondrous skill
In every place
Who in short space   555
Should help their bags to fill.
    At Walsingham[5]
Was Notre Dame,
At Ely good Audrey,[6]
And at Willesden[7]   560
Were great cures done,
By bolstering of bawdry.
    At Hailes[8] there was
One in a glass
That wrought wonders full great,   565
And at Winchcombe
Were cured some
That could Kenelm entreat.[9]
    There were also
A thousand mo'   570
Leeches of his [ap]pointing,
That could heal all
Both great and small
That would anything bring.
    They would not stick   575
To heal the sick
In body and in soul,

They had such wit
They could do it
By drinking of a bowl.[10]   580
    When this was done
Then was all won,
They need to seek no more,
They had all thing
At their liking   585
To spend and keep in store.
    Hypocrisy
Thought then to sty
Up to Nodnoll anon,
To see what was   590
There brought to pass
After he was thence gone.
    But ere he went
More gold he sent
To his god Philargyrie,   595
Than thousands ten
Of brutish men
Could bear, to make him merry.
    Which he ate up
All at one sup   600
And yet was not content,
But said that they
Had by the way
Spent some of that [which] was sent.
    All raging then   605
This god began
On them his wrath to wreak,
He laid about
Among the rout
Till none of them could speak. . . .   610
    Then with a key
He made his way
Into his treasury,
Where was more gold,
I dare be bold,
Than would in Paul's Church lay. . . .

[Philargyrie devoured all the treasure that Hypocrisy amassed. When Hypocrisy decided to rebel, Philaute (Self-Love) revealed his intention to Philargyrie and then went to Nodnoll.]

How the People Forsook Hypocrisy

The people anon
Much mused on
These words that seemed strange,
Yet did they embrace
Them, in short space
Because they love to change. 1240
And naturally
You know, pardie,[11]
Each man will love himself,
Then a small thing
May him soon bring 1245
In love with this world's pelf.[12]
The brutes therefore
Took Philaute's lore
And left Hypocrisy,
Then rang the bell 1250
To a council
That thing to ratify.
In this synod
Ten score and odd
Took Hypocrisy's part, 1255
Yet all they lost
For all their boast
In despite of all their heart.
It was decreed
There and agreed 1260
That Philaute should possess
Forevermore
Hypocrisy's store,
His lands and his riches. . . .
Great lands also 1295
Philaute let go
For gold that was full fine,

And sent it all
To Philargyrie's hall
For him therewith to dine.   1300
    But all was gone
And spent anon
And he looked for more,
But yet in vain
For naught certain   1305
Remained then in store.
    "Well," thought he then,
"I trow I can
Make right fine gold of brass,"
And so he did   1310
But it framed
Full evil as reason it was.
    Well, yet he sent
And raised rent
From five groats to a pound,   1315
Yet there was not
Much won by that
For more was lost than found.
    Well thus at the last
All hope was passed   1320
His god he could not fill,
Unless he should
Be found so bold
The king and his realm to sell.
    Then gan this god   1325
To take the rod
Of hunger in his fist,
And said that he
Would filled be
No man should him resist.   1330
    Then with strokes sore
He smote the poor
And then they gan to cry
To God almight[y]
For them to fight   1335
Against Philargyrie.

How Truth Told All to the King

But then took Truth
Pity and ruth
And to the king he went
And said, "Sir King,   1340
Amend this thing
The realm else will be shent.[13]
    Philargyrie,
Hypocrisy,
And Philaute have spent all,   1345
Thy people are
So full of care
That now to God they call.
    Vengence, therefore,
Is at thy door   1350
Ready the[m] to destroy,
Unless thou will
Purge out the ill
That doth thy flock[14] annoy.
    An horrible thing   1355
It is Sir King
To fall into God's hand,
Thou mayst trust me
No man can be
Able him to withstand. . . ."   1360

How the King Drove That Wicked Sort Out of His Realm

With that the King
For fear gan spring   1380
Unto the Bible book,
And by and by
Right reverently
That sword in hand he took.
    "No wight," quoth he,   1385
"Shall spared be
That doth my flock oppress,
God hath me set

Such things to let
And all wrongs to redress."   1390
    Then he let cry
That low and high
In whom God's fear did dwell,
Should never rest
But do their best   1395
God's enemies to expel.
    Then he fell down
And cast his crown
And diadem aside,
And looking on high   1400
Up to the sky
To God aloud he cried.
    "Lord God," quoth he,
"Thou hast chosen me
Over thy flock to reign,   1405
Make me of might
All wrongs to right
And make all well again."
    Then God him sent
Men that were bent   1410
Oppression to expel,
Who chased out
This giant stout
And then all things were well.

Notes

    1. With a pun on British.
    2. Wizard.
    3. Lines 548–50: monasteries and almshouses.
    4. Physicians.
    5. The shrine of Our Lady at Walsingham, located at one of the wealthiest monasteries in England, attracted violent hostility from reformers.
    6. Although iconoclasts have destroyed the relics of Saint Audrey (Ethelreda), her shrine survives at Ely Cathedral.
    7. An abbey in the suburbs of London where Thomas Bilney preached an iconoclastic sermon in 1527.
    8. The shrine of the relic of Christ's blood at this abbey was one of the wealthiest in England.

9. The abbey at Winchcombe enshrined the body of Saint Kenelm (Cynhelm), who was widely venerated during the Middle Ages.

10. Mass chalice.

11. "By God" (from French "par dieu"), a mild oath.

12. Wealth.

13. Disgraced.

14. The English people as a Christian congregation.

3.4. William Baldwin, from
Beware the Cat (c. 1553, pub. 1570)

The Marvelous History Entitled Beware the Cat supports the ban on the Roman-rite Mass during Edward VI's reign, a time when William Baldwin (1518–63?) flourished as a writer, printer, and preacher. His familiarity with the London printing trade informs the description of the printing house of John Day, the printer, where Gabriel Streamer regaled companions with tales about cats at the outset of the reign of Mary I (see Figure 7). Because this time was inhospitable to the publication of Protestant satire, it remained in manuscript until 1570. During the 1550s and early 1560s, Baldwin occupied himself with editing *A Mirror for Magistrates*, a collection of *de casibus* tragedies that influenced Shakespeare and his contemporaries.

Mixing genres such as proverb, tale, oration, and beast fable, *Beware the Cat* incorporates seriocomic notes that mock Streamer's absurd retelling of testimony delivered by a cat named Mouse-slayer when she was accused before a feline tribunal of violating the feline law of promiscuity. Her picaresque wanderings enabled her to witness forbidden Catholic ceremonies, thereby providing an ironic vision of resistance to official religious policy during the Edwardian reformation. This tale assimilates antifeminist lore, ribald humor associated with fabliaux, and Protestant hostility to devotion to the Virgin Mary and Church of Rome as sheltering "mothers."

When William Baldwin and several companions joined in production of the Christmas revels at the court of Mary I, they engaged in dispute with Gabriel Streamer concerning the question of whether animals are capable of reason. As proof for his belief in the rationality of animals, Streamer told this fantastic story about his encounter with talking cats when he lodged at the printing house of John Day, the London printer.

SOURCE AND EDITION: Baldwin 1988, pp. 9–11, 36–41, 46–53. Reprinted with the permission of the Henry E. Huntington Library.

REFERENCES: Terence N. Bowers, "The Production and Communication of Knowledge in William Baldwin's *Beware the Cat*: Toward a Typographic Culture," *Criticism* 33 (1991): 1–29; Hadfield; King 1982.

Being lodged (as, I thank him, I have been often) at a friend's house of mine, which, more roomish within than garish without, standeth at Saint Martin's Lane end and hangeth partly upon the town wall that is called Aldersgate. . . .

While I lay at the foresaid house for the causes aforesaid, I was lodged in a chamber hard by the printing house, which had a fair bay window opening into the garden, the earth whereof is almost as high as Saint Anne's Church top, which standeth thereby. At the other end of the printing house, as you enter in, is a side door and three or four steps which go up to the leads[1] of the Gate, whereas sometime quarters of men,[2] which is a loathely and abominable sight, do stand up upon poles. . . . In this foresaid leads . . . many cats assembled, and there made such a noise that I could not sleep for them.

Wherefore, on a time as I was sitting by the fire with certain of the house, I told them what a noise and what a wawling the cats had made there the night before from ten o'clock till one, so that neither I could sleep nor

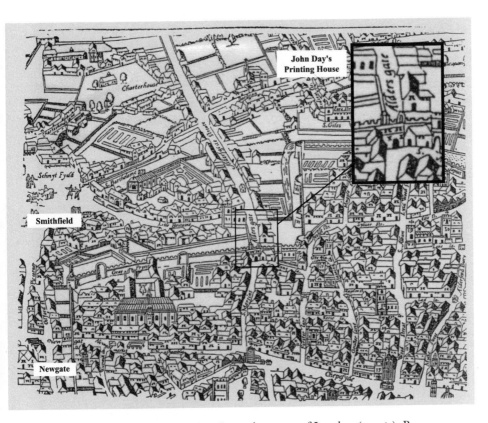

Figure 7. *Environs of Aldersgate.* "Agas" woodcut map of London (c. 1565). By permission of Guildhall Library, London. Incorrectly attributed to Ralph Agas, the surveyor, the "Agas" map of London consists of woodcuts printed on eight sheets. This view portrays the neighborhood around Aldersgate within London Wall, where John Day printed and sold the first four editions of the *Book of Martyrs* (see 6.5 and 7.5). Foxe used Day's premises as the address for his correspondence and worked there one day each week. Day's printing house provides the setting for William Baldwin's *Beware the Cat* (3.4), in which Master Gabriel Streamer witnesses cats scavenging among the remains of executed traitors whose dismembered limbs were displayed upon pikes above the gate. Anne Askew and other individuals condemned for heresy were imprisoned at Newgate, to the southwest, and burned alive at Smithfield, to the northwest (see 6.1).

study for them; and by means of this introduction we fell in communication[3] of cats.[a] . . .

[Streamer claimed that he compounded a concoction that enabled him to understand deliberations of a feline law court that assembled by night outside the window of Day's printing house.]

And by this time all the cats which were there the night before were assembled with many other, only the great grey one excepted. Unto whom, as soon as he was come, all the rest did their [o]beisance as they did the night before.[b] And when he was set, thus he began in his language (which I understood as well as if he had spoken English).

"Ah my dear friends and fellows, you may say I have been a lingerer this night and that I have tarried long; but you must pardon me for I could come no sooner. For when this evening I went into an ambry[4] where was much good meat to steal my supper,[c] there came a wench not thinking I had been there and clapped the lid down, by means whereof I have had much to do to get forth. Also, in the way as I came hither over the housetops, in a gutter were thieves breaking in at the window, who 'fraid me[d] so that I lost my way and fell down into the street and had much to do to escape the dogs. But seeing that by the grace of Hagat and Heg[e] I am now come, although I perceive by the tail of the Great Bear and by Alhabor,[5][f] which are now somewhat southward, that the fifth hour of our night approacheth; yet seeing this is the last night of my charge and that tomorrow I must again to my lord Cammoloch[g] (at this all the cats spread along their tails and cried, 'Hagat and Heg save him'), go to now good Mouse-slayer." quod he, "and that time which my misfortune hath lost, recover again by the briefness of thy talk."[h]

"I will my lord," quod Mouse-slayer, which is the cat which as I told you stood before the great cat the night before continually mewing; who in her language, after that with her tail she had made courtesy, shrunk in her neck and said, "Whereas by virtue of your commission from my lord Cammoloch (whose life Hagat and Heg defend), who by inheritance and our free election enjoyeth the empire of his traitorously murdered mother the goddess Grimolochin,[i] you his greffier[6] and chief counselor, my lord Grisard, with Isegrim and Pol-noir your assistants, upon a complaint put up in your high dais by that false accuser Catch-rat, who beareth me malice because I refused his lecherously offered delights, have caused me, in purging myself before this honorable company, to declare my whole life since the blind days of kitlinghood. You remember, I trust, how in the two nights passed I have declared my life for four years' space, wherein you perceive how I behaved me all that time.

"Wherefore, to begin where I last left, ye shall understand that my lord and lady, whose lives I declared unto you yesternight, left the city and went to dwell in the country, and carried me with them. And being there strange[7] I lost their house, and with Bird-hunt my mate, the gentlest in honest venery that ever I met with, went to a town where he dwelt called Stratford—either Stony, upon Tine, or upon Avon, I do not well remember which[8]—where I dwelled half a year - and this was in the time when preachers had leave to speak against the Mass, but it was not forbidden till half a year after. In this time I saw nothing worthy to certify my lord of, save this.

"My dame, with whom I dwelt, and her husband were both old, and therefore hard to be turned from their rooted belief which they had in the Mass, which caused divers young folk, chiefly their sons and a learned kinsman of theirs, to be the more earnest to teach and persuade them.[j] And when they had almost brought the matter to a good point, I cannot tell how it chanced, but my dame's sight failed her, and she was so sick that she kept her bed two days. Wherefore she sent for the parish priest, her old ghostly father; and when all were voided the chamber save I and they two,[k] she told him how sick she was and how blind, so that she could see nothing, and desired him to pray for her and give her good counsel. To whom he said thus, 'It is no marvel though you be sick and blind in body which suffer your soul willingly to be blinded. You send for me now, but why send you not for me when these new heretics teach you to leave the Catholic belief of Christ's flesh in the sacrament?' 'Why sir,' quod she, 'I did send for you once, and when you came they posed[9] you so with Holy Writ and saints' writings that you could say nothing but call them "heretics," and that they had made the New Testament themselves.'[l]

"'Yea,' quod he, 'but did I not bid you take heed then, and told you how God would plague you?' 'Yea, good sir,' quod she, 'you did, and now to my pain I find you too true a prophet.[m] But I beseech you forgive me and pray to God for me, and whatsoever you will teach me, that will I believe unto the death.' 'Well,' quod he, 'God refuseth no sinners that will repent, and therefore in any case believe that Christ's flesh, body, soul, and bone is as it was born of our Blessed Lady in the consecrated Host, and see that therefore you worship it, pray, and offer to it.[n] For by it any of your friends' souls may be brought out of Purgatory (which these new heretics say is no place at all—but when their souls fry in it, they shall tell me another tale). And that you may know that all I say is true, and that the Mass can deliver such as trust in it from all manner of sins, I will by and by say you a Mass that shall restore your sight and health.'[o]

"Then took he out of his bosom a wafer cake and called for wine. And then, shutting the door unto him,[p] revised[10] himself in a surplice, and upon

a table set before the bed he laid his portas, and thereout he said Mass. And
when he came to the elevation, he lifted up the cake and said to my dame
(which in two days afore saw nothing), 'Wipe thine eyes thou sinful woman
and look upon thy Maker.'q With that she lifted up herself and saw the cake,
and had her sight and her health as well as ever she had before. When Mass
was done she thanked God and him exceedingly, and he gave charge that she
should tell to no young folks how she was holp, for his bishop had throughout the diocese forbidden them to say or sing any Mass, but commanded her
that secretly unto old honest men and womenr she should at all times most
devoutly rehearse it. And by reason of this miracle, many are so confirmed in
that belief that, although by a common law all Masses upon penalty were
since forbidden, divers have them privily and nightly said in their chambers
until this day."s

"Marry sir," quod Pol-noir, "this was either a mighty miracle or else a
mischievous subtlety of a magistical[11] minister. But sure if the priest by magical art blinded her not afore,t and so by like magical sorcery cured her again,
it were as good for us to hire him or other priests at our delivery to sing a
Mass before our kitlings, that they might in their birth be delivered of their
blindness.u And sure, if I knew the priest, it should scape me hard but I
would have one litter of kitlings in some chamber where he useth now to
say his privy night Masses." "What need that?' quod Mouse-slayer, "it would
do them no good. For I myself, upon like consideration, kittened since in
another mistress's chamber of mine where a priest every day said Mass; but
my kitlings saw naught the better, but rather the worse."v

"But when I heard the Lord with whom I went into the country would
to London to dwell again, I kept the house so well for a month before that
my Lady when she went carried me with her.w And when I was come to London again, I went in visitation to mine old acquaintance. And when I was
great with kitling, because I would not be unpurveyed of a place to kitten
in, I got in favor any household with an old gentle-woman, a widow, with
whom I passed out this whole year.

"This woman got her living by boarding young gentlemen, for whom
she kept always fair wenches in store, for whose sake she had the more resort.
And to tell you the truth of her trade, it was fine and crafty, and not so dangerous as deceitful. For when she had soaked from young gentlemen all that
they had, then would she cast them off, except they fell to cheating.x Wherefore many of them in the nighttime would go abroad and bring the next
morning home with them sometimes money, sometime jewels (as rings or
chains), sometime apparel; and sometime they would come again cursing
their ill fortune, with nothing save per-adventure dry blows or wet wounds.

But whatsoever they brought, my dame would take it and find the means either so to gage[12] it that she would never fetch it again, or else melt it and sell it to the goldsmiths.[y]

"And notwithstanding that she used these wicked practices, yet was she very holy and religious.[z] And therefore, although that all images were forbidden, yet kept she one of Our Lady in her coffer. And every night, when everybody were gone to bed and none in her chamber but she and I, then would she fetch her out, and set her upon her cupboard, and light up two or three wax candles afore her,[aa] and then kneel down to her, sometime an whole hour, saying over her beads and praying her to be good unto her and to save her and all her guests both from danger and shame, and promising that then she would honor and serve Her during all her life.[bb]

"While I was with this woman I was alway much cherished and made of,[cc] for on nights while she was a-praying, I would be playing with her beads and alway catch them as she let them fall, and would sometime put my head in the compass of them and run away with them around my neck, whereat many times she took great pleasure, yea and so did Our Lady too.[dd] For my dame would say sometimes to her, 'Yea, Blessed Lady, I know though hearest me by thy smiling at my cat.' . . . "

[The old woman then engaged in an elaborate stratagem in order to convince a young wife to commit adultery. It involved the lie that a necromancer spell had transformed her daughter into Mouse-slayer.]

"Shortly after, this young woman begged me of my dame; and to her I went, and dwelled with her all that year. In which year, as all the cats in the parish can tell, I never disobeyed or transgressed our holy law in refusing the concupiscential[13] company of any cat nor the act of generation, although sometimes it were more painful to me than pleasant, if it were offered in due and convenient time.[ee] Indeed, I confess I refused Catch-rat, and bit him and scrat him, which our law forbiddeth.[ff] For on a time this year when I was great with kitlings, which he of a proud stomach refused to help to get, although I earnestly wooed him thereto; what time he loved so much his own daughter Slick-skin that all other seemed vile in his sight, which also esteemed him as much as he did the rest—that is, never a whit. In this time (I say) when I was great with kitling, I found him in a gutter eating a bat which he had caught that evening; and as you know not only we, but also women in our case, do oft long for many things,[gg] so I then longed for a piece of the reremouse,[14] and desired him, for saving of my kitten, to give me a morsel, though it were but of the leather-like wing. But he, like an unnatural, ravenous churl,[hh] eat it all up and would give me none. And as men do nowadays to their wives, he gave me bitter words, saying we longed for wantonness and not for any need. This grieved me so sore, chiefly for the lack of that I longed for, that I was sick two days after, and had not it been for good dame Isegrim, who brought me a piece of a mouse and made me believe it was of a back,[ii] I had lost my burden by kittening ten days before my time.

"When I was recovered and went abroad again, about three days, this cruel churl met me and needs would have been doing with me.[jj] To whom, when I had made answer according to his deserts, and told him withal, which he might see too by my belly what case I was in, tush, there was no remedy (I think he had eaten savory),[kk] but for all that I could say, he would have his will. I, seeing that, and that he would ravish me perforce, I cried out for help as loud as ever I could squawl, and to defend myself till succor came I scrat and bit as hard as ever I could. And this notwithstanding, had not Isegrim and her son Lightfoot come the sooner (who both are here and can witness), he would have marred me quite. Now, whether I might in this case refuse him, and do as I did without breach of our holy law, which forbiddeth us females to refuse any males not exceeding the number of ten in a night,[ll] judge you, my lords, to whom the interpretation of the laws belongeth."

"Yes, surely," quod Grisard, "for in the third year of the reign of Glascalon,[mm] at a court holden in Catwood, as appeareth in the records, they decreed upon that exception, forbidding any male in this case to force any female, and that upon great penalties. But to let this pass, whereof we were satisfied in your purgation the first night, tell us how you behaved you with your new mistress, and that as briefly as you can; for lo where Corleonis[15] is almost plain west, whereby ye know the goblins' hour approacheth."[nn]

"After I was come to my young mistress," quod Mouse-slayer, "she made much of me, thinking that I had been my old dame's daughter, and many tales she told thereof to her gossips. My master also made much of me, because I would take meat in my foot and therewith put it in my mouth and feed. In this house dwelt an ungracious fellow who, delighting much in unhappy turns [tricks],[oo] on a time took four walnut shells and filled them full of soft pitch, and put them upon my feet, and then put my feet into cold water till the pitch was hardened, and then he let me go.[pp] But Lord, how strange it was to me to go in shoes, and how they vexed me, for when I ran upon any steep thing they made me slide and fall down. Wherefore all that afternoon, for anger that I could not get off my shoes, I hid me in a corner of the garret which was boarded, under which my master and mistress lay. And at night when they were all in bed, I spied a mouse playing in the floor; and when I ran at her to catch her,[qq] my shoes made such a noise upon the boards that it waked my master, who was a man very fearful of spirits. And when he with his servants harkened well to the noise, which went pit-pat, pit-pat, as it had been the trampling of a horse, they waxed all afraid and said surely it was the Devil.^{rr}

"And as one of them, an hardy fellow (even he that had shoed me), came upstairs to see what it was, I went downward to meet him and made such a rattling that, when he saw my glistering eyes, he fell down backward and brake his head,^{ss} crying out, 'The Devil, the Devil, the Devil.' Which his master and all the rest hearing ran naked as they were into the street and cried the same cry.

"Whereupon the neighbors arose and called up, among other, an old priest, who lamented much the lack of holy water which they were forbidden to make. Howbeit, he went to church and took out of the font some of the christening water,^{tt} and took his chalice, and therein a wafer unconsecrate, and put on a surplice, and his stole about his neck, and fet¹⁶ out of his chamber a piece of holy candle which he had kept two year.^{uu} And herewith he came to the house, and with his candle-light in the one hand and a holy-water sprinkle in the other hand, and his chalice and wafer in sight of his bosom, and a pot of font-water at his girdle,^{vv} up he came praying towards the garret, and all the people after him.

"And when I saw this, and thinking I should have seen some Mass that night, as many nights before in other places I had,^{ww} I ran towards them thinking to meet them. But when the priest heard me come, and by a glimpsing had seen me, down he fell upon them that were behind him, and with his chalice hurt one, with his water pot another, and his holy candle fell into another priest's breech beneath (who, while the rest were hawsoning¹⁷ me, was conjuring^{xx} our maid at the stair foot) and all to-besinged him, for he was so afraid with the noise of the rest which fell that he had not the power to put it out. When I saw all this business, down I ran among them where they lay on heaps. But such a fear as they were all in then I think was never seen afore; for the old priest, which was so tumbled among them that his face lay upon a boy's bare arse, which belike was fallen headlong under him, was so astonished that, when the boy, which for fear had beshit himself, had all to-rayed¹⁸ his face, he neither felt nor smelt it, nor removed from him.^{yy}

"Then went I to my dame, which lay among the rest God knoweth very madly, and so mewed and curled about her that at last she said, 'I ween it be my cat.' That hearing the knave that had shoed me, and calling to mind that erst he had forgot,^{zz} said it was so indeed and nothing else. That hearing the priest, in whose holy breech the holy candle all this while lay burning, he took heart a grace, and before he was spied rose up and took the candle in his hand, and looked upon me and all the company, and fell a-laughing at the handsome lying of this fellow's face. The rest, hearing him, came every man to himself[aaa] and arose and looked upon me, and cursed the knave which had shoed me, who would in no case be a-known of it. This done, they got hot water and dissolved the pitch and plucked off my shoes. And then every man (after they desired each other not to be a-known of this night's work[bbb]) for shame departed to their lodgings, and all our household went to bed again."

When all the cats, and I too for company, had laughed at this space,[ccc] Mouse-slayer proceeded and said, "After this about three-quarters of a year, which was at Whitsuntide last, I played another prank, and that was this. The gentleman, who by mine old dame's lying and my weeping was accepted and retained of my mistress, came often home to our house, and always in my master's absence was doing with my dame.[ddd] Wherefore, desirous that my master might know it (for they spent his goods so lavishly between them that, notwithstanding his great trade of merchandise, they had, unwitting to him, almost undone him already[eee]), I sought how I might bewray them. Which as hap would, at the time remembered afore, came to pass thus. While this gentleman was doing with my dame, my master came in[fff]—so suddenly that he had no leisure to pluck up his hose,[19] but with them about his legs ran into a corner behind the painted cloth,[20] and there stood (I warrant you) as still as a mouse. As soon as my master came in, his wife, according to her old wont, caught him about his neck and kissed him, and devised many means to have got him forth again.[ggg] But he, being weary, sat down and called for his dinner. And when she saw that there was none other remedy, she brought it him, which was a mess of potage and a piece of beef, whereas she and her franion[21] had broke their fast with capons, hot venison, marrow bones, and all other kind of dainties.[hhh]

"I, seeing this, and minding to show my master how he was ordered, got behind the cloth, and to make the man speak I all to-pawed him with my claws upon his bare legs and buttocks. And for all this, he stood still and never moved.[iii] But my master heard me and, thinking I was catching a mouse, bade my dame go help me.[jjj] Who, knowing what beast was there, came to the cloth and called me away, saying, 'Come puss, come puss,' and cast me meat into the floor. But I, minding another thing, and seeing that scratching could not move him, suddenly I leaped up and caught him by the genitals with my teeth,[kkk] and bote[22] so hard that, when he had restrained more than I thought any man could, at last he cried out, and caught me by the neck thinking to strangle me. My master, not smelling but hearing such a rat as was not wont to be about such walls, came to the cloth and lift it up, and there found this bare-arsed gentleman strangling me who had his stones in my mouth.[lll] And when I saw my master I let go my hold, and the gentleman his. And away I ran immediately to the place where I now dwell, and never came there since. So that how they agreed among them I cannot tell, nor never durst go see for fear of my life.

"Thus have I told you, my good lords, all things that have been done and happened through me, wherein you perceive my loyalty and obedience to all good laws, and how shamelessly and falsely I am accused for a transgressor.[mmmm] And I pray you, as you have perceived, so certify my liege great Cammoloch (whose life both Hagat and Heg preserve) of my behavior."

When Grisard, Isegrim, and Pol-noir, the commissioners, had heard this declaration and request of Mouse-slayer, they praised her much.[nnn] And after that they had commanded her, with all the cats there, to be on Saint Catherine's' day next ensuing at Caithness[23] where, as they said, Cammoloch would hold his court, they departed. And I, glad to have heard that I heard, and sorry that I had not understood what was said the other two nights before, got me to my bed and slept a-good.[ooo]

And the next morning, when I went out into the garden, I heard a strange cat ask of our cat what Mouse-slayer had done before the commissioners those three nights. To whom our cat answered that she had purged herself of a crime that was laid to her charge by Catch-rat, and declared her whole life for six years' space.[ppp] Whereof in the first two years as she said, said she, she had five masters: a priest, a baker, a lawyer, a broker, and a butcher; all whose privy deceits which she had seen she declared the first night. In the next two years she had seven masters: a bishop, a knight, a pothecary, a goldsmith, an usurer, an alchemist, and a lord[qqq]; whose cruelty, study, craft, cunning, niggishness,[24] folly, waste, and oppression she declared the second night, wherein this doing was notable. Because the knight, having a fair lady to his wife, gave his mind so much to his book that he seldom lay with her, this cat, pitying her mistress and minding to fray him from lying alone,[rrr] on a night when her master lay from her, got to his mouth and drew so his breath that she almost stifled him. A like part she played with the usurer, who, being rich and yet living miserably and feigning him poor,[sss] she got one day, while his treasure chest stood open, and hid here therein; whereof he not knowing locked her in it. And when at night he came thither again and heard one stirring there, and thinking it had been the Devil,[ttt] he called the priest and many other persons to come and help him to conjure. And when in their sight he opened his chest, out leaped she and they saw what riches he had and cessed[25] him thereafter. As for what was done and said yesterday, both of my lord Grisard's hard adventure and of Mouse-slayer's bestowing her other two last years, which is nothing in comparison of any of the other two years before,[uuu] I need not tell you for you were present and heard it yourself.

This talk, lo, I heard between these two cats. And then I got me in, and brake my fast with bread and butter, and dined at noon with common meat, which so repleted my head again and my other powers in the first digestion, that by nighttime they were as gross as ever they were before.[vvv] For when I harkened at night to other two cats, which as I perceived by their gestures spake of the same matter, I understood never a word.

Lo, here have I told you all (chiefly you, my lord)[26] a wonderful matter, and yet as incredible as it is wonderful.[www] Notwithstanding, when I may have convenient time, I will tell you other things which these eyes of mine have seen and these ears of mine have heard, and that of mysteries so far passing this, that all which I have said now shall in comparison thereof be nothing at all to be believed.[xxx] In the meanwhile, I will pray you to help to get me some money to convey me on my journey to Caithness, for I have been going thither these five years and never was able to perform my journey.[yyy]

When Master Ferrers had promised that he would, every man shut up his shop windows,[27] which the foresaid talk kept open two hours longer than they should have been.

Marginal Glosses

[a] A wise man may in some things change his opinion.

[b] Good manners among cats.

[c] Sour meat must have sour sauce.

[d] Cats are afraid of thieves.

[e] Hagat and Heg are witches which the cats do worship.

[f] Cats are skilled in astronomy.

[g] Cammoloch is chief prince among cats.

[h] Gentleness becometh officers.

[i] Grimolochin is the same that was late called Grimalkin.

[j] Old errors are hard to be removed.

[k] Cats are admitted to all secrets.

[l] Railing and slandering are the papists' Scriptures.

[m] A true coal prophet.

[n] Ghostly counsel of a popish confessor.

[o] No such persuasion as miracles chiefly in helping one from grief.

[p] *Veritas quaerit angulos* [The truth seeks hidden places].

[q] A young knave made an old woman's maker.

^r Old folk are lighter of credit than young.

^s Cats hear many privy night Masses.

^t Sorcerers may make folk blind.

^u Why Masses may serve well.

^v Devout kitlings that heard mass so young.

^w Flatterers are diligent when they spy a profit.

^x Whores, gaming, and good hostesses make many gentlemen make shameful shrifts.

^y All is fish that cometh to the net.

^z A Catholic queen.

^{aa} Images cannot see to hear, except they have much light.

^{bb} Our Lady is hired to play the bawd.

^{cc} Old women love their cats well.

^{dd} The image laughed to see the cat play with her dame's beads.

^{ee} Cats have laws among them which they keep better than we do ours.

^{ff} He that despiseth those that love him shall be despised of them that he loveth.

^{gg} Cats do long while they be with kitten.

^{hh} There be churls among cats as well as among Christian folk.

ⁱⁱ It is the conceit of a thing and not the thing itself that is longed for.

^{jj} Churls must be churlishly sever'd.

^{kk} Savory is a hot herb provoking lust in cats.

^{ll} A law for adultery among cats.

^{mm} Glascalon was chief prince of the cats after Grimolochin.

ⁿⁿ After one o'clock at midnight the goblins go abroad, and as soon as any cock croweth, which is their hour, that is at three, they return homeward.

^{oo} Divers men delight in divers fond things.

^{pp} A cat was shoed.

^{qq} Natural delight expelleth melancholy.

^{rr} The fearful are always suspicious.

^{ss} Wickedness is a scourge itself to such as invent it.

^{tt} Holy water was good for conjurers.

^{uu} This fellow thought to beguile the Devil.

^{vv} A conjurer can have no better apparel.

^{ww} Cats hear more Masses than all men hear of.

^{xx} Priests have been good conjurers of such kind of spirits.

^{yy} Fear taketh away the senses.

^{zz} A liar and a doer of shrewd turns out to have a good memory.

^{aaa} One hardy man encourageth many cowards.

^{bbb} Silence is the best friend that shame hath.

^{ccc} The author laughed in a cat's voice.

^{ddd} Adulterers are diligent in waiting their times.

^{eee} A wanton wife and a back door will soon make a rich man poor.

^{fff} Chance oftentimes betrayeth evil.

^{ggg} None seem outwardly so loving as whores.

^{hhh} *Sine Baccho et cerere friget Venus* [Without Bacchus (wine) and food, Venus grows cold; from Terence's *Eunuchus*].

ⁱⁱⁱ Fear overcometh smart.

^{jjj} All are not mice that are behind painted cloths.

^{kkk} It is justice to punish those parts that offend.

^{lll} Whoredom will be known be it never so warily hid.

^{mmm} There be false accusers among all kinds of creatures.

ⁿⁿⁿ Justices should cherish the innocents accused.

^{ooo} Travail and watching maketh sound sleeping.

^{ppp} Mouse-slayer was six years old.

^{qqq} Cats change their dwellings often.

^{rrr} Men ought to lie with their wives.

^{sss} A niggard is neither good to his self nor to any other.

^{ttt} The Devil delighteth to dwell among money.

^{uuu} All in this book is nothing in comparison of that the cat told before.

^{vvv} Gross meats make gross wits.

^{www} Wonders are incredible.

^{xxx} In comparison of a diamond, crystal hath no color.

^{yyy} Poverty hindreth many excellent attempts.

Notes

1. Roof.
2. Dismembered traitors.
3. Discussion.
4. Cupboard.
5. Sirius.
6. Clerk.
7. Unaccustomed.
8. One of three different towns.
9. Ecclesiastical examiners questioned the priest.
10. Dressed.
11. Expert in magic.
12. Pawn.
13. Licentious.
14. Bat.
15. A star in constellation Leo.
16. Procured.

17. Exorcising.
18. Made filthy.
19. Trousers.
20. Tapestry.
21. Lover.
22. Bit.
23. 25 November, in the north of Scotland (with puns on "cat").
24. Stinginess.
25. Taxed.
26. Streamer addresses another associate, Master George Ferrers, a distinguished lawyer who had served as Master of the King's Pastimes during the reign of Edward VI. He contributed verse to the *Mirror for Magistrates*, a set of *de casibus* tragedies initially collected by William Baldwin c. 1554.
27. Shut his eyes.

3.5. Miles Hogarde, from
The Assault of the Sacrament of the Altar (1549, pub. 1554)

Composed in 1549 as a gift for Princess Mary, *The Assault of the Sacrament of the Altar*, a religious allegory by Miles Hogarde (fl. 1553–58), remained in manuscript until after the death of Edward VI. Robert Caly, a Catholic printer recently returned from exile in France, published it in 1554 with Hogarde's later revisions and dedication to "the Queen's most excellent majesty, being then Lady Mary, in which time (heresy then reigning) it could take no place." As a medieval dream vision akin to *Piers Plowman* and Chaucer's *Book of the Duchess*, this allegory resists interpretation until an old man arrives to explain key meanings. The narrative recounts how Lady Faith, defended by the Four Evangelists (Matthew, Mark, Luke, and John) and Saint Paul, protects the Roman rite Mass from Reason (i.e., infidelity), who identifies veneration of the elements of bread and wine with idolatry. The poem allegorizes attacks on the doctrine of transubstantiation over the centuries until the present reign of Mary I. The poem concludes with praise of her as the first Virgin Queen of England, prior to her marriage to Prince Philip of Spain (see 7.2), who presides over the triumph of the Roman Catholic Church.

SOURCE: *STC* 13556, A3ʳ–A5ᵛ, C1ᵛ–C2ᵛ, C4ᵛ–D1ᵛ, E1ʳ–E3ʳ.

When Sagittary[1] had dominion,
The nights then being very long and cold
I mused on the strange opinion,
The which diverse men did diversely hold
Against our Savior's own words plainly told,   5
Which troubled me so, that as it did chance,
With the same study, I fell into a trance.

Then with that I had a wonderful dream,
In the which me thought Morpheus[2] drew near,
And took me by the hand and with strength extreme,   10
He drew me forth, and bade me nothing fear,
But go with him, and as we going were,
"Let not my coming," quod he, "thee displease,
For thou shalt find, it shall be for thine ease.

I know that thou dost sore trouble thy mind   15
With the roundness[3] of men which thou dost see,
Against Christ's words cavillation[4] to find,
The which in the scripture so plain written be,

And how one with an other do not agree:
Is not this thy trouble, I pray thee tell true."　　　20
"It is truth," quod I, "even as thou dost show."

"Well," quod he, "I shall show thee more anon."
Then came we into a hall long and wide,
The like before I never looked upon.
Most gorgeously hung it was on each side,　　　25
With noble stories which I will not hide,
Wrought in fine arrays, with pure silk and gold,
It ravished my wit this hall to behold.

Then did I look upon the left hand,
There saw I the Ark of God purely wrought　　　30
Of fine gold as it orderly doth stand
In the Bible, which seeing I me bethought
Of the stories there, which to my mind brought,
What the Ark, and all the rest do signify,
Which on the left side of this hall did lie.　　　35

First there I saw Melchizedek[5] the king
Meeting Abraham the great patriarch
From slaughter of the four kings, for which thing
He offered to God in a mystery dark,
Bread and wine, the which thing as I did mark,　　　40
A hand in the clouds wrote this him before:
"Thou art a priest," it said "forever more."

Then stood their king David ready with his pen,
And wrote it in the spirit of prophecy,
Pointing to that priest, which should save all men,　　　45
Saying "Thou art a priest eternally,
After Melchizedek's order truly."
The which when I saw, I burnt in desire,
To see all the rest my heart was on fire.

There I saw how that the Jews also　　　50
Did eat the paschal lamb[6] as God commanded,
When he did save them from wicked Pharaoh,
Which with all his army was there confounded

In the Red Sea, where he delivered,
His people dry foot, to show his power great,   55
In remembrance whereof, the lamb they did eat.

Next to this story I saw richly wrought,
Now that manna[7] from above did descend,
To feed those whom God out of thrall had brought
Thus God his goodness to them did extend: 60
King David stood by and this truly penned,
Prophesying thereby a mystery great,
Saying, "Man the bread of angels hath ate."[8]

A goodly table then saw I there spread,
By the which the high priests stood honorably,   65
And did set thereon the holy show bread,
Of the which none might eat, but they only.[9]
Then in that place I did also espy,
Where King David did writ this sentence clear:
"God giveth meat[10] to those that him truly fear."[11]   70

Then as I stood musing these things to scan
I could not with all my wits them define,
Then came there to me an ancient man,
Which seemed to be some noble divine,
He bade me mine ears to him incline,   75
And he would open to me by and by,
What all these things did truly signify.

Of that I was glad, and gave attendance,
To hear how he would these figures discuss,
Which he did truly with noble utterance,   80
And first of the Ark his saying was thus:
"The Ark," quod he, "which is so glorious,
Doth signify Christ his church be thou sure,
Which hath in it the sweet manna most pure.

This manna is the holy sacrament,   85
Of the blessed body and blood of our Lord,
Which he left here to be permanent,
As a pledge most sure of our soul's comfort.

Aaron's rod also doth signify his word,
By the which his church is governed here,   90
But by manna is figured his body most near.

Secondly where Melchizedek the king
Brought forth bread and wine before Abraham,
That did signify Christ's holy offering,
Which he offered when he to his maundy[12] came,   95
Christ's order of priesthood consisteth in the same,
Since Melchizedek's order in his sacrifice,
Was none other than that, scripture plain trice.[13]

And where he saith thou art a priest forever,
Did not only signify Christ's eternity,   100
But also his order which end shall never,
Which he ordained, here at his maundy,
Fulfilling Melchizedek's order truly,
Yet is he the priest which doth work this thing
In his ministers, daily ministering. . . ."   105

[The old man continues to provide allegorical interpretations that explain
Egypt, Pharaoh, Moses, the paschal lamb, and the Exodus as respective figures for sinfulness, the Devil, Christ, the Eucharist, and redemption.]

Now when he had all these figures declared,
Suddenly he vanished from me away.
Then when I saw that, I myself prepared
To see more in this hall. And then without stay,   400
I looked on my right hand, on the which side lay
But two stories of the New Testament,
Which were the verities that the figures meant.

The first was the solemn supper of our Lord,
At the which his body he did consecrate,   405
Placing a new sacrifice for the comfort
Of his new church, which shall not consummate
Until he come again her to congregate,
To reign with him which sacrifice he did ordain,   410
In place of all the old, till then to remain.

Next unto this was very richly wrought,
How Christ on the cross suffered passion,
Whereby all mankind with his blood he bought,
Procuring thereby eternal redemption,   415
Leaving on his part, scripture doth mention,
Not one iota concerning his death and sufferance,
Therefore he is not now offered, but in remembrance.

For there remaineth no sacrifice for sin,
By any shedding of blood or death suffering: 420
For Christ once by death God's favor so did win,
He needs to die no more, for that one offering
Was sufficient, which death as remembering,
We offer to God, as was told me before,
As our chief mean of mercy to him evermore.   425

Then between these stories stood David the king,
With a scroll in his hand all along spread,
And indifferently to these stories pointing,
This verse he had written which I thereon read:
"Thou art a priest for evermore," it said,   430
"After Melchizedek's order then in fine."14
I thought of the word told me by the divine.

This done even suddenly I did espy,
A goodly lady of beauty excellent,15
Decked with gold and stone wondrous costly,   435
Which glistened like the stars in the firmament.
Then the Evangelists I saw ready bent,
Her to defend with the Apostle Saint Paul,
And also there was the ancient doctors all.16

This lady on a three cornered stone did stand,   440
In the which, *Christus* was graven very well,
And an host consecrate she held in her hand,
With much more reverence than I can tell,
Then stood the Evangelists each with his Gospel,
And Saint Paul also, each showing evident,   445
The place where they defend this holy sacrament.

Then all the doctors took of them for their defense,
Each of them a sword sharp and durable,
And faith took them targets[17] of noble science,
By which to withstand all men they were able.   450
Thus they stood stoutly like men firm and stable,
Always ready with these weapons to fight
Against all that would not Lady Faith use right.

Then saw I on their targets written plain
Scutum Fidei,[18] and furthermore like case,   455
Upon their swords *Verbum Dei*[19] certain,
Thus orderly they stood each in his place,
This lady to defend assisted with grace,
Which had on her breast, in letters of gold,
Fides Catholica,[20] most goodly to behold   460

Then I seeing all this with great reverence,
On my knees to Christ I kneeled by and by,
And with divine honor as God in one essence,
With the Father and the Holy Ghost truly,
I did him there worship in that mystery.   465
Then Reason in a corner spied me right soon,
And called me idolater for that I had done.

Then cry I to him, "Why dost thou reprove me
For giving of honor, where honor is due?"
"I would agree," quod he, "if I that could see,   470
But till then, I will not think it to be true.
I see but very bread, therefore doth ensue,
It is but bread, which is not honor worthy,
For which I call it plain idolatry." . . .

[After Berenger of Tours, an eleventh-century opponent of transubstantiation, leads the first assault on the sacrament of the altar, the second assault
begins.]

Then came in Reason with a standard new,
Which had thereon the same superscription,   575
That the other had, which did Faith pursue,

Changing but only in one condition
There captains' names, which had the tuition,
Of that wicked host, then was John Wyclif,
Jerome of Prague, and Hus workers of mischief.[21]   580

All their weapons were of the same sort
As the other were, saving as I did here
Their outcry was so terrible and short,
As though Lady Faith they would clean overbear.
Their arrows flew so thick, my flesh shook for fear.   585
Then all their chief cry as these arrows came
Was these words, *caro non prodest quicquam*.[22]

Then the doctors all their targets forth did hold
From their cruel shot faith for to defend,
And with their swords, like warriors most bold,   590
They stroke at them four, but yet they would not bend,
But arrogantly much time they did spend
Against Lady Faith, but nothing prevailing,
The doctors so well with their assailing.

Who all with one voice did wholly agree,   595
That this text, "the flesh he doth profit nothing,"
Was in this sense only taken to be,
Nothing it profits after the Jews' meaning,
For they understood a carnal eating,
As though they should eat it in gobbets dead,   600
As we do eat flesh wherewith we are fed.

Which error to remove, Christ before sayeth,
"The spirit is that quickeneth," as he would say,
"To eat this flesh of mine as your judgments hath
Conceived, so would profit you no way,   605
But because thereby profit have ye may,
Joined with the Holy Spirit ye shall have it plain,
By which to give life, the flesh shall attain.

Think ye that I mean that ye my flesh shall eat
In this form, as I stand here before you all   610
Mangled out in pieces, as ye do other meat?

Nay, that ye are deceived well perceive ye shall.
For this body ye shall see by power potential,
Ascend where it came from. What will ye say then?
Then shall ye well know I am more than a man."   615

Thus the doctors all did affirm and say,
That of Christ's words this was the perfect sense,
Proving that Christ these words to the Jews did lay
Because of his godhead they should have intelligence,
And then to his words to have given credence.   620
But yet they would not believe more than they saw
Which was his manhood, his godhead they would not know.

Needs would they know how they his flesh should eat,
Or else they would not believe him at all.
Plainly he told them of this heavenly meat,   625
But in contention with Christ they would fall,
The time they would not tarry, but still on Christ call
With a doubtful, "How," which Christ knew full well,
Therefore how they should eat it, Christ would not tell.

But afterward to those that would not contend,   630
But whose humble silence Christ's words did believe,
At the time which he before did intend,
He gave them his flesh their souls to relieve,
Under such a form, that it did not grieve
Their stomachs, for under the form of bread it lay   635
With which their bodies were fed every day. . . .

[After Martin Luther, Johannes Oecolampadius, Andreas Carlstadt, and
their adherents mount the third, fourth, and fifth assaults on the sacrament,
the sixth assault begins in England.]

Then stood Lady Faith quietly in rest,
Holding the sacrament honorably,
Yet some now and then would have her oppressed,   845
Which were soldiers of wicked heresy,[a]
Assaulting her oft very cruelly,
Whom for to hurt when they saw they lacked power,
They fled back all to the tent of error.

Wherein they did rest; I saw them no more.   850
Then kneeled I down doing reverence,
Unto Christ there as I had done before,
Supposing the Devil's deadly diligence
Had been debarred by the doughty defense,
Of all the doctors, and as I there stood,   855
I heard horses bray as they had been wood.[23]

Then began my heart for great fear to quake
Me thought all the world against faith was bent,
But then Faith bade me a good heart to take,
"For this assault," quod she, "will be fervent,   860
But look that from me thou be not absent,
And take here," quod she, "this target and sword."
Glad was I then of her to hear that word.

Then as I took these myself to defend,
In came Reason which a standard did bear,   865
Upon the which in black letters was penned,
The names of all those which his captains were.
Whom when I beheld like bishops did appear,
Which in my mind was a strange sight to see,
Bishops on that sort disguised to be.   870

The first was two archbishops whom I did know,
The third Ridley, which on the queen did rail,
The fourth was Hooper, the fifth was Barlow,
The sixth was Ponet, and the seventh was Bale,
The eighth was Brown, and the ninth Coverdale,   875
Farrar and Taylor made twelve with Scory,
To see them in this case my heart was sorry.

Their footmen they had which by them did roam
As Rogers, Rose, Horne, Saunders and Harley,
Cardmaker, Becon, Crowley and Sampson,   880
Peter Hart, Carter, and old Bilney,
Thomson, Kirkham, Douglas, Knox, and Macbray
Bradford, old Stevens and young Samuel,
With the two Turners, and more than I can tell.[24]

For whom I did then most heartily pray,   885
That our Lord in time would turn their hearts all,
For by their ill doctrine many a day,
They have caused many from faith to fall,
But God grant that his church catholical
They may learn to know and to her to come,   890
Then shall they reign with her in his kingdom.

In armor as black as any ink there were,
And on the crest of their helmets on high,
A woman's foresleeve each of them did bear,
The which as I took it, did signify,   895
That for women's loves their manhoods they would try,
Turkey bows each of them had ready bent,
To shoot out thereof their errors pestilent.

Then saw I the chief bishop of them all,[b]
Rush to the doctors unreverently,   900
And rent out of their books in gobbets small,
Pieces for his purpose, which perversely
He chewed with his teeth, and then spitefully
Shot them at Lady Faith in pellet wise,
And beastly did the sacrament despise.[25]   905

Then certain bishops[c] on Lady Faith's part
Began against him her stoutly to defend,
Which when I saw did comfort my heart,
But then over this their debate had an end,
The Devil new soldiers against faith did send,   910
Which came under the standard of ignorance,
Of whom Self Wit[26] had the church governance.

My help of these bishops effeminate,
Against Lady Faith did so much prevail,
That certain of her men to them was captivate,   920
And for her sake was laid fast in jail,
Then before he was drawn such a veil,
That she was so hid, few men could her see,
Till God saw time, that seen she should be.

For the which as I a long time did pray,   925
I heard trumpets blow very sweet and high,
Then did my heart rejoice putting care away,
Me thought the sound was of some victory,
With that coming in I saw suddenly,
A noble standard all of white and green,
Embroidered with roses royally beseen.   930

After the which standard did enter in,
One triumphantly as the chief captain,
Which was a crowned queen and virgin,
Who seeing Lady Faith so had in disdain,
Drew back the veil that I might see plain,
Lady Faith still holding the sacrament,   935
To the which the queen did kneel continent.

Giving to our Lord hearty lauds and praise,
Which had given to her so a great a victory,
Against her enemies in so few days,
Without bloodshed most miraculously,
Commanding straight to set at liberty,   940
All these which imprisonment did take,
And were punished for Lady Faith's sake.

Which done even suddenly as I there stood,
All that I had seen vanished from my sight,
The which sudden change made me change my mood,   950
But then Morpheus came again to me right,
And bade me fear nothing, then fast as he might
He brought me to my bed, and with that I did wake,
Then to write this vision some pains I did take.

Marginal Glosses

   [a] Mean soldiers. Frith, Lambert, Tyndale, etc.

   [b] Cranmer.

   [c] Catholic bishops: Winchester, London, Dorchester, Chichester, and Durham.

Notes

1. Sagittarius, the ninth sign of the zodiac (about 22 November to 21 December).

2. Classical god of sleep.

3. Unruliness.

4. Scoffing.

5. King and high priest of Salem, who blesses Abraham (Gen. 14:17–20) and came to be regarded as the ideal priest-king and, by Christians, as a type for Christ (Heb. 6–8).

6. The lamb eaten on the first day of Passover (Exod. 12:3–11).

7. The bread miraculously given to the Israelites while in the wilderness (Exod 16:14–36).

8. Ps. 78.25.

9. An offering of twelve loaves of unleavened bread eaten only by priests (Lev. 24:5–9).

10. Food.

11. Ps. 111:5.

12. The Last Supper.

13. Understood immediately.

14. Ps. 110:4.

15. Lady Faith.

16. Fathers of the Church.

17. Shields.

18. "Shield of Faith."

19. "Word of God," i.e., the Bible.

20. "Catholic Faith."

21. Protestants and Catholics commonly regarded these medieval religious reformers, the latter of whom were burned alive as heretics, as proto-Protestants.

22. John 6:63 (see line 596).

23. Crazy.

24. This catalogue of English and Scottish Protestant reformers includes Bale, Coverdale, Crowley, and Ridley (see 1.1.B, 3.1, 3.3, 6.2–3, 6.5.B).

25. Hogarde accuses Cranmer of selective quotation from patristic texts.

26. Knowledge.

4

LAITY VERSUS CLERGY: DIALOGUE AND MONOLOGUE

4.1. Luke Shepherd,
John Bon and Master Parson (c. 1548)

Jon Bon and Master Parson, a satire against the Mass and Roman clergy, is by Luke Shepherd (fl.1548–54), an enigmatic figure active during the reign of Edward VI. He was probably a physician who lived on Coleman Street in London. When Shepherd and his publisher, John Day, were jailed at Fleet Prison for circulating religious propaganda, they obtained release on the ground that this satire had a great following at the royal court. Day and his partner, William Seres, may have timed publication of this chapbook to coincide with the 1548 ban on the festival of Corpus Christi, which commemorated the last supper and doctrine of transubstantiation on the sixtieth day after Easter.

The feigned naïveté and humility of the countryman, who speaks an invented rural dialect, thinly disguise an agrarian radical who mockingly misconstrues Corpus Christi as "copsi cursty" and "cropsy cursty." His homespun wisdom brings to life ideals stated by Erasmus, who called for humble people including women and plowmen to read the Bible, and William Tyndale, who vowed to make a mere plowboy more learned in the Bible than a cleric (see 6.5.A). John Bon's skepticism concerning how the body of Christ can be compressed into the host on display in a tiny monstrance is akin to his rational perception that his ox is black rather than white. This dialogue highlights the clash between religious formalism and Protestant insistence upon inward faith rather than external practice.

SOURCE: *STC* 3258.5, A1–4.

EDITION: Shepherd.

REFERENCES: King 1982; Norbrook.

Parson. What John Bon, good morrow to thee.

John Bon. Now good morrow, Mast Parson, so must I thee.

Parson. What meanest thou John to be at work so soon?

John. The zoner[1] I begin the zoner shall I have done,

    For I [in]tend to work no longer than noon.   5

Parson. Marry John, for that God's blessing on thy heart,

    For surely some there be will go to plow and cart

    And set not by this holy Corpus Christi eve.

John. They are the more to blame, I swear by Saint Steven.

    But tell me, Mast Parson one thing, and you can   10

    What saint is Copsi Cursty, a man or a woman?

Parson. Why John knowest not that? I tell thee it was a man,

    It is Christ, his own self, and tomorrow is his day.

    We bear him in procession and thereby know it ye may.

John. I know, Mast Parson? And not by my fay,[2]   15

But methink it is a mad thing that ye say.
That it should be a man, how can it come to pass,
Because ye may him bear within so small a glass?[3]
Parson. Why neighbor John, and art thou now there?
 Now I may perceive ye love this new gear.   20
John. God forbod,[4] master, I should be of that fashion.
 I question why your maship,[5] in way of cumlication.[6]
 A plain man ye may see will speak as cometh to mind,
 Ye must hold us ascused,[7] for low men be but blind.
 I am an eld[8] fellow of fifty winter and more,   25
 And yet in all my life I knew not this before.
Parson. No did?[9] Why sayest thou so? Upon thyself thou liest.
 Thou hast ever known the sacrament to be the body of Christ.
John. Yea sir, ye say true, all that I know indeed.
 And yet as I remember it is not in my creed.   30
 But as for Cropsy Cursty to be a man or no,
 I knew not till this day, by the way, my soul shall to.
Parson. Why foolish fellow, I tell thee it is so,
 For it was so determined by the Church long ago.
 It is both the sacrament and very Christ himself.   35
John. No spleaser,[10] Mast Parson, then make ye Christ an elf
 And the maddest made man that ever [a] body saw.
Parson. What? Peace madman, thou speakest like a daw.[11]
 It is not possible his manhood for to see.
John. Why sir, ye tell me it is even very he   40
 And if it be not his manhood, his godhead it must be.
Parson. I tell ye none of both, what meanest thou, art thou mad?
John. No nother[12] mad nor drunk, but to learn I am glad,
 But to displease your maship I would be very loath.
 Ye grant me here plainly that it is none of both.   45
 Then is it but a cake, but I pray ye be not wroth.[13]
Parson. Wroth, quod ha, by the Mass, thou makest me swear an oath.
 I had lever[14] with a doctor of divinity to reason
 Then with a stubble cur that eateth beans and peason.
John. I cry ye mercy, Mast Parson, patience for a season.   50
 In all this cumlication is nother felony nor treason.
Parson. No by the Mass, but hearest thou, it is plain heresy.
John. I am glad it chanced so, there was no witness by
 And if there had I cared not, for ye spake as ill as I.
 I speak but as I heard you say, I wot not what ye thought.   55

Ye said it was not God nor man and made it worse than naught.

Parson. I meant not so, thou tookest me wrong.

John. Ah sir, ye sing another song.

    I dare not reason with you long;

    I see well now ye have a knack   60

    To say a thing and then go back.

Parson. No John, I was but a little overseen,

    But thou meantest not good faith I ween

    In all this talk that was us between.

John. I? No trow it shall not so been   65

    That John Bon shall an heretic be called,

    Then might he say him so foul befalled.[15]

Parson. But now if thou wilt mark me well,

    From beginning to ending I will thee tell

    Of the godly service that shall be tomorrow,   70

    That or I have done no doubt thou wilt sorrow

    To hear that such things should be fordone.

    And yet in many places they have begun

    To take away the old and set up new.

    Believe me John, this tale is true.   75

John. Go to, Mast Parson, say on and well to thrive,

    Ye be the jolliest gemman[16] that ever [I] saw in my life.

Parson. We shall first have matins, is it not a godly hearing?

John. Fie? Yes, methink tis a shameful gay cheering,

    For oftentimes on my prayers, when I take no great keep[17]   80

    Ye sing so arrantly[18] well, ye make me fall asleep.

Parson. Then have we procession and Christ about we bear.

John. That is a poison[19] holy thing for God himself is there.

Parson. Then come we in and ready us dress,

    Full solemnly to go to Mass.   85

John. Is not here a mischievous thing?

    The Mass is vengeance holy for all their saying.

Parson. Then say we *Confiteor* and *Miseriatur*.[20]

John. Jeze Lord, tis abominable matter.

Parson. And then we stand up to the altar.   90

John. This gear is as good as Our Lady's Psalter.[21]

Parson. And so goes forth with the other deal

    Till we have read the Pistell and Gospel.[22]

John. That is good. Mast Parson, I know right well.

Parson. Is that good? Why what sayest thou to the other?   95

John. Marry, horrible good, I say none other.
Parson. So is all the Mass, I dare avow this,
    As good in every point as Pistell or Gospel is.
John. The foul evil it is, who would think so much?
    In faith I ever thought that it had been no such.   100
Parson. Then have we the canon[23] that is holiest.
John. A spitefull gay thing of all that ever I wist.
Parson. Then have we the memento even before the sacring.[24]
John. Ye are murrainly[25] well learned. I see by your reckoning
    That ye will not forget such an elvish thing.   105
Parson. And after that we consecrate very God and man
    And turn the bread to flesh with five words[26] we can.
John. The devil ye do I trow. There is pestilent business.
    Ye are much bound to God, for such a spital holiness.
    A gallows gay gift with five words alone   110
    To make both God and man and yet wese[27] none
    Ye talk so unreasonably well, it maketh my heart yearn.
    As old a fellow as iche[28] am, I see well I may learn.
Parson. Yea, John and then with words holy and good
    Even by and by we turn the wine to blood.   115
John. Lo will ye say lie? Who would have thought it
    That ye could so soon, from wine to blood ha' brought it
    And yet except your mouth, be better tasted than mine?
    I cannot feel it other but that it should be wine,
    And yet I wot ne'er a cause there may be why.   120
    Perchance ye ha' drunk blood ofter[29] than ever did I.
Parson. Truly, John, it is blood though it be wine in taste,
    As soon as the word is spoke the wine is gone and past.
John. A sessions on it[30] for me, my wits are me benumb.
    For I cannot study where the wine should become.   125
Parson. Study, quod ha, beware and let such matter go.
    To meddle much with this may bring ye soon to woe.
John. Yea but, Mast Parson, think ye it were right
    That if I desired you to make my black ox white
    And you say it is dun, and still is black in sight,   130
    Ye might me deem a fool for to believe so light.
Parson. I marvel much ye will reason so far.
    I fear if ye use it, it will ye mar.
John. No, no, sir, I trust of that I will beware.
    I pray you with your matter again forth to fare.   135

Parson. And then we go forth and Christ's body receive,
　　Even the very same that Mary did conceive.
John. The devil it is, ye have a great grace
　　To eat God and man in so short a space.
Parson. And so we make an end as it lieth in an order, 140
　　But now the blessed mean[31] is hated in every border
　　And railed on and reviled, with words most blasphemous.
　　But I trust it will be better with the help of the catechismus,
　　For though it came forth but even that other day,
　　Yet hath it turned many to their old way. 145
　　And where they hated Mass and had it in disdain,
　　There have they Mass and matins in Latin tongue again.
　　Yea even in London [it]self, John, I tell thee truth,
　　They be full glad and merry to hear of this, God knoweth.
John. By my troth, Mast Parson, I like full well your talk. 150
　　But mass me no more massings. The right way will I walk,
　　For though I have no learning, yet I know cheese from chalk,
　　And iche can perceive your niggling as crafty as ye walk.
　　But leave your devilish Mass and the communion to you take,
　　And then will Christ be with you even for his promise's sake. 155
Parson. Why art thou such a one and kept it so close?
　　Well all is not gold that hath a fair gloss.
　　But farewell John Bon, God bring thee in better mind.
John. I thank you sir for that you seem very kind,
　　But pray not so for me for I am well enough. 160
　　Whistle,[32] boy, drive forth. God speed us and the plow.
　　Ha brown done,[33] forth that whoreson crab.[34]
　　Kee[35] comomyne,[36] geld[37] white hait,[38] black ha.
　　Have again bold[39] before, hait ree whoa,
　　Cherely[40] boy, come off that, homeward we may go. 165

Notes

　　1. Sooner.
　　2. Faith.
　　3. Monstrance
　　4. Forbid.
　　5. Mastership (disrespectful).
　　6. Conversation (invented dialect).
　　7. Excused.
　　8. Old (dialect).
　　9. Indeed?

10. If it please you?

11. Simpleton.

12. Neither.

13. Angry.

14. Would rather.

15. Befallen.

16. Gentlemen (colloquial).

17. Heed.

18. Notoriously.

19. Peisant (i.e., ponderous).

20. "I confess . . . " (preparatory prayer of confession) and "May [God] have mercy . . . " (prayer for absolution that usually follows the Confiteor in the Mass).

21. The rosary.

22. Epistle and Gospel, opening readings in the Mass.

23. Part of the Mass.

24. Consecration.

25. Plaguely.

26. Ironic misunderstanding of the four words of institution, *hoc est corpus meum* ("this is my body").

27. Imperative of "to be" (archaic).

28. I (dialect).

29. Oftener.

30. "May it be committed to the quarter sessions of justices of the peace" (an expletive)

31. Sacrament.

32. Hush (dialect).

33. Name for a horse.

34. Ill-tempered beast.

35. Cow (dialect).

36. Come on you? (invented dialect).

37. Cow.

38. A command to move forward.

39. Stop.

40. Carefully.

4.2 Luke Shepherd,
Doctor Double Ale (c. 1548)

Shepherd composed *Doctor Double Ale*,[1] a satire on the Latin-rite liturgy and clerical ignorance, at about the same time as *John Bon and Master Parson* (see 4.1). The narrator exemplifies Protestant belief in a literate laity and popular Bible reading, in contrast to Harry George, a curate in the London parish of Saint Sepulchre's who frequents alehouses, confuses his ale pot with the Mass chalice, and violates prohibitions against the Latin Mass under Edward VI.

Plain speech and rationality align the narrator with the cobbler's boy, an apprentice whose understanding of the Bible contradicts the cleric's belief in nonscriptural traditions. The imprisonment of this apprentice may recall the execution in 1540 of a youth, Richard Mekins, on grounds of heresy. The proletarian origins of the cobbler's boy identify him with William Tyndale's ideal of a learned plowboy (see 6.5.A).

The priest's ironic confession recalls alehouse scenes in goliardic verse, Chaucer's *Pardoner's Tale*, *Piers Plowman* (see introduction to 3.3), and John Skelton's *Tunning of Eleanor Rumming*. These medieval poems afford models for Shepherd's use of alliteration and Skeltonics, an idiosyncratic verse form notable for long internal and terminal monorhymes. Sir Philip Sidney and George Puttenham, Elizabethan critics unsympathetic to native English verse, attacked skeltonics as doggerel.

SOURCE: *STC* 7071, A1–7.
EDITION: Shepherd.
REFERENCES: King (1982); Norbrook.

Although I lack intelligence	1
And cannot skill of eloquence,	
Yet will I do my diligence	
To say something ere I go hence	
Wherein I may demonstrate	5
The figure, gesture, and estate	
Of one that is a curate	
That hard is and indurate	
And earnest in the cause	
Of peevish popish laws	10
That are not worth two straws,	
Except it be with daws[2]	
That knoweth not good from evils,	
Nor God's word from the Devil's,	
Nor will in no wise hear	15
The word of God so clear,	

But popishness uprear,
And make the Pope God's peer.
And so themselves they lade
With babies[3] that he made,   20
And still will hold his trade.
No man can them persuade,
And yet I daresay
There is no day
But that they may   25
Hear sincerely
And right truly
God's word to be taught
If they would have sought,
But they set at naught   30
Christ's true doctrine
And themselves decline
To men's ordinance
Which they enhance
And take in estimation,   35
Above Christ's Passion
And so this foolish nation
Esteem their own ration[4]
And all dumb ceremonies
Before the sanctimonies   40
Of Christ's holy writ,
And think their own wi[t]
To be far above it
That the scripture to them teaches
Or honest man preaches.   45
They follow perilous leeches[5]
And doctors dulpatis[6]
That falsely to them pratis[7]
And bring them to the gates
Of Hell and bitter darkness,   50
And all by stubborn starkness
Putting their full trust
In things that rot and rust,
And papistical provisions
Which are the Devil's divisions.   55
Now let us go about

To tell the tale out
Of this good fellow stout
That for no man will doubt
But keep his old conditions 60
For all the new commissions,
And use his superstitions
And also men's traditions,
And sing for dead folks' souls,[8]
And read his bead rolls,[9] 65
And all such things will use
As honest men refuse.
But take him for a cruse[10]
And ye will tell me news,
For if he once begin 70
He leaveth naught therein,
He careth not a pin
How much there be within
So he the pot may win.
Nor will it make full thin, 75
And where the drink doth please,
There will he take his ease,
And drink thereof his fill
Till ruddy be his bill,[11]
And fill both cup and can. 80
Who is so glad a man
As is our curate than?[12]
I would ye knew it a curate,
Not far without Newgate,[13]
Of a parish large; 85
The man hath mickle[14] charge,
And none within this border
That keepeth such an order,
Nor one this side Naverne[15]
Loveth better the ale tavern. 90
But if the drink be small,[16]
He may not well withal.
"Tush, cast it on the wall,"
It fretteth out his gall.
Then seek another house, 95
"This is not worth a louse."

As drunken as a mouse,
"Monsieur, gibbet a vous."[17]
And there will bib and booze,
Till heavy is his brewse.[18]   100
Good ale he doth so haunt,
And drink a due taunt,
That the alewives make their vaunt
Of many a penny round
That some of them hath found.   105
And sometime mickle strife is
Among the alewives,
And sure I blame them not,
For wrong it is, God wot,
When this good drunken sot   110
Helpeth not to empty the pot,
For sometimes he will go
To one and to no mo'.
Then will the whole rout
Upon that one cry out,   115
And say she doth them wrong
To keep him all day long
From coming them among.
Wherefore I give counsel
To them that good drink sell   120
To take in of the best,
Or else they lose their guest.
For he is ready and prest[19]
Where good ale is to rest,
And drink till he be dressed.   125
When he his book[20] should study
He sitteth there full ruddy
Till half the day be gone
Crying, "Fill the pot, Joan!"
And will not be alone   130
But call some other one
At window or at fenester.[21]
That is an idle minister
As he himself is,
Ye know full well this   135
The kind of carrion crows

Ye may be sure grows
The more for carrion stinking,
And so do these in drinking.
This man to some men's thinking 140
Doth stay him much upon the king
As in the due demanding,
Or that he calleth an headpenny[22]
And of the paschal halfpenny.[23]
For the cloth of Corpus Christi[24] 145
Four pence he claimeth swiftly
For which the sexton and he truly
Did tug by the ears earnestly
Saying he cannot the king well pay
If all such dribblers be take away. 150
Is not this a gentle tale
Of our Doctor Double Ale,
Whose countenance is never pale
So well good drink he can uphale.[25]

A man of learning great, 155
For if his brain he would beat
He could within days fourteen
Make such a sermon as never was seen.
I wot not whether he spake in drink,
Or drink in him, how do ye think? 160
I never heard him preach, God wot,
But it were in the good ale pot.
Also he saith that fain he would
Come before the council[26] if he could,
For to declare his learning 165
And other things concerning
Goodly counsels that he could give.
Beyond all measure, ye may me believe,
His learning is exceeding,
Ye may know by his reading. 170
Yet could a cobbler's boy him tell
That he read a wrong Gospel,
Wherefore indeed he served him well,
He turned himself as round as a bell
And with loud voice began to call, 175

"Is there no constable among you all,
To take this knave that doth me trouble?"
With that all was on a hubble shubble,
There was drawing and dragging,
There was lugging and lagging,   180
And snitching and snatching,
And ketching and catching,
And so the poor lad
To the Counter[27] they had.
Some would he should be hanged   185
Or else he would be wranged,[28]
Some said it were a good turn
Such an heretic to burn,
Some said this and some said that,
And some did prate they wist not what.   190
Some did curse and some did ban[29]
For chafing of our curate than.[30]
He was worthy no less
For vexing with his pertness
A gemman[31] going to Mass.   195
Did it become a cobbler's boy
To show a gemman such a toy?

But if it were well weighed
Ye should find I am afraid
That the boy were worthy   200
For his reading and sobriety
And judgment in the verity,
Among honest folk to be
A curate rather than he.
For this is known for certainty,   205
The boy doth love no papistry,
And our curate is called no doubt
A papist London throughout.
And the truth is it, they do not lie,
It may be seen with half an eye.   210
For if there come a preacher,
Or any godly teacher
To speak against his trumpery,[32]
To the alehouse goeth he by and by,

And there he will so much drink   215
Till of ale he doth so stink,
That whether he go before or behind,
Ye shall him smell without the wind.
For when he goes to it he is no hafter[33]
He drinketh drunk for two days after   220
With, "Fill the cup, Joan,
For all this is gone.
Here is ale alone,
I say for all my drinking,
Tush, let the pot be clinking   225
And let us merry make.
No thought will I take,
For though these fellows crake[34]
I trust to see them slake
And some of them to bake   230
In Smithfield[35] at a stake.
And in my parish be some,
That if the time come
I fear not will remember
(Be it August or September,   235
October or November,
Or month of December)
To find both wood and timber
To burn them every member
And goeth to board and bed   240
At the sign of the King's Head.[36]

And let these heretics preach
And teach what they can teach,
My parish I know well
Against them will rebel   245
If I but once them tell
Or give them any warning
That they were of the new learning.[37]
For with a word or twain,
I can them call again.   250
And yet, by the Mass,
Forgetful I was,
Or else in a slumber.

There is a shrewd number
That curstly[38] do cumber   255
And my patience prove
And daily me move.

For some of them still
Continue will
In this new way   260
Whatsoever I say.

It is not so long ago
Since it changed so,
That a burial here was
Without dirge or Mass,   265
But at the burial
They sang a Christmas carol.
By the Mass, they will mar all,
If they continue shall.
Some said it was a godly hearing   270
And of their hearts a gay cheering.
Some of them fell on weeping,
In my church I make no leasing
They heard never the like thing.
Do you think that I will consent   275
To these heretics' intent
To have any sacrament
Ministered in English?
By them I set not a rish[39]
So long as my name is Harry George.   280
I will not do it, [in] spite of their gorge.
Oh, Dankester[40] and Doncaster,
None between this and Lancaster,
Knoweth so much my mind,
As thou my special friend.   285
It would do thee much good
To wash thy hands in the blood
Of them that hate the Mass.
Thou covetest no less,
So much they us oppress   290
Poor priests doubtless.

And yet what then,
There is no man
That sooner can,
Persuade his parishons[41]   295
From such conditions
Then I pierce[42] I,
For by and by
I can them convert
To take my part,   300
Except a few
That hack and hew,
And against me show
What they may do
To put me to   305
Some hindrance.
And yet may chance
The Bishop's visitor[43]
Will show me favor.
And therefore I   310
Care not a fly,
For oft have they
Sought by some way
To bring me to blame
And open shame,   315
But I will bear them out,
In spite of their snout
And will not cease
To drink a pot the less
Of ale that is big,[44]   320
Nor pass not a fig[45]
For all their malice.
Away the mare go walis.[46]
I set not a whiting[47]
For all their writing,   325
For yet I deny not
The Masses private
Nor yet forsake
That I of a cake
My maker may make."   330

But hark a little hark
And a few words mark,
How this calvish[48] clerk
For his purpose could work.
There is an honest man   335
That kept an old woman
Of alms in her bed,
Lying daily bedrid,
Which man could not I say
With popishness away,   340
But fain this woman old
Would have Mass if she could.
The which this priest was told
He hearing this anon,
As the goodman was gone   345
Abroad about his business,
Before the woman he said Mass
And showed his pretty popishness
Against the goodman's will.
Wherefore it is my skill   350
That he should him indite
For doing such despite
As by his popish wile
His house with Mass defile.

Thus may ye behold   355
This man is very bold,
And in his learning old
Intendeth for to sit.
I blame him not a whit
For it would vex his wit   360
And clean against his earning
To follow such learning
As nowadays is taught.
It would soon bring to naught
His old popish brain,   365
For then he must again
Apply him to the school
And come away a fool:
For nothing should he get,

His brain hath been so het,[49] 370
And with good ale so wet.
Wherefore he may now jet[50]
In fields and in meeds
And pray upon his beads.
For yet he hath a pair 375
Of beads that be right fair,
Of coral, jet, or amber
At home within his chamber
For Matins or Mass.
Primer and portas 380
And pots[51] and beads,
His life he leads.

But this I wota[52]
That if ye nota
How this idiota 385
Doth follow the pota.
I hold you a groata
Ye will read by rota
That he may wear a coata
In a cock losel's boata.[53] 390

Thus the dirty doctor,
The pope's own proctor,
Will brag and boast
With ale and a toast,
And like a rutter[54] 395
His Latin will utter
And turn and toss him
With "Tu non possum
Loquere latinum.
This alum finum 400
Is bonus than vinum.
Ego volo quare
Cum tu drinkare
Pro tuum caput,
Quia apud 405
Te propiciacio
Tu non potes facio

Tot quam ego
Quam librum tu lego,
Cave de me   410
Apponere te
Juro per deum.
Hoc est lifum meum[55]
Quia drinkum stalum,
Non facere malum."[56]   415
Thus our dominus dodkin[57]
With ita vera bodkin[58]
Doth lead his life
Which to the alewife
Is very profitable.   420
It is pity he is not able
To maintain a table
For beggars and tinkers
And all lusty drinkers.
Or captain or beadle   425
With drunkards to meddle,
Ye cannot I am sure
For keeping of a cure
Find such a one well
If ye should rake Hell.   430

And therefore now,
No more to you.
Sed perlegas ista,
Si velis papista.[59]
Farewell and adieu,   435
With a whirlary whew
And a tirlary tip,
Beware of the whip.
        Finis.
Take this till more come.

Notes

    1. Double-strength ale.
    2. Fools.
    3. Idols.
    4. Reason.

5. Physicians.
6. Of dull pate, dim witted (mock Latin).
7. Prate (mock Latin).
8. Celebrate a Requiem Mass.
9. Prayer lists.
10. Drinking vessel.
11. Nose.
12. Then.
13. Gate in London Wall.
14. Much.
15. A made-up place name?
16. Weak.
17. Mock French.
18. Ale.
19. Prepared.
20. Bible.
21. Window.
22. Ecclesiastical payment.
23. Easter payment due to a cleric.
24. Body of Christ.
25. Drink up.
26. Church council.
27. A London prison.
28. Tortured.
29. Curse.
30. Then.
31. Gentleman.
32. Rubbish (anti-Catholic jargon).
33. Dodger.
34. Boast.
35. Site for burning heretics (see 6.1, Figure 7).
36. A tavern.
37. Protestantism.
38. Cursedly.
39. Rush.
40. A made-up name for a cleric.
41. Parishioners.
42. Discern.
43. Church inspector.
44. Strong.
45. Not give a fig.
46. Perhaps proverbial, its meaning is unclear.
47. Fish.
48. Calflike.
49. Heated.
50. Walk.
51. Ale pots.

52. Lines 383–90 contain mock Latin word endings.

53. Cock Lorell's boat (a ship of fools).

54. Swindler.

55. Parody of "hoc est corpus meum."

56. Lines 398–415: "You are not able / to speak Latin / This fine ale / Is better than wine / For that reason I wish / To drink with you / For your head / Because with / You . . . / Aren't able to do / So many or much as I am / . . . / Beware of me / To serve you / I swear to God / This is my life: / To drink urine / Not to do evil."

57. Mock honorific for a foolish cleric.

58. "And so true bodkin" (i.e., dagger; mock Latin).

59. Lines 433–34: "But scan this / if you hide a papist."

4.3. George Gifford, from
The Country Divinity (1581)

The Country Divinity is the short title of *A Brief Discourse of Certain Points of Religion, Which Is Among the Common Sort of Christians*. George Gifford (c. 1548–1620) cast it in the form of a dialogue that incorporates vigorous arguments by superstitious Atheos ("ungodly one"), who condones traditional festivity and neighborly fellowship among the indulgent laity and ale-drinking clergy, and precisian Zelotes ("zealous one"). He favors evangelical preaching, as opposed to rote reading from the *Book of Homilies* (2.2), and the strict code of religious practice that came to be known as Puritanism. Based on Gifford's own experience as a parson in a rural parish, this book's harsh view of a stubbornly irreligious laity represents a sharp departure from the views of William Tyndale, Luke Shepherd, and other members of earlier generations of English Protestants, who claimed that plainspoken peasants and artisans were capable of scriptural understanding superior to that of ignorant clerics (see 4.1–2, 6.5.A). Gifford underwent suspension from preaching because of his nonconformist convictions until William Cecil, chief minister of Elizabeth I, interceded on his behalf. Enjoying a reputation for rousing preaching, he wrote many religious treatises and served as chaplain and deathbed confessor to Sir Philip Sidney, a zealot Protestant.

SOURCE: *STC* 11846, fol. 1ʳ–4ʳ.

Zelotes. Well overtaken my friend.

Atheos. I thank you sir.

Zelotes. How far do ye travel this way?

Atheos. Twenty miles.

Zelotes. Do you dwell in Essex?

Atheos. Yea, not far from Clelmeford.[1]

Zelotes. What call ye the town where ye dwell?

Atheos. G. B.

Zelotes. Have ye a preacher there?

Atheos. We have an honest man, our curate.

Zelotes. Doth he teach his flock?

Atheos. He doth his good will and more ye cannot require of a man.

Zelotes. Ye did commend him even now to be an honest man.

Atheos. Commend him, yea I may commend him; I am persuaded we have the best priest in this country, we would be loath to forgo him for the learnedst of them all.

Zelotes. I pray ye let me hear what his virtues be for which ye do commend him so highly.

Atheos. He is as gentle a person as ever I see; a very good fellow, he will not stick when good fellows and honest men meet together to spend his groat at the alehouse; I cannot tell, they preach and preach, but he doth live as well as the best of them all. I am afraid when he is gone we shall never have the like again.

Zelotes. Be these the great virtues which ye do commend him for? He may have all these and yet be more meet for to keep swine, than to be a shepherd over the flock of Christ. Is he able to teach the people, and doth he instruct them in God's word?

Atheos. I know not what teaching ye would have, he doth read the service, as well as any of them all, and I think there is as good edifying in those prayers and homilies, as in any that the preacher can make; let us learn those first.

Zelotes. That is not all which is required in a minister, for a boy of ten years old can do all this. Doth he not teach them to know the will of God and reprove naughtiness among the people?

Atheos. Yes, that he doth, for if there be any that do not agree, he will seek for to make them friends; for he will get them to play a game or two at bowls or cards and to drink together at the alehouse. I think it a godly way to make charity. He is none of these busy controllers; for if he were, he could not be so well liked of some (and those not of the meanest) as he is.

Zelotes. Do ye call the preachers of God's word busy controllers? Do they go further than God's word doth lead them?

Atheos. We may call them busy controllers. I think we shall do nothing shortly. As poor a man as I am, I would not for forty shillings that we had one of them; there be more of my mind.

Zelotes. Some poor men perhaps.

Atheos. Nay, the best in the parish, who would not so well like of our curate, if he should meddle that way.

Zelotes. I perceive now what manner of man your curate is, and I see like master, like scholar.

Atheos. Why so, I pray thee?

Zelotes. Why so, I smell how unmeet he is, and also how ignorant you are. Let me question a little while with ye concerning that which ye have uttered.

Atheos. I trust I have uttered nothing but that which doth become an honest man.

Zelotes. Nay all your speech doth bewray that ye are a carnal man, for you have made a very fine description of a good curate. What mean ye when ye say he is a good fellow, and will not stick to spend his money among good fellows? Is it not because he is a pot[2] companion?

Atheos. Do ye mislike good fellowship? Is it not lawful for honest men to drink and be merry together?

Zelotes. I do not mislike true friendship, which is in the Lord, knit in true godliness, but I mislike this vice, which overfloweth everywhere, that drunkards meet together and sit quaffing and the minister which should reprove them to be one of the chief; when he should be at his study, to be upon the ale bench at cards or dice.

Atheos. I perceive you are one of those curious and precise fellows, which will allow no recreation. What would ye have men do? We shall do nothing shortly. You would have them sit moping always at their books. I like not that.

Zelotes. Nay my friend, I do not allow that recreation, which profane men call so, which is no recreation, but a torment to a godly mind, to see men drunken, to hear them swear and rail, to spend their goods and their time so lewdly, and he that should teach them, to be a ringleader; as there be as many as it seemeth, which are entered into the ministry for none other purpose, but to live an idle life, to have leisure to play at cards, or tables, and bowls all the week. And therefore they have no skill to teach, but like unsavory salt are not good enough even for the dunghill.[3]

Atheos. These things were used before you were born, and will be when you are gone. So long as men think no hurt when they play and be merry. . . .

Zelotes. But let us pull this old fellow out of his new coat, and ye shall see what a lean shrimp he is, and so feeble, that he cannot go on stilts. These things were used say you, before you were born, so were all other naughty vices. Are they now good because they be old? Because men committed them before I was born, and will do when I am dead?

Notes

1. Chelmsford (?).
2. Ale pot.
3. Matt. 5:13.

4.4. Anthony Gilby, from
A Pleasant Dialogue Between a Soldier of Berwick and an English Chaplain (1581)

Anthony Gilby (d. 1585) was a minister prominent in the English exile community at Strasbourg during the reign of Mary I. Having collaborated on the Geneva Bible (see 1.1), Gilby returned to England, where he received a clerical appointment in the gift of the earl of Huntington, a prominent Puritan patron. Although Gilby composed the two tracts that make up his *Pleasant Dialogue* during the early 1570s, they remained in manuscript until a decade later. He dedicates this book to a group of London ministers, including Miles Coverdale and Robert Crowley (see 3.3), who were leaders of the emergent Puritan movement. It opposed ecclesiastical policies condoned by Elizabeth I. At its inception, their attack focused on the retention of ecclesiastical vestments, but they did not advocate Presbyterianism or separatism.

Gilby frames arguments in the form of extended speeches by a Soldier of Berwick,[1] an adherent of the London ministers who believes in preaching by learned divines and worship based upon New Testament precedent. A chaplain named Bernard defends formalistic practices that Puritans attacked as idolatrous remnants of Roman Catholicism. They include fasting, ritualism, and kneeling during communion. The Soldier's colorful language typifies invective employed by Puritans to vilify opponents as adherents of the pope as Antichrist. His prophetic voice recalls the confidence of William Tyndale and the Edwardian gospellers that unlearned members of the laity could interpret the Bible without clerical intercession (see 4.1–2, 6.5.A).

SOURCE: *STC* 11888, B8ᵛ–C1ᵛ, C2ʳ⁻ᵛ, C3ᵛ, C4ʳ–C5ʳ,D4ᵛ–D5ʳ, E4ʳ–E5ᵛ, E6ʳ⁻ᵛ, E8ᵛ–F1ʳ. The Latin name Miles is translated as Soldier in this edition.

Soldier. If I knew what your proctor[2] were, whether he be a priest of the popish order, or of the English order, or a man of the lay and lewd sort, as the papists are wont to term them, I could show in him greater lewdness,[3] and more folly, than you or he can prove in them. But because I do not know his person, I will answer the cause of Christ's servants, and let him and you alone to your Lord and Master: giving you both warning, that you shall give an answer before the great Judge, for that which you do or say, against these his little ones, whom you call fools. But is the matter, answer me plain. Is it not meet that they, which should bring others to obedience of Christ, should first practice in themselves the same obedience; and that they should do nothing without the warrant and commandments of Christ; that so not only by doctrine, but also by their example of obedience, they may teach their auditors only to depend on Christ?

Bernard. No man will deny this thing to be meet and reasonable.

Soldier. This is the sum of the request and supplication of the godly ministers of London (as far as I can hear) that after so long preaching of Christ in London (almost these thirty years)[4] they may put in practice the doctrine of Christ and minister his holy sacraments in that simplicity, that Christ and his apostles hath left them, without the ceremonies and garments abused by the papists (the enemies of Christ's his Gospel) which cannot in any wise make for education in Christ: and that seeing their fathers and brethren, and they with their own mouths, have so long cried out against all popish ceremonies; as kneeling before the sacrament, whereby much idolatry hath been and is committed; as the ministration in the wafer cake, whereby the people hath been brought into vain imaginations, and have not felt the comfort, that our Savior Christ would have sensibly to be presented in the vital bread of many grains, and many crumbs, making one body, and being the vital food; as also against other monuments of superstition and idolatry, as the garments of the popish priesthood, and as the popish Mass. Now (I say) at the length, after so many years teaching, and so much blood of God's saints shed for the abolishing of Antichrist, they themselves should not be compelled to give any signification in their own persons and bodies, that they have any concord or agreement with that Roman Antichrist, but that they go before their flock, to practice in work that thing, which they have taught in words, for the banishing from their own bodies at the least, such things as they know not grounded on God's word, but man's mere inventions, superstitions, idolatrical, papistical, and therefore very hurtful to Christ's flock committed to their charge, because that such traditions are only cloaks to the transgression of God's commandments. . . .

Bernard. I cannot reason with scriptures (fellow Soldier) but me think that they are stark fools, that will lose such good livings, for a cope[5] of two shillings, or a surplice that shall cost them nothing. . . . It was never good world with us priests, since every soldier and every serving man could talk so much of the scripture, and these foolish ministers are the cause thereof, which would make all men as wise as themselves. . . .

Soldier. You think that the London ministers, and we that take their parts, are so foolish as yourselves are, that we should only stay upon our own wits and wills. Nay we settle our consciences herein, upon the express commandment of God, and the examples of the most godly in all ages, and especially upon our Master Christ and his apostles. And as poor and unlearned a soldier as I am, yet shalt thou know, that I have enough to say against them. And as the Christian soldiers under Julian that wicked Emperor[6] would not yield to any show of superstition, not so much as in the taking of their wages, to burn a little incense, nor to wear a garland upon their heads, because the Christian soldier is commanded to abstain from all show of evil, and to fight and thrive against the works of darkness, and to reprove them, and so striving as he ought to do, wait for the garland. So rather would I serve under Berwick walls, than do as thou doest and have counseled me to do, either in taking of a benefice by such unlawful means, or to enter into the Pope's livery, my sworn enemy, because I am an English man, and to me most detestable of all other earthly creatures, because I am a Christian man, for I know, and am fully persuaded by the word of God, that the Pope is the very Antichrist, the son of perdition: against whom, with hear and hand I do think myself most bound to fight. Therefore my heart ariseth in my body, when I see thee and thy fellows clothed like his chaplains, that burned the blessed Bible, and our faithful fathers, and dear brethren in our eyes.

You say that it is great wisdom for you to wear this popish gear, and call other men fools that will not do it. Then was there greater wisdom (say I) in the Pope and his priests, that have taught you thus to do. So may men say of a hundred points of popery, that you maintain, buying and selling licenses, dispensations, pluralities, absolutions, and other merchandise of that Roman Antichrist. And I do ask you all, as you will answer before God, what do you by these your deeds, but approve that Romish beast, and labor to heal his deadly wound, and so to make a mock of a reformation of religion. But God will not be mocked. There was never yet any reformation begun, and after repented, but it was terribly punished. . . .

Bernard. I pray thee, Soldier, hold thy peace, thou makest me tremble with thy terrible words, and by calling old things to remembrance. And I tell thee that though the papists were thieves, and robbers, and sodomites, and foul quellers,[7] and what thou wilt, yet are we none such, for we do all for policy.

Soldier. Nay all your doings are not policy. Have you no religion? Your church service is not policy, and in the Archbishop's advertisements, you have laws temporal, mere ecclesiastical. Your fasting days are not mere policy, for your Archbishop granteth dispensations, for forty shillings, that men may eat flesh in the days forbidden *Sana conscientia*,[8] as though he had authority over men's consciences, unless they have his license. And (unless hypocrisy may be counted policy) there be many things in your reformation, that will be found fond policy. For what is this, that both the physician of body and soul must be consulted withal, before you may eat flesh? Was not this once plain popery?. . . . What fellowship hath light with darkness? Righteousness with unrighteousness? What concord hath God with belief? Christ and Antichrist, the sincere gospeller, and the polluted papist? Wherefore separate yourselves from them, touch none of their filthy gear, so have you a promise, that God will receive you, and be father unto you.

There is no such warranty of your proctor's policies. And how can this be good policy, to compel the ministers of God against God's warranty, to be like the idolatrous priest, and to wear their garish gear? How can they be like that blasphemous priesthood, which fight with all force against that priesthood, and labor by all means to abolish it? Or how can this be a good policy, to bring God's plagues upon England to set godly men at variance, to stay and hinder the course of God's word, to cause the enemies, Harding[9] and his fellows to triumph, and to wait for an overthrow of both parts? But the maintenance of these superstitious and idolatrous monuments causeth all this, therefore there is in them no good policy, but a manifest hastening of God's great plagues, that have so long hanged over England.

Bernard. I can see no cause why God's plagues should come upon England for this, seeing the most part of popery is put down, and we live quietly.

Soldier. Is not this a great plague of God, thinkest thou, that the chiefest gospellers are together by the ears? One spoileth another of liberty and living, and the papists live quietly indeed, and laugh in their sleeves. Is not this a plague, that where there be so few preachers of God's Gospel, in so great a realm, the most painful laborers are put to silence by them, that should seek for laborers? And the Israelites destroying many of the Amorites and Canaanites, according to God's commandment, yet living quietly for a while with the rest, and leaving some relics and remnants of them, by their own negligence, fond affection, and foolish policy, were continually corrupted, polluted, and plagued with these wicked remnants, by God's just judgment. So is it to be feared here in England, that the abolishing of much popery according to God's will, and the reserving of some superstitious and idolatrous relics of the same by negligence, affection, or policy to have quietness, should cause this realm still to be polluted, corrupted, and plagued with papists and popery.

Bernard. If you could prove these things superstitious and idolatrous, you said somewhat to the purpose. But that I cannot see.

Soldier. Was there anything more idolatrous or superstitious about the idols, than the disguised garments, the cope and the surplice, wherein they were censed[10] and served? Were not they so misshapen and altered in form, from all other garments, that they were in fashion monstrous, to any other use, but about those idols cumbersome and superfluous? Wilt thou be blind within and without? Hast thou not seen them occupied about the idols an hundred times? Again, to prove them superstitious or idolatrous, small disputation serveth to them that will grant popery to be superstition and idolatry. For wherein played the papists all their popish pageants, but in this garish gear? And David counteth himself polluted, with the naming of the idols. Therefore would he never command any of his subjects to wear any of their garments.

The serpent was accursed, because it was an instrument of Satan to tempt man to sin, and so is this garish gear, that hath tempted man to superstition and idolatry. Not, but that the serpent, and the Devil also, the idol, and the idolite,[11] the cope or surplice, and the matters whereof they are made, are good by creation but in that all these are altered from their creation, to be the instruments of sin, they have gotten strange names and forms for the idols (and so the Devil to be served therein) so are they superstitious, idolatrous and abominable. And for their copes and tippets, were they not for that idolatrous and blasphemous priesthood, and them that take profit by the same, as they are now appointed for you English chaplains?

Bernard. Nay man, thou wottest not what thou sayeth, for many young scholars did wear them in the universities, that were no priests at all. . . .

Soldier. For this cause it is said, that Bonner was much aggrieved at those men, which were not of his religion, and yet would wear these garments and apparel. For said he, they are ornaments belonging only to our religion. And therefore after his scoffing manner, he counted them the honester men, that would not wear them, nor challenge that to themselves which was none of theirs. If any did forsake the pope, were he bishop or archbishop, they plucked these rags from him with all violence, as they did from Cranmer, Ridley, and Hooper.[12] So that it is no good policy for this realm of England that are enemies to the Pope, and the Pope unto it, to leave so many soldiers in their enemies liveries. Neither is it good policy of the gospellers that wear this gear, to continue in that livery, forth of the which of necessity, they must be turned, by their own band, if any Queen Mary (which GOD forbid) reign over us. . . .

Bernard. What, you are too hot and too hasty, you think that Rome may be builded upon one day. There be many yet infirm and weak in England, with whom the governors must bear for a season, until they be stronger, and that is very good policy, seeing they cannot reform all things at once. And because such things have been creeping in by little and little, and have now been long shed, they cannot be taken away, but by a long continuance.

Soldier. Now I do ask thee in God's name, if thou do think that they go about to build Rome again, or to destroy it? A thing is much sooner destroyed then builded. Or canst thou tell me this, how long they will be weak? Or when all will be strong? It is almost forty years,[13] since the Pope and popery hath been so long written and spoken against, and about thirty years, that his name (as a thing most odious) was commanded by law of Parliament, to be erased out of all books and places in England, and the Testament of Jesus Christ hath been so long restored and published amongst us. Now if men be not yet confirmed in the knowledge of Christ, against that Roman Antichrist, the Pope and his blasphemous priesthood, when will they be confirmed? When they are fifty or three score years old peradventure, and have been taught so many years? But you know that the most part die before forty, and who shall answer for them? Either[14] how knowest thou that God's word shall continue in England ten or twenty years longer, until men be no more weak? Either will you tarry till men learn it in another world? Either is God so behind to England, that he will not forsake England, as he hath done his own people, and many other nations for the greatest of their sins?

Notes

1. Fortified town on England's border with Scotland.

2. Deputy.

3. Ignorance.

4. Since the reign of Edward VI.

5. Cloaklike vestment.

6. Julian the Apostate, Roman emperor (361–63) who renounced Christianity and attempted to destroy it.

7. Destroyers.

8. "Sound conscience" (Lat.).

9. Thomas Harding (1516–72), recusant exile who attacked the Elizabethan settlement of religion

10. Perfumed with incense.

11. Idolater.

12. John Hooper (d. 1555), proto-Puritan cleric who was burned at the stake. For Cranmer and Ridley, see 6.5.B and 9.1.

13. Since the schism from the Church of Rome in 1534.

14. Or.

4.5. The Marprelate Controversy, from *Oh Read Over Doctor John Bridges, For It Is a Worthy Work* (1588)

The first of seven satires published under the pseudonym Martin Marprelate, Gentleman, *Oh Read Over John Bridges, For It Is a Worthy Work* resorts to a verbal flood of ribald mockery, puns and wordplay, invective, ironic epithets, alliteration, and rhyming prose in order to refute *A Defense of the Government Established in the Church of England* (1587), in which John Bridges, Dean of Salisbury Cathedral, defends the authority of John Whitgift, Archbishop of Canterbury, and other formalistic bishops (notably John Aylmer, Bishop of London) against Thomas Cartwright's presbyterian manifestos in favor of the autonomy of individual congregations. The printer, Robert Waldegrave, concealed his identity and the location of his secret printing press at East Molesey with this facetious imprint: "Printed oversea, in Europe, within two furlongs of a bouncing priest."

Job Throckmorton, a radical preacher, appears to have written this tract and its successors. The Marprelate Tracts exemplify the breakdown of both the Edwardine alliance between evangelical bishops and zealous Protestant laypersons, who lodged heated allegations concerning the ignorance and negligence of Catholic clerics (see 4.1–2), and the uneasy truce between supporters of episcopacy and nonseparatist Puritans that existed under Edmund Grindal (d. 1583), who preceded Whitgift as incumbent of the see of Canterbury.

SOURCE: *STC* 17453, 1–4.

EDITION: W. Pierce, ed., *The Marprelate Tracts* (London: J. Clark, 1911).

REFERENCE: Leland Carlson, *Martin Marprelate, Gentleman: Master Job Throckmorton Laid Open in His Colors* (San Marino, Calif.: Huntington Library, 1981).

Martin Marprelate, Gentleman, Primate and Metropolitan of All the Martins in England

To the right puissant and terrible priests, my clergy masters of the Convocation-house, whether Fickers-General, worshipful Paltripolitans,[1] or any other of the Holy League of Subscription: this work I recommend unto them with all my heart, with a desire to see them all so provided for one day, as I would wish, which I promise them shall not be at all to their hurt.

Right poisoned, persecuting, and terrible priests: the theme of mine epistle unto your venerable masterdoms is of two parts (and the *Epitome* of our Brother Bridges' book shall come out speedily). First, most pitifully complaining, Martin Marprelate, etc. Secondly, may it please your good worships, etc.[2]

Most pitifully complaining therefore, you are to understand that Dean Bridges hath written in your defense, a most senseless book, and I cannot very often at one breath come to a full point, when I read the same.

Again, may it please you to give me leave to play the dunce[3] for the nonce, as well as he. Otherwise dealing with Master Doctor's book, I cannot keep *decorum personae*. And, may it please you, if I be too absurd in any place (either in this epistle, or that epitome), to ride to Sarum,[4] and thank his Deanship for it. Because, I could not deal with his book commendably according to order, unless I should be sometimes tediously dunstical and absurd. For I have heard some clergymen say that Master Bridges was a very patch[5] and a dunce when he was in Cambridge. And some say, saving your reverence that are bishops, that he is as very a knave and enemy unto the sincerity of religion, as any popish prelate in Rome. But the patch can do the cause of sincerity no hurt. Nay, he hath in this book wonderfully graced the same by writing against it. For I have heard some say that whosoever will read his book shall as evidently see the goodness of the cause of reformation, and the poor, poor, poor nakedness of your government, as almost in reading all Master Cartwright's works. This was a very great oversight in his Grace of Canterbury to suffer such a book to come out. For besides that an archbishop is very weakly defended by Master Dean, he hath also by this means provoked many to write against his gracious fatherhood, who perhaps never meant to take pen in hand. And Brother Bridges, mark what Martin tells you. You will shortly, I hope, have twenty fists about your ears more than your own. Take heed of writing against Puritans while you live. Yet they say that his Grace would not have the book to be published; and, if you mark, you shall not find "seen and allowed"[6] in the title of his book.

We'll fare, old Mother Experience, yet. The burnt child dreads the fire. His Grace will carry to his grave, I warrant you, the blows which Master Cartwright gave him in this cause, and therefore no marvel though he was loath to have any other so banged as he himself was to his woe. Others say that John Canterbury[7] oversaw every proof. If he did, then he oversaw many a foul solecism, many a senseless period,[8] and far more slanders. "Slanders, my friend?" I think so. For what will you say if our Brother Bridges, and our Cousin Cosins,[9] with many others have had their grace of the bishop *ad practicandum*[10] in Flanders? How could their government stand, unless they should slander their brethren, and make Her Majesty believe that the church government prescribed in the Word would overthrow her regiment, if it were received into our church; and that seekers of reformation are a sort of malcontents, and enemies unto the state.

Item: May it please you worthy worships to receive this courteously to favor at my hand, without choler or laughing? For my Lord of Winchester is very choleric and peevish. So are his betters at Lambeth.[11] And Doctor Cosins hath a very good grace in jesting, and I would he had a little more grace, and a handful or two more of learning against he answer the abstract next. . . . And I am none of the malicious sectaries whereof John of London[12] spake the last Lent, 1588, in his letters written to the Archdeacon of Essex to forbid public fasts. Ha, ha, Doctor Copcot, are ye there? Why do not you answer the confutation of your sermon at Paul's Cross? It is a shame for your grace, John of Canterbury, that Cartwright's books have been now a dozen years almost unanswered. You first provoked him to write, and you first have received the foil. If you can answer those books, who do you suffer the Puritans to insult and rejoice at your silence? If you cannot, why are you an Archbishop? He hath proved the calling to be unlawful and antichristian. You dare not stand to the defense of it.

Now, most pitifully complaineth Master Marprelate: desireth you either to answer what hath been written against the gracelessness of your archbishopric, or to give over the same, and to be a means that no bishop in the land be a lord any more? I hope one day Her Majesty will either see that the lord bishops prove their calling lawful by the Word, or, as John of London prophesied, saying "Come down, you bishops from your thousands, and content you with your hundreds; let your diet be priestlike and not princelike, etc." Quoth John Aylmer in the *Harbor of Faithful Subjects*.[13] But, I pray you, Brother John, dissolve this one question to your Brother Martin: if this prophecy of yours come to pass in your days, who shall be Bishop of London? And will you not swear, as commonly you do, like a lewd swag, and say, "By my faith, by my faith, my masters, this gear goeth hard with us." Now may it please your grace, with the rest of your worships, to procure that the Puritans may one day have a free disputation with you about the controversies of the church, and if you be not set at a flat *non plus*[14] and quite overthrown, I'll be a lord bishop myself. Look to yourselves. I think you have not long to reign. Amen.

And take heed, brethren, of your reverend and learned brother, Martin Marprelate. For he meaneth in these reasons following, I can tell you, to prove that you ought not to be maintained by the authority of the magistrate in any Christian commonwealth. Martin is a shrewd fellow, and reasoneth thus. Those that are petty popes and petty Antichrists ought not be maintained in any Christian commonwealth. But every lord bishop in England as, for illsample,[15] John of Canterbury, John of London, John Exeter, John Rochester, Thomas of Winchester, the Bishops of Lincoln, of Worcester, of Peterborough, and to be brief, all the bishops in England, Wales, and Ireland, are petty popes and petty Antichrists. Therefore no lord bishop (now, I pray thee good Martin, speak out, if ever thou didst speak out, that Her Majesty and the Council may hear thee) is to be tolerated in any Christian commonwealth. And therefore, neither John of Canterbury, John of London, etc., are to be tolerated in any Christian commonwealth. What say you now, Brother Bridges? Is it good, writing against Puritans? Can you deny any part of your learned Brother Martin's syllogism? "We deny your minor,[16] Master Marprelate," say the bishops and their associates. Yea, my learned Masters, are you good at that? What do you brethren? Say me that again? Do you deny my minor? And that be all you can say to deny lord bishops to be petty popes, turn me loose to the priests in that point. For I am old Suresby[17] at the proof of such matters. I'll presently mar the fashion of their Lordships.

Notes

1. Inversion of "metropolitans," a title for bishops.
2. Common phrases used to begin formal petitions.
3. By consistently employing the spelling "duns" instead of "dunce," the original text of this pamphlet calls attention to the derivation of this word from the name of Duns Scotus, the Scholastic philosopher.
4. Salisbury.
5. Fool.
6. Permission to publish.
7. Whitgift.
8. Sentence.
9. Dr. Richard Cosin, Dean of Arches and Master in Chancery.
10. "For the sake of practicing" (mock Latin).
11. London palace of the Archbishop of Canterbury.
12. John Aylmer, Bishop of London.
13. A defense of the capacity of Elizabeth I to govern as a woman.
14. "No more" (Lat.).
15. Wordplay on "example."
16. Minor premise.
17. One who may be relied upon.

5

THEATRICAL
CONTROVERSY

5.1. Lewis Wager, Prologue to *The Life and Repentance of Mary Magdalene* (c. 1550)

Early Protestants were ambivalent about using drama to advance religious reform. In contrast to the pre-Reformation church, which condoned traditional festivity in addition to edifying entertainment, many Protestants associated drama with the theatricality of the Mass and Roman-rite ritual. Nonetheless, clerics such as John Bale, Lewis Wager, and Richard Weaver adapted techniques and conventions of mystery plays and moral interludes for propagandistic purposes. In dramatizing backsliding and religious conversion among professed Protestants, early plays such as *The Three Laws* and *Lusty Juventus* (see 3.1–2) contradict later belief that drama is ungodly.

Composed during the reign of Edward VI, *The Life and Repentance of Mary Magdalene* remained in manuscript until 1566. Lewis Wager (fl. 1547–53), a Franciscan friar who became a Protestant preacher, designed it for production by an itinerant troupe made up of four men. In the hybrid manner of John Bale's Protestant mystery plays, this interlude intermingles biblical figures with personified Virtues (e.g., Knowledge of Sin, Faith, and Repentance) and Vices (e.g., Pride of Life, Cupidity, and Carnal Concupiscence). In response to an anonymous attack on theatrical entertainment, the prologue included in the present anthology echoes Bucer's *Concerning the Kingdom of Christ* by insisting that "true" drama excels at bringing to life edifying examples for the purpose of didactic instruction in religion and politics.

SOURCE: *STC* 24932, A2ʳ–A3ʳ.

REFERENCE: Collinson 1988; King 1982; White.

Prologue

There is no state, however modest and happy,
    That is able to escape the bite of malice.[1]
No state of man, be it never so modest,
    Never so unrebukeable and blameless,
No person, be he never so good and honest,   5
    Can escape at any season now harmless,
    But the wicked teeth of such as be shameless,
        Are ready most maliciously him for to bite,
        Like as Valerius in his fourth book doth write.

We and other persons have exercised   10
    This comely and good faculty[2] a long season,
Which of some have been spitefully despised,
    Wherefore I think they can allege no reason,

Where affect ruleth, there good judgement is geason.[3]
   They never learned the verse of Horace doubtless,   15
   Nec tua laudabis studia, aut aliena reprehendes,[4]

Thou shalt neither praise thine own industry,
   Nor yet the labor of other men reprehend,
The one proceedeth of a proud arrogancy,
   And the other from envy, which doth discommend,   20
   All things that virtuous persons do intend.
      For evil will never said well, they do say,
      And worse tongues were never heard before this day.

I marvel why they should detract our faculty:
   We have ridden and gone many sundry ways,   25
Yea, we have used this feat at the university,
   Yet neither wise nor learned would it dispraise:
   But it hath been perceived ever before our days,
      That fools love nothing worse than fools to be called:
      A horse will kick if you touch where he is galled.   30

Doth not our faculty learnedly extol virtue?
   Doth it not teach, God to be praised above all things?
What faculty doth vice more earnestly subdue?
   Doth it not teach true obedience to the king?
   What godly sentences to the mind doth it bring?   35
      I say, there was never [a] thing invented
      More worth, for man's solace to be frequented.

Hypocrites that would not have their faults revealed
   Imagine slander our faculty to let,
Fain would they have their wickedness still concealed   40
   Therefore maliciously against us they be set,
   O (say they) much money they do get.
      Truly I say, whether you give halfpence or pence,
      Your gain shall be double, before you depart hence.

Is wisdom no more worth than a penny trow you?   45
   Scripture calleth the price thereof incomparable.
Here may you learn godly sapience now,
   Which to body and soul shall be profitable.

To no person truly we covet to be chargeable,
    For we shall think to have sufficient recompense,   50
    If ye take in good worth our simple diligence.

In this matter which we are about to recite,
    The ignorant may learn what is true belief,
Whereof the Apostles of Christ do largely write,
    Whose instructions here to you we will give,   55
    Here an example of penance the heart to grieve,
        May be learned, a love which from faith doth spring,
        Authority of scripture for the same we will bring.

Of the Gospel, we shall rehearse a fruitful story,
    Written in the seven[5] of Luke with words plain   60
The story of a woman that was right sorry
    For that she had spent her life in sin vile and vain,
    By Christ's preaching she was converted again,
        To be truly penitent by her fruits she declared,
        And to show herself a sinner she never spared.   65

Her name was called Mary of Magdalene,
    So named of the title of her possession,
Out of her Christ rejected seven spirits unclean,
    As Mark and Luke make open profession.
Doctors of high learning, wit, and discretion,   70
        Of her diverse and many sentences do write,
        Which in this matter we intend now to recite.

Of the place aforesaid, with the circumstance,
    Only in this matter (God willing) we will treat.
Where we will show that great was her repentance,   75
    And her love towards Christ was also as great.
    Her sin did not her conscience so grievously fret,
        But that faith erected her heart again to believe,
        That God for Christ's sake would all her sins forgive.

We desire no man in this point to be offended,   80
    In that virtues with vice we shall here introduce,
For in men and women they have depended:
    And therefore figuratively to speak, it is the use.

I trust that all wise men will accept our excuse.
Of the preface for this season here I make an end,   85
In godly mirth to spend the time we do intend.

Notes

1. Valerius Maximus, *Factorum ac dictorum memorabilium* (IV.vii).
2. Dramatic performance.
3. Uncommon.
4. Translated in the following lines.
5. Seventh chapter.

5.2. Martin Bucer, from
Concerning the Kingdom of Christ (1550)

Martin Bucer (1491–1551), the irenic German reformer, attempted to mediate among different theological positions including those of Martin Luther and Ulrich Zwingli concerning the presence of Christ in the Lord's Supper. In 1549 he accepted Thomas Cranmer's invitation to migrate to England, where he received appointment as Regius Professor of Divinity at Cambridge University. In *De regno Christi* (*Concerning the Kingdom of Christ*), a manuscript dedicated to Edward VI, he advocates the performance of comedies and tragedies based upon scriptural subjects for the purpose of instructing audiences concerning the Bible. During the heresy prosecutions under Mary I, the headsman burned Bucer's exhumed remains along with his books.

SOURCE: Reproduced from Wilhelm Pauck, ed., *Melanchthon and Bucer*, Library of Christian Classics 19 (Philadelphia: Westminster Press, 1969), pp. 349–53. Used by permission of Westminster John Knox Press.

Youth could also perform comedies and tragedies, and by such means a useful form of entertainment, honorable and contributing toward an increase of piety, may be staged for the people; but it will be necessary that devout and wise men experienced in the kingdom of Christ compose these comedies and tragedies, in which there may be presented on the stage the plans, actions, and events of mankind, whether common and ordinary as it occurs in comedies or unique and eliciting admiration as it is characteristic of tragedies. All this will contribute toward a correction of morals and a pious orientation to life.

If a comedy is presented, take, for example, the quarrel of the shepherds of Abraham and Lot and their separation from each other.[1] For although Abraham and Lot are heroic figures appropriate to tragedy, yet the quarrels that arose among their shepherds because they had too many sheep were common and ordinary. It was also common and ordinary that these holy householders were somewhat disturbed with each other by the quarrels of their servants, so much so that Abraham rightly decided that they should separate from one another. . . .

A not dissimilar plot could be derived also from the story of Jacob, in the part in which it is described that in fear of his brother, leaving his parents, he went to his uncle Laban and there was enriched with two wives, children, and great wealth, by the goodness of God, because of the faithful service he performed for his uncle. Likewise, how on his return he was restored to the favor of his brother.[2] There is also a tragic aspect to this story in the apparition of the Lord on the way and the struggle with the angel. But these consolations of God are not foreign to any real Christians, although they are not set forth to all in visions and signs of this sort as they were to Jacob. For it is clearly a mark of all Christians that they live in God and before God, and have the Father and the Son abiding in them and angels ministering to them.

Although the scriptures contain very many stories from which holy comedies befitting Christians can be portrayed, apt and pious poets can nevertheless produce many such things from other stories and from occurrences in daily life.

The scriptures everywhere offer an abundant supply of material for tragedies, in almost all the stories of the holy patriarchs, kings, prophets, and apostles, from the time of Adam, the first parent of mankind. For these stories are filled with divine and heroic personages, emotions, customs, actions, and also events, which turned out contrary to what was expected, which Aristotle calls a reversal. Since all such things have so wonderful a power of confirming faith in God and enkindling a desire and love for God and likewise an admiration of piety and righteousness, and of engendering and increasing the horror of impiety and all perversity, how much more does it befit Christians to derive their poems from these things, in which they can represent the great and illustrious plans, efforts, characters, emotions, and events of mankind, rather than from the godless fables and stories of the pagans.

It must be observed, however, that when in both kinds of poetic material, comic and tragic, the activities and sins of men are described and actively presented to be seen with the eyes, it should be done in such a way that although the crimes of reprobate men are related, yet a certain terror of divine judgment and horror of sin should appear in these things, and a shameless daring and an exultant delight in crimes should not be expressed. It is better here to take something away from poetic fitness rather than from the concern for edifying the piety of the spectators, which demands that in every representation of sin there be felt the condemnation of one's conscience and the horrible fear of God's judgment.

But when pious and good actions are shown, they should express as clearly as possible a happy, secure, and confident sense of the divine mercy, but moderate and diffident as regards the self, and a joyful trust in God and his promises, with holy and spiritual pleasure in doing good. This is the way by which one can present most skillfully the saints' character, way of life, and emotion for the establishment of all piety and virtue among the people.

In order that the people of Christ may receive this enjoyment from holy comedies and tragedies, men must be put in charge also of this matter who have a singular understanding of poetry as well as a known and constant zeal from the Kingdom of Christ so that no comedy or tragedy is enacted which these persons have not seen and decreed fit for performance. These will also take care that nothing shallow, or histrionic is admitted in the acting, but that everything is shown by means of a holy and grave, though agreeable action, for the saints alone, in which there are represented not so much the actualities and activities of men and their feelings and troubles, but rather their morals and character; these should be presented in such a way that what has been piously planned and rightly done arouses the spectators to an eager imitation, but what has been wrongly designed and done, strengthens them in their detestation of it and stimulates them to a vigilant avoidance of it.

When these precautions are observed, much material for the diversion of youth can certainly be presented which is indeed useful for nourishing and promoting virtue, especially when a desire and an interest have been aroused for this sort of comedies and tragedies, both in the vernacular language and in Latin and Greek. There are now available some of these comedies and tragedies with which one cannot be displeased. Although in the comedies of our time the scholars miss that acumen and wit and pleasantness of speech which people admire in Aristophanes, Terence, and the tales of Plautus, and in the tragedies the gravity, cleverness, and elegance of dialogue of Sophocles, Euripides, and Seneca, yet those who want to know the Kingdom of Christ and who desire to learn the wisdom of living unto God do not miss, in this poetry of our people, heavy doctrine, emotions, behavior, speech, and adventures worthy of the sons of God. It is desirable, however, that those to whom God has given more of a talent for this sort of thing will prefer to use it for his glory rather than to retard the pious enthusiasms of others by their untimely criticisms, seeing that it is more satisfactory to stage comedies and tragedies in which, even if they lack poetic art, the knowledge of eternal life is excellently exhibited, rather than those in which for the sake of some contribution to the cultivation of genius and language, spirit and behavior are dirtied by filthy and scurrilous imitation.

Notes

1. Gen. 13:5–12
2. Gen. 28:10–33:20

5.3. Philip Stubbes, from
The Anatomy of Abuses (1583)

Philip Stubbes (c. 1555–c. 1610) lacks the confidence concerning the usefulness of drama for purposes of moral edification expressed by members of an earlier generation, who included John Bale, Martin Bucer, and Lewis Wager. Published during the reign of Elizabeth I, *The Anatomy of Abuses* (1583) is cast in the form of a dialogue between Spudeus ("zealous one") and Philoponus ("lover of toil"), in which the latter condemns all forms of theater including religious drama because of his conviction that play-going supplants attendance at sermons and encourages adherence to Roman Catholicism, idleness, whoredom, and sodomy. (Nevertheless, a preface unique to the first edition acknowledges the validity of moralistic plays.) Stubbes's prose is notable for colorful catalogs of vices that are filled with vivid doublets and alliterative language.
SOURCE: *STC* 23376, L5ʳ⁻ᵛ, L7ʳ–M1ᵛ.

Of Stage-Plays and Interludes, With Their Wickedness

Philoponus. All stage-plays, interludes, and comedies are either of divine or profane matter. If they be of divine matter, then are they most intolerable, or rather sacrilegious, for that the blessed Word of God, is to be handled, reverently, gravely, and sagely, with veneration to the glorious majesty of God, which shineth therein, and not scoffingly, floutingly, gibingly, as it is upon stages in plays and interludes, without any reverence, worship, or veneration to the same. The Word of our salvation, the price of Christ his blood, and the merits of his Passion were not given to be derided, and jested at as they be in these filthy plays and interludes on stages and scaffolds, or to be mixed and interlaced with bawdry, wanton shows and uncomely gestures as is used (every man knoweth) in these plays and interludes. . . . They are no fit exercises for a Christian man to follow. But if there were no evil in them save this, namely, that the arguments of tragedies are anger, wrath, immunity, cruelty, injury, incest, murder, and suchlike. The persons or actors are gods, goddesses, furies, fiends, hags, kings, queens, or potentates. Of comedies, the matter and ground is love, bawdry, cozening, flattery, whoredom, adultery. The persons or agents whores, queens, bawds, scullions, knaves, courtesans, lecherous old men, amorous young men, with suchlike of infinite variety. If I say there were nothing else but this, it were sufficient to withdraw a good Christian from the using of them. For so often as they go to those houses where players frequent, they go to Venus's palace[1] and Satan's synagogue[2] to worship devils and betray Christ Jesus.

Spudeus. But notwithstanding, I have heard some hold opinion that they be as good as sermons, and that many a good example may be learned out of them.

Philoponus. Oh blasphemy intolerable. Are filthy plays and bawdy interludes comparable to the Word of God, the food of life and life itself? It is all one, as if they had said, bawdry, heathenry, paganry, scurrility, and devilry itself is equal with the Word of God. Or that the Devil is equipolent[3] with the Lord.

The Lord our God hath ordained his blessed Word, and made it the ordinary means of our salvation; the Devil hath inferred the other as the ordinary means of our destruction, and will they yet compare the one with the other? If he be accursed that calleth light darkness and darkness light, truth falsehood and falsehood truth, sweet sour and sour sweet, then *a fortiori*[4] is he accursed that saith that plays and interludes be equivalent with sermons. Besides this, there is no mischief which these plays maintain not. For do they not nourish idleness? And *odia dant vita*, idleness is the mother of vice. Do they not draw the people from hearing the Word of God, from godly lectures and sermons? For you shall have them flock thither thick and threefold, when the church of God shall be bare and empty. And those that will never come at sermons will flow thither apace. The reason is for that the number of Christ his elect is but few, and the number of the reprobate is many, the way that leadeth to life is narrow, and few tread the path; the way that leadeth to death is broad, and many find it.[5] This showeth they are not of God, who refuse to hear his Word (for he that is of God heareth God his Word saith our savior Christ) but of the Devil, whose exercises they go to visit. Do they not maintain bawdry, infinite foolery, and renew the remembrance of heathen idolatry? Do they not induce whoredom and uncleanness? Nay, are they not rather plain devourers of maidenly virginity and chastity? For proof whereof, but mark the flocking and running to theaters and curtains,[6] daily and hourly, night and day, time and tide to see plays and interludes, where such wanton gestures, such bawdy speeches, such laughing and fleering,[7] such kissing and bussing, such clipping and culling, such winking and glancing of wanton eyes, and the like is used, as is wonderful to behold. Then these goodly pageants being done, every mate sorts to his mate, every one brings another homeward of their way very friendly, and in their secret conclaves (covertly) they play the sodomites, or worse. And these be the fruits of plays and interludes, for the most part. And whereas, you say, there are good examples to be learned in them.

Truly, so there are. If you will learn falsehood, if you will learn cozening, if you learn to deceive. If you will learn to play the hypocrite, to cog, lie, and falsify. If you will learn to jest, laugh, and fleer, to grin, nod, and mow. If you will learn to play the vice, to swear, tear, and blaspheme both heaven and earth. If you will learn to become a bawd, unclean, and to devirginate maids, to deflower honest wives. If you will learn to murder, slay, kill, pick, steal, rob, and rove. If you will learn to rebel against princes, to commit treasons, to consume treasures, to practice idleness, to sing and talk of bawdy love and venery. If you will learn to deride, scoff, mock, and flout, to flatter and smooth. If you will learn to play the whoremaster, the glutton, drunkard, or incestuous person. If you will learn to become proud, haughty, and arrogant. And finally, if you will learn to contemn God and all his laws, to care neither for heaven nor hell, and to commit all kind of sin and mischief, you need to go to no other school, for all these good examples, may you see painted before your eyes in interludes and plays. Wherefore, that man who giveth money for the maintenance of them, must needs incur the damage of praemunire,[8] that is, eternal damnation except they repent. For the Apostle[9] biddeth us beware, lest we communicate with other men's sins, and this their doing is not only to communicate with other men's sins and maintain evil to the destruction of themselves and many others, but also a maintaining of a great sort of idle lubbers and buzzing dronets[10] to suck up and devour the good honey, whereupon the poor bees should live.

Therefore, I beseech all players and founders of plays and interludes, in the bowels of Jesus Christ, as they tender the salvation of their souls, and others, to leave of that cursed kind of life and give themselves to such honest exercises and godly ministries, as God hath commanded them in his Word to get their livings withal. For who will call him a wise man that playeth the part of a fool and a vice? Who can call him a Christian, who playeth the part of a devil, the sworn enemy of Christ? Who can call him a just man that playeth the part of a dissembling hypocrite? And to be brief, who can call him a straight dealing man, who playeth a cozener's trick? And so of all the rest. Away therefore with this so infamous an art, for go they never so brave, yet are they counted and taken but for beggars. And is it not true? Live they not upon begging of every one that comes? Are they not taken by the laws of the realm for rogues and vagabonds? I speak of such as travel the countries with plays and interludes, making an occupation of it, and ought to be punished if they had their deserts. But hoping that they will be warned now at the last, I will say no more of them, beseeching them to consider what a fearful thing it is to fall into the hands of God and to provoke his wrath and heavy displeasure against themselves and others, which the Lord of his mercy turn from us.

Notes

1. Brothel.
2. Catholic church (jargon).
3. Equally powerful.
4. All the more.
5. Matt. 7:13–14.
6. Playhouses.
7. Mock.
8. Obeying a foreign authority.
9. Saint Paul.
10. Bees.

6

BIOGRAPHY,
AUTOBIOGRAPHY,
AND MARTYROLOGY

6.1. Anne Askew, from
The Latter Examination (1546, pub. 1547)

Government officials condemned Anne Askew (1521–46) to be burned alive as a heretic because of her denial of Catholic beliefs and practices including transubstantiation, the ritual of the Mass, and auricular confession (see Figure 8). She arrived at her views through reading the Bible in vernacular translation. Officials including William Paget, secretary of state under both Henry VIII and Edward VI, justified the use of torture in an unsuccessful effort to force her to recant.

Her blunt language and unruly talkativeness violated the expectation that women would remain silent and obey patriarchal authority. She employed rhetorical questions, smiles, and gestures to puzzle her interrogators. She even claimed that after racking by Richard Rich and Thomas Wriothesley, the lord chancellor, rendered her incapable of standing, she sat on the floor in order to debate theology and law. Her enemies included the bishops of Winchester and London, Stephen Gardiner and Edmund Bonner. She refused to acknowledge financial support from aristocratic women associated with Queen Catherine Parr, such as the Duchess of Suffolk and Anne Stanhope, Lady Hertford and wife to Edward Seymour, leader of the Protector faction at court (see 6.5.D, 7.5.B–C).

Like other condemned heretics, Askew smuggled manuscript accounts of interrogation and condemnation out of prison. It seems likely that German merchants transported her moving personal narrative to continental Europe, where it came into the hands of John Bale. Driven into exile by the persecution of Protestant partisans late in the reign of Henry VIII, Bale remained actively engaged in the publication of Protestant propaganda in the English language and edited the two parts of Askew's *Examinations*, to which he added a lengthy commentary here omitted. Derik van der Straten printed the *Examinations* in 1547. Although this printer resided in Wesel in the duchy of Cleves, a German principality on the Rhine River, false information concealed the origin of copies smuggled into England. Relaxation of censorship under Edward VI enabled Askew's *Examinations* to circulate in England without restraint. John Foxe assimilated this text into the *Book of Martyrs*.

SOURCE: *STC 850*, fol. 11ʳ–29ʳ, 31ʳ–34ʳ, 36ᵛ–49ʳ, 54ʳ–64ʳ.

EDITIONS: Askew; Foxe, *Acts and Monuments*.

REFERENCES: Beilin; Brigden; King 1982.

I do perceive (dear friend in the Lord) that thou art not yet persuaded thoroughly in the truth concerning the Lord's Supper, because Christ said unto his Apostles, "Take, eat; this is my body, which is given for you." In giving forth the bread as an outward sign or token to be received at the mouth, he minded them in a perfect belief to receive that body of his which should die for the people, or to think the death thereof the only health and salvation of their souls. The bread and the wine were left us for a sacramental

Figure 8. *The Execution of Anne Askew*. From Foxe's *Book of Martyrs* (1563), p. 678, woodcut. By permission of The Ohio State University Libraries. This woodcut portrays Askew prior to being burned alive in the company of several men on 16 July 1546. Nicholas Shaxton, who saved his life by recanting on the same day, delivers an unsuccessful appeal from a portable pulpit for her to recant as well. Because torture on the rack had disjointed her, a chain holds her upright at the stake. Members of the Privy Council overlook the scene from a dais erected before a building that walls in the churchyard around Saint Bartholomew the Great (see Figure 7). John Day, the printer, commissioned this woodcut as an illustration for Robert Crowley's *Confutation of the Twelve Articles, Whereunto Nicholas Shaxton Subscribed* (1548), which he published in partnership with William Seres, a bookseller. Day retained ownership, or knew of the location, of the woodblock when he went underground during the reign of Mary I, because he reused it on page 678 of Foxe's *Book of Martyrs* (1563) and in later editions.

communion or a mutual participation of the inestimable benefits of his most precious death and bloodshedding. And that we should in the end thereof be thankful together for that most necessary grace of our redemption. For in the closing up thereof, he said thus, "This do ye in remembrance of me. Yea, so oft as ye shall eat it or drink it," Luke 22 and 1 Corinthians 2. Else should we have been forgetful of that we ought to have in daily remembrance, and also been altogether unthankful for it.

Therefore it is meet that in prayers we call unto God to graft in our foreheads the true meaning of the Holy Ghost concerning this communion. For Saint Paul doth say that the letter slayeth. The spirit is it only that giveth life, 2 Corinthians 3. Mark well the sixth chapter of John, where all is applied unto faith. Note also the fourth chapter of Saint Paul's First Epistle to the Corinthians, and in the end thereof ye shall find plainly that the things which are seen are temporal, but they that are not seen are everlasting. Yea, look in the third chapter to the Hebrews and ye shall find that Christ, as a son and no servant, ruleth over his house (whose house are we, and not the dead temple) if we hold fast the confidence and rejoicing of that hope to the end. Wherefore, as saith the Holy Ghost, "Today if you shall hear his voice, harden not your hearts," etc., Psalm 94.

The Sum of My Examination Afore the King's Council at Greenwich

Your request as concerning my prison fellows, I am not able to satisfy because I heard not their examinations. But the effect of mine was this: I, being before the Council, was asked of Master Kyme. I answered that my Lord Chancellor knew already my mind in that matter. They with that answer were not contented but said it was the king's pleasure that I should open the matter to them. I answered then plainly that I would not so do. But if it were the king's pleasure to hear me, I would show him the truth. Then they said it was not meet for the king with me to be troubled. I answered that Solomon was reckoned the wisest king that ever lived, yet misliked not he to hear two poor common women,[1] much more His Grace a simple woman and his faithful subject. So, in conclusion, I made them none other answer in that matter.

Then my lord chancellor asked me of my opinion in the sacrament. My answer was this, "I believe that so oft as I in a Christian congregation do receive the bread in remembrance of Christ's death and with thanksgiving according to his holy instruction, I receive therewith the fruits also of his most glorious passion. The bishop of Winchester bade me make a direct answer. I said I would not sing a new song to the Lord in a strange land.[2]

Then the bishop said I spake in parables. I answered it was best for him.

"For if I show the open truth," quoth I, "ye will not accept it." Then he said I was a parrot. I told him again I was ready to suffer all things at his hands, not only his rebukes, but all that should follow besides, yea, and that gladly. Then had I diverse rebukes of the Council because I would not express my mind in all things as they would have me. But they were not in the meantime unanswered for all that, which now to rehearse were too much, for I was with them there above five hours. Then the clerk of the Council conveyed me from thence to my Lady Garnish.

The next day I was brought again before the Council. Then would they needs know of me what I said to[3] the sacrament. I answered that I already had said that [which] I could say. Then, after diverse words, they bade me, "Go by." Then came my Lord Lisle, my lord of Essex,[4] and the Bishop of Winchester, requiring me earnestly that I should confess the sacrament to be flesh, blood, and bone. Then said I to my Lord Parr and my Lord Lisle that it was great shame for them to counsel contrary to their knowledge. Whereunto in few words they did say that they would gladly all things were well.

Then the bishop said he would speak with me familiarly. I said, "So did Judas when he unfriendly betrayed Christ." Then desired the bishop to speak with me alone. But that I refused. He asked me, "Why?" I said that in the mouth of two or three witnesses every matter should stand, after Christ's and Paul's doctrine, Matthew 18 and 2 Corinthians 13.

Then my lord chancellor began to examine me again of the sacrament. Then I asked him how long he would halt on both sides? Then would he needs know where I found that? I said in the scripture, 3 Kings 18.[5] Then he went his way.

Then the bishop said I should be burned. I answered that I had searched all the scriptures, yet could I never find there that either Christ or his Apostles put any creature to death. "Well, well," said I. "God will laugh your threatenings to scorn," Psalm 2. Then was I commanded to stand aside.

Then came Master Paget to me with many glorious words, and desired me to speak my mind to him. "I might," he said, "deny it again if need were." I said that I would not deny the truth. He asked me how I could avoid the very words of Christ: "Take, eat. This is my body, which shall be broken for you." I answered that Christ's meaning was there, as in these other places of the Scripture: "I am the door," John 10. "I am the vine," John 15. "Behold the lamb of God," John 1. "The rock stone was Christ," 1 Corinthians 10, and such other like. "Ye may not here," said I, "take Christ for the material thing that he is signified by, for then ye will make him a very door, a vine, a lamb, and a stone, clean contrary to the Holy Ghost's meaning. All these indeed do signify Christ, like as the bread doth his body in that place. And though he did say there, "Take, eat this in remembrance of me," yet did he not bid them hang up that bread in a box and make it a God or bow to it.

Then he compared it unto the king and said that the more His Majesty's honor is set forth, the more commendable it is. Then said I that it was an abominable shame unto him to make no better of the eternal Word of God, than of his slenderly conceived fantasy. A far other meaning requireth God therein than man's idle wit can devise, whose doctrine is but lies without his heavenly verity. Then he asked me if I would commune with some wiser man? That offer, I said, I would not refuse. Then he told the Council. And so went I to my lady's[6] again.

Then came to me Doctor Cox and Doctor Robinson.[7] In conclusion we could not agree. Then they made me a bill[8] of the sacrament, willing me to set my hand thereunto, but I would not. Then on the Sunday I was sore sick, thinking no less than to die. Therefore I desired to speak with Latimer; it would no be. Then was I sent to Newgate in my extremity of sickness. For in all my life afore was I never in such pain. Thus the Lord strengthen you in the truth. Pray, pray, pray.

The Confession of Me, Anne Askew, for the Time I was in Newgate, Concerning My Belief

I find in the scriptures that Christ took the bread and gave it to his disciples, saying, "Eat; this is my body, which shall be broken for you," meaning in substance his own very body, the bread being thereof an only sign or sacrament. For after like manner of speaking, he said he would break down the temple and in three days build it up again, signifying his own body by the temple, as Saint John declareth it, John 2, and not the stony temple itself. So that the bread is but a remembrance of his death or a sacrament of thanksgiving for it, whereby we are knit unto him by a communion of Christian love. Although there be many that cannot perceive the true meaning thereof, for the veil that Moses put over his face before the children of Israel, that they should not see the clearness thereof, Exodus 34 and 2 Corinthians 3. I perceive the same veil remaineth to this day. But when God shall take it away, then shall these blind men see.

For it is plainly expressed in the story of Bel in the Bible that God dwelleth in nothing material. "Oh, king," saith Daniel, "be not deceived," Daniel 14, "for God will be in nothing that is made with hands of men," Acts 7. Oh what stiff-necked people are these, that will always resist the Holy Ghost. But as their fathers have done, so do they, because they have stony hearts. Written by me, Anne Askew, that neither wish death nor yet fear his might, and as merry as one that is bound towards heaven. Truth is laid in prison, Luke 21; the law is turned to wormwood, Amos 6. And there can no right judgement go forth, Isaiah 59.

Oh, forgive us all our sins and receive us graciously. As for the works of our hands, we will no more call upon them. For it is thou, Lord, that art our God. Thou showest ever mercy unto the fatherless. "Oh, if they would do this," saith the Lord, "I should heal their sores; yea, with all my heart would I love them. O Ephraim, what have I to do with idols any more? Whoso is wise shall understand this. And he that is rightly instructed will regard it. For the ways of the Lord are righteous. Such as are godly will walk in them. And as for the wicked, they will stumble at them," Hosea 14. . . .

The Sum of the Condemnation of Me, Anne Askew, at Guildhall

They said to me there that I was an heretic and condemned by the law if I would stand in my opinion. I answered that I was no heretic; neither yet deserved I any death by the law of God. But as concerning the faith which I uttered and wrote to the Council, I would not, I said, deny it, because I knew it true. Then would they needs know if I would deny the sacrament to be Christ's body and blood. I said, "Yea, for the same Son of God that was born of the Virgin Mary is now glorious in heaven and will come again from thence at the latter day like as he went up, Acts 1. And as for that ye call your God, is but a piece of bread. For a more proof thereof (mark it when ye list) let it lie in the box but three months, and it will be mold and so turn to nothing that is good. Whereupon I am persuaded that it cannot be God."

After that they willed me to have a priest. And then I smiled. Then they asked me if it were not good? I said I would confess my faults to God, for I was sure that he would hear me with favor. And so we were condemned without a quest.[9]

My belief which I wrote to the Council was this: that the sacramental bread was left us to be received with thanksgiving, in remembrance of Christ's death, the only remedy of our soul's recover[y]. And that thereby we also receive the whole benefits and fruits of his most glorious passion. . . .

My Faith Briefly Written to the King's Grace

I, Anne Askew, of good memory, although God hath given me the bread of adversity and the water of trouble, yet not so much as my sins have deserved, desire this to be known to your grace. That forasmuch as I am by the law condemned for an evildoer, here I take heaven and earth to record that I shall die in my innocency. And according to that I have said first and will say last, I utterly abhor and detest all heresies. And as concerning the Supper of the Lord, I believe so much as Christ hath said therein, which he confirmed with his most blessed blood. I believe also so much as he willed me to follow and believe, and so much as the Catholic Church of him doth teach. For I will not forsake the commandment of his holy lips. But look what God hath charged me with his mouth, that have I shut up in my heart. And thus briefly I end, for lack of learning. Anne Askew.

The Effect of My Examination and Handling Since My Departure from Newgate

On Tuesday I was sent from Newgate to the sign of the Crown,[10] where as Master Rich and the Bishop of London with all their power and flattering words went about to persuade me from God. But I did not esteem their glossing pretenses. Then came there to me Nicholas Shaxton and counseled me to recant as he had done. Then I said to him that it had been good for him never to have been born, with many other like words.

Then Master Rich sent me to the Tower, where I remained till three of the clock. Then came Rich and one of the Council, charging me upon my obedience to show unto them if I knew man or woman of my sect. My answer was that I knew none. Then they asked me of my lady of Suffolk, my lady of Sussex, my lady Hertford, my lady Denny, and my lady Fitzwilliams. I said, if I should pronounce anything against them, that I were not able to prove it.

Then said they unto me that the king was informed that I could name, if I would, a great number of my sect. Then I answered that the king was as well deceived in that behalf as dissembled with in other matters.

Then commanded they me to show how I was maintained in the Counter[11] and who willed me to stick by my opinion. I said that there was no creature that therein did strengthen me. And, as for the help that I had in the Counter, it was by the means of my maid. For, as she went abroad in the streets, she made to[12] the prentices, and they by her did send me money. But who they were, I never knew.

Then they said that there were diverse gentlewomen that gave me money. But I knew not their names. Then they said that there were diverse ladies which had sent me money. I answered that there was a man in a blue coat which delivered me ten shillings and said that my lady of Hertford sent it me. And another in a violet coat did give me eight shillings and said that my Lady Denny sent it me. Whether it were true or no, I cannot tell, for I am not sure who sent it me, but as the men did say.

Then they said there were of the Council that did maintain me. And I said no. Then they did put me on the rack because I confessed no ladies nor gentlewomen to be of my opinion, and thereon they kept me a long time.

And because I lay still and did not cry, my lord chancellor and Master Rich took pains to rack me [with] their own hands till I was nigh dead.

Then the lieutenant caused me to be loosed from the rack. Incontinently I swooned, and then they recovered me again. After that I sat two long hours reasoning with my lord chancellor upon the bare floor, where as he with many flattering words persuaded me to leave my opinion. But my Lord God (I thank his everlasting goodness) gave me grace to persevere, and will do (I hope) to the very end.

Then was I brought to an house and laid in a bed with as weary and painful bones as ever had patient Job, I thank my Lord God thereof. Then my Lord Chancellor sent me word, if I would leave my opinion, I should want nothing. If I would not, I should forth to Newgate and so be burned. I sent him again word that I would rather die than to break my faith. Thus the Lord open the eyes of their blind hearts, that the truth may take place. Farewell, dear friend, and pray, pray, pray. . . .

The Confession of Her Faith Which Anne Askew Made in Newgate Afore She Suffered

I, Anne Askew, of good memory, although my merciful Father hath given me the bread of adversity and the water of trouble, yet not so much as my sins hath deserved, confess myself here a sinner before the throne of His Heavenly Majesty, desiring his eternal mercy. And forsomuch as I am by the law unrighteously condemned for an evildoer concerning opinions, I take the same most merciful God of mine which hath made both heaven and earth to record that I hold no opinions contrary to his most Holy Word.

And I trust in my merciful Lord, which is the giver of all grace, that he will graciously assist me against all evil opinions which are contrary to his blessed verity. For I take him to witness that I have, do, and will do, unto my life's end, utterly abhor them to the uttermost of my power. But this is the heresy which they report me to hold: that, after the priest hath spoken the words of consecration, there remaineth bread still.

But they both say and also teach it for a necessary article of faith that after those words be once spoken, there remaineth no bread but even the selfsame body that hung upon the cross on Good Friday, both flesh, blood, and bone. To this belief of theirs say I nay. For then were our common creed false, which saith that he sitteth on the right hand of God the Father Almighty, and from thence shall come to judge the quick and the dead. Lo, this is the heresy that I hold, and for it must suffer the death.

But as touching the holy and blessed Supper of the Lord, I believe it to be a most necessary remembrance of his glorious sufferings and death.

Moreover, I believe as much therein as my eternal and only redeemer Jesus Christ would I should believe. Finally, I believe all those Scriptures to be true, whom he hath confirmed with his most precious blood.

Yea, and as Saint Paul saith, those scriptures are sufficient for our learning and salvation that Christ hath left here with us, so that I believe we need no unwritten verities[13] to rule his church with. Therefore, look what he hath laid unto me with his own mouth in his Holy Gospel; that have I, with God's grace, closed up in my heart. And my full trust is, as David saith, that it shall be a lantern to my footsteps, Psalm 118.

There be some do say that I deny the Eucharist, or sacrament of thanksgiving. But those people do untruly report of me. For I both say and believe it that, if it were ordered like as Christ instituted it and left it, a most singular comfort it were unto us all. But as concerning your Mass as it is now used in our days, I do say and believe it to be the most abominable idol that is in the world. For my God will not be eaten with teeth, neither yet dieth he again. And upon these words that I have now spoken will I suffer death.

O Lord, I have more enemies now than there be hairs on my head. Yet, Lord, let them never overcome me with vain words. But fight thou, Lord, in my stead; for on thee cast I my care. With all the spite they can imagine, they fall upon me, which am thy poor creature. Yet, sweet Lord, let me not set by[14] them which are against thee. For in thee is my whole delight.

And, Lord, I heartily desire of thee that thou wilt of thy most merciful goodness forgive them that violence which they do and have done unto me. Open also thou their blind hearts, that they may hereafter do that thing in thy sight which is only acceptable before thee. And to set forth thy verity aright, without all vain fantasies of sinful men. So be it, O Lord; so be it. By me, Anne Askew.

The Ballad Which Anne Askew Made and Sang When She Was in Newgate

Like as the armed knight
Appointed to the field,
With this world will I fight,
And faith shall be my shield.

Faith is that weapon strong
Which will not fail at need.
My foes, therefore, among,
Therewith will I proceed.

As it is had in strength
And force of Christ's way,

It will prevail at length
Though all the devils say nay.
    Faith in the fathers old
Obtained rightwiseness,
Which make[s] me very bold
To fear no world's distress.
    I now rejoice in heart,
And hope bid me do so;
For Christ will take my part
And ease me of my woe.
    Thou sayest, Lord, whoso knock,
To them wilt thou attend.
Undo therefore the lock,
And thy strong power send.
    More enemies now I have
Than hairs upon my head.
Let them not me deprave,
But fight thou in my stead.
    On thee my care I cast;
For all their cruel spite,
I set not by their haste,
For thou art my delight.
    I am not she that list
My anchor to let fall;
For every drizzling mist,
My ship substantial.
    Not oft use I to write
In prose nor yet in rhyme,
Yet will I show one sight
That I saw in my time.
    I saw a royal throne
Where justice should have sit;
But in her stead was one
Of moody, cruel wit.
    Absorbed was rightwiseness,
As of the raging flood;
Satan in his excess,
Sucked up the guiltless blood.
    Then thought I, Jesus, Lord,
When thou shalt judge us all,

Hard is it to record
On these men what will fall.
　　Yet, Lord, I thee desire,
For that they do to me,
Let them not taste the hire
Of their iniquity.[15]

Notes

1. 1 Kings 3:16–28.
2. Ps. 137:4.
3. Concerning.
4. John Dudley, Viscount Lisle, and William Parr, Earl of Essex, were members of the Privy Council.
5. I.e, 1 Kings 18.
6. I.e., Lady Garnish.
7. Two clerics.
8. Written document.
9. Inquest.
10. An inn located near Newgate.
11. A prison.
12. Set to work.
13. Nonscriptural traditions.
14. Set any store in.
15. This poem is based on the allegory of the Armor of God (Eph. 6:11–17).

6.2. John Bale, from
The Vocation of John Bale (1553)

This book is a vigorous autobiographical account of Bale's experience as Bishop of Ossory in Ireland until his flight into exile upon the accession of Mary I. A satirical colophon claims that publication took place at "Rome, before the castle of Sant' Angelo at the sign of Saint Peter" in December 1553. Even though this device protects the identity of the printer, most likely Joos Lambrecht of Wesel in the duchy of Cleves, the text proclaims Bale's identity. Addressing a consolatory message to beleaguered Protestants in England, he interprets his deliverance as an example of providential intervention.

Bale's chief goal as an uncompromising missionary bishop was to replace the doctrine of transubstantiation and Roman rite Mass with a Protestant communion service, to stamp out clerical violations of poverty and chastity, and to educate the laity. This uncommonly brisk narrative recounts the poisoning of an archbishop, the murder of Bale's servants for mowing hay on a Catholic feast day, and his own flight from murderous priests into captivity by a pirate who eventually released him in the Low Countries. He retells ludicrous anecdotes about a cleric who boasts about being sired by an abbot, about another who fathers bastards in order to increase church offerings, about a third who uses Eucharistic bread as fish bait, and about another who "pissed" in the mouth of a congregant who fell asleep in church. Bale's staging his own plays in an effort to convert Irish Catholics coexisted with his rejection of the theatricality of the Mass (see 5.1–3). See Bale's *Image of Both Churches* and *Three Laws* (1.1.B, 3.1).

SOURCE: STC 1307, fol. 17ʳ–18ʳ, 18ᵛ–19ʳ, 19ʳ⁻ᵛ, 20ʳ–22ᵛ, 23ʳ–24ʳ, 24ʳ⁻ᵛ, 25ᵛ, 26ʳ⁻ᵛ, 27ʳ⁻ᵛ, 28ʳ–29ʳ, 31ᵛ–32ʳ, 33ʳ⁻ᵛ, 34ʳ–35ʳ, 35ᵛ–36ʳ, 36ᵛ–38ʳ, 38ᵛ–39ʳ, 39ᵛ–41ᵛ, 42ʳ⁻ᵛ.
EDITION: Bale 1990.
REFERENCES: Hadfield; Happé; Kendall; King 1982.

On the nineteenth day of December I took my journey from Bishopstoke with my books and stuff toward Bristol,[1] where as I tarried twenty-six days for passage and diverse times preached in that worshipful city at the instant desire of the citizens. Upon the twenty-first day of January we entered into the ship, I, my wife, and one servant. And being but two nights and two days upon the sea, we arrived most prosperously at Waterford in the coldest time of the year, so merciful was the Lord unto us.

In beholding the face and order of that city, I see many abominable idolatries maintained by the epicurish priests for their wicked bellies' sake. The communion or Supper of the Lord was there altogether used like a popish Mass, with the old apish toys of Antichrist, in bowings and beckings, kneelings and knockings, the Lord's death after Saint Paul's doctrine neither preached nor yet spoken of. There wailed they over the dead with prodigious

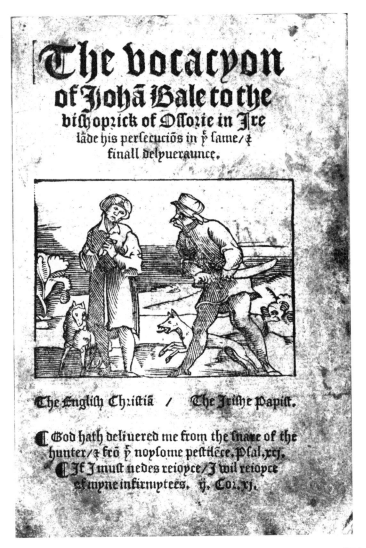

The vocacyon
of Johā Bale to the
bischoprick of Ossorie in Ire
lāde his persecuciōs in ȳ same/ȝ
finall delyueraunce.

The English Christiā / The Irishe Papist.

❡ God hath deliuered me from the snare of the
hunter/ȝ frō ȳ noysome pestilēce. Psal,xcj.
❡ Jf J must nedes reioyce/ J wil reioyce
of myne infirmytees. ij. Cor.xj.

Figure 9. *The English Christian Versus the Irish Papist.* From *The Vocation of John Bale* (Wesel, 1553), Title page woodcut. By permission of the British Library. This woodcut portrays a victim, cowering alongside a lamb symbolic of Christlike innocence, under assault from an attacker accompanied by a hunting dog or wolf. In addition to identifying these generic figures respectively as an English colonialist and an Irish Catholic, Bale supplies consolatory epigraphs (Ps. 90:1–2 [Vulgate Ps. 91:1–2], 2 Corinthians 11:30) concerning providential rescue. The second tag likens Bale's escape from Ireland to Saint Paul's deliverance from Damascus. The possession of the woodblock by Joos Lambrecht, who worked as a printer in Wesel from 1553 until 1556, suggests that he may have printed *The Vocation of John Bale* in partnership with Hugh Singleton. This illustration had appeared in Andries van der Meulen's *Een zuverlic boucxkin vander ketyvigheyt der menschelicker naturen* ("A fine tract on the misery of the condition of man"), a Flemish poem printed at Ghent in 1543.

howlings and patterings, as though their souls had not been quieted in Christ and redeemed by his Passion, but that they must come after and help at a pinch with Requiem Eternam[2] to deliver them out of hell by their sorrowful sorceries. . . . The next day after, I rode toward Dublin and rested the night following in a town called Knocktopher in the house of Master Adam Walsh, my general commissary[3] for the whole diocese of Ossory.

At supper the parish priest, called Sir Philip,[4] was very serviceable and in familiar talk described unto me the house of the White Friars which sometime was in that town, concluding in the end that the last prior thereof called William was his natural father. I asked him if that were in marriage? He made me answer, no. For that was, he said, against his profession. Then counseled I him that he never should boast of it more. Why, saith he, it is an honor in this land to have a spiritual man, as a bishop, an abbot, a monk, a friar, or a priest to father. With that I greatly marveled, not so much of his unshamefast talk as I did that adultery, forbidden of God and of all honest men detested, should there have both praise and preferment, thinking in process for my part to reform it. . . .

Upon the purification day[5] of Our Lady, the lord chancellor of Ireland, Sir Thomas Cusack, our special good lord and earnest aider in all our proceedings, appointed us to be invested, or consecrated as they call it, by George the Archbishop of Dublin. . . . As we were coming forth to have received the imposition of hands[6] according to the ceremony, Thomas Lockwood, Blockhead he might well be called, the dean of the cathedral church there, desired the lord chancellor very instantly that he would in no wise permit that observation to be done after that book of consecrating bishops which was last set forth in England by act of Parliament,[7] alleging that it would be both an occasion of tumult and also that it was not as yet consented to by act of their Parliament in Ireland. For why he much feared the new changed order of the communion therein to hinder his kitchen and belly. The lord chancellor proponed[8] this matter unto us. The archbishop consented thereunto. . . .

When I see no other way, I stepped forth and said, if England and Ireland be under one king, they are both bound to the obedience of one law under him. And as for us, we came hither as true subjects of his, sworn to obey that ordinance. It was but a bishopric, I said, that I came thither to receive that day. Which I could be better contented to tread under my foot there than to break from that promise or oath that I had made. I bade them in the end set all their hearts at rest, for came I once to the church of Ossory, I would execute nothing for my part there but according to the rules of that latter book. Then went the ass-headed dean away more than half confused.

Neither followed there any tumult among the people, but every man saving the priests was well contented. Then went the archbishop about that observation, very unsavorily and as one not much exercised in that kind of doing, especially in the administration of the Lord's Holy Supper. In the end, the lord chancellor made to us and to our friends a most friendly dinner to save us from exceeding charges, which otherwise we had been at that day.

Within two days after was I sick again, so eagerly[9] that no man thought I should have lived, which malady held me till after Easter. Yet in the meantime I found a way to be brought to Kilkenny, where as I preached every Sunday and holy day in Lent till the Sunday after Easter was fully past, never feeling any manner of grief of my sickness for the time I was in the pulpit. Whereat many man and myself also greatly marveled. . . .

My first proceedings in that doing were these. I earnestly exhorted the people to repentance for sin and required them to give credit to the Gospel of salvation. To acknowledge and believe that there was but one God, and him alone without any other sincerely to worship. To confess one Christ for an only savior and redeemer and to trust in none other man's prayers, merits, nor yet deservings, but in his alone, for salvation I treated at large both of the heavenly and political state of the Christian church, and helpers I found none among my prebendaries and clergy, but adversaries a great number. I preached the Gospel of the knowledge and right invocation of God; I maintained the political order by doctrine and moved the commons always to obey their magistrates. But when I once sought to destroy the idolatries and dissolve the hypocrites' yokes, then followed angers, slanders, conspiracies, and in the end the slaughter of men. Much ado I had with the priests, for that I had said among other that the white gods[10] of their making such as they offered to the people to be worshipped were no gods but idols and that their prayers for the dead procured no redemption to the souls departed, redemption of souls being only in Christ, of Christ, and by Christ. I added that their office by Christ's straight commandment was chiefly to preach and instruct the people in the doctrine and ways of God, and not to occupy so much of the time in chanting, piping, and singing.

Much were the priests offended also for that I had in my preachings willed them to have wives of their own and to leave the unshamefast occupying of other men's wives, daughters, and servants. But hear what answer they made me always, yea the most vicious men among them. "What, should we marry," said they, "for half a year and so lose our livings?" Think ye not that these men were ghostly inspired? Either yet had knowledge of some secret mischief working in England? I for my part have not a little since that time marveled when it hath fallen to my remembrance. Well the truth is I could never yet by any godly or honest persuasion bring any of them to marriage, neither yet cause them which were known for unshamefast whorekeepers to leave that filthy and abominable occupying, what though I most earnestly labored it. . . .

In the week after Easter, when I had once preached twelve sermons among them and established the people, as I thought, in the doctrine of repentance and necessary belief of the Gospel in the true worshippings of one God our eternal Father and no more and in that hope of one redeemer Jesus Christ and no more, I departed from Kilkinney to another place of mine five miles off called Holmes Court,[11] where as I remained till Ascension Day. In the meantime came sorrowful news unto me that Master Hugh Goodacre, the archbishop of Armagh, that goodly preacher and virtuous learned man, was poisoned at Dublin by procurement of certain priests of his diocese for preaching God's verity and rebuking their common vices. And letters by and by were directed unto me by my special friends from thence to beware of the like in my diocese of Ossory, which made me peradventure more circumspect than I should have been. Upon the Ascension Day I preached again at Kilkenny, likewise on Trinity Sunday and on St. Peter's Day at midsummer then following.

On the twenty-fifth day of July the priests were as pleasantly disposed as might be and went by heaps from tavern to tavern to seek the best Rob Davie[12] and *aqua vitae*,[13] which are their special drinks there. They caused all their cups to be filled in with *Gaudeamus in dolio*,[14] the mystery thereof only known to them and at that time to none other else. Which was that King Edward was dead and that they were in hope to have up their masking[15] Masses again. As we have in Saint John's Revelation that they which dwell on the earth, as do our earthly minded massmongers, should rejoice and be glad when God's true witnesses were once taken away and should send gifts one to another for gladness because they rebuked them of their wicked doings (Revelation 11). For ye must consider that the priests are commonly the first that receive such news. The next day following a very wicked justice called Thomas Howth with the Lord Mountgarret resorted to the cathedral church, requiring to have a communion in honor of Saint Anne. Mark the blasphemous blindness and willful obstinacy of this beastly papist. The priests made him answer that I had forbidden them that celebration, saving only upon the Sundays. . . .

Thus was the wicked justice not only a violator of Christ's institution but also a contemner of his prince's earnest commandment and a provoker of the people by his ungracious example to do the like. This could he do with other mischiefs more by his long being there by a whole month's space, but for murders, thefts, idolatries, and abominable whoredoms, wherewith all that nation aboundeth, for that time he sought no redress, neither appointed any correction. The priests thus rejoicing that the king was dead and that they had been that day confirmed in their superstitious obstinacy resorted to the foresaid false justice the same night at supper to gratify him with Rob Davie and *aqua vitae* for that he had been so friendly unto them and that he might still continue in the same. The next day after was the Lady Jane Guildford[16] proclaimed their queen, with solemnity of processions, bonfires, and banquets, the said justice, as I was informed, sore blaming me for my absence that day, for indeed I much doubted that matter.

So soon as it was there rumored abroad that the king was departed from this life, the ruffians of that wild nation not only rebelled against the English captains, as their lewd custom in such changes hath been always, chiefly no English deputy[17] being within the land, but also they conspired into the very deaths of so many English men and women as were left therein alive: minding, as they then stoutly boasted it, to have set up a king of their own. And to cause their wild people to bear the more hate to our nation, very subtly but yet falsely they caused it to be noised over all that the young earl of Ormond[18] and Barnaby, the baron of Upper Ossory's son, were both slain in the court at London.

Upon this wily practice of mischief they raged without order in all places and assaulted the English forts everywhere.

And at one of them by a subtle train[19] they got out nine of our men and slew them.

On the thirteenth day of August a gentlewoman, the wife of Matthew King,[20] having a castle not far off, her husband then being at London, fled with her family and goods in carts toward the foresaid Kilkenny and in the highway was spoiled of all, to her very petticoat, by the kerns and galloglasses[21] of the forenamed baron of Upper Ossory, Michael Patrick, and of the Lord Mountgarret, which ought rather to have defended her. In this outrage had she after long conflict with those enemies, four of her company slain, besides other mischiefs more.

On the twentieth day of August was the Lady Mary with us at Kilkenny proclaimed Queen of England, France, and Ireland, with the greatest solemnity that there could be devised of processions, musters, and disguisings, all the noble captains and gentlemen thereabout being present. What ado I had that day with the prebendaries and priests about wearing the cope, crosier, and miter in procession, it were too much to write. . . .

With that I took Christ's testament in my hand and went to the market cross, the people in great number following. There took I the thirteenth chapter of Saint Paul to the Romans declaring to them briefly what the authority was of the worldly powers and magistrates, what reverence and obedience were due to the same. In the meantime had the prelates gotten two disguised priests, one to bear the miter afore me and another the crosier, making three procession pageants of one. The young men in the forenoon played a tragedy of God's promises in the old law at the market cross with organ playings and songs very aptly. In the afternoon again they played a comedy of Saint John Baptist's preachings, of Christ's baptizing, and of his temptation in the wilderness,[22] to the small contentation of the priests and other papists there.

On the Thursday next following, which was Saint Bartholomew's Day, I preached again among them, because the prebendaries and other priests there had made their boasts that I should be compelled to recant all that I had preached afore. . . . The same day I dined with the mayor of the town, whom they named their sovereign, called Robert Shea, a man sober, wise, and godly, which is a rare thing in that land. . . . The next day I departed from thence and went home with my company to Holmes Court again.

Whereas I had knowledge the next day following that the priests of my diocese, especially one Sir Richard Routh, treasurer of the church of Kilkenny, and one Sir James Joys, a familiar chaplain of mine, by the help of one Barnaby Bolgar, my next neighbor and my tenant at the said Holmes Court, had hired certain kerns of the Lord Mountgarret and of the baron of Upper Ossory, whom they knew to be most desperate thieves and murderers, to slay me. And I am in full belief that this was not all without their knowledge also, for so much as they were so desirous of my lands in diverse quarters and could neither obtain them by their own importunate suits nor yet by the friendship of others. As for the Lord Mountgarret, I suspect him by this: a horse groom of his, with another of his breechless gallants besides, came into my court one day and made a stout brag among my servants that he would both steal my horses, as it is there reckoned no great fault to steal, and also that he would have my head if I came abroad. . . .

On the Thursday after, which was the last day of August, I being absent, the clergy of Kilkenny, by procurement of that wicked Justice Howth, blasphemously resumed again the whole papism or heap of superstitions of the bishop of Rome, to the utter contempt of Christ and his holy Word, of the king and council of England, and of all ecclesiastical and politic order, without either statute or yet proclamation. They rang all the bells in the cathedral minster and parish churches, they flung up their caps to the battlement of the great temple[23] with smilings and laughings most dissolutely, the justice himself being therewith offended. They brought forth their copes, candlesticks, holy-water stock, cross, and censers.[24] They mustered forth in general procession most gorgeously, all the town over, with *Sancta Maria ora pro nobis*[25] and the rest of the Latin litany. They chattered it, they chanted it, with great noise and devotion. They banqueted all the day after, for that they were delivered from the grace of God into a warm sun. For they may now from thence forth again deceive the people as they did afore time with their Latin mumblings and make merchandise of them (2 Peter 2). They may make the witless sort believe that they can make every day new gods of their little white cakes and that they can fetch their friends' souls from flaming purgatory if need be, with other great miracles else.

They may now without check have other men's wives in occupying or keep whores in their chambers or else play the buggery knaves, as they have done always, and be at an utter defiance with marriage, though it be the institution of God, honorable, holy, righteous, and perfect. . . .

On the Friday next following, which was the eighth day of September, five of my household servants, Richard Foster, a deacon; Richard Headley; John Cage, an Irish horse groom; and a young maid of sixteen years of age went out to make hay about half a mile off, betwixt eight and nine of the clock, after they had served God according to the day. And as they were come to the entrance of that meadow, the cruel murderers, to the number of more than a score, leaped out of their lurking bushes with swords and with darts and cowardly slew them all unarmed and unweaponed, without mercy. This did they in their wicked fury, as it was reported, for that they had watched so long afore, yea, an whole month space they say, and sped not of their purpose concerning me. They feloniously also robbed me of all my horses and of all Master Cooper's horses, which that time sojourned with me for safeguard of his life, to the number of seven, driving them afore them. In the afternoon, about three of the clock, the good sovereign of Kilkenny, having knowledge thereof, resorted to me with an hundred horsemen and three hundred footmen, and so with great strength brought me that night to the town, the young men singing psalms and other godly songs all the way, in rejoice of my deliverance.

As we were come to the town the people in great number stood on both sides of the way both within the gates and without, with candles lit in their hands, shouting out praises to God for delivering me from the hands of those murderers. The priests the next day to color their mischief caused it to be noised all the country over that it was by the hand of God that my servants were slain, for that they had broken, they said, the great holy day of our Lady's nativity. But I would fain know what holy day those bloodthirsty hypocrites and malicious murderers kept, which had hired those cruel kerns to do that mischief? O abominable traitors, both to God and to all godly order. . . .

And as I had continued there certain days, I chanced to hear of many secret mutterings that the priests would not so leave me, but were still conspiring my death. It was also noised abroad by the bishop of Galway and others that the Antichrist of Rome should be taken again for the supreme head of the Church of Ireland. And to declare a contemptuous change from religion to superstition again, the priests had suddenly set up the altars and images in the cathedral church. Beholding therefore so many inconveniences to ensue and so many dangers toward, having also, which was worst of all, no English deputy or governor within the land to complain to for remedy, I shook the dust off my feet against those wicked collegianers[26] and priests, according to Christ's commandment (Matthew 10), that it might stand against them as a witness at the day of judgment. The next day early in the morning by help of friends I conveyed myself away to the Castle of Leighlin, and so forth to the city of Dublin, where as I for a certain time among friends remained.

As the epicurous archbishop had knowledge of my being there, he made boast upon his ale bench with the cup in his hand, as I heard the tale told, that I should for no man's pleasure preach in that city of his. But this needed not. For I thought nothing less at that time than to pour out the precious pearls of the Gospel afore so brockish[27] a swine as he was, becoming then of[28] a dissembling proselyte a very pernicious papist. And as touching learning, whereof he much boasted among his cups, . . . his preachings, twice in the year, of the plowman in winter, by *Exit qui seminat*,[29] and of the shepherd in summer, by *Ego sum pastor bonus*,[30] are now so well known by rote of every gossip in Dublin that afore he cometh up into the pulpit,[31] they can tell his sermon. . . .

After certain days within my host's house, a young man of Essex called Thomas was coming and going, which for his master's affairs into Scotland had hired a small ship, there called a picard. I rejoiced at the chance, as one that had found great treasure, and thought it a thing provided of God for my safeguard and deliverance at that present. Anon I covenanted with him to pay the half charges of that ship that I might pass thither with him, and delivered to him out of hand the more part thereof. . . .

And as he and I were together in the ship, there tarrying upon the tide for passage, an Irish pirate, yea, rather a cruel tyrant of hell, called Walter, being pilot as they call them, or loads-man in a Flemish ship-of-war, made the covetous captain thereof to believe that I was a Frenchman and that I had about me innumerable treasure. The captain, hearing of this, with an exceeding fierceness invaded our poor ship and removed both the young man, Thomas, and me from thence into his great ship of war. Where as he searched us both to the very skins and took from us all that we had in money, books, and apparel. He took also from the master of our picard, or little ship, five pound, which I and the said Thomas had given to him in part of payment, with all his beer and victuals, notwithstanding that he perfectly knew us to be Englishmen and no Frenchmen. . . .

"Since ye came to our ship," said he, "I heard you wish yourself in Dutchland,[32] and I promise you we will honestly bring you thither and not long tarry by the way." My chance was indeed to find there among them an Hollander called Leonard, which knew me in Northwich,[33] with my Master John Sartorius. To him in familiar talk I had wished myself there at that present. "But how will ye lead me," said I to the captain, "as ye have done hitherto, like a captive prisoner, or like a free passenger?" "No," said he, "I take ye now for no prisoner, but for a man of worship and for a most honest passenger, and so will I deliver you there." But all this time he had my money in his own keeping. Within two days after, we were driven into Saint Ives in Cornwall by extremity of weather. Where as the foresaid wicked pirate Walter get him[self] aland afore us, so fast as ever he could, and accused me there for an heinous traitor, yea, for such a one as for that cause had fled out of Ireland.

And to bring his wicked purpose to pass of winning somewhat by me, for he thought then to have half my money which was in the captain's hands, he fetched thither one Downings from seven miles off, by the counsel of the mariners of that town, which was noised to be the most cruel termagant of that shire, yea, such a one as had been a beginner of the last commotion there, both to examine me and apprehend me.

And as I was come to that examination before one of the bailiffs, the constables, and other officers, I desired the said bailiff, appearing to me a very sober man, as he was indeed, to ask of the said Walter how long he had known me and what treason I had done since that time of his knowledge? He answered that he never saw me, neither yet had heard of me afore I came into that ship of war a four or five days afore. "Then," said the bailiff, "what treason hast thou known by this honest gentleman since? For I promise thee, he seemeth to be an honest man." . . .

Then came in the captain and his purser and reviled the said Walter, reporting him to be a very naughty fellow and a common drunkard and that I was a very honest man. For they feared at that time the discharge of my money out of their hands, I offering myself, for my trial against him, to be brought to the sessions,[34] which were then not far off. Then said the foresaid

Downings in great displeasure, God's soul, what do I hear? This is but a drunken matter, by the mass. And so went his way in a fume, and for anger would not once drink with us. So that I went clear away in this prodigious conflict. The next day being Sunday, I resorted to the temple to see the fashions there. As the peals were all ended, they sang matins, hours, holy water making, and Mass all in Latin. Nothing was there in English but the poor litany, which the priest, a stout sturdy lubber, said with least devotion of all, much of the people lamenting to behold so miserable a mutation and saying, "Afore time might we have learned somewhat by our coming to the church, but now nothing at all to our understanding. Alas, what shall become of us?"

After dinner that priest resorted unto us, as bold as great Hercules, and after a little talk fell to flat railing of good Miles Coverdale,[35] their bishop, after this sort: "Where is that heretic knave now," saith he, "and other of his companions, vagabonds, apostates, and renegades?" With other uncomely words. And as I was bent to have made him an answer, a gentleman of the country thereabout rubbed me on the elbow and bade me in mine ear to let him alone and I should hear wonders. And the said gentleman brought him into another talk of old familiarities. Wherein he confessed that he had in one day begotten two men's wives of that parish with child to increase the church's profit in chrisms[36] and offerings, whereas their husbands were not able to do it. "Yea, marry Sir James"[37] saith the gentleman, "and ye have done more miracles that that. Went ye not one day a-fishing?" saith he. "Yes, by the mass did I," said the priest again, "and made the fishes more holy than ever the whoresons were afore. For I sent out my maker[38] among them, whom I had that day received at the altar." "By the mass," quoth he, "I was able to hold him no longer." "Since that day I am sure," quoth he, "that our fishers hath had better luck than ever they had afore." . . .

When supper was done, certain of the mariners resorted to us, declaring what an uncomely part the priest had played with their piper as that he had pissed in his mouth, being gaping asleep in the church after evensong. This is the beauteous face of our Irish and English churches at this present. The poor people are not taught but mocked of their ministers, their servants abused, their wives and daughters defiled, and all Christian order confounded.

As the weather waxed fair, the captain went away with the ship and was more than two miles on his way, minding, as it appeared, to have gone away with all that I had, money, apparel, and books, if the wind had served him well. The customer's[39] servant, an Irishman also, being admonished by his countryman Walter of my money in the captain's hands, came to my lodging in the morning and told me thereof, thinking as I had been in possession thereof, if I had come to land again therewith, to have raised new rumors upon me and so to have deprived me thereof. For he showed himself very serviceable in providing me a boat and in bringing me to the ship. But when he once perceived that I would not demand my money of the captain and return again with him, though I gave him a crown for his boat and pains, yet went he away in great displeasure with no small reproaches. And at that present was the foresaid Walter banished the ship for his only troubling of me, so benevolent that hour was the captain unto me.

The next day after I demanded my money of the captain, and it was very honestly delivered me, all schisms, as I thought, pacified. Howbeit that wretched mammon most strongly wrought in the unquietous heart of the captain, so that continually after that time he threatened to set us on land, and marvel it was that he threw us not both over the board. Always were we well contented to have gone to land, but yet still he drove it off till we came into Dover Road, I not understanding the mystery concerning the said money, as that it was in my hand and not in the captain's, which marred all the whole matter. In the meantime they went a-roving by a whole week's space and more. And first they took an English ship of Totnes, going toward Brittany and loaden with tin, and that they spoiled both of ware and money under the color of Frenchmen's goods. The next day in the afternoon beheld they two English ships more, whom they chased all that night long and the next day till ten of the clock, and of them they took one by reason that his topsail broke, and that was a ship of Lynn.[40] In this had they nothing but apples, for he went for his loading. After that traced they the seas over more than half a week and found none there but their own countrymen, being men-of-war and sea robbers as they were.

At the last they came to Dover Road, and there would the captain need to land with his purser. My companion Thomas and I, taking ourselves for free passengers, desired to go aland with them, "but that might not be," he said, "till he had been there afore." "Yes," saith Thomas, "I will go aland if any man go, for I have nothing to do here." "Thou shalt not go," saith the captain, "but I will lay thee fast by the feet if thou prate any more." With that, one Cornelius stood forth and said, "We are much to blame that we have not dispatched him ere this and thrown him over the board." . . .

After midnight he returned to the ship, prating among his company what he had done aland and how he had almost lost all by his busy talk. But he had heard of me, he said, much more than he knew afore, and he trusted that I should be to him and to all the ship a profitable prize. The next day in the morning after his first sleep, he arose and with stout countenance boasted that he would straight to London with his most dangerous carriage,

which were we two poor innocent souls that had done ill to no man, saving
that we could not bear with the blasphemies of the papists against God
and his Christ. Much to and fro was among them about that passage. In the
end they all concluded that better it was to tarry still there with the ship
whiles one or two of them went to the council of England in message and
came again then thither to travail with ship and all. To land goeth the purser
and other besides to hire their horses towards London, for mountains of
gold would be gotten that ways, they said. . . .

"I am contented, Master Captain," said I, "to be ordered as ye will
reasonably have me." "What will ye give, then," said the captain, "to be delivered into Flanders and our purser to be called again?" I answered that I
would give as himself would reason and conscience require. "If ye had told
us so much yesternight," said he, "this matter had been at a point,[41] and we
by this time had been in Zeeland."[42] Then was all the rabble of the ship, hag,
tag, and rag,[43] called to the reckoning, rushing together as they had been the
cooks of hell with their great Cerebus, an whole hundred pound demanded
for my deliverance. In the end it was concluded that no less might assuage
that hungry heat than fifty pound at the least, with this proviso that all
the money that I had in my purse, with part of my garments also, should be
out of hand divided among them and the captain, which was twenty-one
pound in the whole. I instantly desired that it might be received in part payment of the other sum. They cried all with one voice, "Nay, we will none
of that." Then I besought them that I might have at the least an honest portion thereof for payment of my charges whiles I should be providing of so
great a ransom as they had laid to me.

In fine they assented that I should have six crowns of mine own money
allowed me for my costs till I had found out my friends. Then caused the
captain a piece of ordnance to be fired and a gun to be let[44] to call back the
purser and his companion. In whose return there was much to and fro. For
some would needs to London, thinking that way to win more than to bring
me into Flanders. And of them which would into Flanders, some would
to land for a barrel of drink, for in the ship at that time was neither bread,
beef, nor beer. Some feared the coming of the mayor and captain of the castle for searching their ship. So that our captain commanded them at the last
to hoist up the sails and speedily to pass towards Flanders. In the meantime
was I, poor soul, compelled to set my hand to a false bill of their devising,
as that I had hired their ship in Ireland for fifty pound to bring me without
delay or tarriance into Zeeland. Which I never did, as the Almighty Lord
well knoweth, but came from thence with them against my will and was
tossed to and fro upon the seas by the space of twenty-four days in following

prizes, as they call their robberies. And I was by that time so full of lice as I could swarm.

As we came once thither, they brought me into the house of one of the four owners of the ship, which was a man fearing God, and his wife, a woman of much godliness also, which was to me [a] careful[45] creature, a singular comfort provided of God. The next day were all the four owners called to the reckoning and a Latin interpreter with them to know how, where, and when this ransom of fifty pound should be paid? And more than twenty-six days of leisure for the payment thereof might not be granted. I desired to have had liberty to go abroad to seek my friends, but that I could not obtain, though it were in my former covenant when the six crowns were delivered me. In the afternoon was it noised abroad by the drunken mariners all over that they had brought such a one with them out of Ireland as paid half an hundred pound for his passage, to the wondering of all the town. So that my host was fain to keep me close in his house and to say both to the mariners and others that I was gone to Antwerp, the people there resorted so fast to see me. They reported there also in their drunkenness that I was he which had put down the Mass in England and had thrown Doctor Gardiner into the Tower, with a great sort of lies and slanders more.

Thus continued I there as a prisoner by the space of three weeks, sometime threatened to be thrown in their common jail, sometime to be brought afore the magistrates, sometime to be left to the examination of the clergy, sometime to be sent to London, or else to be delivered to the Queen's ambassadors at Brussels, but always by God's provision I had mine host and hostess to friends. And behold a most wonderful work of God. The parson of the town, a most cruel monk, a master at Louvain and an inquisitor of heretics, as they called those rabbis,[46] the next day after my coming [was] sore sickened and never came out of his bed so long as I was there, which was greatly marked of some of the inhabitants, being godly affected. At the last, in deliberating the matter that they required so much money of me and would not suffer me to go abroad to seek it, mine host bade the captain and mariners consider how far they had run beyond the limits of their commission in misusing the English nation, with whom they had no war. "It may chance hereafter," saith he, "deeply to be laid to your charges. Therefore by my assent ye shall agree with this good man for less money." Then were they contented to receive thirty pound as I should be able to pay it, and so to discharge me.

Thus hath my Lord God most miraculously delivered me from all these dangerous perils and from the greedy mouths of devouring lions into the worthy land of Germany yet once again, I hope to the glory of his most holy name, everlasting praise be to him for it. Amen.

Here have ye, dear friends, a most lively and wonderful example of God's chastenings and of his most gracious deliverance again. . . .

By violence hath he yet once again, as ye in this treatise have read here, driven me out of that glorious Babylon, that I should not taste too much of her wanton pleasures. But with his most dearly beloved disciples to have my inward rejoice in the cross of his son Jesus Christ. The glory of whose church, I see it well, standeth not in the harmonious sound of bells and organs, nor yet in the glittering of miters and copes, neither in the shining of gilt images and lights, as the blind bluddering[47] papists do judge it, but in continual labors and daily afflictions for his name's sake. God at this present in England hath his fan[48] in hand, and after his great harvest[49] there is now sifting the corn from the chaff, blessed shall they be which persevere in faith to the end. In case without doubt is England now, as was Jewry after the heavenly doctrine was there plenteously sown by Christ and by his apostles, the true ministers of his word being partly imprisoned and partly dispersed, as they were. God of his great mercy preserve it from that plague of destruction which not only Jerusalem but also that whole land tasted for their willful contempt of that message of their salvation. Amen.

Notes

1. Port in southwest England.
2. Opening words of introit of the Mass for the dead, *Requiem aeternam dona eis, Domine*.
3. Official representative of a bishop.
4. Mocking name for a priest.
5. Feast of the Purification of the Virgin Mary.
6. Laying on of hands.
7. "The Form of Consecrating of an Archbishop or Bishop" in the second *Book of Common Prayer* of Edward VI (1552).
8. Set forth.
9. Violently.
10. Mass wafers.
11. Bale's residence five miles outside Kilkenny.
12. Metheglin, i.e., spiced mead.
13. Whisky.
14. "Let us rejoice in the wine vat," a parody of *in Domino*, the introit of the Feast of All Saints (and others).
15. Masquelike.
16. Lady Jane Grey (see 7.1).
17. Lord Deputy.
18. Thomas Butler, a member of the old Anglo-Norman community.
19. Stratagem.
20. Clerk of the Check.

21. Foot soldiers and soldiers with poleaxes.

22. Polemical interludes composed by Bale circa 1538 and published in 1547–48.

23. Church, with a derogatory sense of paganism.

24. Ecclesiastical equipment forbidden under Edward VI.

25. "Holy Mary, pray for us."

26. Clerics who belong to a college.

27. Beastly.

28. Turning into.

29. "A man went out to sow" (Luke 8:5).

30. "I am the good shepherd" (John 10:14).

31. Bale accuses Archbishop Brown of preaching only two sermons, which vary only by season.

32. Deutschland (Germany).

33. Noordwijk, a village in Holland.

34. Magistrate's court.

35. Bible translator and Bishop of Exeter.

36. Sacramental oils.

37. Popular name for a priest.

38. Consecrated host.

39. Collector of customs duties.

40. King's Lynn, a port in Norfolk

41. An end.

42. Dutch province.

43. Riffraff.

44. Discharged.

45. Solicitous.

46. Learned men, a contemptuous reference.

47. Irrational.

48. Matt. 3:12.

49. Rev. 14:15.

6.3. James Cancellar, from
The Path of Obedience (c. 1556)

James Cancellar (fl.1556–64) wrote *The Path of Obedience, Right Necessary for All the King and Queen's Majesty's Loving Subjects* to appeal for obedience to royal authority while serving as chaplain to Mary I, to whom he dedicated the book. A vivid attack on *The Vocation of John Bale* makes up the following excerpt. Reversing symbolism found in the *Vocation*, he claims that Bale is a renegade friar who blasphemously compares himself with Saint Paul at a time when "true" religion has undergone restoration in England.

SOURCE: *STC* 4564, D3ʳ–D4ʳ, D4ᵛ–D5ᵛ, D6ʳ–7ʳ.
EDITION AND REFERENCE: Bale 1990.

As of late many hath risen among us in this realm, and especially that presumptuous heretic, John Bale, who hath taken no small travail to hinder through his abominable heresies, the glory of Christ's gospel. As it doth appear by diverse and sundry books by him made, and especially in his book entitled *The Vocation of John Bale to the Bishopric of Ossory*, where he not a little triumpheth of his dangerous travails which he had in the same, not shaming to compare himself with holy Saint Paul in troubles, in labors, in peril of shipwreck, in peril of the sea, in peril of false brethren, in peril of pirates, robbers, and murderers. This whilst he is comparing himself with the holy Apostle like a mad harehead[1] beginneth to say why should I shrink or be ashamed to boast as the Apostle hath? Who as it appeareth in the second to the Corinthians (saith he) did boast of his labors, perils, and troubles in the gospel. And the like labor and perils had I in my journey with no less trouble than he had from Jerusalem to Rome, saving that (saith he) we lost not our ship. . . .

So do we well understand you to be a notable heretic apostate, and runagate, whereby you are compelled of necessity to run with the thief or murderer from city to city and from country to country for the assurance of your life, but undoubtedly if you had been as you say a true disciple of Christ and as fellow like with Saint Paul as you write yourself to be, when you by chance of weather were driven into Dover Road would like as Paul did at Philippus have set your foot on land and preached Christ but contrariwise as you have written in the fortieth leaf of your book and on the left side you were more desirous to set your hand to a bill of fifty pounds more than you were able to pay to that end you might be set on land in Flanders, for that ye might have speedy travail to the rest of your viperous brethren in Germany, whereas ye say you were received with as much rejoice of your miraculous deliverance (as you term it). . . .

And in the conclusion of his Book the forty-fourth leaf and on the left side also, he hath diverse comparisons, between the prophets, apostles, and the Church of England, and these are his words: "What shall I say more? John Baptist is now derided in the prison, and Jesus the son of God is grinned at upon the Cross," but contrariwise in England, Master Bale, John Baptist is now delivered forth of prison. And Jesus the son of God is truly worshipped upon the Cross, and moreover he saith: "Paul in Athens is hissed at, the poor apostles are slyly laughed to scorn." But now in England praised be our lord Jesus Christ, Paul is truly preached, and the Apostles receive their due honor. . . . The rest of Bale's treachery I will omit at this time and return to my matter.

Note

    1. Harebrain.

6.4. William Roper, from
The Life of Sir Thomas More (c. 1556, pub. 1626)

When William Roper (1496–1578) embarked on legal study at Lincoln's Inn, he joined the household of Sir Thomas More, who persuaded him to abandon Lutheran convictions. Roper constructed this memoir to assist Nicholas Harpsfield, the Jesuit controversialist, in writing More's biography. Roper provides many anecdotes that date from his residence at More's Chelsea household (c. 1523–33) and also relies on his wife Margaret, More's daughter, who as her father's confidante attests to More's state of mind during imprisonment in the Tower of London for failure to assent to Henry VIII's supremacy over the Church of England. This moving narrative resembles a traditional saint's life in its emphasis upon More's self-denial, which included wearing a hair shirt and self-flagellation, effecting a miraculous cure, patient suffering, accepting martyrdom on the model of Saint Cyprian, and joy that he would undergo beheading for treason on the feast day of Saint Thomas (1535). Roper mentions More's well-stocked library, and deprivation of books and writing a letter with coal during imprisonment, but he stresses his reputation for wit rather than authorship. By contrast, Foxe's *Book of Martyrs* emphasizes the writing of *monuments* (i.e., documents) by Protestant saints (see 7.5.A). Written during the reign of Mary I (c. 1556), Roper's memoir remained in manuscript until 1626, when Jesuit exiles printed *The Mirror of Virtue in Worldly Greatness; or, The Life of Sir Thomas More* with a false Paris imprint at the English College Press at Saint-Omer, Normandy.

SOURCE: STC 21316, pp. 38–40, 43–45, 77–79, 90–91, 126–28, 135–43, 161–68.

EDITION: Richard Sylvester, ed., *Two Early Tudor Lives* (New Haven, Conn.: Yale University Press, 1962).

REFERENCE: Marius.

Thus did Sir Thomas More through the whole course of his life, by his actions make it appear, that all his travails and pains, without thought of earthly commodity either to himself or any of his, were only for the service of God, his King, and the commonwealth, wholly bestowed and employed. And he was oftentimes, in his latter days heard to say, that he never asked of the King for himself, the value of one penny.

His daily custom was, if he were at home, besides his private prayers with his wife, children, and family, often to retire alone, and exercise himself in private and godly devotions: as also every night before he went to bed, he used to go to his chapel with his whole family aforesaid, and there upon his knees devoutly to say, certain litanies,[1] psalms, and collects with them.

And because he was always desirous of private exercise, and that he might the better withdraw himself from worldly company, he built himself a lodging a good distance from his mansion house, called the New Building, wherein he placed a chapel, library, and a gallery to walk, spending many days in the week in prayer, and study together. And always on the Friday, he did usually continue there from morning until night, bestowing his time only in meditation, reading, and such godly exercises. . . .

Thus he ever delighted, not only to busy himself in virtuous exercises, but also to exhort his wife, children, and household to embrace and follow the same. To whom for his notable virtues, God showed, as it seemed, a miraculous and manifest token of his love, and favor towards him, at such time, as his daughter Roper lay dangerously sick of the sweating sickness (as many other did that year) and continued in such extremity of that disease, that by no skill of physic, or other art in such case, commonly used (although she had diverse both expert and learned physicians continually attendant about her) she could be kept from sleeping, so that the physicians themselves utterly despaired of her recovery, and quite gave her over. Her father Sir Thomas More, as one that most entirely loved and tendered her, being in great grief and heaviness, and seeing all humane helps to fail, determined to have recourse to God by prayer for remedy. Whereupon going up after his accustomed manner, into his aforesaid New Building, he there in his chapel, upon his knees with tears, most devoutly besought almighty God, that it would please his divine goodness, unto whom nothing was impossible, if it were his blessed will, to vouchsafe graciously to hear his humble petition. And suddenly it came into his mind, that a clyster[2] might be the only way to help her; of which when he had told the physicians, they all instantly agreed, that if there were any hope of remedy, that was the most likeliest, and marveled much, that themselves had not before remembered the same. . . .

This lord chancellor, although he was well known, both to God and the world to be a man of most eminent virtue, though not so considered of every man; yet for the avoiding of singularity would he appear to the eye of the world no otherwise than other men, as well in his apparel, as behavior. And albeit he appeared outwardly honorable, like to one of his dignity and calling, yet inward did he esteem all such things for mere vanity: for next to his naked body he wore almost continually a shirt of hair; the which a young gentlewoman, named Mistress More, by chance one day espying as he sat in his doublet and hose at dinner in the summertime, and seemed to smile thereat, his daughter Roper perceiving the same (being not ignorant of this his austerity) gave him private notice thereof, and he did presently amend the fault, seeming withal sorry that she had seen it. He also wore another plain coarse shirt without ruff or collar, upon his shirt of hair; and many times he likewise punished his body with whips, made of knotted cords; the which thing was only known to his daughter Roper, who for her secrecy, above all the rest he especially trusted, for that as need required she did always wash and mend his shirt of hair, which he would not discover unto any other whatsoever. . . .

In the time, before his troubles, he would talk with his wife and children of the joys of heaven, and the pains of hell, and the lives of the holy martyrs, of their grievous martyrdoms, of the marvelous patience, and of their sufferings and deaths, and that they died most willingly rather than they would offend God: also what a happy and blessed thing it was for the love of God to suffer loss of goods, imprisonment, loss of life, and lands. Moreover he would further say unto them, that upon his faith, if he could but perceive, that his wife and children would encourage him to die in a good cause, it would be such a comfort unto him, that for very joy thereof he would run merrily to his death. . . .

[Because of More's refusal to deny papal authority, he was imprisoned in the Tower of London on 17 April 1534.]

After he had remained in the Tower about a month, his daughter Roper (having greatly desired to see her father) made earnest suit, and got leave to visit him: at whose coming (after the saying of the seven psalms[3] and litanies, which he was ever accustomed to say with her) before they fell into discourse of any other matter, among other speeches he said unto her, "I believe, Meg, that they who have put me here, think they have done me a great displeasure: but I assure thee on my faith (mine own good daughter) if it had not been for my wife and you my children, whom I account the chief part of my charge, I would not have failed long ere now, to have enclosed myself in a straighter room than this. But since I am come hither, without mine own desert, I trust that God of his goodness will disburden me of my care, and with his gracious help supply my want amongst you. And I find no cause (I thank God, Meg) to reckon myself in worse case here, than in mine own house. For methinks in this case, God maketh me even a wanton, setting me upon his knee and dandling me."

Thus by his patient suffering, and cheerful demeanor in all his tribulations and disasters, it plainly appeared, that nothing seemed painful unto him, but rather a profitable exercise, for the good of his soul. Then when he had questioned a while with his daughter about his wife and children, and household state in his absence, he asked her how Queen Anne did.[4] "Never better, Father," quoth she. "Never better, Meg," quoth he, "alas, alas, it pitieth me to remember into what misery (poor soul) she will shortly come." . . .

Within a while after, Master Secretary[5] came to him from the king, and pretending much friendship towards him said that the King's Highness was his good and gracious Lord, not minding any matter thenceforward, wherein he should have cause of scruple to trouble his conscience. As soon as Master Secretary was departed to express what comfort he received of his speeches, he took a coal (for pen and ink then he had none) and wrote these lines following:

Aye, flattering Fortune, look thou never so fair,
Nor never so pleasantly, begin to smile,
As though thou wouldst my ruin all repair;
During my life thou shalt not me beguile!
Trust I shall God to enter in a while
Thy heaven of heavens, sure and uniform:
  Even after a calm, look I for a storm.

Now Sir Thomas More had continued almost six weeks in the Tower, before the Lady his wife could obtain license to visit him. Who at her first coming to him (like a good simple worldly woman) bluntly saluted him in this manner: "What a good care Master More, I marvel that you, who have been always hitherto taken for so wise a man, will now so play the fool to lie here in this close filthy prison, and be content to be thus shut up amongst mice and rats, when you might be abroad at your liberty, with the favor and goodwill both of the King and his council, if you would but do as all the bishops, and best learned of the realm have done? And since you have at Chelsea a right fair house, your library, your books, your garden, your orchard, and all other necessaries handsome about you where also you might, in the company of me your wife, children and household be merry; I muse what a God's name you mean thus fondly to tarry here?"

After he had a while quietly heard her, with a cheerful countenance he said unto her, "I pray thee, good Mistress Alice tell me one thing." "What is that?" quoth she. "Is not this house as near heaven as mine own?" Whereto after her accustomed homely fashion not liking such speeches she answered: "Tilly-valle, tilly-valle!" "How say you Mistress Alice, is it not so?" quoth he. "Bene deus, bene deus,[6] man, will your old tricks never be left?" quoth she again. "Well then, Mistress Alice," said he, "if it be so, it is very well; for I see no great cause, why I should joy much either in my gay house, or in anything belonging thereunto, when as if I should but live seven years underground and then rise again and come thither, I should not fail to find some dwelling therein, that would bad me get out of doors, and tell me it were none of mine. What cause then have I to love such a house, as would so soon forget his old Master?" So as her persuasions moved him nothing at all.

Not long after this there came unto him the lord chancellor,[7] the dukes of Norfolk and Suffolk, with Master Secretary, and divers of the Privy Council, at two several times, who used all possible policy to procure him either precisely to confess the supremacy, or directly to deny it. Whereunto (as appeareth by the book of his examinations[8]) they could never bring him or justly tax him for the contrary.

Shortly hereupon, one Master Rich (created afterward Lord Rich) that then was newly made the king's solicitor, Sir Richard Southwell, and one Master Palmer, servant to the secretary, were sent unto Sir Thomas More under color of fetching his books away from him. And whilst Sir Richard Southwell and Master Palmer were busy in picking them up, Master Rich pretending friendly discourse with him, amongst other things (of set purpose as it seemed) said thus unto him: "For as much as it is well known, Master More, that you are a man both wise, and well learned, as well in the laws of the realm, as otherwise, I pray you therefore, let me in courtesy, and good will be so bold to put you this cause. Admit there were, sir," quoth he, "an act of Parliament, that all the kingdom should take me for king, would not you then Master More, take me for king?" "Yes, marry," quoth Sir Thomas More, "that would I." "Then I put case further," quoth Master Rich, "Admit there were an act of Parliament that all the realm should take me for pope, would not you then Master More take me for pope?" "For answer," quoth Sir Thomas More, "to your first case, the Parliament may well (Master Rich) meddle with the state of temporal princes; but to make answer to your latter case: suppose the Parliament would make a law, that God should not be God: would you Master Rich, then say, that God were not God?" "No, sir," quoth he, "that would I not." "No more," quoth Sir Thomas More, as Master Rich after reported of him, "could the Parliament make the king supreme head of the church." And so Master Rich with the rest departed.

Now upon the only report of this speech Sir Thomas More was indicted of treason, upon the statute, whereby it was made treason to deny the king to be Supreme Head of the Church: unto which indictment, were put these heinous words, "Maliciously, traitorously, and diabolically." . . .

So remained he in the Tower more than eight days after his condemnation, from whence, the day before he suffered, he sent his shirt of hair (not willing to have it seen) to his said daughter Roper, and a letter written with a coal (printed in the . . . book of his works[9]) expressing plainly the fervent desire he had to suffer on the morrow, in these words following: "I cumber you, good Margaret very much, but I would be sorry if it should be any longer than tomorrow; for tomorrow is Saint Thomas of Canterbury his Eve, and the Octave[10] of Saint Peter, and therefore tomorrow long I to go to God; it were a day very meet, and convenient for me. I never liked your manner better towards me than when you last embraced me, and when daughterly love, and dear charity, have no leisure to look towards worldly courtesy."

Upon the next morrow, according as he wished, early in the morning there came unto him Sir Thomas Pope, his singular good friend, with a message from the king and council, that he must before nine of the clock, the same morning, suffer death, and that he should forthwith prepare himself thereto. "Master Pope," quoth he, "for your good tidings, I most heartily thank you. I have always been bound to the King's Highness, for the many benefits, and honors that he hath still from time to time most bountifully heaped upon me; especially that it hath pleased His Majesty, to put me here in this place, where I have had convenient time and leisure to remember my last end; and now most of all am I bound unto His Grace, that I shall be so shortly rid out of the miseries of this wretched life, and therefore will I not fail to pray earnestly for His Grace, both here and in the other world also."

"The King's pleasure is further," quoth Sir Thomas Pope, "that at your execution you shall not use many words." "Master Pope," quoth he, "You do well to give me warning of the King's pleasure, for otherwise I might have offended his Majesty against my will. I had indeed purposed at that time to have spoken somewhat, but of no matter of offense to his Grace; nevertheless whatsoever I intended, I am ready to conform myself obediently to his commandment. And I beseech you, good Master Pope, be a means[11] unto His Majesty that my daughter Margaret may be at my burial." "The King is contented already," quoth Sir Thomas Pope, "that your wife, children, and other of your friends have liberty to be present thereat." "Oh how much am I bound unto his grace," quoth Sir Thoms More, "that vouchsafeth to have so gracious a consideration of my poor burial." Whereupon Sir Thomas Pope taking his leave could not forbear weeping: which Sir Thomas More perceiving, comforted him in this wise, "Quiet yourself good Master Pope, and be not discomforted, for I trust we shall one day see each other in heaven, where we shall be sure to live, and love together in joyful bliss eternally."

Upon Sir Thomas Pope's departure, he changed himself into his best apparel, as one that had been invited to some solemn feast, which Master Lieutenant seeing, advised him to put it off, saying that he that was to have it was but a javel.[12] "What, Master Lieutenant," quoth he, "Shall I account him a javel that shall do me this day so singular a benefit? Nay, I assure you, were it cloth of gold, I would account it very well bestowed upon him, as Saint Cyprian[13] did, who gave to his executioner thirty pieces of gold." Yet through the lieutenant's persuasions he altered his apparel, and after the example of the foresaid holy martyr, he gave that little money he had left to his executioner, which was one angel of gold.

Then was he by Master Lieutenant brought out of the Tower, and from thence led towards the place of executions upon the Tower Hill, where going up the scaffold which was weak and ready to fall, he said smilingly to Master Lieutenant: "I pray you, good Master Lieutenant, see me safe up, and for my coming down let shift for myself." Then desired he all the people about him to pray for him, and to bear witness, that he should now there suffer death in and for the faith of the Holy Catholic Church. Which done he kneeled down, and after his prayers said he turned to the executioner, and with a cheerful countenance spake thus merrily unto him: "Pluck up thy spirits, man, and be not afraid to do thine office: my neck is somewhat short, therefore take heed thou striketh not awry, for saving of thine honesty: but if thou doest, upon my word I will not hereafter cast it in thy teeth." So at one stroke of the executioner passed Sir Thomas More out of this world, to God, upon the same day, which himself had most desired. 6 July 1535.

Soon after his death, intelligence thereof came unto the Emperor Charles the Fifth, whereupon he sent for Sir Thomas Eliot, then ambassador there, and said unto him, "My Lord Ambassador, we understand that the King your master hath put his faithful servant, and grave counselor to death, Sir Thomas More." Whereunto Sir Thomas Eliot answered, that he had heard nothing thereof. "Well," quoth the Emperor, "it is too true, and this will I say, that if I had been master of such a servant (of whose counsels and performance in state matters myself have had those many years no small experience), I would rather have lost the best city of my dominions, than such a worthy counselor." Which speech of the Emperor was afterward related by Sir Thomas Eliot unto Master William Roper, and his wife, being with him at supper in the presence of one Master Clement,[14] Master Heywood,[15] and their wives.

Notes

1. Liturgical prayers.
2. Enema.
3. The Seven Penitential Psalms.
4. Anne Boleyn, charged with adultery, convicted, and beheaded in 1536.
5. Thomas Cromwell (see Appendix).
6. "Good God, Good God."
7. Sir Thomas Audley.

8. Register of interrogations.

9. More's *English Works*, ed. William Rastell (1557).

10. Eighth day following a feast day.

11. Mediator.

12. Rascal.

13. Executed by the Romans in 258 C.E., this theologian served as bishop of Carthage in North Africa.

14. John Clement (d. c. 1570).

15. John Heywood (c. 1497–c. 1580).

6.5. John Foxe, from
The Book of Martyrs

John Foxe (1516–87) compiled the *The Book of Martyrs* under the auspices of John Day, the zealously Protestant printer. They collaborated on four ever-expanding editions (1563, 1570, 1576, and 1583) that ballooned to more than three million words before they died. The collection contains hundreds of martyrologies from the time of the Roman emperors onward, but its focus is the burning of more than three hundred Protestants during the reign of Mary I. This book and its famous illustrations (see Figures 5, 8, 10, 12, and 13) were widely known in Elizabethan England because ordinary people could read, hear, or look at pictures in chained copies placed in churches, guildhalls, and schools.

Foxe identifies "true" sainthood with the act of witnessing to religious faith. In contrast to medieval legends of saints that celebrate alleged miracles, cures, and magical feats, he supplies instances of providential intervention to deliver the faithful or punish their opponents. The compiler inflamed Protestant fervor against the pope and the Church of Rome by attaching partisan comments to his narratives. In addition to scores of stories about ordinary individuals, the collection features well-known persons such as Anne Askew (see 6.1). Her *Examinations* typify the conventional movement from apprehension to interrogation by authorities to being burned alive after refusing to recant and delivering an eloquent testimonial of faith. In many instances, Foxe assimilates separately printed texts into the collection. Its reliability came under attack soon after its initial publication (see 6.9).

EDITION: Foxe 2000.

REFERENCES: Gregory; King 1989; Loades 1997; Loades 1999; White 1963.

A. From the Life of William Tyndale (1570)

Constructed out of divergent manuscripts and printed books, Foxe's martyrology celebrates William Tyndale (c. 1495–1536) as "the Apostle of England." The 1570 life differs markedly from the 1563 version, having undergone careful revision and expansion based upon research into diocesan registers and Tyndale's own books. The preamble summarizes the translator's education at Oxford University, where he instructed students and fellows in the Bible. The narrative then recounts how he outwitted unlearned clerics at Little Sodbury, Gloucester, because of his mastery of the Bible. Foxe's source preserves the echo of Erasmus's *Paraclesis* in Tyndale's famous claim that he would cause a plowboy to surpass the biblical knowledge of a Catholic cleric.

Foxe resorts to *The Obedience of a Christian Man* (see 1.2.A) to recount Tyndale's goal of translating the Bible so that common people might understand it without mediation through nonscriptural traditions of the Catholic clergy. The compiler uses other writings by Tyndale to flesh out the story of how Cuthbert Tunstall, Bishop of London and trusted servant of Henry VIII, declined to patronize the translation project. The narrative concludes with Tyndale's migration to

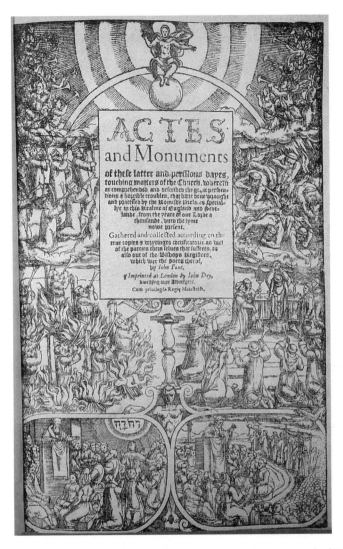

Figure 10. *The Persecuted Church and the Persecuting Church*. Foxe, *Book of Martyrs* (1563), title page woodcut. Courtesy of The Ohio State University Libraries. This polemical title page depicts the Protestant and Catholic churches. In the 1570 edition, John Day added an epigraph that alludes to Bale's *Image of Both Churches*: "The Image of the persecuted Church. The Image of the persecuting Church." An upward movement at the left-hand side conveys homage to Christ the Judge from ranked hierarchies of martyrs in flames, martyrs in heaven, and angels. A descending movement at the right-hand side portrays disobedient angels falling from heaven toward a celebration of the Roman-rite Mass. The lower left inset portrays a minister preaching to Bible-reading believers. Inspiration of their peers who kneel beneath the Tetragrammaton alludes to the birth of the Christian church at Pentecost. The other inset depicts a priest preaching to a congregation that tells its rosary beads opposite a Corpus Christi procession.

Figure 11. *Portrait Device of John Day. The Works of Thomas Becon*, vol. 1 (1564), 3C3ʳ, woodcut. Courtesy of The Ohio State University Libraries. John Day employed this bold woodcut device above the colophons of the *Book of Martyrs* and other books he published during the reign of Elizabeth I. Crafted in 1562, it depicts him at the age of forty. Day's motto, "Life is Death, and Death is Life," symbolizes the Resurrection in the manner of his other devices. At one time, he sold books at the sign of the Resurrection, which portrayed a rising sun.

the Continent, where he settled in Antwerp at a lodging for English merchants run by Thomas Poyntz. The story details the treachery of Henry Phillips, an Englishman who ingratiated himself into Tyndale's company in order to hand him over to imperial authorities. The life concludes with a poignant account of his last words prior to execution (see Figure 12).

SOURCE: STC 11223, pp. 1224–30.

EDITION: Foxe 2000.

REFERENCES: Daniell; Greenblatt.

William Tyndale, the faithful minister and constant martyr of Christ, was born about the borders of Wales, and brought up from a child in the University of Oxford, where he by long continuance grew up, and increased as well in the knowledge of tongues, and other liberal arts, as especially in the knowledge of the scriptures. Whereunto his mind was singularly addicted, in so much that he lying there in Magdalen Hall, read privily to certain students and fellows of Magdalen College, some parcel of divinity, instructing them in the knowledge and truth of the scriptures. Whose manners also and conversation being correspondent to the same, were such that all they which knew him, reputed and esteemed him to be a man of most virtuous disposition and of life unspotted. Thus he in the University of Oxford increasing more and more in learning and proceeding in degrees of the schools, spying his time, removed from thence to the University of Cambridge,[1] where after he had likewise made his abode a certain space, being now further ripened in the knowledge of God's word. Leaving that university also, he resorted to one Master Walsh a knight of Gloucestershire, and was there schoolmaster to his children, and in good favor with his master. This gentleman, as he kept a good ordinary[2] commonly at his table, there resorted to him many times sundry abbots, deans, archdeacons, with other divine doctors and great beneficed men, who there together with Master Tyndale sitting at the same table, did use many times to enter communications and talk of learned men, as of Luther and of Erasmus, also of diverse other controversies and questions upon the scripture.

Then Master Tyndale, as he was learned and well practiced in God's matters, so he spared not to show unto them simply and plainly his judgment in matters, as he thought. And when as they at any time did vary from Tyndale in opinions and judgment, he would show them in the book, and lay plainly before them the open and manifest places of the scriptures, to confute their errors and to confirm his sayings. And thus continued they for a certain season, reasoning and contending together diverse and sundry times, till at length they waxed wary, and bare a secret grudge in their hearts against him.

Figure 12. *The Execution of William Tyndale*. Foxe, *Book of Martyrs* (1563), p. 519, woodcut. Courtesy of The Ohio State University Libraries. This execution scene portrays Tyndale chained to the stake at Vilvorde Castle in Brabant, a province in the Low Countries, as the headsman garrotes him before burning. The crowd surrounding the scaffold includes jeering friars, soldiers, officials, and townspeople. We may read the translator's dying words in the banderole, "Lord, open the King of England's eyes." The printer, John Day, instructed the compositor to set them by means of movable type in an aperture within the wood block. These words allude to the New Testament motif of blindness versus seeing spiritual light, which is a commonplace feature of Tyndale's nontranslation prose and other Reformation texts.

Not long after this, it happened that certain of these great doctors had invited Master Walsh and his wife to a banquet, where they had talk at will and pleasure, uttering their blindness and ignorance without any resistance or gainsaying. Then Master Walsh and his wife, coming home and calling for Master Tyndale, began to reason with him about those matters whereof the priests had talked before at their banquet. Master Tyndale answering by scriptures, maintained the truth and reproved their false opinions. Then said the Lady Walsh, a stout and wise woman (as Tyndale reported) "Well" (said she) "there was such a doctor which may dispend one hundred pounds and another two hundred pounds and another three hundred pounds and what were it reason, think you, that we should believe you before them?" Master Tyndale gave her no answer at that time, nor also after that (because he saw it would not avail) he talked but little in those matters. At that time he was about the translation of a book called *Enchiridion Militis Christiani*,[3] which being translated he delivered to his Master and Lady. Who after they had read and well perused the same, the doctors and prelates were no more so often called to the house, neither had they the cheer and countenance when they came, as before they had. Which thing they marking and well perceiving, and supposing no less but it came by the means of Master Tyndale, refrained themselves, and at last utterly withdrew themselves, and came no more there.

As this grew on, the priests of the country clustering together, began to grudge and storm against Tyndale, railing against him in alehouses and other places. Of whom Tyndale himself in his prologue before the first book of Moses, this testifieth in his own words, and reporteth that he suffered much in that country by a sort of unlearned priests, being full rude and ignorant (sayeth he) God knoweth, which have seen no more Latin than that only which they read in their portases and missals. . . .

It was not long after, but Master Tyndale happened to be in the company of a certain divine recounted for a learned man. And in summoning and disputing with him, he drove him to that issue, that the said great doctor burst out into these blasphemous words and said, "we were better to be without God's law than the Pope's." Master Tyndale hearing this, full of godly zeal and not bearing that blasphemous saying, replied again and said, "I defy the Pope and all this laws," and further added that if God spared him life, ere many years he would cause a boy that driveth the plow to know more of the scripture, than he did.

After this the grudge of the priests increasing still more and more against Tyndale, they never ceased barking and rating at him, and laid many sore things to his charge, saying that he was an heretic in sophistry, an heretic in logic, and an heretic in divinity, and said moreover to him that he bare himself bold of the gentlemen there in that country. But not withstanding, shortly he should be otherwise talked withal. To whom Master Tyndale answering again thus said that he was contented they should bring him into any country in all England, giving him one pound a year to live with, and binding him to no more but to teach children and to preach.

To be short, Master Tyndale being so molested and detested in the country by the priests, was constrained to leave that country and to seek another place. And so coming to Master Welsh he desired him of his good will, that he might depart from him, saying on this wise to him: "Sir I perceive I shall not be suffered to tarry long here in this country, neither shall you be able though you would to keep me out of the hands of the spirituality, and also what displeasure might grow thereby to you by keeping me, God knoweth, for the which I should be right sorry." So that in time, Master Tyndale with the good will of his master, departed and eftsoons came up to London, and there preached a while, according as he had done in the country before, and specially about the town of Bristol, and also in the said town, in the common place called Saint Austin's Green. At length, he bethinking himself of Cuthbert Tunstall, then Bishop of London, and especially for the great commendation of Erasmus, who in his annotations[4] so extoleth him for his learning, thus cast with self that if he might attain unto his service, he were a happy man. And so coming to Sir Henry Guilford, the King's Controller, and bringing with him an oration of Isocrates, which he had then translated out of Greek into English, he desired him to speak with the said Bishop of London for him. Which he also did, and willed him moreover to write an epistle to the bishop, and to go himself with him. Which he did likewise, and delivered his epistle to a servant of his named William Hebilthwayte, a man of his old acquaintance. But God who secretly disposeth the course of things saw that was not best for Tyndale's purpose nor for the profit of his church, and therefore gave him to find little favor in the bishop's sight. The answer of whom was this, that his house was full. He had more than he could well find, and advised him to seek in London abroad, where he said he could lack no service, etc. And so remained he in London the space almost of a year, beholding and marking with himself the course of the world, and especially the demeanor of the preachers, how they boasted themselves and set up their authority and kingdom, beholding also the pomp of the prelates, with other things more which greatly misliked him. In so much that he understood, not only there to be no room in the bishop's house for him to translate the New Testament, but also that there was no place to do it in all England. And therefore finding no place for his purpose within the realm, and having some aid and provision, by God's providence ministered unto him by Humphrey Monmouth . . . and certain other good men, he took his leave of the realm and departed into Germany. Where the good man keeping inflamed with a tender care and zeal of his country, refused no travail nor diligence how by all means possible to reduce his brethren and countrymen of England to the same taste and understanding of God's holy word and verity, which the Lord had endued him withal.

Whereupon he considering in his mind, and partly also conferring with John Frith, thought with himself no way more to conduce thereunto than if the scripture were turned into the vulgar speech, that the poor people might also read and see the simple plain word of God. For first he wisely casting in his mind, perceived by experience how that it was not possible to establish the laypeople in any truth, except the scripture were so plainly laid before their eyes in their mother tongue, that they might see the process, order, and meaning of the text. For else what so ever truth should be taught them, these enemies of the truth would quench it again, either with apparent reasons of sophistry and traditions of their own making, founded without all ground of scripture, either else juggling with the text, expounding it in such a sense as impossible it were to gather of the text, if the right process, order, and meaning thereof were seen.

Again, right well he perceived and considered this only or most chiefly to be the cause of all mischief in the church, that the scriptures of God were hidden from the people's eyes. For so long the abominable doings and idolatries maintained by the pharisaical clergy could not be espied, and therefore all their labor was with might and main to keep it down, so that either it should not be read at all, or if it were, they would darken the right sense with the mist of their sophistry, and so entangle them which rebuked or despised their abominations, with arguments of philosophy and with worldly similitudes, and apparent reasons of natural wisdom. And with wrestling the scripture unto their own purpose, contrary unto the process, order, and meaning of the text, would so delude them in descanting upon it with allegories, and amaze them, expounding it in many senses laid before the unlearned lay people, that though thou felt in thy heart, and were sure that all were false that they said, yet could not thou solve their subtle riddles.[5]

For these and other such considerations, this good man was moved (and no doubt stirred up of God) to translate the scripture into his mother tongue, for the public utility and profit of the simple vulgar people of his country. First, setting in hand with the New Testament, which he first translated about the Year of Our Lord 1527. After that, he took in hand to translate the Old Testament, finishing the first books of Moses, with sundry most learned and godly prologues prefixed before every one, most worthy to be read and read again of all good Christians. As the like also he did upon the New Testament.

He wrote also diverse other works under sundry titles, among the which is that most worthy monument of his entitled the *Obedience of a Christian Man*, wherein with singular dexterity he instructeth all men in the office and duty of Christian obedience. With diverse other treatises, as of the *The Parable of the Wicked Mammon, The Practice of Prelates*, with expositions upon certain parts of the scripture, and other books also answering to Sir Thomas More and other adversaries of the truth no less delectable, than also most fruitful to be read, which partly yet being unknown to many, partly also being almost abolished and worn out by time, the printer hereof intendeth (good reader) for conserving and restoring such singular treasures, shortly (God willing) to collect and set forth in print the same in one general volume all and whole together, as also the works of John Frith, Barnes, and other as shall seem most special and profitable for thy reading.[6]

These books of William Tyndale being compiled, published, and sent over into England, it cannot be spoken what a door of light they opened to the eyes of the whole English nation, which before were many years shut up in darkness.

At his first departing out of the realm, he took his journey into the further parts of Germany, as into Saxony, where he had conference with Luther, and other learned men in those quarters. Where, after that he had continued a certain season, he came down from thence into the Netherlands and had his most abiding in the town of Antwerp, until the time of his apprehension. Whereof more shall be said God willing hereafter.

Among his other books which he compiled, one work he made also for the declaration of the sacrament (as it was then called) of the altar. The which he kept by him, considering how the people were not as yet fully persuaded in other matters tending to superstitious ceremonies and gross idolatry. Wherefore he thought as yet time was not come to put forth that work, but rather that it should hinder the people from other instructions, supposing that it would seem to them odious to hear any such thing spoken or set forth at that time, sounding against their great goddess Diana, that is, against their Mass, being had everywhere in great estimation, as was the goddess Diana among the Ephesians whom they thought to come from heaven.

Wherefore, Master Tyndale being a man both prudent in his doings, and no less zealous in the setting forth of God's holy truth, after such sort as it might take most effect with the people, did forbear the putting forth of that work, not doubting but by God's merciful grace, a time should come to have that abomination openly declared, as it is at this present day, the Lord almighty be always praised therefore, Amen.

These godly books of Tyndale, and specially the New Testament of his translation, after that they began to come into men's hands, and to spread abroad, as they wrought great and singular profit to the godly. So the ungodly, envying and disdaining that the people should be anything wiser than they, and again fearing lest by the shining beams of truth, their false hypocrisy and works of darkness should be discerned, began to stir with no small ado, like as at the birth of Christ, "turbatus est Herodes et tota Hierosolyma cum eo."[7] But especially, Satan the Prince of Darkness, maligning the happy course and success of the Gospel set to his might also how to impeach and hinder the blessed travails of that man, as by this, and also by sundry other ways may appear. . . .

[After publication of Tyndale's translation of the New Testament, he migrated to Antwerp, where he resided in a lodging for English merchants run by Thomas Poyntz, a relative of Lady Anne Walsh. He there befriended Henry Phillips, who betrayed him to imperial authorities.]

Then said Phillips, "Master Tyndale you shall be my guest here this day." So said Master Tyndale, "I go forth this day to dinner, and you shall go with me and be my guest, where you shall be welcome." So when it was dinner time Master Tyndale went forth with Phillips, and at the going forth of Poyntz's house was a long narrow entry, so that two could not go in a front. Master Tyndale would have put Phillips before him, but Phillips would in no wise, but put Master Tyndale afore, for that he pretended to show great humanity. So Master Tyndale being a man of no great stature, went before, and Phillips a tall comely person followed behind him, who had set officers on either side of the door upon two seats, which being there, might see who came in the entry, and coming through the same entry, Phillips pointed with his finger over Master Tyndale's head down to him, that the officers which sat at the door might see that it was he whom they should take, as the officers that took Master Tyndale afterward told Poyntz, and said to Poyntz when they had laid him in prison, that they pitied to see his simplicity when they took him. Then they took him and brought him to the emperor's attorney or Procurer General, where he dined. Then came the Procurer General to the house of Poyntz, and sent away all that was there of Master Tyndale's, as well his books as other things, and from thence Tyndale was had to the castle of Vilvorde, eighteen English miles from Antwerp, and there he remained until he was put to death. . . .

At last, after much reasoning, when no reason would serve, although he deserved no death, he was condemned by virtue of the Emperor's decree made in the assembly in Augsberg . . . and upon the same brought forth to the place of execution. Was there tied to the stake and then strangled first by the hangman, and afterward with fire consumed in the morning at the town of Vilvorde, anno 1536, crying thus at the stake with a fervent zeal and a loud voice: "Lord open the King of England's eyes."

Such was the power of his doctrine and sincerity of his life, that during the time of his imprisonment (which endured a year and a half) it is said he converted his keeper, his daughter, and other of his household. Also the rest that were with him conversant in the castle reported to him, that if he were not a good Christian man, they could not tell whom to trust.

The Procurer General, the emperor's attorney being there, left this testimony of him, that he was *homo doctus, pius, et bonus*, that is, a learned, a good, and a godly man.

The same morning in which he was had to the fire, he delivered a letter to the keeper of the castle, which the keeper himself brought to the house of the foresaid Poyntz in Antwerp shortly after. Which letter, with his examinations and other his disputations, I would might have come to our hands. All which I understand did remain, and yet perhaps do, in the hands of the keeper's daughter. For so it is of him reported that, as he was in the castle prisoner, there was much writing and great disputation to and fro between him and them of the University of Louvain (which was not past nine or ten miles from the place where he was prisoner) in such sort, that they all had enough to do, and more than they could well wield, to answer the authorities and testimonies of the scripture, whereupon he most pithily grounded his doctrine.

Notes

1. A site associated with Lutheranism.
2. Meal.
3. Erasmus's chief devotional handbook.
4. Latin commentary on the New Testament.
5. Foxe refers to the fourfold method of biblical interpretation that Tyndale rejects in *The Obedience of a Christian Man* (1.2.A).
6. Foxe edited a collection gathered and published by John Day, *The Whole Works of William Tyndale, John Frith, and Doctor [Robert] Barnes* (1573).
7. "Herod was troubled, and all Jerusalem with him" (Matt. 2:3).

B. The Burning of Hugh Latimer and Nicholas Ridley (1570)

Perhaps the most poignant narrative in the *Book of Martyrs*, the double marty-rology of Hugh Latimer and Nicholas Ridley recounts the execution of the for-mer bishops of Worcester and London. They exerted great influence during the reign of Edward VI (see 2.3), but their religious convictions were anathema to his sister, Mary I. A partisan narrator, possibly Ridley's brother-in-law George Ship-side, narrates their suffering in a manner both horrifying and uplifting. After they arrive at a stake in a ditch beside Balliol College at the University of Oxford on 16 October 1555, Richard Smith, Regius Professor of Divinity, preaches a "wicked sermon" on 1 Corinthians 13:3: "If I yield my body to the fire to be burned, and have not charity, I shall gain nothing thereby" (see Figure 13). The martyrs tes-tify to their religious faith, refuse to recant, and demonstrate scorn for death by uttering witty asides and, in Latimer's case, donning his own burial shroud. A fic-tional speech added in 1570 augments his words of comfort with what may be the best-known words in Foxe's collection: "Be of good comfort, Master Ridley, and play the man. We shall this day light such a candle by God's grace in Eng-land, as, I trust, shall never be put out." Their friends hang bags of gunpowder around their necks in order to guarantee a speedy death. This effort fails in Rid-ley's case because tightly packed wood caused intense pain as it smoldered with-out consuming his upper body.

SOURCE: *STC* 11223, pp. 1376–79.

EDITION: Foxe 2000.

REFERENCES: Chester; Loades 1997; Loades 1999.

Upon the north side of the town, in the ditch over against Balliol College, the place of execution was appointed, and, for fear of any tumult that might arise to let[1] the burning of them, the Lord Williams was commanded by the queen's letters and the householders of the city to be their assistant, suffi-ciently appointed. And when everything was in a readiness, the prisoners were brought forth by the mayor and bailiffs.

Master Ridley had a fair black gown furred and faced with foins,[2] such as he was wont to wear being bishop, and a tippet of velvet furred likewise about his neck, a velvet nightcap upon his head, and a corner cap upon the same, going in a pair of slippers to the stake, and going between the Mayor and an Alderman, etc. After him came Master Latimer in a poor Bristol frieze frock all worn, with his buttoned cap and a kerchief on his head, all ready to[3] the fire, a new long shroud hanging over his hose down to his feet, which at the first sight stirred men's hearts to rue upon them, beholding on the one side the honor they sometime had, on the other, the calamity where-unto they were fallen.

Master Doctor Ridley, as he passed toward Bocardo,[4] looked up where

Master Cranmer did lie, hoping belike to have seen him at the glass window, to have spoken unto him. But then Master Cranmer was busy with Friar Soto and his fellows disputing together, so that he could not see him through that occasion. Then Master Ridley, looking back, espied Master Latimer coming after. Unto whom he said, "Oh, be ye there?" "Yea," said Master Latimer, "have after as fast as I can follow." So, he following a pretty way[5] off, at length they came both to the stake one after the other, where first Doctor Ridley entering the place, marvelous earnestly holding up both his hands, looked towards heaven: then shortly after espying Master Latimer, with a wonderous cheerful look, ran to him, embraced and kissed him, (and

Figure 13. *The Burning of Hugh Latimer and Nicholas Ridley*. Foxe, *Book of Martyrs* (1563), p. 1375, woodcut. Courtesy of The Ohio State University Libraries. A woodcut commissioned by John Day supplements Latimer and Ridley's martyrologies. Banderoles extending from their mouths contain the opening words of their dying prayers: "Father of heaven receive my soul" and "In manus tuas domine" ("Into thy hands, Lord"). This picture portrays the condemned men at the center of an empty space amid a large crowd of hostile onlookers. Master Smith preaches from a portable wooden pulpit as Thomas Cranmer looks down from the Bocardo Prison, stating, "O Lord strengthen them."

as they that stood near reported) comforted him saying: "Be of good heart brother, for God will either assuage the fury of the flame, or else strengthen us to abide it."

With that went he to the stake, kneeled down by it, kissed it, most effectuously[6] prayed, and behind him Master Latimer kneeled, as earnestly calling upon God as he. After they arose, the one talked with the other a little while, till they which were appointed to see the execution, removed themselves out of the sun. What they said, I can learn of no man.

Then Doctor Smith of whose recantation in King Edward's time, ye heard before, began his sermon to them, upon this text of Saint Paul in the thirteenth chapter of the first epistle to the Corinthians: *Si corpus meum tradam igni, charitatem autem non habeo, nihil inde utilitatis capio.* That is: "If I yield my body to the fire to be burned and have not charity, I shall gain nothing thereby."[7] Wherein he alleged that the goodness of the cause, and not the order of death, maketh the holiness of the person: which he confirmed by the examples of Judas and of a woman in Oxford that of late hanged herself, for that they and such like, as he recited, might then be adjudged righteous, which desperately sundered their lives from their bodies, as he feared that those men that stood before him would do. But he cried still to the people to beware of them, for they were heretics and died out of the Church. And on the other side he declared their diversity in opinions, as Lutherans, Oecolampadians, Zwinglians,[8] of which sect they were, he said, and that was the worst. But the old Church of Christ and the Catholic faith believed far otherwise. At which place they lifted up both their hands and eyes to heaven, as it were calling God to witness of the truth. The which countenance they made in many other places of his sermon, whereas they thought he spake amiss. He ended with a very short exhortation to them to recant and come home again to the Church, and save their lives and souls, which else were condemned. His sermon was scant[9] in all a quarter of an hour.

Doctor Ridley said unto Master Latimer: "Will you begin to answer the sermon, or shall I?" Master Latimer said: "Begin you first, I pray you." "I will," said Master Ridley.

Then, the wicked sermon being ended, Doctor Ridley and Master Latimer kneeled down upon their knees towards my Lord Williams of Thame,[10] the Vice Chancellor of Oxford, and diverse other commissioners appointed for that purpose, which sat upon a form[11] thereby. Unto whom Master Ridley said: "I beseech you my lord even for Christ's sake, that I may speak but two or three words"; and whilst my lord bent his head to the Mayor and Vice Chancellor, to know (as it appeared) whether he might give him leave to speak, the bailiffs and Doctor Marshall,[12] Vice Chancellor, ran hastily unto him, and with their hands stopped his mouth and said: "Master Ridley, if you will revoke your erroneous opinions and recant the same, you shall not only have liberty so to do, but also the benefit of a subject, that is, have your life." "Not otherwise?" said Master Ridley. "No," quod Doctor Marshall. "Therefore, if you will not do so, then there is no remedy but you must suffer for your deserts." "Well," quod Master Ridley, "so long as the breath is in my body, I will never deny my Lord Christ and his known truth; God's will be done in me." And with that he rose up and said with a loud voice: "Well, then, I commit our cause to Almighty God, which shall indifferently judge all."

To whose saying Master Latimer added his old poesy,[13] "Well, there is nothing hid but it shall be opened." And he said he could answer Smith well enough, if he might be suffered.[14] Incontinently they were commanded to make them ready, which they with all meekness obeyed. Master Ridley took his gown and his tippet and gave it to his brother-in-law, Master Shipside, who all his time of imprisonment, although he might not be suffered to come to him, lay there at his own charges to provide him necessaries, which from time to time he sent him by the sergeant that kept him. Some other of his apparel that was little worth, he gave away, other the bailiffs took.

He gave away besides diverse other small things to gentlemen standing by and diverse of them pitifully weeping; as to Sir Henry Lee[15] he gave a new groat, and to diverse of my Lord Williams' gentlemen some napkins, some nutmeg, and resins of ginger,[16] his dial,[17] and such other things as he had about him, to everyone that stood next to him. Some plucked the points[18] off his hose. Happy was he that might get any rag of him.

Master Latimer gave nothing, but very quietly suffered his keeper to pull off his hose, and his other array, which to look unto was very simple. And being stripped into his shroud, he seemed as comely a person to them that were there present, as one should lightly[19] see. And whereas in his clothes he appeared a withered and crooked silly[20] old man, he now stood bolt upright, as comely a father as one might lightly behold.

Then Master Ridley, standing as yet in his truss,[21] said to his brother: "It were best for me to go in my truss still." "No," quoth his brother, "it will put you to more pain, and the truss will do a poor man good." Whereunto Master Ridley said: "Be it in the name of God," and so unlaced himself. Then being in his shirt, he stood upon the foresaid stone and held up his hands and said: "Oh heavenly Father, I give unto thee most hearty thanks for thou hast called me to be a professor[22] of thee, even unto death. I beseech thee, Lord God, take mercy upon this realm of England, and deliver the same from all her enemies."

Then the smith took a chain of iron and brought the same about both Doctor Ridley's and Master Latimer's middles. And as he was knocking in a staple,[23] Doctor Ridley took the chain in his hand and shaked the same, for it did gird in his belly, and looking aside to the smith, said: "Good fellow, knock it in hard, for the flesh will have his course." Then his brother did bring him gunpowder in a bag, and would have tied the same about his neck. Master Ridley asked what it was. His brother said, "Gunpowder." Then said he, "I take it to be sent of God; therefore, I will receive it as sent of him." "And have you any," said he, "for my brother?" meaning Master Latimer. "Yea sir, that I have," quod his brother. "Then give it unto him," said he, "betime, lest you come too late." So his brother went and carried of the same gunpowder unto Master Latimer. . . .

Then brought they a faggot kindled with fire, and laid the same down at Doctor Ridley's feet. To whom Master Latimer spake in this manner: "Be of good comfort, Master Ridley, and play the man. We shall this day light such a candle by God's grace in England, as, I trust, shall never be put out."

And so the fire being given unto them, when Doctor Ridley saw the fire flaming up toward him, he cried in a wonderful loud voice: "*In manus tuas domine commendo spiritum meum. Domine recipe spiritum meum.*"[24] And after repeated this latter part often in English: "Lord, Lord, receive my spirit." Master Latimer crying vehemently on the other side, "Oh Father of Heaven receive my soul," who received the flame as it were embracing of it. After, as he had stroked his face with his hands and, as it were, bathed them a little in the fire, soon died (as it appeared) with very little pain or none. And thus much concerning the end of this old and blessed servant of God, Master Latimer, for whole laborious travails, fruitful life, and constant death, the whole realm hath cause to give great thanks to almighty god.

But Master Ridley, by reason of the evil[25] making of the fire unto him, because the wooden faggots were laid above the gorse[26] and over-high built, the fire burned first beneath, being kept down by the wood. Which when he felt, he desired them for Christ's sake to let the fire come unto him. Which when his brother-in-law heard, but not well understood, intending to rid him out of his pain (for which cause he gave attendance) as one in such sorrow not well advised what he did, heaped faggots upon him, so that he clean covered him, which made the fire more vehement beneath, that it burned clean all his nether parts before it once touched the upper, and that made him leap up and down under the faggots and often desire them to let the fire come unto him, saying, "I cannot burn," which indeed appeared well. For after his legs were consumed by reason of his struggling through the pain (whereof he had no release but only his contentation[27] in God) he showed that side towards us clean, shirt and all untouched with flame. Yet in all this torment he forgot not to call unto God still, having in his mouth, "Lord, have mercy upon me," intermeddling[28] this cry, "Let the fire come unto me; I cannot burn." In which pains he labored till one of the standers-by with his bill[29] pulled off the faggots above, and where he saw the fire flame up, he wrested himself unto that side. And when the flame touched the gunpowder, he was seen [to] stir no more, but burneth on the other side, falling down at Master Latimer's feet. Which some said happened by reason that the chain loosed; other said that he fell over the chain by reason of the poise[30] of his body and the weakness of the nether limbs.

Some say that before he was like to fall from the stake, he desired them to hold him to it with their bills. Howsoever it was, surely it moved hundreds to tears in beholding the horrible sight. For I think there was none that had not clean exiled all humanity and mercy which would not have lamented to behold the fury of the fire so to rage upon their bodies. Signs there were of sorrow on every side. Some took it grievously to see their deaths whose lives they held dear. Some pitied their persons that thought their souls had no need thereof. His brother moved many men, seeing his miserable case; seeing (I say) him compelled to such infelicity, that he thought then to do him best service when he hastened his end. Some cried out of the luck, to see his endeavor who most dearly loved him and sought his release, turn to his greater vexation and increase of pain. But whoso considered their preferments in time past, the places of honor that they sometime occupied in this commonwealth, the favor they were in with their princes, and the opinion of learning they had, could not choose but sorrow with tears to see so great dignity, honor, and estimation, so necessary members sometime accounted, so many godly virtues, the study of so many years, such excellent learning, to be put into the fire and consumed in one moment. Well, dead they are, and the reward of this world they have already. What reward remain for them in Heaven, the day of the Lord's glory when he cometh with his Saints, shall shortly, I trust, declare.

Notes

1. Prevent.
2. Marten furs.
3. Prepared for.
4. A prison.
5. Considerable distance.
6. Earnestly.
7. 1 Cor. 13:3.
8. Protestant groups.

9. Scarcely.
10. John Williams (1500–1559), lord of Thame, also figures in 7.5.B).
11. Platform.
12. Richard Marshall, dean of Christ Church.
13. Motto.
14. Permitted.
15. Courtier, Master of the Leash.
16. Medicinal extract.
17. Timepiece.
18. Laces attaching hose to doublet.
19. Readily.
20. Pitiable.
21. Snug garment.
22. Worshipper.
23. Metal attachment of a chain to the stake.
24. "Into your hands, Lord, I commend my spirit" (Luke 23:46).
25. Unskillful.
26. Kindling.
27. Acceptance of one's lot.
28. Intermingling.
29. Halberd or pickaxe.
30. Weight.

C. The Examination and Execution of Alice Driver
and Alexander Gouch (1570)

Alice Driver and Saunder (Alexander) Gouch were condemned for heresy and burned alive at Ipswich on 4 November 1558, two weeks before the death of Queen Mary brought a halt to the persecution of Protestants. Driver was the literate daughter and wife of farmers and Gouch a literate weaver. They brought to life the ideal articulated by Erasmus and Tyndale that ordinary individuals including women, children, weavers, and plowmen were entitled to read and interpret the Bible in their native language without intercession by clerics (see 1.2.A).

No account of Gouch's interrogation remains extant, but Foxe prints transcriptions of two examinations of Driver by Dr. Spenser, chancellor of Norwich, and Dr. Gascoigne. The source of these documents is unknown, but we may presume that she recorded them from memory. Driver's rejection of transubstantiation on the ground that it lacks scriptural warrant and her willingness to debate points of biblical and theological interpretation with learned men recall the refusal of Anne Askew to bow to patriarchal authority (see 6.1). Her ears had been cut off because she compared Mary I to Jezebel, an idolatrous queen who persecuted Hebrew prophets (1 Kings 18–21). Driver's argument that the word *church* exists nowhere in the New Testament reflects knowledge of Tyndale's translation of the Greek word *ekklesia* as *congregation*, a translation that Thomas More and other Roman Catholics rejected.

SOURCE: *STC* 11222, pp. 1670–72.

EDITION: Foxe 2000.

Master Noone, a justice in Suffolk, dwelling in Martlesham, hunting after good men to apprehend them (as he was a bloody tyrant in the days of trial) at the length had understanding that one Gouch of Woodbridge, and Driver's wife of Grousborough, to be at Grousborough together, a little from his house, immediately took his men with him and went thither, and made diligent search for them, where the poor man and woman were compelled to step into an haygolph[1] to hide themselves from their cruelty. At the last they came to search the hay for them, and by gauging thereof with pitchforks at the last found them. So they took them and led them to Melton jail, where they remaining a time, at the length were carried to Bury, against the assize at Saint James's tide, and being there examined of matters of faith, did boldly stand to confess Christ crucified, defying the pope with all his papistical trash. And among other things, Driver's wife likening Queen Mary in her persecution to Jezebel, and so in that sense calling her Jezebel, for that, Sir Clement Higham, being chief judge there, adjudged her ears immediately to be cut off, which was accomplished accordingly, and she joyfully yielded herself to the punishment, and thought herself happy that she was counted worthy to suffer anything for the name of Christ.

After the assize at Bury, they were carried to Melton jail again, where they remained a time. This Saunder Gouch was a man of the age of thirty-six years or thereabout, and by his science[2] he was a weaver of shredding coverlets, dwelling at Woodbridge in Suffolk, and born at Ufford in the same county. Driver's wife was a woman about the age of thirty years, and dwelt at Grousborough, where they were taken in Suffolk; her husband did use husbandry. These two were carried from Melton jail to Ipswich, where they remained and were examined, the which their examination, as it came to our hands, hereafter followeth.

The Examination of Driver's Wife Before Doctor Spenser, the Chancellor of Norwich

First, she coming into the place where she should be examined, with a smiling countenance, Doctor Spenser said, "Why, woman, dost thou laugh us to scorn?"

Driver's Wife. Whether I do or no, I might well enough, to see what fools ye be."

Then the chancellor asked her wherefore she was brought before him, and why she was laid in prison.

Driver's Wife. "Wherefore? I think I need not tell you, for ye know it better than I."

Chancellor. "No, by my troth, woman, I know not why."

"Then have ye done me much wrong" (quoth she) "thus to imprison me and know no cause why; for I know no evil that I have done, I thank God, and I hope there is no man that can accuse me of any notorious fact that I have done justly."

Chancellor. "Woman, woman, what sayest thou to the blessed sacrament of the altar? Dost thou not believe that it is very flesh and blood after the words be spoken of consecration?"

Driver's wife unto those words held her peace, and made no answer. Then a great chuff-headed[3] priest that stood by spake and asked her why she made not the chancellor an answer. With that, the said Driver's wife looked upon him austerely and said, "Why, priest, I come not to talk with thee, but I come to talk with thy master; but, if thou wilt, I shall talk with thee. Command thy master to hold his peace." And with that the priest put up his nose in his cap and spake never a word more. Then the chancellor bade her make answer to that he demanded of her.

Driver's Wife. "Sir," said she, "pardon me though I make you no answer, for I cannot tell what you mean thereby; for in all my life I never heard nor read of any such sacrament in all the scripture."

Chancellor. "Why, what scriptures have you read, I pray you?"

Driver's Wife. "I have (I thank God) read God's book."

Spenser. "Why, what manner of book is that you call God's book?"

Driver's Wife. "It is the New Testament. What call you it?"

Chancellor. "That is God's book indeed, I cannot deny."

Driver's Wife. "That same book have I read throughout, but yet never could find any such sacrament there; and for that cause I cannot make you answer to that thing I know not. Notwithstanding yet for all that I will grant you a sacrament, called the Lord's Supper; and therefore, seeing I have granted you a sacrament, I pray you show me what a sacrament is."

Chancellor. "It is a sign." And one Doctor Gascoigne, being by, confirmed the same, that it was a sign of an holy thing.

Driver's Wife. "You have said the truth, sir," said she, "it is a sign indeed, I must needs grant it; and therefore seeing it is a sign, it cannot be the thing signified also. Thus far we do agree; for I have granted your own saying."

Then stood up the said Gascoigne, and made an oration with many fair words, but little to purpose, both offensive and odious to the minds of the godly. In the end of which long talk, he asked her if she did not believe the omnipotency of God, and that he was almighty, and able to perform that he spake. She answered, "Yes," and said, "I do believe that God is almighty, and able to perform that he spake and promised."

Gascoigne. "Very well. Then he said to his disciples, 'Take, eat, this is my body.' Ergo, it was his body. For he was able to perform that he spake. For God useth not to lie."

Driver's Wife. "I pray you, did he ever make any such promise to his disciples that he would make the bread his body?"

Gascoigne. "Those be the words. Can you deny it?"

Driver's Wife. "No, they be the very words indeed, I cannot deny it; but I pray you, was it not bread that he gave unto them?"

Gascoigne. "No, it was his body."

Driver's Wife. "Then was it his body that they did eat over night?"

Gascoigne. "Yea, it was his body."

Driver's Wife. "What body was it, then, that was crucified the next day?"

Gascoigne. "It was Christ his body."

Driver's Wife. "How could that be, when his disciples had eaten him up over night, except he had two bodies, as by your argument he had: one they did eat over night, and another was crucified the next day? Such a doctor, such doctrine! Be you not ashamed to teach the people, that Christ had two bodies? In the twenty-second of Luke, 'he took bread and brake it, and gave it to his disciples, saying, 'Take, eat, and do this in the remembrance of me.' Saint Paul also sayeth (1 Corinthians 11) 'Do this in the remembrance of me; for as often as ye shall eat this bread, and drink this cup, ye shall show the Lord's death till he come.' And therefore I marvel ye blush not before all this people, to lie so manifestly as ye do?"

With that Gascoigne held his peace, and made her no answer. For, as it seemed, he was ashamed of his doings. Then the chancellor lift up his head off on his cushion, and commanded the jailer to take her away.

Driver's Wife: "Now" (said she) "ye be not able to resist the truth, ye command me to prison again. Well, the Lord in the end shall judge our causes, and to him I leave it. I wis, I wis, this gear will go for no payment then."

So went she with the jailer away.

The Second Examination Before Doctors Spenser and Gascoigne

The next day she came before them again, and the chancellor then asked her what she said to the blessed sacrament of the altar.

Driver's Wife. "I will say nothing to it. For you will neither believe me nor yourselves. For yesterday I asked you what a sacrament was, and you said it was a sign, and I agreed thereto, and said it was the truth, confirming it by the scriptures, so that I went not from your own words; and now ye come and ask me again of such a sacrament as I told you I never read of in the scriptures."

Chancellor. "Thou liest, naughty woman. We did not say so, that it was a sign."

Driver's Wife. "Why masters, be ye not the men that you were yesterday? Will ye eat your own words? Are ye not ashamed to lie before all this multitude here present, who heard you speak the same?"

Then stood up Doctor Gascoigne, and said she was deceived. For there were three churches: the malignant church, the church militant, and the church triumphant. So he would fain have made matter, but he could not tell which way.

Driver's Wife. "Sir, is there made mention of so many churches in the scripture?"

Gascoigne. "Yea."

Driver's Wife. "I pray you, where find you this word 'church' written in the scripture?"

Gascoigne. "It is written in the New Testament."

Driver's Wife. "I pray you, sir, show the place where it is written."

Gascoigne. "I cannot tell the place, but there it is."

With that she desired him to look in his Testament. Then he fumbled and sought about him for one; but at that time he had none, and that he knew well enough, though he seemed to search for it. At the last she said, "Have ye none here, sir?"

Gascoigne. "No."

Driver's Wife. "I thought so much indeed, that ye were little acquainted withal. Surely, you be a good doctor. You say you sit here to judge according to the law, and how can you give true judgment, and have not the book of the law with you?"

At which words Gascoigne was out of countenance, and asked her if she had one.

Driver's Wife. "No."

Gascoigne. "Then," said he, "I am as good a doctor as you."

Driver's Wife. "Well, sir, I had one, but you took it from me (as you would take me from Christ if you could) and since would ye not suffer me to have any book at all, so burning is your charity. But you may well know (I thank God) that I have exercised the same. Else could I not have answered you (to God's glory be it spoken) as I have."

Thus she put them all to silence, that one looked on another, and had not a word to speak.

Driver's Wife. "Have you no more to say? God be honored. You be not able to resist the spirit of God in me, a poor woman. I was an honest poor man's daughter, never brought up in the university, as you have been, but I have driven the plow before my father many a time (I thank God); yet notwithstanding in the defense of God's truth, and in the cause of my master Christ, by his grace I will set my foot against the foot of any of you all, in the maintenance and defense of the same. And for that, if I had a thousand lives, they should go for payment thereof."

So the chancellor rose up, and read the sentence in Latin of condemnation, and committed her to secular power, and so went she to prison again as joyful as the bird of day, praising and glorifying the name of God.

At that time also was examined one Gouch, who was taken with her, as before is said of, whose examination hereafter followeth.

This Alexander Gouch was examined chiefly of the sacrament and other ceremonies of the popish church, and for that his belief was that Christ was ascended into heaven, and there remaineth, and that the sacrament was the remembrance of his death and passion, refusing the Mass, and the pope to be the supreme head of Christ's church. For these causes was he condemned and died with Alice Driver at Ipswich, the fourth of November, which was the Monday after All Saints, 1558. They both ending their lives with earnest zeal, nothing fearing to speak their conscience, when they were commanded to the contrary.

Notes

1. Haystack.
2. Skill.
3. Fat-headed.

D. The Hairbreadth Escape and Exile of the Duchess of Suffolk (1576)

Foxe added this rousing story about Catherine Brandon (née Willoughby, 1520–80), widow of Charles Brandon, duke of Suffolk, to the 1576 edition of the *Book of Martyrs*. Although she shared Queen Mary's Spanish descent, the Duchess Dowager was a zealous Protestant who belonged to Catherine Parr's pietistic circle and patronized Hugh Latimer and other reformers (see 2.3, 6.5.B, 7.5.C). According to Stephen Gardiner, Bishop of Winchester, who spent Edward VI's reign in prison, she once travestied the Roman rite by dressing a dog in episcopal vestments, calling it by his name, and having it carried about in a mock religious procession. As lord chancellor under Mary I, the bishop alludes to Protestant attacks upon him as the "Winchester Wolf" who preyed upon Protestant "lambs" (see Figure 14).

This sensational story recounts how the duchess flees across the English Channel in the middle of winter with her infant daughter and an unlikely retinue that includes her fool, a gentlewoman, a cook, a laundress, a horse rider, a joiner, and a brewer. After reuniting with Richard Bertie, her second husband, they endure many hairbreadth escapes during an odyssey that passes across the Low Countries and through Germany to safe haven in Poland, where they receive protection from Baron Johannes à Lasco, who had been a prominent immigrant to London during Edward VI's reign. This romance-like narrative is filled with providential interventions that precede a "happy ending" in which Bertie becomes a Polish earl.

SOURCE: *STC* 22224, pp. 1971–73.
EDITION: Foxe 2000.

Stephen Gardiner, bishop of Winchester, surmising the Lady Catherine, Baroness Willoughby de Eresby, and Duchess Dowager of Suffolk, to be one of his ancient enemies, because he knew he had deserved no better of her, devised in the holy time of the first Lent in Queen Mary's reign a holy practice of revenge, first by touching her in the person of her husband, Master Richard Bertie, Esquire. . . .

[When Gardiner summoned Bertie for interrogation, he resisted the bishop's demand for repayment of a sizable debt already paid during the reign of Edward VI.]

"If it be true that you say," quoth the bishop, "I will show you favor. But of another thing, Master Bertie, I will admonish you, as meaning you well. I hear evil of your religion, yet I hardly can think evil of you, whose mother I know to be as godly and Catholic as any within this land, yourself brought up with a master whose education, if I should disallow, I might be charged as author of his error. Besides, partly I know you myself and understand of my friends enough to make me your friend; wherefore, I will not doubt of

Figure 14. *The Roman Wolves* (c. 1555). Engraving. Courtesy Department of Prints and Drawings, British Museum; © The British Museum. This caricature vilifies Stephen Gardiner, Bishop of Winchester and Lord Chancellor, as a wolfish butcher who slaughters Christ as the Lamb of God. It elaborates Protestant use of the term *wolf* as jargon for Catholic prelates. In this instance bishops conceal their vestments beneath "sheep's clothing" (Matt. 7:15) as they drink the Lamb's blood in a grotesque parody of the Roman-rite Mass. The satire also implicates Bishop Edmund Bonner in the persecution of "lambs" whose carcasses bear the names of the most famous Marian martyrs, including Hugh Latimer and Nicholas Ridley (see 6.5.B and Figure 13). Christ as the slaughtered Lamb rejects the doctrine of transubstantiation: "Why do you crucify me again, for with one oblation have I for ever made perfect those that are sanctified?" The "Winchester Wolf" acknowledges that "now I feed on men."

you, but I pray you if I may ask the question of my lady, your wife. Is she now as ready to set up the Mass as she was lately to pull it down, when she caused in her progress[1] a dog in a rochet to be carried and called by my name, or doth she think her lambs now safe enough, which said to me when I vailed my bonnet[2] to her out of my chamber window in the Tower, that it was merry with the lambs now the wolf was shut up? Another time my lord, her husband,[3] having invited me and diverse ladies to dinner, desired every lady to choose him whom she loved best and so place themselves. My lady, your wife, taking me by the hand for that my lord would not have her to take himself, said that, for so much as she could not sit down with my lord, whom she loved best, she had chosen me, whom she loved worst."

"Of the device of the dog," quoth Master Bertie, "she was neither the author nor the allower. The words, though in that season they sounded bitter to your lordship, yet if it should please you without offense to know the cause, I am sure the one will purge the other. As touching setting up of Mass, which she learned not only by strong persuasions of diverse excellent learned men but by universal consent and order whole six years past inwardly to abhor, if she should outwardly allow, she should both to Christ show herself a false Christian and to her prince a masking[4] subject. You know, my lord, one by judgement reformed is more worth than a thousand transformed temporizers. To force a confession of religion by mouth, contrary to that in the heart, worketh damnation where salvation is pretended."

"Yea, marry," quoth the bishop, "that deliberation would do well if she never required to come from an old religion to a new. But now she is to return from a new to an ancient religion, wherein, when she made me her gossip,[5] she was as earnest as any."

"For that, my lord," said Master Bertie, "not long since she answered a friend of hers, using your lordship's speech, that religion went not by age but by truth, and therefore she was to be turned by persuasion and not by commandment."

"I pray you," quoth the bishop, "think you it possible to persuade her?"

"Yea, verily," said Master Bertie, "with the truth, for she is reasonable enough."

The bishop, thereunto replying, said, "It will be a marvelous grief to the Prince of Spain[6] and to all the nobility that shall come with him when they shall find but two noble personages of the Spanish race within this land, the queen and my lady, your wife, and one of them gone from the faith."

[Government officials permitted Bertie to travel to the Continent, but the duchess remained in England at risk of death for heresy.]

So he passed the seas at Dover about the beginning of June in the first year of her reign, leaving the duchess behind, who, by agreement and consent betwixt her and her husband, followed, taking barge at Lyon Quay very early in the morning on the first day of January next ensuing, not without some peril.

There was none of those that went with her made privy to her going till the instant but one old gentleman called Master Robert Cranwell, whom Master Bertie had specially provided for that purpose. She took with her her daughter, an infant of one year, and the meanest of her servants, for she doubted the best would not adventure that fortune with her. They were in number four men: one a Greek born, which was a rider of horses; another a joiner; the third a brewer; the fourth a fool; one of the kitchen; one gentlewoman; and a laundress.

As she departed her house, called the Barbican,[7] betwixt four and five of the clock in the morning with her company and baggage, one Atkinson, a herald, keeper of her house, hearing noise about the house, rose and came out with a torch in his hand as she was yet issuing out of the gate. Wherewith, being amazed, she was forced to leave a mail[8] with necessaries for her young daughter and a milk pot with milk in the same gatehouse, commanding all her servants to speed them away before to Lyon Quay, and, taking with her only the two women and her child, so soon as she was forth of her own house, perceiving the herald to follow, she stepped in at Charterhouse hard by. The herald, coming out of the duchess' house and seeing nobody stirring, not assured, though by the mail suspecting, that she was departed, returned in, and while he stayed ransacking parcels left in the mail, the duchess issued into the street and proceeded in her journey, knowing the place only by name where she should take her boat, but not the way thither, nor none with her. Likewise her servants, having divided themselves, none but one knew the way to the said quay.

So she, appareled like a mean merchant's wife, and the rest like mean servants, walking in the streets unknown, she took the way that led to Finsbury Field, and the others walked the city streets as they lay open before them till, by chance more than discretion, they met all suddenly together a little within Moorgate, from whence they passed directly to Lyon Quay and there took barge in a morning so misty that the steersman was loath to launch out, but that they urged him. So soon as the day permitted, the Council[9] was informed of her departure, and some of them came forthwith to her house to inquire of the manner thereof and to take an inventory of her goods, besides further order devised for search and watch to apprehend and stay her.

The fame of her departure reached to Leigh, a town at the Land's End.[10] . . . When the time came that she should take ship, being constrained to lie that night at an inn in Leigh, where she was again almost bewrayed,[11] yet notwithstanding, by God's good working she escaping that hazard, at length, as the tide and wind did serve, they went aboard and, being carried twice into the seas almost to the coast of Zeeland,[12] by contrary wind were driven to the place from whence they came. And at the last recoil certain persons came to the shore, suspecting she was within that ship; yet, having examined one of her company that was aland for fresh achates[13] and finding by the simplicity of his tale only the appearance of a mean merchant's wife to be aship-board, he ceased any further search.

To be short, so soon as the duchess had landed in Brabant, she and her women were appareled like the women of Netherland with hukes,[14] and so she and her husband took their journey towards Cleveland,[15] and being arrived at a town therein called Santon, took a house there until they might further devise of some sure place where to settle themselves.

About five miles from Santon is a free town called Wesel under the said Duke of Cleves' dominion and one of the Hansetowns,[16] privileged with the company of the Steelyard[17] in London, whither diverse Walloons[18] were fled for religion. . . . Which practice discovered by a gentleman of that country to Master Bertie, he without further delay, taking no more than the duchess, her daughter, and two other with them, as though he meant no more but to take the air, about three of the clock in the afternoon in February, on foot, without hiring of horse or wagon for fear of disclosing his purpose, meant privily that night to get to Wesel, leaving his other family still at Santon.

After the duchess and he were one English mile from the town, there fell a mighty rain of continuance whereby a long frost and ice before congealed was thawed, which doubled more the weariness of those new lackeys. But being now on the way and overtaken with the night, they sent their two servants, which only went with them, to villages as they passed to hire some carry for their case, but none could be hired. In the meantime Master Bertie was forced to carry the child, and the duchess his cloak and rapier. At last betwixt six and seven of the clock in the dark night, they came to Wesel, and repairing to their inns for lodging and some repose after such a painful journey, found hard entertainment, for going from inn to inn, offering large money for small lodging, they were refused of all the innholders, suspecting Master Bertie to be a lance-knight[19] and the duchess to be his woman. The child for cold and sustenance cried pitifully; the mother wept as fast; the heavens rained as fast as the clouds could pour.

Master Bertie, destitute of all other succor of hospitality, resolved to bring the duchess to the porch of the great church in the town and so to buy coals, victuals, and straw for their miserable repose there that night, or at least till by God's help he might provide her better lodging. Master Bertie at that time understood not much Dutch, and by reason of evil weather and late season of the night, he could not happen upon any that could speak English, French, Italian, or Latin, till at last going toward the church porch, he heard two striplings talking Latin, to whom he approached and offered them two stivers[20] to bring him to some Walloon's house.

By these boys and God's good conduct he chanced at the first upon the house where Master Perusell supped that night, who had procured them the protection of the magistrates of that town. At the first knock, the goodman of the house himself came to the door and, opening it, asked Master Bertie what he was. Master Bertie said, an Englishman that sought for one Master Perusell's house. The Walloon willed Master Bertie to stay awhile, who went back and told Master Perusell that the same English gentleman of whom they had talked the same supper had sent, by likelihood, his servant to speak with him. Whereupon Master Perusell came to the door and, beholding Master Bertie, the duchess, and their child, their faces, apparels, and bodies so far from their old form, deformed with dirt, weather, and heaviness, could not speak to them, nor they to him, for tears. At length recovering themselves, they saluted one another, and so together entered the house, God knoweth full joyfully. Master Bertie changing all his apparel with the goodman, the duchess with the goodwife, and their child with the child of the house.

Within a few days after, by Master Perusell's means, they hired a very fair house in the town and did not let to show themselves what they were, in such good sort as their present condition permitted. It was by this time through the whole town what discourtesy the innholders had showed unto them at their entry, insomuch as on the Sunday following, a preacher in the pulpit openly in sharp terms rebuked that great incivility towards strangers by allegation of sundry places out of Holy Scriptures, discoursing how not only princes sometime are received in the image of private persons but angels in the shape of men[21] and that God of his justice would make the[m] strangers one day in another land,[22] to have more sense of the afflicted heart of a stranger.

The time thus passing forth, as they thought themselves thus happily settled, suddenly a watchword came from Sir John Mason, then Queen Mary's ambassador in Netherland, that my Lord Paget[23] had feigned an errand to the baths that ways; and whereas the Duke of Brunswick was shortly with ten ensigns to pass by Wesel for the service of the House of Osterreich[24] against the French king, the said duchess and her husband should be with the same charge and company intercepted.

Wherefore, to prevent the cruelties of these enemies, Master Bertie with his wife and child departed to a place called Weinheim in High Dutchland[25] under the Palsgrave's[26] dominion, where, under his protection, they continued till their necessaries began to fail them and they, almost fainting under so heavy a burden, began to fail of hope. . . .

The said duchess and her husband with their family entered the journey in April 1557 from the castle of Weinheim where they before lay towards Frankfurt. In the which their journey it were long here to describe what dangers fell by the way upon them and their whole company by reason of the landgrave's[27] captain, who, under a quarrel pretensed for a spaniel of Master Bertie's, set upon them in the highway with his horsemen, thrusting their boarspears through the wagon where the children and women were, Master Bertie having but four horsemen with him. In the which brabble it happened the captain's horse to be slain under him.

Whereupon a rumor was sparsed[28] immediately through towns and villages about that the landgrave's captain should be slain by certain Walloons, which incensed the ire of the countrymen there more fiercely against Master Bertie, as afterward it proved. For as he was motioned by his wife to save himself by the swiftness of his horse and to recover[29] some town thereby for his rescue, he so doing was in worse case than before, for the townsmen and the captain's brother, supposing no less but that the captain had been slain, pressed so eagerly upon him that he had been there taken and murdered among them had not he, as God would, spying a ladder leaning to a window, by the same got up into the house and so gone up into a garret in the top of the house, where he with his dag[30] and rapier defended himself for a space; but at length the burgomaster coming thither with another magistrate which could speak Latin, he was counseled to submit himself to the order of the law. Master Bertie, knowing himself clear and the captain to be alive, was the more bolder to submit himself to the judgment of the law, upon condition that the magistrate would receive him under safe conduct and defend him from the rage of the multitude. Which being promised, Master Bertie putteth himself and his weapon in the magistrate's hand and so was committed to safe custody while the truth of his cause should be tried. . . .

And thus Master Bertie and his wife, escaping that danger, proceeded in their journey toward Poland, where in conclusion they were quietly entertained of the king and placed honorably in the earldom of the said king of Poles in Sanogelia, called Crozan,[31] where Master Bertie with the duchess, having the king's absolute power of government over the said earldom, continued both in great quietness and honor till the death of Queen Mary.

Notes

1. Procession.
2. Tipped my hat.
3. Her late husband, Charles Brandon.
4. Hypocritical.
5. Intimate friend (in an ironic sense).
6. Prince Philip of Spain, whom Mary I married on 25 July 1554.
7. Willoughby House was located in an aristocratic neighborhood north of London Wall.
8. Valise.
9. Privy Council.
10. At the mouth of the River Thames.
11. Betrayed.
12. Dutch province.
13. Provisions.
14. Hooded capes.
15. Duchy of Cleves.
16. Cities of the Hanseatic League.
17. A Hanseatic commercial enclave on the River Thames.
18. French-speaking residents of the Low Countries.
19. Mercenary.
20. Silver coins.
21. Gen. 18:2.
22. Exod. 2:22, 18:3.
23. William Paget, secretary of state under Henry VIII and Edward VI.
24. Hapsburg rulers of Austria.
25. Germany.
26. Count Palatine's.
27. A German count.
28. Spread.
29. Arrive at.
30. Pistol.
31. Earldom of Kroze in Samogitia.

6.6. Chidiock Tichborne, Poems (1586)

Chidiock Tichborne (1558?–86) was a well-born Catholic who supported the Jesuit Mission to England and became a reluctant adherent of the conspiracy of Anthony Babington to assassinate Queen Elizabeth in 1586. His three extant poems reflect circumstances at the end of his life, when, after delivering a moving final speech, he was hung, drawn, and quartered at Tyburn because of his complicity in the Babington Plot. Composed in the Tower of London as he awaited execution, "Tichborne's Lament" poignantly articulates the lost promises of youth. It circulated widely in contemporary manuscript miscellanies. "The Housedove" explores the unfortunate downfall of an innocent victim of a cunning pursuer. Written in fourteener couplets, "To His Friend" stands alone in its overt articulation of religious faith by means of an allegorical conceit that explores life in terms of a tortuous sea voyage. Tichborne's antithetical style anticipates verse by Robert Southwell (see 6.8).

SOURCE AND EDITION: The present modernized selection from *The Works of Chidiock Tichborne* (text), ed. Richard M. Hirsch, is reprinted from *English Literary Renaissance* 16 (1986): 303–18 with the permission of the editors.

Tichborne's Lament

My prime of youth is but a frost of cares,
My feast of joy is but a dish of pain,
My crop of corn[1] is but a field of tares,[2]
And all my good is but vain hope of gain.
The day is gone, and yet I saw no sun.   5
And now I live and now my life is done.

The spring is past, and yet it hath not sprung.
The fruit is dead, and yet the leaves are green.
My youth is gone, and yet I am but young.
I saw the world and yet I was not seen.   10
My thread is cut, and yet it was not spun.
And now I live, and now my life is done.

I sought my death, and found it in my womb.
I looked for life, and saw it was a shade.
I trod the earth, and knew it was my tomb,   15
And now I die, and now I am but made.
The glass is full, and now the glass is run,
And now I live, and now my life is done.

The Housedove

A silly housedove happed to fall
    amongst a flock of crows.
Which fed and filled her harmless craw
    amongst her fatal foes.
The crafty fowler drew his net—   5
    all his that he could catch—
The crows lament their hellish chance,
    the dove repents her match.
But too, too late! It was her chance
    the fowler did her spy,   10
And so did take her for a crow—
    which thing caused her to die.

To His Friend

Good sorrow cease, false hope be gone, misfortune once farewell;
Come, solemn muse, the sad discourse of our adventures tell.
A friend I had whose special part made mine affections his;
We ruled tides and streams ourselves, no want was in our bliss.
Six years we sailed, sea-room enough, by many happy lands,   5
Till at the length, a stream us took and cast us on the sands.
There lodged we were in a gulf of woe, despairing what to do,
Till at the length, from shore unknown, a pilot to us drew,
Whose help did sound our grounded ship from out Charybdis'[3] mouth,
But unadvised, on Scylla[4] drives the wind which from the south   10
Did blustering blow the fatal blast of our unhappy fall,
Where driving, leaves my friend and I to fortune ever thrall;
Where we be worse beset with sands and rocks on every side;
Where we be quite bereft of aid, of men, of wind, of tide;
Where vain it is to hail for help so far from any shore.   15
So far from pilot's course: despair shall we, therefore?
No! God from out his heap of helps on us will some bestow,
And send such mighty surge of seas, or else such blasts to blow.
As shall remove our grounded ship, far from this dangerous place;
And we shall joy each other's chance through God's almighty grace,   20
And keep ourselves on land secure, our sail on safer seas.
Sweet friend, till then content thyself, and pray for our release.

Notes

1. Grain.
2. Matt. 13:25–29.
3. Whirlpool in the Straits of Messina.
4. Sea monster metamorphosed into a rock facing Charybdis.

6.7. Robert Southwell, from
An Epistle of Comfort (1587)

Robert Southwell, S.J. (1561–95) studied at the Jesuit seminary founded at Douai by William Allen (see 2.7) and the English College in Rome prior to his ordination. He returned to England in 1586 as part of the mission to England spearheaded by Edmund Campion and Robert Parsons (see 1.2.C, 2.5, 2.7, 6.9). Southwell's devotional pamphlets and poetry circulated in manuscript and surreptitiously printed books. He served as chaplain in Catholic households including the London residence of Henry Fitzalan and Anne Howard, Earl and Countess of Arundel. The earl was a leader of the surviving Catholic aristocracy. Located on the Strand, Arundel House concealed the secret printing press that produced Southwell's first publication, *An Epistle of Comfort* (1587). Originating in letters to Fitzalan when he was imprisoned for recusancy, its eloquent prose extends consolation to Catholic priests and laypeople subject to persecution by Elizabethan authorities and encourages them to persevere in religious faith. The following excerpt articulates a powerful appeal for and definition of martyrdom. After Richard Topcliffe, the infamous priest-hunter, apprehended Southwell, he underwent torture prior to execution for treason at Tyburn, which serves as a pilgrimage site to the present day. For Southwell's poetry, see 6.8.

SOURCE: *STC* 22946, S2ᵛ–S4ʳ, S5ᵛ, X8ᵛ–Y2ʳ, Z7ʳ–&1ᵛ,
REFERENCE: Brownlow.

Chapter II

What greater preeminence is there in God's church, than to be a martyr? What more renowned dignity, than to die in this cause of the Catholic faith? And this crown do our greatest enemies set upon our heads. The glory whereof, though none can sufficiently utter, but such as by experience have proved the same, yet may we gather conjectures, no small part of the greatness of it. For if we consider it in itself, it is the noble act of fortitude, death being the hardest thing for nature to overcome. It is also the greatest point of charity by God's own testimony, who said "Maiorem charitatem nemo habet, quam vt animam suam ponat quis, pro amicis suis."[1] It is the principalest act of obedience commended so highly in Christ. "Factus obediens vsque ad mortem." Become obedient even unto death. It is by Saint Augustine's verdict more honorable than virginity. It is finally the very chiefest act or effect of all virtues. If therefore as the divines say, that work or action is more perfect or meritorious, which proceedeth of the greatest number of good causes concurring to the same, then must martyrdom be a most glorious thing, which requireth the concourse of all virtues, and that in the highest degree, to the accomplishment thereof.

Martyrdom hath the privilege of the sacrament of baptism, and by Saint Augustine is compared therewith. In martyrdom saith he all the mysteries of baptism are fulfilled. "He that must be baptized conferreth his faith before the priest, and answereth when he is demanded. This doth also the martyr before the persecutor, he acknowledgeth his faith and answereth the demand. The baptized is either sprinkled, or dipped in water, but the martyr is either sprinkled with his blood, or not dipped but burned in fire. The baptized by imposition of the bishops' hands receiveth the holy ghost. The martyr is made a habitacle[2] of the same spirit, while it is not he that speaketh but the spirit of his heavenly Father that speaketh within him. The baptized receiveth the blessed sacrament in remembrance of the death of our Lord, the martyr suffereth death itself for our Lord. The baptized protesteth to renounce the vanities of the world, the martyr besides this renounces his own life. To the baptized all his sins are forgiven."[3] In the martyr all his sins are quite extinguished. Saint Cyprian also alleging a reason, why no crime nor surpassed offense could prejudice a martyr, sayeth "Ideo martirium appellatur, tam corona quam baptisma, quia baptisat pariter et coronat."[4]

Therefore is martyrdom called as well a crown, as a baptism, for that it baptizeth and crowneth together. So that as no offense committed before baptism can do the baptized any harm, so also doth martyrdom so cleanse the soul from all spot of former corruption, that it giveth thereunto a most undefiled beauty. Yea and in this, martyrdom seemeth to have a prerogative above baptism. For though baptism perfectly cleanse the soul, and release not only the offense, but also the temporal punishment due unto the same; yet sticketh the root of sin in the flesh, and the party baptized retaineth in him, the badge and cognizance, yea the scars and tokens of a sinner. But martyrdom's virtue is such, that it not only worketh the same effect of baptism, but purchaseth also to the soul, forthwith a perfect riddance of all concupiscence and inclination to sin, and maketh it not only without offense, but unable to offend anymore. It doth not only gather the fruits, or lop the branches, or fell the tree, but plucketh it up by the very roots, and disableth it from springing up again. With the brood it killeth the dame, it consumeth both the weed and the seed together, and cleanseth us both from the mire and from the stain and spot that remaineth after it. . . .

In the baptism of water (saith St. Thomas) the Passion of Christ worketh, by a certain figurative representation, in the baptism of spirit by a desire and affection, in the baptism of blood by perfect imitation. Likewise the power of the Holy Ghost worketh in the first by secret virtue, in the second by commotion of the mind, in the third by fervor of perfect love. So much therefore in imitation in deed, is better than representation in the

figure, and desire in the thought: So much doth the baptism of blood surpass those of water and spirit. . . .

Chapter 12

O how unhappy are they,[5] that for the saving of goods, credit temporal
authority, or such worldly respects, forsake these so glorious and divine honors, and purchase a most lamentable and ignominious style. . . . What are
they but ruins of religion, dismembered offals and limbs of Satan. Many
of them yielding before the battle, and foiled before they fought, have not
left themselves so much as this excuse, to say that they went to church un-
willingly. They offer themselves voluntarily, they run wittingly to their own
ruin, and seem rather to embrace a thing before desired, than to yield to an
occasion that they would fain have eschewed. And did not your feet stumble, your eyes dazzle, your heart quake and your body tremble, when you
came into the polluted synagogue? And could Christ's servant abide in that
place to do any reverence and renounce Christ, or to do any homage to his
enemy whom he had in baptism renounced? And could you come there to
offer your prayers unto God, where your very presence offered you body and
soul to the devil? And could Catholic ears sustain without glowing, the blasphemous, reproachful, and rallying speeches against your true mother the
Catholic Church? Was it no pain to hear the corrupt translations, abuses and
falsifyings of God's own word? Was not the law of going to church, and
being there present at that which they call divine service, made and published
purposefully to the abolishing of the Catholic faith, to the contempt, re-
proof, and overthrow of the true church, to the establishing of their untrue
doctrine? And can any Catholic knowing this (as none can be ignorant
thereof) imagine, but that in obeying this law he consenteth unto it, and to
the accomplishing of that, which the law intendeth, that is the impugning of
the true and setting up of a false faith.

Do you not remember Saint Paul's words, "They are worthy of death
not only that do such things, but also those that consent to such as do
them?"[6] Even as he is worthy to be punished, who though in mind he favor
his prince, yet in deed he cleaveth to his enemy. Moreover was not this law
made, to force men to show and profess a conformableness in external
behavior to this new faith? Is it not required as a sign of renouncing the true
church, and approving this new form of service, sacraments, and religion? To
deny this, is against experience. For to this effect found all the penal laws and
statutes, this do the examinations, and arrangements and executions, make
manifest, wherein still things punished, and condemned are, not going to
the divine service as they call it, the hearing Mass, the receiving priests, using

the benefit of their function, or acknowledging of the authority of the See Apostolic. In all which, what can we think is meant, but that their laws, and all their endeavors tend to make us deny our, and receive their belief. And therefore when we obey them in these points, what do we but that which they pretend at our hands? . . .

Chapter 13

For though it hath been the property of heretics, to vaunt of such as died for their religion, and to term them martyrs, as they did their heresy true religion: yet in fine it hath always appeared, that as their doctrine was heresy, so their death desperation. . . . How is it possible for them to have the truth of martyrdom, that want the truth of Christ? The manna when it was used agreeably to the precept of God, had all kind of delightsome tastes, was fit to nourish and very pleasant to eat. But when in the use thereof his commandment was not observed, that most comfortable viand rotted, and turned into worms. So though martyrdom, if it be well used, be an act of singular virtue, yea of all virtues together, and turn to the incomparable glory of the martyr: yet when it is not taken for a right cause, and in due sort, it is to the sufferer but a beginning of an eternal corruption, and breedeth an everlasting worm of conscience. And upon such alighteth that curse of God mentioned in Deuteronomy, that they shall sow much seed, and reap little corn; because the locust shall devour it. They shall plant and dig a vineyard, but never drink the wine thereof; because the worms shall destroy it. They shall have olive trees in their grounds, and yet not be anointed with the oil; because their olives shall fall and perish.[7]

And so what torturing so ever the wicked or heretics suffer, it shall avail them to nothing but to their pain. For if all were martyrs, that die for their religion, then many heresies both contrary among themselves, and repugnant to the evident doctrine of Christ, should be truths, which is impossible. . . . He can be no martyr that is not in the church: he cannot achieve the kingdom, that forsaketh her that shall be Queen. They can make no abode with God, that refuse to be peaceable in his church. Well may they broil in flames, and being thrown into the fire, or whirled to wild beasts cast away their lives. It shall be no crown of their faith but a punishment of their perfidiousness, it shall not be a glorious end of their religious virtue, but a death of desperation. Well may such a one be killed: but he cannot be crowned. He so professeth himself to be a Christian, as the devil falsely sayeth himself to be Christ. As our Lord forewarned us saying, "Many shall come in my name saying I am Christ, and shall deceive diverse."[8] In the same fire (saith Saint Augustine)[9] the gold shineth and straw smoketh. Under the same flail the corn is purged and husks broken. Neither is the oil and dregs confounded together, because they are both under the weight of the same press. Even so the same violence that proveth, purifieth, and cleanseth the good; damneth, wasteth, and spoileth the bad. And in the same affliction the wicked curse and blasphemy God, and the good praise him and pray unto him, so much importeth it, not what things, but in what state and cause everyone suffereth. For by the like stirring the mire breatheth out a horrible, and the sweet ointment a delightsome savor.

The Red Sea of martyrdom, though to the true Israelite it yield dry way without impediment, yet Pharaoh and the false Egyptians are drowned therein and sink to the bottom like stones.[10] Who were ever more ready to die for the religion than the *Donatistesi?*[11] who did not only die obstinately when they were condemned, but provoked men to kill them for their religion. Have we not the same furious spirit, likewise in the Anabaptists,[12] who though they deny the scripture, the humanity of Christ, though they stick only to their own dreams, and revelations, though they permit such brutish community and plurality of wives, and marriage of sister and brother together: yet die they in defense of these damnable paradoxes, and that with such pertinacity, as though they had bodies of steel, that felt no pain or torment. But let not this move anyone to think the truth on their side.

Notes

1. John 15:13.
2. Habitation.
3. Southwell bases this passage on Saint Cyprian of Carthage's *Ad Fortunatum* and on a pseudo-Augustinian treatise commonly attributed to Gennadius of Marseilles, *De ecclesiasticis dogmatibus*, 3.74.
4. "For that reason one speaks of martyrdom as a crown as well as a baptism, for it baptizes as well as crowns." *De singularitate clericorum* 34, *Corpus Scriptorum Ecclesiasticorum Latinorum* (Vienna, 1866–present), 3.3.86.
5. Nonmartyrs.
6. Rom. 1:32.
7. Deut. 28:38–40.
8. Matt. 24:5.
9. Augustine, *The City of God*, Book 1, Chapter 8.
10. Exod. 14.
11. Donatists.
12. Radical religious sect.

6.8. Robert Southwell,
Poems (c. 1590)

Robert Southwell began to compose devotional poetry and prose during his residence as a seminarian and priest in Rome, but he completed most of his writing during residence in England as a Jesuit missionary (1586–95). Copies of his poems circulated in manuscript prior to the publication in 1595 of *Saint Peter's Complaint, With Other Poems* and *Mœoniæ; or, Certain Excellent Poems and Spiritual Hymns*. Domesticating techniques and conventions of Counter-Reformation verse, he adopted Continental meditative modes. The strained conceits, hyperbole, stirring antitheses, and paradoxy of his Manneristic verse anticipate poems by Richard Crashaw. Composed in fourteener couplets, which is metrically equivalent to ballad measure, "The Burning Babe" is a vivid Christmas carol whose meditative allegory explores intimations of the Crucifixion present in the Incarnation. This virtuoso lyric rivals devotional poetry by John Donne and George Herbert. "Of the Blessed Sacrament of the Altar" (originally entitled "The Christian's Manna") celebrates the Roman-rite Mass and doctrine of transubstantiation in a manner antithetical to contemporary Protestant thinking. It circulated in the form of a broadside ballad printed at Douai in 1606 (not in *STC*). See Southwell's *Epistle of Comfort* (6.7).

SOURCE: *STC* 22960, L4ᵛ and *STC* 22963, L7ʳ–L8ᵛ.

EDITION: *The Poems of Robert Southwell*, ed. Nancy Pollard Brown and James H. McDonald (Oxford: Clarendon Press, 1967).

REFERENCE: Brownlow.

The Burning Babe

As I in hoary winter's night stood shivering in the snow,
Surprised I was with sudden heat, which made my heart to glow;
And lifting up a fearful eye, to view what fire was near,
A pretty babe all burning bright did in the air appear;
Who scorched with excessive heat, such floods of tears did shed,
As though his floods should quench his flames, which with his tears were bred:
"Alas" (quoth he) "but newly born, in fiery heats I fry,
Yet none approach to warm their hearts or feel my fire, but I;
My faultless breast the furnace is, the fuel wounding thorns;
Love is the fire and sighs the smoke, the ashes, shames and scorns;
The fuel Justice layeth on, and Mercy blows the coals,
The metal in this furnace wrought are men's defiled souls;
For which, as now on fire I am to work them to their good,
So will I melt into a bath, to wash them in my blood."
With this he vanished out of sight, and swiftly shrunk away,
And straight I called unto mind, that it was Christmas day.

Of the Blessed Sacrament of the Altar

In paschal feast, the end of ancient rite,
An entrance was to never fading grace:
Types to the truth, dim glimpses to the light:
Performing deed presaging signs did chase:
      Christ's final meal was fountain of our good,   5
      For mortal meat, he gave immortal food.

That which he gave he was, O peerless gift,
Both God and man he was, and both he gave.
He in his hands himself did truly lift:
Far off they see whom in themselves they have.   10
      Twelve did he feed, twelve did their feeder eat:[1]
      He made, he dressed, he gave, he was their meat.

They saw, they heard, they felt him sitting near:
Unseen, unfelt, unheard, they him received,
No diverse thing, though diverse it appear,   15
Though senses fail, yet faith is not deceived.
      And if the wonder of the work be new:
      Believe the work, because his word is true.

Here true belief of force inviteth love,
So sweet a truth love never yet enjoyed.   20
What thought can think, what will doth best approve,
Is here attained, where no desire is void.
      The grace, the joy, the treasure here is such:
      No wit can wish, nor will embrace so much.

Self love here cannot crave more than it finds: 25
Ambition to no higher worth aspire.
The eagerest famine of most hungry minds,
May fill, yea far exceed their own desire.
      In sum here's all, and that in some expressed:
      Of much the most, of every good the best.   30

Here to delight the wit true wisdom is:
To woo the will of every good the choice.
For memory, a mirror showing bliss:

Here all that can both sense and soul rejoice.
     And if to all, all this it doth not bring,   35
     The fault is in the men, not in the thing.

Though blind men see no light, the sun doth shine:
Sweet cates[2] are sweet though soured tastes deny it.
Pearls precious are, though trodden on by swine:[3]
Each truth is true, though all men do not try it.   40
     The best still to the bad doth work the worst:
     Things bred to bliss doth make them more accursed.

The angels' eyes, whom veils cannot deceive:
Might best disclose what best they do discern.
Men must with sound and silent faith receive: 45
More than they can by sense or reason learn.
     God's power our proof, his works our wit exceed:
     The doer's might is reason for his deed.

A body is endowed with ghostly rights:
A nature's work from nature's law is free.   50
In heavenly sun lies hid eternal lights:
Lights clear, and near, yet them no eye can see.
     Dead forms a never dying life doth shroud,
     A boundless sea lies in a little cloud.

The God of hosts in slender hosts doth dwell: 55
Yea God, and man, withal to either due.
That God that rules the heavens, and rifted hell:
That man whose death did us to life renew.
     That God and man it is that angels bless:
     In form of bread and wine our nurturess.   60

Whole may his body be, in smallest bread:
Whole in the whole, yea whole in every crumb.
With which be one, or be ten thousand fed:
All to each one, to all but one doth come.
     And though each one, as much as all receive: 65
     Nor one too much, nor all to little have.

One soul in man is all in every part,
One face at once in many glasses shines.
One fearful noise doth make a thousand start:
One eye at once of countless things defines.   70
    If proof of one in many, nature frame,
    Why may not God much more perform the same?

God present is at once in every place:
Yet God in every place is always one.
So may there be by gifts of ghostly grace: 75
One man in many rooms yet filling none.
    Since angels may effects of bodies show:
    God angels gifts on bodies may bestow.

What God as author made, he alter may,
No change so hard, as making all of naught.   80
If Adam framed were of slimy clay:
Bread may to Christ's most sacred flesh be wrought.
    He still doth this, that made with mighty hand,
    Of water wine, a snake of Moses' wand.[4]

Notes

  1. The Last Supper.
  2. Delicacies.
  3. Matt. 7:6.
  4. Exod. 4:3.

6.9. Robert Parsons, from
A Treatise of the Three Conversions of England (1603)

Robert Parsons published his *Treatise of the Three Conversions of England* (Saint-Omer, 1603) in response to the *Book of Martyrs*. Asserting that "Foxe playeth the fox," Parsons was one of many early Catholic readers who claimed that this collection contains an extraordinarily large number of falsifications and errors. Parsons rejects Foxe's replacement of the majority of saints in the traditional church calendar with Protestant "confessors" (i.e., believers) and martyrs, notably those who were burned alive during the reign of Mary I. In the present selection, Parsons reinterprets the accounts of Anne Askew and Catherine Parr found in the *Book of Martyrs* (6.1, 7.5.C). He regards the former as an unruly dissident whose misinterpretation of the vernacular Bible led her to flout patriarchal authorities ranging from her husband to statesmen, and the latter as a misguided heretic whom Askew led into error. See Parsons's *Temperate Ward-Word* (1.2.C) and *Christian Directory* (2.5).

SOURCE: *STC* 19416, vol. 3, pp. 1–2, 17–18; vol. 2, pp. 491–96.

An Observation to the Reader About the Multitude of Foxean Martyrs, Which in the Former Calendar Are Recorded to Have Suffered Death, and Other Punishments for Their Opinions

It may be (gentle reader), and so commonly it falleth out in the best natures, that thou wilt have a certain horror of mind, to see under one view so many burned for their opinions in religion, as in this Calendar, hath been laid before thee; and to some it may seem perhaps great rigor and cruelty (and so Foxe endeavoreth everywhere to make it appear) and to others this cogitation may offer itself, that at least ways these men and women, that have offered their lives so willingly for defense of their religion, had some great inward testimony of the truth thereof. . . .

This willing or rather willful suffering death in sectaries[1] for their particular opinions, is not to be called constancy, but rather pertinacity . . . or rather audacity, much more to utter appearance than Catholic martyrs did. And yet further for thy better instruction herein, I thought good to set down a brief note of sundry heretics, condemned and put to death in our country, different from the Protestants' religion; yea condemned and executed for the most part by Protestants themselves. So as hereby thou might see, that neither only Protestant sectaries do offer themselves to go to the fire, nor only the Catholic clergy and magistrate hath, or doth exercise such punishment upon them. And finally I have thought good also, to lay before thee here at the beginning certain sentences of Holy Father's concerning this matter, whereby thou might the better be directed to judge of all the rest, that ensueth throughout the whole book. . . .

Another Animadversion About the Story of Foxean Martyrs That Ensueth Throughout Every Month

To prevent all occasions of cavil (gentle reader) to him that will seek to wrangle, I do here fore-signify first, that I do not prosecute in my narration all particulars that Foxe setteth down of his martyrs and confessors, for that had been to write as large a volume, as he hath done. Secondly, I do not lay forth such praises of them as he dilateth everywhere, with all his art of oratory skill, and this partly for that I do not believe them (finding him so false in other narrations, as I have done) partly also for that though some of them had moral virtues, yet were they neither eminent nor extraordinary, as will appear by the view of this our history, and whatsoever they were or might have been. Yet they being sectaries, and out of the church, could receive no avail by them towards salvation, as by the former doctrine of the Fathers you have seen. Thirdly then, whatsoever I have here written of them, I have taken it commonly out of Foxe himself, or of some other good author, whose words I do ever recite, as also the place and page where they are to be found, which Foxe often doth not. So that whatsoever I have omitted, or left out touching them, I have done it of purpose for brevity sake, and upon good causes; and what I have written and affirmed, I have done it with all truth and fidelity, and so will he find that shall read my narration, and confer it with Foxe himself; and this animadversion being premised, let any heretic cavil or wrangle that listeth, his arguments are answered before he begin. . . .

The Discussion of the Month of June, and What Martyrs and Confessors John Foxe Doth Place in the Catalogue and Calendar Thereof, as Appertaining to the Triumphant Church

After this upon the second day of the same, there ensue four other burned together at one fire in Smithfield, upon the last year of the reign of King Henry the Eighth for Zwinglianism, Calvinism, and denying the real presence in the sacrament of the altar. Three were men; to wit, Nicolas Balenian, priest of Salopshire,[2] John Lascelles, gentleman of the house of King Henry the Eighth, John Adams, tailor of London. But the captain of all was a young woman of some twenty-four or twenty-five years old, named Anne Askew. Who having left the company of her husband John Kyme, a gentleman of Lincolnshire, did follow the liberty of the new gospel, going up and down at her pleasure, to make new gospellers and proselytes of her religion until King Henry restrained her by imprisonment. This young woman's story is so pitifully related by John Foxe, as he would move compassion on her side, and hatred against the King and his council, that particularly handled this matter, and sought to save her, if it had been possible. And twice she recanted publicly, once upon the twentieth of March, 1545. . . .

Another recantation also she made, or at least an abnegation, upon the thirteenth of June next following in the very same year in the Guildhall of London. Where Holinshed declareth, "that she was arraigned before the King's justices, for speaking words against the sacrament of the altar, contrary to the Statute of Six Articles,[3] together with one Robert Luken, and Joan Sawtry." And that she was quit and dismissed thence, for that there was no witness to prove the accusation against her. Which in such matters of heresy is not likely would have happened, except there also she had made profession of her faith to the contrary. But yet the next year following, King Henry being informed, that, contrary to her oaths and protestations she did in secret seek to corrupt diverse people, but especially women, with whom she had conversed; and that she had found means to enter with the principal of the land, namely with Queen Catherine Parr herself, and with his nieces, the daughters of the Duke of Suffolk and others. He caused her to be apprehended and put to the rack, to know the truth thereof. And finding her guilty, he commanded her also to be burned. And by her confession he learned so much of Queen Catherine Parr, as he had purposed to have burned her also, if he had lived. As may appear by that, which Foxe relateth himself of her danger, presently after the burning of Anne Askew in the same year 1546, which was the last of King Henry; prefixing this title before his treatise thereof, "The Story of Queen Catherine Parr, Late Queen and Wife to King Henry the Eighth, Wherein Appeareth, in What Danger She Was for the Gospel, et cetera."

In which narration though Foxe, according to his fraudulent fashion, doth disguise many things, and lay the cause of all her trouble upon Bishop Gardiner and others, and that the King did kindly and lovingly pardon her; yet the truth is, that the King's sickness and death shortly ensuing, was the chief cause of her escape. And the error of the Lord Chancellor Wriothesley (afterward Earl of Southampton) who let fall out of bosom the King's hand, and commission for carrying her to the Tower, gave her occasion (the paper being found and brought to her) to go and humble herself to the King. At what time Foxe concludeth, that the King said unto her: "You are become a Doctor Kate, etc." And the truth is, that the principal occasion against her was for heretical books found in her closet, brought or sent her in by Anne Askew. Whereof the witnesses were the Lady Herbert, Lady Lane, Lady Tyrwit, and others. And by that occasion was the said Anne Askew put to the rack, for the discovery of the truth.

And this is the story of Anne Askew, whom John Bale . . . calleth "Anne Askew, *Iuvencula*," a young heifer or steer that abideth no yoke. He seemeth not to be far amiss, for that she was a coy dame, and of very evil fame for wantonness, in that she left the company of her husband, Master Kyme, to gad up and down the country a gospelling and gossiping where she might, and ought not.[a] And this for diverse years before her imprisonment, but especially she delighted to be in London near the court. And for so much as John Bale so highly commendeth her beauty and youth, affirming besides that she was but twenty-five years of age, when she was put to death. It is easily seen, what may be suspected of her life, and that the mystical speeches and demands, which herself relateth in Foxe to have been used to her by the King's council, about the leaving of her husband, were grounded in somewhat. Especially, seeing that she seemed in a sort to disdain the bearing of his name, calling herself Anne Askew, alias Kyme. And Bale in his description of her, never so much as nameth her husband or the name Kyme, but only calleth her Askew after her father's name.

By all which, and by the public opinion and same, that was of her lightness and liberty in that behalf. Every man may guess, what a *Iuvencula* she was and how fit for Bale's pen, and for Foxe his Calendar. And the proud and presumptuous answers, quips, and nips, which she gave both in matter of religion and otherwise to the King's council, and bishops, when they examined her, and dealt with her seriously for her amendment, do well show her intolerable arrogancy. And if she had lived but few years longer, it is very likely, she would have come to the point, that her dear sister, disciple and handmaid Joan of Kent (alias Knell, alias Bocher)[4] did. Whom she used most confidently in sending heretical books hither and thither, but especially into the court.

Marginal Gloss

[a] Anne Askew suspected of dishonest life.

Notes

1. Sectarians.
2. Shropshire.
3. Act of Six Articles (1539), which Protestants detested because of its imposition of harsh penalties on Bible reading and other practices (see Bray, no. 20).
4. Anabaptist who was burned alive for heresy in 1550.

QUEENLY PAGEANTRY
AND TEXTS

7.1. Lady Jane Grey,
Prison Writings (1553–54)

After the death of Edward VI, Protestant aristocrats attempted to retain power by engineering the succession to the throne of Lady Jane Grey (1537–54), the "nine-day queen." She functioned as a pawn in a plot in which her father, Henry Grey, Duke of Suffolk, collaborated with John Dudley, Duke of Northumberland, whose son, Lord Guildford Dudley, married Lady Jane. According to a legally dubious version of Henry VIII's will, her claim to the crown as the descendant of Henry's younger sister Mary was superior to that of his once-illegitimatized daughters Mary and Elizabeth. Lady Jane had attained a legendary reputation for learning acquired during residence in the household of Catherine Parr (see 7.5.C).

Wyatt's Rebellion (February 1554), a Protestant effort to depose Mary I, endangered Elizabeth (see 7.5.B) at the same time that it ensured Jane's condemnation for treason. She documented her spiritual experience in hortatory letters and a formal prayer as she awaited execution in the Tower of London. They were printed surreptitiously, possibly by John Day, as antigovernment propaganda. One letter castigates her one-time tutor John Harding for apostasy and urges him to return to "true" religion. Another is a remarkable document addressed to her sister Catherine, which she inscribed with the head of a pin on the flyleaf of her Greek New Testament during the night before she died. Her prose is notable for dense scriptural allusion, antithetical language that corresponds to John Bale's interpretation of the book of Revelation (see 1.1.B), and martyrological claims compatible with Foxe's later incorporation of her writings into the *Book of Martyrs* (see 6.5, 7.5).

SOURCE: *STC* 7279, A2ʳ–A5ᵛ, B1ᵛ–B2ʳ, B6ʳ–8ʳ.
EDITION: Bentley; Foxe 2000.
REFERENCES: Beilin; Hannay; King 1982.

A. An Epistle to a Learned Man of Late Fallen from the Truth

So oft as I call to mind the dreadful and fearful sayings of God: that he which layeth hold upon the plow and looketh back again is not meet for the kingdom of heaven.[1] And, on the other side, to remember the comfortable words of our Savior Christ to all those that, forsaking themselves, do follow him,[2] I cannot but marvel at thee and lament thy case. That thou, which sometime wast the lively member of Christ,[3] but now the deformed imp of the Devil; sometime the beautiful temple of God, but now the stinking and filthy kennel of Satan; sometime the unspotted spouse of Christ, but now the unshamefast paramour of Antichrist; sometime my faithful brother, but now a stranger and apostate; yea, sometime a stout Christian soldier, but now a cowardly runaway. So oft as I consider the threatenings and promises of God to all those that faithfully love him, I cannot but speak to thee, yea, rather cry out upon thee, "Thou seed of Satan, and not of Judah,"[4] whom the Devil hath deceived and the world hath beguiled, and desire of life hath subverted and made thee, of[5] a Christian, an infidel. Wherefore hast thou taken upon thee the testament of the Lord in thy mouth? Wherefore hast thou hitherto yielded thy body to the fire and bloody hands of cruel tyrants? Wherefore hast thou instructed other[s] to be strong in Christ, when thou thyself dost now so horribly abuse the testament and law of the Lord? When thou thyself preachest not to steal, yet most abominably stealest not from men, but from God and, as a most heinous sacrileger, robbest Christ, thy Lord, of his right of[6] his members: thy body and thy soul? When thou thyself dost rather choose to live miserably, with shame, to the world than to die and gloriously with honor to reign with Christ, in whom even in death there is life? And when, I say, thou thyself art most weak, thou oughtest to show thyself most strong. For the strength of a fort is not known before the assault, but thou yieldest thy hold before any battery be made.

Oh wretched and unhappy man, what art thou but dust and ashes?[7] And wilt thou resist thy maker that formed thee and fashioned thee; wilt thou now forsake him that called thee from custom, gathering among the Romish and anti-Christians[8] to be ambassador and messenger of his eternal Word; he that first framed thee and since thy creation and birth preserved thee, nourished thee, and kept thee, yea, and inspired thee with the spirit of knowledge, I cannot say of grace; shall he not possess thee? Darest thou deliver up thyself to another, being not thine own but his? How canst thou, having knowledge, or how darest thou neglect the law of the Lord and follow the vain traditions of men; and, whereas thou hast been a public professor of his name, become now a defacer of his glory? Ay, will thou refuse the true God and worship the invention of man: the Golden Calf,[9] the Whore of Babylon, the Romish religion, the abominable idol, the most wicked Mass. Wilt thou torment again, rent, and tear the most precious body of our Savior Christ with thy bodily and fleshly teeth, without the breaking whereof upon the cross, our sinful sins could else noways be redeemed? Wilt thou take upon thee to offer up any sacrifice unto God for our sins, considering that Christ offered up himself, as Paul saith, upon the cross, a lively sacrifice once for all?

Can neither the punishment of the Israelites, which for their idolatry so oft they received, move thee; neither the terrible threatenings of the ancient prophets stir thee; nor the curses of God's own mouth fear thee[10] to honor any other god than him? Wilt thou so regard him that spared not his dear and only son for thee, so diminishing, yea utterly extinguishing, his glory that thou wilt attribute the praise and honor to idols which have mouths and speak not, eyes and see not, ears and yet hear not; which shall perish with them that made them? What saith the prophet Baruch, where he reciteth the Epistle of Jeremiah,[11] written to the captive Jews? Did he not forewarn them that in Babylon they should see gods of gold, silver, wood, and stone borne upon men's shoulders to cast a fear before the heathen? "But be not ye afraid of them," saith Jeremiah, "nor do as other[s] do. But when you see other[s] worship them, say you in your hearts, 'It is thou, Oh Lord, that oughtest only to be worshipped; for as for the timber of those gods, the carpenter framed them and polished them; yea, gilded be they and laid over with silver and vain things and cannot speak.'"[12] He showeth, moreover, the abuse of their deckings,[13] how the priests took off their ornaments and appareled their women withal. How one holdeth a scepter, another a sword in his hand, and yet can they judge in no matter nor defend themselves, much less any other, from either battle or murder, nor yet from gnawing of worms nor any other evil thing.[14] These and such like words speaketh Jeremiah unto them, whereby he proveth them but vain things and no gods. And at last he concludeth thus: "Confounded be they that worship them."[15] They were warned by Jeremiah, and thou, as Jeremiah, hast warned other[s], and art warned thyself, by many scriptures, in many places.

God saith he is a jealous God,[16] which will have all honor, glory, and worship given to him only. And Christ saith, in the fourth [chapter] of Luke, to Satan, which tempted him, even to the same Satan, the same Beelzebub, the same devil which hath prevailed against thee: "It is written," saith he, "thou shalt honor the Lord thy God, and him only shalt thou serve."[17] These and such like do prohibit thee and all Christians to worship any other God than which was before all worlds and laid the foundations both of heaven and earth. And wilt thou honor a detestable idol invented by Romish popes and the abominable college of crafty cardinals? Christ offered himself up once for all, and wilt thou offer him up again daily[18] at thy pleasure? But thou wilt say thou dost it for a good intent. Oh sink of sin! Oh child of perdition! Dost thou dream therein a good intent where thy conscience beareth the witness, the promise of God's wrath toward thee? How did Saul, who, for that he disobeyed the word of God for a good intent, was thrown from his worldly and temporal kingdom? Shalt thou then, that so deface God's honor and rob him of his right, inherit the eternal and heavenly kingdom? Wilt thou, for a good intent, pluck Christ out of heaven and make his death void and deface the triumph of his cross, offering him up daily? Wilt thou, either for fear of death or hope of life, deny and refuse thy God, who enriched thy poverty, healed thine infirmity, and yielded to this victory, if thou couldst have kept it? Dost thou not consider that the third of life hangeth upon him that made thee, who can, as his will is, either twine it hard to last the longer or untwine it again to break it the sooner? Dost thou not remember the saying of David, a notable king, which teacheth thee, a miserable wretch, in his one hundred and fourth Psalm, where he saith: "When thou takest away thy spirit, O Lord, from men, they die and are turned again to their dust, but when thou lettest thy breath go forth, they shall be made, and thou shalt renew the face of the earth"?[19] . . .

Remember the horrible history of Julian,[20] of old, and the lamentable case of Francis Spira,[21] of late, whose case, me thinketh, should be yet so green in your remembrance, that, being a thing of our time, you should fear the like inconvenience, seeing that you are fallen into the like offense. Last of all, let the lively remembrance of the last day be always afore your eyes, remembering the terror that such shall be in at that time, with the runagates and fugitives from Christ, which, setting more by the world than by heaven, more by their life than by him that gave them their life, did shrink, yea, did clean fall away from him that never forsook them. And, contrariwise, the inestimable joys prepared for them that feared no peril, nor dreading death, have manfully sought and victoriously triumphed over all power of darkness, over hell, death, and damnation, through their most redoubted[22] captain Christ, who now stretcheth out his arms to receive you, ready to fall upon your neck and kiss you and last of all to feast you with the dainties and delicates of his own precious blood, which undoubtedly, if it might stand with his determinate purpose, he would not let to shed again, rather than you should be lost. To whom with the Father and the Holy Ghost be honor, praise, and glory everlastingly. Amen.

Be constant; be constant; fear not for pain:
Christ hath redeemed thee, and heaven is thy gain. . . .

B. An Exhortation Written by the Lady Jane the Night Before She Suffered, in the End of the New Testament in Greek, Which She Sent to Her Sister, Lady Catherine

I have here sent you, good sister Catherine, a book: which, although it be not outwardly trimmed with gold, yet inwardly it is more worth than precious stones. It is the book, dear sister, of the law of the Lord. It is his testament and last will, which he bequeathed unto us wretches, which shall lead you to the path of eternal joy. And if you with a good mind read it, and with an earnest desire follow it, it shall bring you to an immortal and everlasting life. It will teach you to live and learn[23] you to die. It shall win you more than you should have gained by the possession of your woeful father's lands. For as, if God had prospered him, you should have inherited his lands; so, if you apply diligently this book, seeking to direct your life after it, you shall be an inheritor of such riches as neither the covetous shall withdraw from you, neither the thief shall steal, neither yet the moths corrupt.[24] Desire with David, good sister, to understand the law of the Lord your God.[25] Live still to die, that you by death may purchase eternal life. And trust not that the tenderness of your age shall lengthen your life; for as soon, if God call, goeth the young as the old. And labor alway[s] to learn to die. Deny the world, defy the devil, and despise the flesh and delight yourself only in the Lord. Be penitent for your sins, and yet despair not. Be strong in faith, and yet presume not, and desire with Saint Paul to be dissolved and to be with Christ,[26] with whom even in death there is life. Be like the good servant, and even at midnight be waking. Lest, when death cometh and steal upon you like a thief in the night, you be with the devil's servant found sleeping;[27] and lest, for lack of oil, ye be found like the five foolish women;[28] and like him that had not on the wedding garment, and then you be cast out from the marriage.[29] Rejoice in Christ, as I trust ye do. And seeing ye have the name of a Christian, as near as ye can, follow the steps of your master, Christ, and take up your cross;[30] lay your sins on his back,[31] and always embrace him. And, as touching my death, rejoice as I do, good sister, that I shall be delivered of this corruption and put on uncorruption.[32] For I am assured that I shall, for losing of a mortal life, win an immortal life. The which I pray God grant you; send you of his grace to live in his fear and to die in the true Christian faith. From the which, in God's name, I exhort you that ye never swerve, neither for hope of life nor fear of death. For if ye will deny his truth to lengthen your life, God will deny you and yet shorten your days. And if ye will cleave to him, he will prolong your days to your comfort and his glory. To the which glory, God bring me now and you hereafter, when it shall please God to call you. Farewell, good sister, and put your only trust in God, who only must help you. Amen.

Your loving sister,
Jane Dudley.

C. The Lady Jane's Words upon the Scaffold

"Good Christian people, I am under a law and by a law I am condemned to die, not for anything I have offended the Queen's Majesty, for I will wash my hands guiltless thereof, but only for that I consented to the thing which I was enforced[33] unto. Notwithstanding, I have offended almighty God, for that I have followed overmuch the lust of my flesh and the pleasure of this wretched world, and I have not lived according to the knowledge that God hath given me, wherefore God hath plagued me now with this kind of death, and that worthily according to my deserts. Howbeit, I thank him heartily that he hath given me time to repent my sins here in this world. Wherefore, good Christian people, I shall desire you all to pray with me and for me while I am now alive, that God of his goodness will forgive me my sins. And I pray you all to bear me witness that I here die a true Christian woman and that I trust to be saved by the blood of Jesus Christ and by none other means, and now I pray you all, pray for me and with me"; and so said the Psalm of *Miserere mei*.[34] That done, she said, "Lord, save my soul, which now I commend into thy hands," and so prepared herself meekly to the block.

Notes

1. Luke 9:62.
2. Luke 5:11.
3. Christian.
4. God's chosen people.
5. From.
6. To.
7. Gen. 18:27.
8. Followers of Antichrist.
9. Exod. 32:35.
10. Make you afraid.
11. Apocryphal Letter of Jeremiah (Bar. 6).
12. Bar. 6: 4–9.
13. Decorations.
14. Bar. 6:14–21.
15. Bar. 6: 39.
16. Exod. 20:5, 34:14.
17. Luke 4:8.
18. In the Mass.
19. Ps. 104:29–30.
20. Julian the Apostate, Roman emperor who abjured Christianity and attempted to destroy it.
21. Italian jurist who renounced Christianity.
22. Revered.
23. Teach.
24. Matt. 6:19–20, Luke 12:33.
25. Ps. 19.
26. 2 Cor. 5:1.
27. Matt. 24:42–50.
28. Parable of the Wise and Foolish Virgins (Matt. 25:1–13).
29. Matt. 22:11–14.
30. Matt. 16:24.
31. Isa. 38:17.
32. 1 Cor. 15:52–53.
33. Compelled, against her will, to become queen.
34. Ps. 51.

7.2. John Elder, from
A Copy of a Letter Sent into Scotland (1555)

It was customary for citizens in late medieval and early modern northern Europe to organize pageantry in celebration of rulers upon their formal entry into important cities. Festivities involved elaborate tableaux vivants that featured allegorical scenes, emblazoning of verses or recitation of quasi-dramatic speeches, and musical performances.

John Elder (fl. 1555) provides a detailed account of the entry into London of Mary and her husband-to-be, Prince Philip of Spain, on 18 August 1554. The pageant of the Four Philips and other tableaux praised him as a consort suitable to father offspring who would inherit the throne of England in a line descended from Edward III. At Saint Paul's Cathedral, Mary and Philip received praise as "godly" rulers when they paused at a pageant in which actors representing them were flanked by Justice and Equity, on the one hand, and Bible-bearing Truth, on the other. This scene also alluded to the queen's motto, "Veritas Temporis Filia" ("Truth, the Daughter of Time"), an adage that symbolized her restoration of the old religion (see Figure 15). The pageant designer, Richard Grafton, had planned a different version of the tableau of the Nine Worthies from the one described by Elder by incorporating a portrayal of Henry VIII bearing a vernacular Bible (see Figure 1). The familiarity of this scene as a Reformation emblem suggests that the Lord Mayor and aldermen of London responsible for this entry harbored residual Protestant sympathies. Prior to the royal entry, Stephen Gardiner brought this tableau in line with official policy by ordering that the Bible be painted out and replaced with a pair of gloves.[1]

SOURCE: *STC* 7552, B4ᵛ–C4ᵛ.
REFERENCES: King 1989; Kipling.

Their most excellent Majesties made their most noble and triumphing entries into the noble city of London, first of Southwark Place, the next Saturday, which was the eighteenth of August, at two of the clock at afternoon. Where, after all the lords of their most honorable Privy Council, and the ambassadors of all nations, with the nobility of England and Spain, and diverse other noble and gentlemen, as well English as strange,[2] were all on horseback, two and two in a rank, the Lord Mayor of London, as the two princes came out at the gate, kneeled and delivered a mace, which signified his power and authority within the city of London, to the Queen's Grace. Whose majesty delivering the said mace to the Lord Mayor again, the King's Highness and she ascended their horses, and so marching towards London Bridge, the queen of the right hand, and the king of the left, with two swords of honor before them, and before the swords the Lord Mayor of London bearing the mace, the Tower of London beginneth to shoot. And

Figure 15. *Mary I as Truth the Daughter of Time*. Frans Huys. Engraving. Antwerp, 1555. By permission of the Department of Prints and Drawings, British Museum; © The British Museum. This portrait depicts the stern-looking queen above her personal motto, "Veritas Temporis Filia." She converted a classical tag used as a Reformation emblem into an argument for the validity of Catholic tradition, rescued by Time from oppression. As the embodiment of the traditions of the Church of Rome, Veritas occupied a central position in a pageant that greeted Mary and her husband-to-be, Philip of Spain, upon their 1554 entry into London (see 7.2). Elizabeth I appropriated her sister's motto and struck a histrionic pose as Protestant Truth during her precoronation entry into London (see 7.3).

when they came to the drawbridge, there they made the first stay, where there was in the height thereof, a fair table, holden up with two great giants: the one named Corineus Britannus, and the other Gogmagog Albionus. In which table, in a field silver, with fair roman letters of sable, these twelve verses[3] following were written: . . .

O noble Prince sole hope of Caesar' s side
By God appointed all the world to guide,
Right hastily welcome art thou to our land
The archer Britain yieldeth thee her hand
And noble England openeth her bosom
Of hearty affection for to bid thee welcome
But chiefly London doth her lone vouchsafe
Rejoicing that her Philip is come safe
She seeth her citizens love thee on each side
And trusts they shall be happy of such a guide
And all do think thou art sent to their city
By the only mean of God's paternal pity,
So that their mind, voice, study, power, and will
Is only set, to love thee Philip still.

Here also the Tower of London (the sign given that the king and the queen were in sight thereof) shot such peals of ordinance in, and about every quarter thereof, and specially out of the top of the White Tower and of the wharf, as never was heard the like in England heretofore.

Which being done, they proceeded forward until they came in Grace-church Street, where in their way the conduit thereof was finely trimmed, whereon was painted very ingeniously the Nine Worthies with many notable proverbs and adages, written with fair roman letters on every side thereof. And at the sign of the Splayed Eagle, they made the second stay where the first pageant was devised and made by the merchant strangers of the Steelyard.[4]

Where amongst diverse notable stories there was in the top thereof, the picture of the king sitting on horseback, all armed very gorgeously and richly set out to the quick. Under which picture were written in field silver with fair roman letters of sable, these words following after this manner. . . : "In honor of worthy Philip the fortunate, and most mighty, Prince of Spain, most earnestly wished for." And under that were written in a field blue, which heralds call azure, with fair roman letters of silver, these two verses following. . . :

Most might Philip, neither hope, nor fear may fright,
Thy strong and valiant heart, away from night.

Which picture and all other notable stories and writings in the said pageant pleasing their Majesties very well, they marched forward until they came to Cornhill, where the conduit also there being very excellently painted, at the west end of the street was the second pageant which was right excellently handled and set out, where their Majesties made the third stay. In which pageant were four lively persons, which represented the four most noble Philips of whose most noble acts and doings we read in ancient stories. That is to say, Philip King of Macedonia,[5] Philip the Roman Emperor,[6] Philip Duke of Burgundy surnamed Bonus,[7] and Philip Duke of Burgundy surnamed Audax,[8] betwixt which four princes, two being of the right side of the pageant, and two of the left, there was a fair table, wherein were written in a field azure, with roman letters of silver, these eight verses following . . . :

We read in time past Philips have been four
Whose glory through about all the world is blown
The first through noble blood past all before,
The second's match in good success unknown,
The third for goodness got eternal fame,
The fourth for boldness used against his son,
In birth, in fortune, boldness, virtuous name,
Thou Philip passest these Philips four alone.

This pageant with the stories therein contained liking the King's Highness and the queen wondrous well, they passed towards Cheapside, and at the east end thereof, the conduit there also being finely painted and trimmed, they made the fourth stay, where the third pageant was made. In the height whereof, was one playing on a harp, who signified the most excellent musician Orpheus,[9] of whom, and of Amphion,[10] we read in the fables of old poets. Where also were nine fair ladies playing and singing on divers sweet instruments, signifying the Nine Muses.[11]

And not far from them were men, and children decked up like wild beasts, as lions, wolves, foxes, and bears. So that the most sweet strokes, noise, and sounds of Orpheus with the Nine Muses playing and singing in the said pageant, and also the counterfeited beasts dancing and leaping, with Orpheus' harp, and the Muses' melody exhilarated and rejoiced their Majesties very much. Under Orpheus in a field silver, with fair roman letters of sable, were written in a very fair table these eight verses following . . . :

The prince that hath the gift of eloquence
May bend his subjects to his most behoof[12]
Which in old times was showed by conference
In Orpheus whose song did wild beasts move,
In the like case now thy grace of speech so frank
Doth comfort us, whose minds afore were bleak
And therefore England giveth thee hearty thanks
Whose chiefest joy is to hear thee Philip speak.

Their Majesties being satisfied with the sight of that pageant, they marched from thence, and passing through Cheapside, where they perceiving the Cross thereof, which was with fine gold richly gilded, they stayed a little looking thereon, which was (no doubt it is) unto them a right excellent view, where also the King's Highness perceiving the crucifix in the top thereof, very humbly put off his cap. This seen, they marched forward, and at the west end of Cheap they made the fifth stay, where was the fourth and most excellent pageant of all. Wherein was contained, declared, and showed their most noble genealogy from King Edward the Third, which genealogy was most excellently and most ingeniously set out, with a great arbor or tree; under the root whereof was an old man lying on his left side, with a long white beard, a close crown on his head, and a scepter in his right hand and a ball imperial in his left. Which old man signified King Edward the Third, of whom both their Majesties are lineally descended. Which green arbor or tree grew up of both the sides with branches, whereon did sit young fair children which represented the persons of such kings, queens, princes, dukes, earls, lords, and ladies as descended from the said King Edward the Third unto their days, whose names were written above their heads in fields azure in fair tables with roman letters of silver. Where also in the said top of the said arbor or tree was a queen of the right hand, and a king of the left, which presented their Majesties. Above whose heads was written their new style and title, with fair roman letters of sable in a field gold. And above that, in the height of all, were both their arms joined in one under one crown imperial. And finally under the old man which lay under the root of the arbor and signified (as I have said) King Edward the Third, were written these six verses following in a field of silver, with letters of gold . . . :

England, if thou delight in ancient men,
Whose glorious acts thy fame abroad did blaze,
Both Mary and Philip their offspring ought thou then
With all thy heart to love and to embrace

Which both descended of one ancient line
It hath pleased God by marriage to combine.

Which pageant being thoroughly viewed and much commended of
their Majesties, they went hence towards Saint Paul's Church. And in their
way a scholar of Paul's school decked up in cloth of gold, delivered unto the
King's Highness a fair book, which he received very gently. Where also a fellow came slipping upon a cord as an arrow out of a bow, from Paul's steeple
to the ground, and lighted with his head forward on a great sort of feather
beds. And after he climbed up the cord again, and done certain feats, their
Majesties lighted, and being in Paul's Church received with procession by
the Bishop of London, and *Te Deum* sung and ended, they departed, and
marched towards Fleet Street, at the conduit whereof they made the sixth
and last stay, where was the fifth and hindermost pageant of all. Wherein was
a queen and a king representing their Highness, having of their right side
Justitia[13] with a sword in her hand, and Equitas[14] with a pair of balance. And
of their left side Veritas[15] with a book in her hand, whereon was written Verbum Dei[16] and Misericordia[17] with a heart of gold. Where also from the
height of the pageant descended one which signified Sapientia[18] with a
crown in each of her hands, whereof the one she put on the head on her that
presented the queen, and the other on the head of him that presented the
king; under which two were written in a field azure with fair roman letters
of silver these six verses following . . . :

When that a man is gentle, just, and true
With virtuous gifts fulfilled plenteously,
If Wisdom then him with her crown endue
He govern shall the whole world prosperously,
And since we know thee Philip to be such
While thou shalt reign we think us happy much.

And after their Majesties had seen the effect of this pageant they proceeded forward towards Temple Bar, where they stayed a little in viewing a
certain oration in Latin, which was in a long table written with roman letters, above the port thereof as they passed departed forth of the city. Which
oration declared that such triumphs and pageants as were devised and made
in the noble City of London by the Lord Mayor thereof, his brethren, and
the citizens, for their entries, whose most happy coming, they most heartily
so long time desired, and wished for, and again the running and rejoicing of
the great number of people as were there calling and crying everywhere "God

save your graces," was an evident token, testimony, and witness of their faithful and unfeigned hearts to the Queen's Highness and the king. For whose most excellent Majesties they prayed unto almighty God long to live, rule, and reign over their most noble Empire of England.

Notes

1. British Library, MS Harleian 419, f. 131.
2. Foreign.
3. The omitted Latin contains twelve lines.
4. A Hanseatic commercial enclave on the River Thames.
5. Father of Alexander the Great.
6. Philip of Swabia.
7. Philip the Good.
8. Philip the Bold.
9. Mythic poet who entranced wild beasts with music.
10. Mythic lyre player.
11. Goddesses of poetic, musical, and artistic inspiration.
12. Advantage, benefit.
13. Justice.
14. Equity.
15. Truth.
16. Word of god.
17. Mercy.
18. Wisdom.

7.3. Richard Mulcaster, from
The Queen's Majesty's Passage Through the City of London (1559)

Richard Mulcaster (1530?–1611), headmaster of Merchant Taylors School, compiled this description of the 14 January 1559 procession of Elizabeth I through the City of London on the day before her coronation. Polemical spectacles represented her accession as a providential deliverance in the manner of Foxe's account of her prior imprisonment at the Tower of London and Woodstock (see 7.5.B). Although both queen and actors pretended that her responses were spontaneous, she actively collaborated in these tableaux.

The first pageant depicted the reunion of the houses of Lancaster and York in the marriage between Henry VII and Elizabeth of York at the end of the Wars of the Roses. Representation of their son, Henry VIII, with Anne Boleyn flatters Elizabeth I by rehabilitating her mother, whom her father executed. The second pageant featured the victory of personified Virtues over Vices in an appeal to the queen for restoration of Protestant religion after its suppression by Mary I.

Another pageant dramatized Elizabeth's motto, "Truth, the Daughter of Time." Artificial hills, one barren and the other fruitful, symbolized the transition from England's ruin under late Queen Mary to the new regime. Emerging from a cave with Father Time, Truth presented Elizabeth with an English Bible in a definitive image of Reformation monarchy (see Figures 1 and 5 [lower left inset]). Having remarked that "Time hath brought me hither," the queen embraced the Bible in a bold proclamation of her Protestant convictions.

The succeeding tableau featured Deborah, the chief biblical precedent for government by a woman (Judg. 4–5). Her consultation with the parliamentary estates mirrored the untested status of a queen who lacked absolute authority.

Mulcaster's fondness of allegory may have influenced Edmund Spenser, a onetime student of the Merchant Taylors School.

SOURCE: *STC* 7589.5, A2^r, A4^r–B1^r, B3^r–B4^r, B4^v–C1^r, C2^{r-v}, C3^v–D1^v, D3^{r-v}, D4^r, E2^v–E3^r, E4^{r-v}.

REFERENCES: Frye; King 1989; Kipling; Mullaney.

Upon Saturday, which was the fourteenth day of January in the year of our Lord God, 1558,[1] at about two of the clock after noon, the most noble and Christian princess, our most dread sovereign Lady Elizabeth, by the grace of God Queen of England, France, and Ireland,[2] defender of the faith, etc., marched from the Tower to pass through the City of London toward Westminster, richly furnished and most honorably accompanied as well with gentlemen, barons, and other the nobility of this realm, as also with a notable train of goodly and beautiful ladies, richly appointed. And entering the City, was of the people received marvelous entirely, as appeared by the assembly, prayers, wishes, welcomings, cries, tender words, and all other signs which

Figure 16. *Elizabeth I and the Four Virtues*. Bishops' Bible (1569), title page woodcut. By permission of the American Bible Society. In the title page woodcut of the 1569 second edition of the Bishops' Bible, Elizabeth I assumes a variation of the conventional royal pose established in the Coverdale Bible. In a manner analogous to the allegorical tableaux staged for her precoronation entry into London, she is surrounded by Justice and Mercy, the Imperial Virtues who respectively bear the Sword and the Book seen in portraits of Henry VIII and Edward VI. (Book 5 of Spenser's *Faerie Queene* allegorizes these virtues.) Fortitude and Prudence also accompany her. The queen's portrayal recalls her histrionic pose as Truth, the Daughter of Time, when she embraced the Bible, according to Mulcaster's *Queen's Majesty's Passage* (see 7.3 and Figure 15).

argue a wonderful, earnest love of most obedient subjects toward their sovereign. And on the other side, Her Grace, by holding up her hands and merry countenance to such as stood far off, and most tender and gentle language to those that stood nigh to Her Grace, did declare herself no less thankfully to receive her people's good will than they lovingly offered it unto her. . . .

[The queen proceeded from the Tower of London along Fenchurch Street to an elaborate arch at Gracechurch Street.]

A stage was made which extended from the one side of the street to the other, richly vaulted with battlements containing three ports, and over the middlemost was advanced three several stages in degrees. Upon the lowest stage was made one seat royal wherein were placed two personages representing King Henry VII and Elizabeth, his wife, daughter of King Edward IV. Either of these two princes sitting under one cloth of estate in their seats, no otherwise divided but that the one of them, which was King Henry VII proceeding out of the house of Lancaster was enclosed in a red rose, and the other, which was Queen Elizabeth, being heir to the house of York, enclosed with a white rose; each of them royally crowned and decently appareled as appertaineth to princes, with scepters in their hands and one vault surmounting their heads wherein aptly were placed two tables,[3] each containing the title of those two princes. And these personages were so set that the one of them joined hands with the other, with the ring of matrimony perceived on the finger. Out of the which two roses sprang, two branches gathered into one, which were directed upward to the second stage or degree, wherein was placed one representing the valiant and noble prince, King Henry VIII, which sprang out of the former stock, crowned with a crown imperial, and by him sat one presenting the right worthy lady, Queen Anne, wife to the said King Henry VIII and mother to our most sovereign lady, Queen Elizabeth that now is, both appareled with scepters and diadems and other furniture due to the [e]state of a king and queen and two tables surmounting their heads wherein were written their names and titles. From their seat also proceeded upwards one branch directed to the third and uppermost stage or degree, wherein likewise was planted a seat royal, in the which was set one representing the Queen's Most Excellent Majesty, Elizabeth, now our most dread sovereign lady, crowned and appareled as the other princes were. Out of the forepart of this pageant was made a standing for a child, which at the Queen's Majesty's coming declared unto her the whole meaning of the said pageant. The two sides of the same were filled with loud noises of music. And all empty places thereof were furnished with sentences concerning unity. And the whole pageant garnished with red roses and white, and in the forefront of the same pageant, in a fair wreath, was written the name and title of the same, which was: *The uniting of the two houses of Lancaster and York*. The pageant was grounded upon the Queen's Majesty's name. For like as the long war between the two houses of York and Lancaster then ended, when Elizabeth, daughter to Edward IV, matched in marriage with Henry VII, heir to the house of Lancaster; so, since that the Queen's Majesty's name was Elizabeth and forsomuch as she is the only heir of Henry VIII, which came of both the houses as the knitting up of concord, it was devised that like as Elizabeth was the first occasion of concord, so she, another Elizabeth, might maintain the same among her subjects, so that unity was the end whereat the whole device shot, as the Queen's Majesty's names moved the first ground. . . .

[The queen proceeded to the second pageant, which was located at Cornhill Conduit, a large water fountain trimmed with banners on top of which musicians played instruments.]

This pageant standing in the nether end of Cornhill was extended from the one side of the street to the other, and in the same pageant was devised three gates, all open, and over the middle part thereof was erected one chair, a seat royal with cloth of estate to the same, appertaining wherein was placed a child representing the Queen's Highness, with consideration had for place convenient for a table which contained her name and title. And in a comely wreath artificially and well devised with perfect sight and understanding to the people. In the front of the same pageant was written the name and title thereof, which is: *The seat of worthy governance*, which seat was made in such artificial manner, as to the appearance of the lookers-on the forepart seemed to have no stay, and therefore of force was stayed by lively personages, which personages were in number four, standing and staying the forefront of the same seat royal, each having his face to the queen and people, whereof everyone had a table to express their effects, which are virtues, namely: *Pure Religion, Love of Subjects, Wisdom, and Justice*, which did tread their contrary vices under their feet, that is, to wit: *Pure Religion* did tread upon *Superstition* and *Ignorance*, *Love of Subjects* did tread upon *Rebellion* and *Insolency*, *Wisdom* did tread upon *Folly* and *Vainglory*, *Justice* did tread upon *Adulation* and *Bribery*. Each of these personages, according to their proper names and properties, had not only their names in plain and perfect writing set upon their breasts easily to be read of all, but also every [one] of them was aptly and properly appareled, so that his apparel and name did agree to express the same person that in title he represented. This part of the pageant was thus appointed and furnished. The two sides over the two side ports had in them placed a noise of instruments, which immediately after the child's speech gave an heavenly melody. Upon the top or uppermost part of the said pageant stood the arms of England royally portraitured with the proper beasts to uphold the same. One representing the Queen's Highness sat in this seat crowned with an imperial crown, and before her seat was a convenient place appointed for one child which did interpret and apply the said pageant as hereafter shall be declared. Every void place was furnished with proper sentences commending the seat supported by virtues and defacing the vices, to the utter extirpation of rebellion and to everlasting continuance of quietness and peace. The Queen's Majesty, approaching nigh unto this pageant thus beautified and furnished in all points, caused her chariot to be drawn nigh thereunto that Her Grace might hear the child's oration, which was this:

> While that Religion true shall Ignorance suppress
> And with her weighty foot break Superstition's head,
> While Love of Subjects shall Rebellion distress
> And with Zeal to the Prince Insolency down tread.
> While Justice can Flattering Tongues and Bribery deface,
> While Folly and Vainglory to Wisdom yield their hands,
> So long shall government not swerve from her right race,
> But wrong decayeth still and rightwiseness upstands.

> Now all thy subjects' hearts, oh prince of peerless fame,
> Do trust these virtues shall maintain up thy throne
> And vice be kept down still, the wicked put to shame,
> That good with good may joy, and naught with naught may moan. . . .

Beside these verses there were placed in every void room of the pageant, both in English and Latin, such sentences as advanced the seat of governance upholden by virtue. The ground of this pageant was that like as by virtues, which do abundantly appear in Her Grace, the Queen's Majesty was established in the seat of government, so she should sit fast in the same so long as she embraced virtue and held vice under foot. For if vice once got up the head, it would put the seat of government in peril of falling. The Queen's Majesty, when she had heard the child and understood the pageant at full, gave the City also thanks there and most graciously promised her good endeavor for the maintenance of the said virtues and suppression of vices. . . .

[The queen then proceeded past the pageant of the Eight Beatitudes at the Great Conduit in Cheapside.]

At the Standard in Cheap, which was dressed fair against the time, was placed a noise of trumpets, with banners and other furniture. The Cross likewise was also made fair and well trimmed. And near unto the same, upon the porch of Saint Peter's Church door, stood the waits[4] of the City, which did give a pleasant noise with their instruments as the Queen's Majesty did pass by, which on every side cast her countenance and wished well to all her most loving people. Soon after that Her Grace passed the Cross, she had espied the pageant erected at the Little Conduit in Cheap and incontinent required what it might signify. And it was told Her Grace that there was placed Time. "Time?" saith she, "and Time hath brought me hither." And so forth the whole matter was opened to Her Grace as hereafter shall be declared in the description of the pageant. But in the opening, when Her Grace understood that the Bible in English should be delivered unto her by Truth, which was therein represented by a child, she thanked the city for that gift and said she would oftentimes read over that book, commanding Sir John Perrot,[5] one of the knights which held up her canopy, to go before and to receive the book. But learning that it should be delivered unto Her Grace down by a silken lace. . . .

[The queen continued to the eastern end of Cheapside, where she received a gift of 1000 marks in gold from the city of London. She then proceeded to the western end, where she witnessed the following tableau at the Little Conduit.]

And in the same pageant was advanced two hills or mountains of convenient height. The one of them being on the north side of the same pageant was made cragged, barren, and stony, in the which was erected one tree, artificially made, all withered and dead, with branches accordingly. And under the same tree, at the foot thereof, sat one in homely and rude apparel crookedly, and in mourning manner, having over his head in a table written in Latin and English, his name, which was *Ruinosa Respublica*, a decayed commonweal. And upon the same withered tree were fixed certain tables wherein were written proper sentences expressing the causes of the decay of a commonweal. The other hill on the south side was made fair, fresh, green, and beautiful, the ground thereof full of flowers and beauty, and on the same was erected also one tree very fresh and fair, under the which stood upright one fresh personage well appareled and appointed, whose name also was written both in English and in Latin, which was *Respublica bene instituta*, a flourishing commonweal. And upon the same tree also were fixed certain tables containing sentences which expressed the causes of a flourishing commonweal. In the middle between the said hills was made artificially one hollow place or cave, with door and lock enclosed, out of the which, a little before the Queen's Highness coming thither, issued one personage whose name was Time appareled as an old man with a scythe in his hand, having wings artificially made, leading a personage of lesser stature than himself which was finely and well appareled, all clad in white silk, and directly over her head was set her name and title in Latin and English, *Temporis filia*, the daughter of Time. Which two so appointed went forward toward the south side of the pageant. And on her breast was written her proper name which was *Veritas*, Truth, who held a book in her hand upon the which was written, *Verbum Veritas*, the word of Truth. And out of the south side of the pageant was cast a standing for a child which should interpret the same pageant. Against whom, when the Queen's Majesty came, he spake unto Her Grace these words:

> This old man with the scythe, old Father Time they call,
> And her his daughter Truth, which holdeth yonder book,
> Whom he out of this rock hath brought forth to us all
> From whence this many years she durst not once out look.
>
> The ruthful wight that sitteth under the barren tree
> Resembleth to us the form when commonweals decay,
> But when they be in state triumphant, you may see
> By him in the fresh attire that sitteth under the bay.
> Now since that Time again his daughter Truth hath brought,
> We trust oh worthy queen, thou wilt this Truth embrace.
> And since thou understandest the good estate and naught,
> We trust wealth thou wilt plant, and barrenness displace.
>
> But for to heal the sore, and cure that is not seen,
> Which thing that book of Truth doth teach in writing plain;
> She doth present to thee the same, oh worthy queen,
> For that, that words do fly, but writing doth remain.

When the child had thus ended his speech, he reached his book towards the Queen's Majesty which a little before Truth had let down unto him from the hill, which by Master Perrot was received and delivered unto the queen. But she as soon as she had received the book, kissed it, and with both her hands held up the same, and so laid it upon her breast with great thanks to the City therefore. And so went forward towards Paul's Churchyard. . . .

[A tablet bore the following text.]

Causes of a ruinous commonweal are these:
Want of the fear of God.   Blindness of guides.

Disobedience to rulers.	Bribery in magistrates.
Rebellion in subjects.	Unmercifulness in rulers.
Civil disagreement.	Unthankfulness in subjects.
Flattering of princes.	

Causes of a flourishing commonweal:

Fear of God.	Obedient subjects.
A wise prince.	Lovers of the commonweal.
Learned rulers.	Virtue rewarded.
Obedience to officers.	Vice chastened.

The matter of this pageant dependeth of them that went before. For as the first declared her Grace to come out of the house of unity, the second that she is placed in the seat of government stayed with virtues to the suppression of vice, and therefore in the third the eight blessings of Almighty God might well be applied unto her, so this fourth now is to put Her Grace in remembrance of the state of the commonweal, which Time with Truth his daughter doth reveal, which Truth also Her Grace hath received, and therefore cannot but be merciful and careful for the good government thereof. From thence the Queen's Majesty passed towards Paul's Churchyard. And when she came over against Paul's School, a child appointed by the schoolmaster thereof pronounced a certain oration in Latin. . . .

[The procession then proceeded through London Wall at Ludgate and across Fleet Bridge to Fleet Street.]

Her Grace went forward toward the Conduit in Fleet Street, where was the fifth and last pageant erected in form following. From the conduit, which was beautified with painting, unto the north side of the street was erected a stage, embattled[6] with four towers, and in the same a square plat rising with degrees, and upon the uppermost degree was placed a chair or seat royal, and behind the same seat in curious, artificial manner was erected a tree of reasonable height and so far advanced above the seat as it did well and seemly shadow the same without endamaging the sight of any part of the pageant, and the same tree was beautified with leaves as green as art could devise, being of a convenient greatness and containing thereupon the fruit of the date, and on top of the same tree in a table was set the name thereof which was *A Palm Tree*, and in the aforesaid seat or chair was placed a seemly and meet personage richly appareled in Parliament robes with a scepter in her hand, as a queen crowned with an open crown, whose name and title was in a table fixed over her head, in this sort: *Deborah the Judge and Restorer of the House of Israel, Judges 4*,[7] and the other degrees on either side were furnished with six personages, two representing the nobility, two the clergy, and two the commonality. And before these personages was written in a table *Deborah with her Estates, Consulting for the Good Government of Israel*. At the feet of these and the lowest part of the pageant was ordained a convenient room for a child to open the meaning of the pageant. When the Queen's Majesty drew near unto this pageant and perceived, as in the other, the child ready to speak, Her Grace required silence and commanded her chariot to be removed nigher that she might plainly hear the child speak, which said as hereafter followeth:

> Jaben[8] of Canaan king had long by force of arms
> Oppressed the Israelites, which for God's people went.
> But God minding at last for to redress their harms,
> The worthy Deborah as judge among them sent.
>
> In war she, through God's aid, did put her foes to flight,
> And with the dint of sword the band of bondage brast.[9]
> In peace she, through God's aid, did alway maintain right
> And judged Israel till forty years were passed.
>
> A worthy precedent, oh worthy queen, thou hast,
> A worthy woman judge, a woman sent for stay.
> And that the like to us endure alway thou mayest
> Thy loving subjects will with true hearts and tongues pray.. . .

The void places of the pageant were filled with pretty sentences concerning the same matter. The ground of this last pageant was that forsomuch as the next pageant before had set before Her Grace's eyes the flourishing and desolate states of a commonweal, she might by this be put in remembrance to consult for the worthy government of her people, considering God ofttimes sent women nobly to rule among men, as Deborah which governed Israel in peace the space of forty years, and that it behooveth both men and women so ruling to use advice of good counsel. . . .

[After the queen heard two final orations, one of which summarized all of the pageants, she bade farewell to the citizens of London with a promise to maintain "truth" and root out "error."]

Thus the Queen's Highness passed through the city, which without any foreign person, of itself beautified itself and received Her Grace at all places as hath been before mentioned with most tender obedience and love due to so gracious a queen and sovereign lady. And Her Grace likewise of her side in all Her Grace's passage showed herself generally an image of a worthy lady and governor, but privately these especial points were noted in Her Grace as signs of a most princelike courage, whereby her loving subjects may ground a sure hope for the rest of gracious doings hereafter.

Certain Notes of the Queen's Majesty's Great Mercy, Clemency, and Wisdom Used in This Passage

. . . But because princes be set in their seat by God's appointing and therefore they must first and chiefly tender the glory of him from whom their glory issueth, it is to be noted in Her Grace that forsomuch as God hath so wonderfully placed her in the seat of government over this realm, she in all doings doth show herself most mindful of his goodness and mercy showed unto her, and amongst all other two principle signs thereof were noted in this passage. First in the Tower, where Her Grace before she entered her chariot lifted up her eyes to heaven and said:

"Oh Lord, Almighty, and Everlasting God, I give thee most hearty thanks that thou hast been so merciful unto me as to spare me to behold this joyful day. And I acknowledge that thou hast dealt as wonderfully and as mercifully with me as thou didst with thy true and faithful servant Daniel[10] thy prophet whom thou deliveredst out of the den from the cruelty of the greedy and raging lions; even so was I overwhelmed and only by thee delivered. To thee therefore only be thanks, honor, and praise forever. Amen."[11]

The second was the receiving of the Bible at the Little Conduit in Cheap. For when Her Grace had learned that the Bible in English should there be offered, she thanked the City therefore, promised the reading thereof most diligently, and incontinent commanded that it should be brought. At the receipt whereof, how reverently did she with both her hands take it, kiss it, and lay it upon her breast to the great comfort of the lookers-on. God will undoubtedly preserve so worthy a prince which at his honor so reverently taketh her beginning. For this saying is true, and written in the book of Truth, "He that first seeketh the kingdom of God shall have all other things cast unto him."[12]

Now, therefore, all English hearts and her natural people must needs praise God's mercy, which hath sent them so worthy a prince, and pray for Her Grace's long continuance amongst us.

Notes

1. This date assumes that the year begins on Lady Day (25 March).

2. Elizabeth claimed the throne of France despite the loss of Calais, England's last foothold in France, in 1558. England controlled the Pale, a district around Dublin, but it elsewhere exerted indirect rule through Irish chieftains endowed with English titles.

3. Tablets.
4. Group of wind instrumentalists maintained by the city.
5. He was believed to be the illegitimate son of Henry VIII.
6. Crenellated.
7. See Judg. 4:4–5.
8. See Judg. 4:2–3.
9. Burst.
10. See Dan. 6.
11. For an account of danger of death alluded to in this prayer, see 7.5.B.
12. See Matt. 6:33.

7.4. Thomas Randolph, Letter on the Entry into Edinburgh of Mary, Queen of Scots (1561)

Upon her return from France, Mary, Queen of Scots, received a rude reception into Edinburgh on 2 September 1561. Presbyterian citizens staged pageantry that mocked her as a demonic queen. Thomas Randolph (1523–90), an English agent, reported by letter to William Cecil that a child costumed as an angel presented the queen with keys to the burgh, a Bible, and a book of Psalms. If a dragon effigy consumed by flames at another tableau represented the Seven-headed Beast (see 1.1), this spectacle suggested that Mary was a latter-day Whore of Babylon, whom hostile Protestants regarded as a personification of the Church of Rome. Before entering the palace of Holyroodhouse, she heard a child deliver an appeal for the abolition of the Mass. Enactment of these pageants not long after Elizabeth I embraced a Bible during her progress through London (see 7.3), a gesture that proclaimed her Protestant sympathies, highlighted local resistance to government of Scotland by a Catholic queen. Supplementing Randolph's report, John Knox, who preached at nearby Saint Giles, the High Kirk of Scotland, reported that the queen "for shame . . . could not refuse" the Bible, but frowned as she handed it to a retainer.

SOURCE AND EDITION: Anna Mill, *Mediaeval Plays in Scotland* (Edinburgh: Blackwood, 1927), pp. 189–91.

REFERENCES: King 1989; Kipling.

And thereafter, when she was riding down the Castle Hill, there met her highness a convoy of the young men of the said burgh, to the number of fifty, or thereby, their bodies and thighs covered with yellow taffetas, their arms and legs from the knee down bare, colored with black, in manner of Moors, upon their heads black hats, and on their faces black visors, in their mouths rings, garnished with intellable[1] precious stones, about their necks, legs, and arms infinite of chains of gold; together with sixteen of the most honest men of the town, clad in velvet gowns and velvet bonnets, bearing and going about the pail[2] under the which her highness rode; which pail was of fine purple velvet lined with red taffetas, fringed with gold and silk; and after them was a cart with certain bairns, together with a coffer wherein was the cupboard and propine[3] which should be propined[4] to her highness; and when her grace came forward to the butter trone[5] of the said burgh, the nobility and convoy foresaid preceded, at the which butter trone there was a port made of timber, in most honorable manner colored with fine colors, hung with sundry arms; upon the which port was hung certain bairns in the most heavenly wise; under the which port there was a cloud opened with four leaves, in the which was put a bonny bairn. And when the Queen's highness was coming through the said port, the said cloud opened, and the bairn descended down as it had been an angel, and delivered to her highness the keys of the town, together with a Bible and a Psalm book, covered with fine purple velvet; and after the said bairn had spoken some small speeches, he delivered also to her highness three writings, the tenor thereof is uncertain. That being done, the bairn ascended in the cloud, and the said cloud steeked;[6] and thereafter the Queen's grace came down to the tollbooth, at the which was[7] upon two scaffolds, one above and one under that; upon the under was situated a fair virgin, called Fortune, under the which were three fair virgins, all clad in most precious attirement, called [Love], Justice and Policy. And after a little speech made there, the Queen's grace came to the cross, where there were standing four fair virgins, clad in the most heavenly clothing, and from the which cross the wine ran out at the spouts in great abundance; there was the noise of people casting the glasses with wine. This being done, our sovereign lady came to the salt throne, where there were some speakers; and after a little speech, they burnt upon the scaffold made at the said throne, the manner of a sacrifice; and with that being done, she departed to the Nether Bow, where there was another scaffold made, having a dragon in the same, with some speeches; and after that the dragon was burnt, and the Queen's grace heard a Psalm sung, her highness passed to her Abbey of Holyroodhouse with the said convoy and nobilities; and there the bairns which was in the cart with the propine made some speech concerning the putting away of the Mass, and thereafter sang a Psalm; and this being done, the cart came to Edinburgh, and the said honest men remained in her utter chalmer,[8] and desired her grace to receive the said cupboard, which was double overgilt; the price thereof was two thousand marks; who received the same, and thanked them thereof.

Notes

1. Innumerable.
2. Canopy (not in OED).
3. Gift.
4. Presented.
5. A pair of market scales.
6. Remained in position.
7. A word is omitted in the original text.
8. Outer chamber.

7.5. John Foxe, from *The Book of Martyrs*
A. Dedication to Queen Elizabeth (1563)

In dedicating the *Book of Martyrs* to Elizabeth I, Foxe praises her for halting the persecution of Protestants. He compares her accession to the designation of Christianity as an official religion of the Roman Empire by Emperor Constantine I (see Figure 17). Foxe aligns the popes as usurpers of political authority with tyrannical emperors such as Nero and Diocletian, who burned Christians or threw them to the lions until Constantine halted persecution. Foxe ironically attacks the Donation of Constantine as a fraudulent conferral of temporal authority on the papacy. By likening the queen to Constantine and himself to Eusebius, whose martyrological chronicle in the *Ecclesiastical History* provides one of his major sources, Foxe optimistically claims that the present moment restores the degree of collaboration between church and state that existed under Constantine. He also appeals for patronage on the model of Constantine's support of Eusebius's historical research. Foxe's praise of the queen for restoring "godly" government constitutes a delicate appeal for her to return to religious policies in place under Edward VI. The compiler's assertion that he collects the "acts and monuments" of martyrs emphasizes the importance of not only their deeds, but also the written documents that monumentalize them in place of the veneration of relics in Catholic devotion. If one reads this dedication in conjunction with the story about Elizabeth's suffering before she became queen (see 7.5.B), they constitute "bookends" for the entire collection in asserting that providential deliverance enabled her to restore "true" religion and government.

SOURCE: *STC* 11222, B1ʳ–B2ᵛ.
REFERENCES: King 1989; Yates.

To the Queen's Most Excellent Majesty, Queen Elizabeth, by the grace of God Queen of England, France, and Ireland, Defender of the Faith, and Supreme Governor of the said realm of England and Ireland, next under the Lord, as well in causes ecclesiastical, as also to the temporal state appertaining, her humble subject, John Foxe, heartily wisheth and desireth with increase of God's holy spirit and grace, long to flourish and reign in perfect health, and much honor, through the mercy and favor of Christ Jesus, our Lord and eternal Savior, to the comfort of his church, and the glory of His holy name.

Constantine, the great and mighty emperor, the son of Helena, an English woman of this your realm and country (most Christian and renowned princess, Queen Elizabeth) after he had pacified and established the church of Christ, being long before under persecution, from the time of our savior Christ almost 400 years: and coming in his progress at length to a city called Caesaria, (where Eusebius writer of the Ecclesiastical story was then placed

Figure 17. *Elizabeth I as Emperor Constantine.* Foxe, *Book of Martyrs* (1563), woodcut initial, unpaginated (signature B1ʳ). Courtesy of The Ohio State University Libraries. As publisher of the *Book of Martyrs*, John Day commissioned this historiated initial C to begin Foxe's dedication of the first edition to Elizabeth I. This woodcut idealizes her as a new Constantine who is said to halt persecution by instituting mild Christian government. The cornucopia of plenty integrated into the letter's head symbolizes her reign as a time of peaceful "harvest" following the discord of Mary I's reign. The iconoclastic scene portrays Elizabeth surmounting the toppled pope, who is entwined with demonic serpents beneath her feet. The man closest to the queen is Day (see Figure 11). Foxe stands in the center alongside a courtier who may represent their sponsor at court, possibly Thomas Norton.

bishop), required of said Eusebius upon his own free motion, to demand and ask of him whatsoever he thought expedient or necessary for the state and commodity of his church, promising to grant unto him the same whatsoever he would ask. Which Eusebius, if he had then required what terrene benefit soever he would, either of possessions to be given, or of impositions to be released, or any other like, etc., he had no doubt obtained his request of that so liberal, and so noble hearted emperor. But the good and godly bishop, more needy than greedy, more spiritually given, than worldly minded, who had learned rather to take a little, than to ask much, setting all other respects aside, made this petition, only to obtain at his majesty's hand, under his seal and letters authentic, free leave and license through all the monarchy of Rome, going to all consuls, proconsuls, tribunes, and other officers in all cities and countries, to search out the names, suffering, and acts of all such as suffered in all that time of persecution before, for the testimony and faith of Christ Jesus. . . .

Two things put me in a variable doubt, whether of these two rather to commend and extol: the good Emperor, or the godly Bishop: the one for his princely proffer, the other for his godly and sincere petition. The Emperor for his rare and singular affection in favoring and furthering the Lord's church, or the Bishop in zealing the public business of the Lord, before the private lucre of himself. Certes in both together may to us appear, what all manner estates may learn to know: not only what in those days was done, but also what ought now to be followed. In the Bishop is to be noted: the goods and ornaments of the church chiefly to consist, not in donates[1] and patrimonies, but in the blood, acts, and life of martyrs, the seeking and setting forth whereof ought to occupy the study of true Christian bishops. In the Emperor also we behold how studiously the nobility in those days were set to tender the state and vitality of the church, and the ministers of the same: in giving to them, not in taking from them, yea, in preventing their tamest modesty, with their princely liberality. Such was then the careful affection of them in those days toward the Lord, that it rebounded also unto his church, and ministry thereof, in furthering and in gratifying them, enlarging them, in privileging and enriching them with ample gifts and princely benefits, that the like affection hath rare been found since those days: as may appear in that which the Roman Church at this present calleth the Donation of Constantine, which although it be forged and counterfeited of themselves (as no doubt it is) yet it cannot be denied, but that the emperors and princes were in those days patrons highly beneficial unto the same. . . .

What a sore and dreadful hand of the Lord in primitive time of the church was seen under so many persecuting Emperors, and cruel consuls? At length the Lord sent this mild Constantine, to cease blood, to stay persecution, to refresh his people. In much like manner what bitter blasts, what smarting storms have been felt in England during the space of certain years, till at last God's pitiful grace sent us your Majesty to quench firebrands, to assuage rage, to relieve innocents. What a multitude of godly martyrs were slain before the time of the said Constantine, is partly above declared. And likewise what a number also before your grace's happy reign were murdered, in this present history here following is comprehended. Over and besides to compare time with time, and place with place: what was in his time found so happy, for which we have not as great cause now to bless God in this so gracious a time of yours. For as God gave then great rest to his church by reign of him: so hath it pleased the Lord with no less abundance of peace to bless us by the means of you. . . .

The second and principal cause why I have induced this foresaid matter of Constantine and Eusebius, is this: for that your Majesty in marking the humble petition of the Bishop, and the gentle grant of the Emperor, may rather be entreated to accept this my poor and simple endeavor, in setting forth this present history touching the acts and monuments of such godly Martyrs as suffered before your reign for the like testimony of Christ and his truth. For if then such care was in searching and setting forth the doings and acts of Christ's faithful servants, suffering for his name in the primitive time of the church, why should they now be more neglected of us in the latter church, such as give their blood in the same cause and like quarrel? For what should we say? Is not the name of Christ as precious now, as then? Were not the torments as great? Is not the cause all one? And if the adversaries will say contrary and repugn again, alleging that those in the primitive time suffered then for Christ, these suffered not for Christ, but for heresy, I will answer them again as Martin Luther answered unto the pope. "Let the Pope," said he, "and his Popelings grant Christ only to be my savior, and that the faith only in Christ justifieth a Christian man, I will take him for a good Bishop, and his religion to be right." But that he will never do, so long as he is Pope. For Pope holy, and faith only, cannot otherwise join together, but that all his idolatrous worship, his superstitious merits, and trifling traditions must needs give place, and lose their authority. For in these three I recount all the Pope's whole religion to consist but of this enough.

Now returning again to our purposed matter, and following the example of Eusebius this worthy bishop, although I cannot achieve it so perfectly as he hath done, yet have I labored and travailed according to my infirm ability, what I may, in collecting and setting forth the acts, fame and memory of these our martyrs of this latter time of the church, which according as my duty doth bind me, next under the Lord, I offer and present here unto your majesty, humbly desiring, and nothing yet misdoubting, but that your highness and singular clemency, likewise following the steps of that noble Constantine, with no less propensity of favor and furtherance, will accept and also assist these my laborious travails to the behoove of the church, against the importunity of the malignant: if peradventure any such spurners against the truth shall appear, as I fear they will, bending themselves to malign and detract the doings hereof, as they do all other things, being contrary to their corrupt religion and affection, except your grace's assistance shall relieve and defend me against the same. Who in so doing not only shall make me think my pains and labors herein the better bestowed: but also shall encourage, by the same your princely benignity, both me and all other my fellow brethren to proceed (the grace of the Lord so assisting us) in further travail, to accomplish that which our diligence can extend unto for the use of Christ's church, utility of your realm, and the glory of His holy name: to whom we give most hearty thanks for exalting your majesty out of adversity: so we beseech him to conserve you in long prosperity, with the days not only of Constantine's reign, but also with them whose reign hath been longest in any commonwealth.

Vivat Regina in Domino.[2]
Your majesty's faithful and
humble subject in the Lord.

J. Foxe

Notes

1. Gifts.
2. "May the Queen live in God."

B. The Miraculous Preservation of the Lady Elizabeth (1563)

It may be that Queen Elizabeth (1533–1603) directly or indirectly aided in the construction of this narrative, because she alone knew what transpired during her imprisonment between March 1554 and April 1555, initially at the Tower of London and later at the royal manor at Woodstock. Coming near the end of early editions of the *Book of Martyrs*, this story affords a capstone for the collection. Focusing almost wholly on her imprisonment, this well-crafted tragicomic and romance-like history moves from initial adversity to a triumphant conclusion based upon repeated interventions of divine providence. The writer embellishes the narrative with artful touches including Elizabeth's witty application of Jesus' Parable of the Two Houses (Matt. 2:24–27) when the imprisoned princess uses the Bible as a symbol for religious faith upon entry into the Tower. This detail may constitute an anachronistic back-formation from her display of the Bible during her precoronation entry into London (see 7.3).

Elizabeth was in mortal peril when agents of Stephen Gardiner tried in vain to link her to Wyatt's Rebellion. This story alludes to his reputation as a wolfish predator on "true" believers (see Figure 14), despite her religious conformity under Mary I, when she strikes a histrionic pose as a Christlike lamb being led to slaughter. In proclaiming that she is "tanquam ovis" ("like a sheep"), Elizabeth applies to her own experience the Vulgate version of Isaiah 53:7, a messianic text that Christians interpret as a prophecy of the Crucifixion.

SOURCE: *STC* 11222, pp. 1711–16.

REFERENCE: Frye.

In the beginning of Queen Mary's reign, mention was made before how the Lady Elizabeth and the Lord Courtney[1] were charged with false suspicion of Sir Thomas Wyatt's rising.[2] Whereupon Queen Mary, whether for that surmise or for what other cause I know not, being offended with the said Lady Elizabeth, her sister, at that time lying in her house at Ashridge, sent to her two lords and Sir John Williams, afterward Lord of Thame,[3] with their retinue and troop of horsemen to the number of two hundred and fifty. . . .

From that place she was conveyed to the court, where by the way came to meet her many gentlemen to accompany Her Highness, which were very sorry to see her in that case; but especially a great multitude of people there were standing by the way who, then flocking about her litter, lamented and bewailed greatly at her estate. Now when she came to the court, Her Grace was there straight ways shut up and kept as close prisoner a fortnight, seeing neither king nor queen nor lord nor friend all that time, but only then the Lord Chamberlain, Sir John Gage,[4] and the Vice Chamberlain, which were attendant unto the doors. About which time Sir William Sentlowe was called before the Council, to whose charge was laid that he knew of Wyatt's rebellion, which he stoutly denied, protesting that he was a true man both to God and his prince, defying all traitors and rebels; but, being straightly examined, was in conclusion committed to the Tower.

The Friday before Palm Sunday, the Bishop of Winchester with nineteen other of the Council, who shall be here nameless as I have promised, came unto Her Grace from the Queen's Majesty and burdened[5] her with Wyatt's conspiracy, which she utterly denied, affirming that she was altogether guiltless therein. They, being not contented with this, charged Her Grace with the business made by Sir Peter Carew[6] and the rest of the gentlemen of the west country, which also she, utterly denying, cleared her innocency therein. In conclusion, after long debating of matters, they declared unto her that it was the queen's will and pleasure that she should go unto the Tower while the matter were further tried and examined. Whereat she, being aghast, said that she trusted the Queen's Majesty would be [a] more gracious lady unto her and that Her Highness would not otherwise conceive of her, but that she was a true woman; declaring furthermore to the lords that she was innocent in all those matters wherein they had burdened her and desired them therefore to be a further mean to the queen her sister that she, being a true woman in thought, word, and deed towards Her Majesty, might not be committed to so notorious and doleful a place; protesting that she would request no mercy at her hand if she should be proved to have consented unto any such kind of matter as they laid unto her charge, and therefore, in fine, desired their lordships to think of her what she was, and that she might not so extremely be dealt withal for her truth. Whereunto the lords answered that there was no remedy, for that the Queen's Majesty was fully determined that she should go unto the Tower, wherewith the lords departed with their caps hanging over their eyes.[7] But not long after, within the space of an hour or little more, came four of the foresaid lords of the Council with the guard, who, warding the next chamber to her, secluded all her gentlemen and yeomen, ladies and gentlewomen; saving that for one gentleman usher, three gentlewomen, and two grooms of her chamber were appointed, in their rooms, three other men of the queen's and three waiting women to give attendance upon her, that none should have access to Her Grace.

At which time there were an hundred of northern soldiers in white coats watching and warding about the gardens all that night, a great fire being made in the midst of the hall, and two certain lords watching there also with their band and company. Upon Saturday, being Palm Sunday Even,[8] two certain lords of the Council, whose names here also we do omit, came and certified Her Grace that forthwith she must go unto the Tower, the barge being prepared for her and the tide now ready, which tarrieth for nobody. In heavy mood Her Grace requested the lords that she might tarry another tide, trusting that the next would be more joyous and better. But one of the lords replied that neither tide nor time was to be delayed. And when Her Grace requested him that she might be suffered to write to the Queen's Majesty, he answered that he durst not permit that, adding that in his judgement it would rather hurt than profit Her Grace in so doing. But the other lord, more courteous and favorable, who was the Earl of Sussex,[9] kneeling down, told Her Grace that she should have liberty to write, and, as he was a true man, he would deliver it to the Queen's Highness and bring an answer of the same, whatsoever came thereof. Whereupon she wrote, albeit she could not ne[10] might not speak with her, to her great discomfort, being no offender against Her Majesty.

And thus the tide and time passed away for that time; till the next day, being Palm Sunday, when about nine of the clock those two came again, declaring that it was time for Her Grace to depart; she answering: "If there be no remedy, I must be contented," willing the lords to go on before. And being come forth into the garden, she did cast up her eyes toward the window, thinking to have seen the queen, which she could not. Whereat she said she marveled much what the nobility of the realm meant, which in that sort would suffer her to be led into captivity, the Lord knew whither, for she did not. After all this she took her barge with two foresaid lords, three of the queen's gentlewomen, and three of her own, her gentleman usher, and two of her grooms, lying and hovering upon the water an hour, for that they could not shoot[11] the bridge, the bargemen being very unwilling to shoot the same so soon as they did because of the danger thereof. For the stern of the boat struck upon the ground: the fall[12] was so big, and the water was so shallow.

Then Her Grace desired of the lords that she might not land at the stairs where all traitors and offenders customably[13] used to land. They answered that it was past their remedy, for that otherwise they had in commandment. "Well," said she, "if it be so, my lords, I must needs obey it, protesting before all your honors that here now steppeth as true a subject as ever was towards the Queen's Highness. And before thee O God I speak it, having none other friends but only thee." The lords declared unto her that there was no time then to try the truth. "You have said well my lords," quod she. "I am sorry that I have troubled you." So then they passed on and went into the Tower, where were a great company of harnessed men and armed soldiers warding on both sides; whereat she, being amazed, called the lords to her and demanded the cause why those poor men stood there. They declared unto her that it was the use and order of the place so to do. "And if it be," quod she, "for my cause, I beseech you that they may be dismissed." Whereat the poor men kneeled down and wit' one voice desired God to preserve Her Grace, who the next day were released of their cold coats.

After this, passing a little further, she sat down upon a cold stone and there rested herself. To whom the lieutenant then being said: "Madam, you were best to come out of the rain. For you sit unwholesomely." She then replying answered again: "Better sitting here than in a worse place. For, God knoweth, I know not whither you will bring me." With that her gentleman usher wept, she demanding of him what he meant so uncomfortably to use her, seeing she took him to be her comforter and not dismayer, especially for that she knew her truth to be such that no man should have cause to weep for her. But forth she went into the prison. The doors were locked and bolted upon her, which did not a little discomfort and dismay Her Grace. At what time she called to her gentlewoman for her book,[14] desiring God not to suffer her to build her foundation upon the sands but upon the rock, whereby all blasts of blustering weather should have no power against her.[15] After the doors thus locked and she close shut up, the lords had great conference how to keep ward and watch; every man declaring his opinion in that behalf, agreeing straightly and circumspectly to keep her; while that one of them—I mean the lord of Sussex—swearing, said: "My lords, let us take heed and do no more than our commission will bear us, whatsoever shall happen hereafter. And further, let us consider that she was the king, our master, his daughter and, therefore, let us use such dealing that we may answer unto it hereafter if it shall so happen. For just dealing," quod he, "is always answerable." Whereunto the other lords agreed that it was well said of him and thereupon departed.

It would make a pitiful and a strange story here by the way to touch and recite what examinations and rackings of poor men there were to find out that knife that should cut her throat, what gaping among my lords of the clergy to see the day wherein they might wash their goodly white rochets in her innocent blood. But especially the Bishop of Winchester, Stephen Gardiner, then Lord Chancellor, ruler of the roost, who then within few days after came unto her with diverse other of the Council and examined her of the talk that was at Ashridge betwixt her and Sir James Croft[16] concerning her removing from thence to Donnington Castle, requiring her to declare what she meant thereby. At the first she, being so suddenly asked, did not well remember any such house; but within a while, well advising herself, she said: "Indeed," quoth she, "I do now remember that I have such a place. But I never lay in it in all my life. And as for any that hath moved me thereunto, I do not remember."

Then to enforce the matter they brought forth Sir James Croft. The Bishop of Winchester demanded of her what she said to that man. She answered that she had little to say to him, or to the rest that were then prisoners in the Tower. "But my lords," quod she, "you do examine every mean prisoner of me, wherein methinks you do me great injury. If they have done evil and offended the Queen's Majesty, let them answer to it accordingly. I beseech you, my lords, join not me in this sort with any of these offenders. And as concerning my going unto Donnington Castle, I do remember that Master Hoby and mine officers and you, Sir James Croft, had such talk; but what is that to the purpose, my lords, but that I may go to my own houses at all times." The lord of Arundel, kneeling down, said: "Your Grace saith true and certainly. We are very sorry that we have so troubled you about so vain matters." She then said: "My lords, you do sift me very narrowly. But well I am assured you shall not do more to me than God hath appointed. And so God forgive you all." At their departing, Sir James Croft kneeled down, declaring that he was sorry to see the day in which he should be brought as a witness against Her Grace. "But I assure Your Grace," said he, "I have been marvelously tossed and examined touching Your Highness, which the Lord knoweth is strange to me. For I take God to record before all your honors, I do not know anything of that crime that you have laid to my charge and will thereupon take my death if I should be driven to so straight a trial."

That day or thereabouts diverse of her own officers, who had made provision for her diet, brought the same to the utter[17] gate of the Tower, the common rascal soldiers receiving it, which was no small grief unto the gentlemen, the bringers thereof. Wherefore they required to speak with the Lord Chamberlain, being then Constable of the Tower. Who, coming before his presence, declared unto his lordship that they were much afraid to bring Her Grace's diet and to deliver it unto such common and desperate persons as they were which did receive it, beseeching His Honor to consider Her Grace and to give such order that her viands might at all times be brought in by them which were appointed thereunto. "Yea sirs," said he, "who appointed you this office?" They answered, "Her Grace's Council." "Council?" quoth he. "There is none of them which hath to do, either in that case or anything else within this place; and I assure you, for that she is a prisoner, she shall be served with the Lieutenant's men as other the prisoners are." Whereat the gentlemen said that they trusted for more favor at his hands, considering her personage, saying that they mistrusted not, but that the queen and her Council would be better to Her Grace than so; and herewith showed themselves to be offended at the ungrateful words of the Lord Chamberlain towards their lady and mistress. At this he swore by God, striking himself upon the breast, that if they did either frown or shrug at him, he would set them where they should see neither sun nor moon. Thus taking their leave, they desired God to bring him into a better mind toward Her Grace and departed from him.

Upon the occasion whereof, Her Grace's officers made great suit unto the Queen's Council that some might be appointed to bring her diet unto her and that it might no more be delivered in to the common soldiers of the Tower; which, being reasonably considered, was by them granted and thereupon were appointed one of her gentlemen, her clerk of the kitchen, and her two purveyors to bring in her provision once a day. All which was done, the warders ever waiting upon the bringers thereof. The Lord Chamberlain himself, being always with them, circumspectly and narrowly watched and searched what they brought and gave heed that they should have no talk with any of Her Grace's waiting servants, and so warded them both in and out. At the said suit of her officers were sent by the commandment of Council to wait upon Her Grace two yeomen of her chamber, one of her robes, two of her pantry and ewery,[18] one of her buttery, another of her cellar, two of her kitchen, and one of her larder, all which continued with her the time of her trouble.

Here the constable, being at the first not very well pleased with the coming in of such a company against his will, would have had his men still to have served with Her Grace's men; which her servants at no hand would suffer, desiring his lordship to be contented, for that order was taken that no stranger would come within their offices. At which answer, being sore displeased, he brake[19] out into these threatening words: "Well," said he, "I will handle you well enough." Then went he into the kitchen and there would needs have his meat roasted with Her Grace's meat and said that his cook should come thither and dress it. To that Her Grace's cook answered: "My lord, I will never suffer any stranger to come about her diet, but her own sworn men, so long as I live." He said they should. But the cook said his lordship should pardon him for that matter. Thus did he trouble her poor servants very stoutly, though afterward he were otherwise advised, and they more courteously used at his hands. And good cause why. For he had good cheer and fared of the best, and Her Grace paid well for it. Wherefore he used himself afterward more reverently toward Her Grace.

After this sort, having lain a whole month there in close prison and being very evil at ease therewithal, she sent for the Lord Chamberlain and the Lord Chandos[20] to come and speak with her. Who coming, she requested them that she might have liberty to walk in some place, for that she felt herself not well. To the which they answered that they were right sorry that they could not satisfy Her Grace's request, for that they had commandment to the contrary, which they durst not in any wise break. Furthermore, she desired of them, if that could not be granted, that she might walk but into the queen's lodging. No, nor that, they answered, could by any means be obtained without a further suit to the queen and her Council. "Well," said she, "my lords, if the matter be so hard that they must be sued unto for so small a thing and that friendship be so strait, God comfort me," and so they departed, she remaining in her old dungeon still without any kind of comfort, but only God.

The next day after, the Lord Chandos came again unto Her Grace, declaring unto her that he had sued unto the Council for further liberty. Some of them consented thereunto; divers others dissented for that there were so many prisoners in the Tower. But in conclusion, they did all agree that Her Grace might walk into those lodgings, so[21] that he and the Lord Chamberlain and three of the queen's gentlewomen did accompany her and the windows were shut and she not suffered to look out at any of them; wherewith she contented herself and gave him thanks for his goodwill in that behalf. Afterward there was liberty granted to Her Grace to walk in a little garden, the doors and gates being shut up, which, not withstanding, was as much discomfort unto her as the walk in the garden was pleasant and acceptable. At which times of her walking there, the prisoners on that side straightly were commanded not to speak or look out at the windows into the garden till Her Grace were gone out again, having, in consideration thereof, their keepers waiting upon them for that time.

Thus Her Grace with this small liberty contented herself in God, to whom be praise therefore. During this time there used a little boy, a man's child in the Tower, to resort to their chambers and many times to bring Her Grace flowers, which likewise he did to the other prisoners that were there; whereupon naughty and suspicious heads, thinking to make and wring out some matter thereof, called on a time the child unto them, promising him figs and apples and asking of him when he had been with the Earl of Devonshire, not ignorant of the child's wonted frequenting unto him. The boy answered that he would go by and by thither. Further they demanded of him when he was with the Lady Elizabeth's Grace. He answered, "Every day." Furthermore they examined him what the Lord Devonshire sent by him to Her Grace. The child said, "I will go [to] know what he will give to carry to her." Such was the discretion of the child, being yet but three years of age. "This same is a crafty boy," quod the Lord Chamberlain. "How say you, my Lord Chandos?" "I pray you my lord," quod the boy, "give me the figs ye promised me." "No, marry," quod he, "thou shalt be whipped if thou come any more to the Lady Elizabeth or the Lord Courtney." The boy answered, "I will bring my lady, my mistress, more flowers." Whereupon the child's father was commanded to permit the boy no more to come up into their chambers. And the next day, as Her Grace was walking in the garden, the child, peeping in at a hole in the door, cried unto her, saying: "Mistress, I can bring you no more flowers." Whereat she smiled but said nothing, understanding thereby what they had done. Wherefore afterward the Lord Chamberlain rebuked highly his father, commanding him to put him out of the house. "Alas, poor infant," quod the father. "It is a crafty knave," quod the Lord Chamberlain. "Let me see him here no more."

The fifth day of May the constable was discharged of his office of the Tower, one Sir Henry Bedingfield[22] being placed in his room,[23] a man unknown to Her Grace and therefore the more feared; which so sudden mutation was unto her no little amaze. He brought with him an hundreth soldiers in blue coats; wherewith she was marvelously discomforted and demanded of such as were about her whether the Lady Jane's scaffold[24] were taken away or no, fearing by reason of their coming lest she should have played her part. To whom answer was made that the scaffold was taken away and that Her Grace needed not to doubt of any such tyranny. For God would not suffer any such treason against her person. Wherewith, being contented but not altogether satisfied, she asked what Sir Henry Bedingfield was and whether he was of that conscience or no that, if her murdering were secretly committed to his charge, he would see the execution thereof. She was answered that they were ignorant what manner of man he was. Howbeit they persuaded her that God would not suffer such wickedness to proceed. "Well," quod she, "God grant it be so. For thou, O God, art the withdrawer[25] and mollifier of all such tyrannous hearts and acts; and I beseech thee to hear me, thy creature which am thy servant, and at thy commandment trusting by thy grace ever so to remain."

About which time it was spread abroad that Her Grace should be carried from thence by this new jolly[26] captain and his soldiers, but whither it could not be learned. Which was unto Her Grace a great grief, especially for that such a kind of company was appointed to her guard, requesting rather to continue there still than to be led thence with such a rascal company. At last plain answer was made by the Lord Chandos that there was no remedy, but from thence she must needs depart to the manor of Woodstock, as he thought. Being demanded of her for what cause: "For that," quod he, "the Tower is like further to be furnished." Whereat she, being more greedy, as far as she durst, demanded wherewith. He answered, with such matter as the queen and Council were determined in that behalf, whereof he had no knowledge and so departed. In conclusion, the sixteenth day of May she was removed from the Tower, the Lord Treasurer being then there for the loading of her carts and discharging the place of the same. Where Sir Henry Bedingfield, being appointed her jailer, did receive her with a company of rakehells[27] to guard her, besides the Lord of Derby's[28] band, wafting in the country about for the moonshine in the water;[29] unto whom at length came my lord of Thame, joined in commission with the said Sir Henry for the safe guiding of her to prison, and they together conveyed Her Grace to Woodstock, as hereafter followeth.

The first day they conducted her to Richmond, where she continued all night, being restrained of[30] her own men, which were laid in outchambers, and Sir Henry Bedingfield his soldiers appointed in their rooms to give attendance on her person; whereat she, being marvelously dismayed, thinking verily some secret mischief a-working toward her, called her gentleman usher and desired him with the rest of his company to pray for her. "For this night," quod she, "I think to die." . . .

The next day, passing over the water at Richmond, going towards Windsor, Her Grace espied certain of her poor servants standing on the other side, which were very desirous to see her; whom, when she beheld, turning to one of her men standing by, said: "Yonder," quod she, "I see certain of my men. Go to them and say these words from me: *'tanquam ovis.'*"[31] . . .

[After a journey from Richmond to Oxfordshire, Elizabeth and her party arrived at the royal manor at Woodstock, where she remained under house arrest for six months.]

After Her Grace's being there a time, she made suit to the Council that she might be suffered[32] to write to the queen, which at last was permitted to Her Grace, so that Sir Henry Bedingfield brought her pen, ink, and paper; and standing by her while she wrote, which he straitly observed, always she being wary, would carry away her letters and bring them again when she called for them. In the finishing thereof, he would have been messenger to the queen of the same; whose request Her Grace denied, saying one of her own men should carry them and that she would neither trust him nor none of his thereabouts. . . .

Then about the eighth day of June came down Dr. Owen and Dr. Wendy, sent by the queen to Her Grace for that she was sickly; who, ministering to her and letting her blood,[33] tarried there and attended on Her Grace five or six days; who, being well amended, they returned again to the court, making their good report to the queen and the Council of Her Grace's behavior and humbleness towards the Queen's Highness, which Her Majesty, hearing, took very thankfully. But the bishops thereat repined, looked black in the mouth, and told the queen they marveled she submitted not herself to Her Majesty's mercy, considering that she had offended Her Highness. Wily champions, ye may be sure, and friends at a need, God amend them. About this time, Her Grace was requested by a secret friend to submit herself to the Queen's Majesty, which would be very well taken and to her great quiet and commodity; unto whom she answered that she would never submit herself to them whom she never offended. "For," quod she, "if I have offended and am guilty, I then crave no mercy but the law, which I am certain," quod she, "I should have had ere this if it could be proved by[34] me. For I know myself, I thank God, to be out of the danger thereof, wishing that I were as clear out of the peril of my enemy, and then I am assured, I should not so be locked and bolted up within walls and doors as I am. God give them a better mind when it pleaseth him."

About this time was there a great consulting among the bishops and gentlemen touching a marriage for Her Grace, which some of the Spaniards wished to be with some stranger, that she might go out of the realm with her portion, some saying one thing and some another. A lord being there at last said that the king[35] should never have any quiet commonwealth in England unless her head were stricken from the shoulders. Whereunto the Spaniards answered, saying: "God forbid that their king and master should have that mind to consent to such a mischief." This was the courteous answer of the Spaniards to the Englishmen, speaking after that sort against their own country. From that day the Spaniards never left off their good persuasions to the king that the like honor he should never obtain as he should in delivering the Lady Elizabeth's Grace out of prison, whereby at length she was happily released from the same. Here is a plain and evident example of the good clemency and nature of the king and his counselors towards Her Grace, praised be God therefore, who moved their hearts therein. Then hereupon she was sent for shortly after to come to Hampton Court.[36] In her imprisonment at Woodstock, these verses she wrote with her diamond in a glass window:

> Much suspected by me,
> Nothing proved can be,
>   Quod Elizabeth the prisoner. . . .

The first night from Woodstock she came to Rycote, the next night to Master Dormer's, and so to Colnbrook, where she lay all that night at the George;[37] and by the way coming to the said Colnbrook, met Her Grace certain of her gentlemen and yeomen, to the number of three score, much to all their comforts, which had not seen Her Grace of long season before; neither could, but were commanded in the queen's name immediately to depart the town, to Her Grace's no little heaviness and theirs, who could not be suffered once to speak with them. So that night all her men were taken from her, saving her gentleman usher, three gentlewomen, two grooms, and one of her wardrobe, the soldiers watching and warding round about the house and she close shut up within her prison.

The next day Her Grace entered Hampton Court on the backside into the prince's lodging, the doors being shut to her; and she, guarded with soldiers as before, lay there a fortnight at the least or[38] ever any had recourse unto her. At length came the lord William Howard,[39] who marvelous honorably used Her Grace, whereat she took much comfort and requested him to be a mean that she might speak with some of the Council; to whom, not long after, came the Bishop of Winchester, the Lord of Arundel,[40] the Lord of Shrewsbury,[41] and Secretary Petre,[42] who with great humility humbled themselves to Her Grace. She again, likewise saluting them, said: "My lords," quod she, "I am glad to see you, for methinks I have been kept a great while from you desolately alone. Wherefore I would desire you to be a mean to the King and Queen's Majesties, that I may be delivered from prison, wherein I have been kept a long space, as to you, my lords, it is not unknown." When she had spoken, Stephen Gardiner, the Bishop of Winchester, kneeled down and requested that she would submit herself to the Queen's Grace, and in so doing, he had no doubt but that Her Majesty would be good unto her; she making answer that, rather than she would so do, she would lie in prison all the days of her life, adding that she craved no mercy at Her Majesty's hand but rather desired the law, if ever she did offend Her Majesty in thought, word, or deed; and besides this, "In yielding," quod she, "I should speak against myself and confess myself to be an offender, which never was towards Her Majesty, by occasion whereof the king and the queen might ever hereafter conceive an ill opinion; and, therefore, I say, my lords, it were better for me to lie in prison for the truth, than to be abroad and suspected of my prince."

And so they departed, promising to declare her message to the queen. On the next day the Bishop of Winchester came again unto Her Grace and, kneeling down, declared that the queen marveled that she would so stoutly use herself, not confessing to have offended, so that it should seem the Queen's Majesty wrongfully to have imprisoned Her Grace. "Nay," quod my lady Elizabeth, "it may please her to punish me as she thinketh good." "Well," quod Gardiner, "Her Majesty willeth me to tell you that you must tell another tale or that you be set at liberty." Her Grace answered that she had as lief[43] be in prison with honesty and truth as to be abroad and suspected of Her Majesty; "And this that I have said I will stand to. For I will never belie myself." The Lord of Winchester again kneeled down and said: "Then Your Grace hath the vantage of me and other the lords for your long and wrong imprisonment." "What vantage I have," quod she, "you know; taking God to record I seek no vantage at your hands for your so dealing with me. But God forgive you and me also." With that the rest kneeled, desiring Her Grace that all might be forgotten, and so departed, she being fast locked up again.

A sennight after, the Queen's Majesty sent for Her Grace at ten of the clock in the night to speak with her, for she had not seen her in two years before. Yet, for all that, she was amazed at the so sudden sending for, thinking it had been worse for her than afterward it proved, and desired her gentlemen and gentlewomen to pray for her, for that she could not tell whether ever she should see them again or no. At which time coming in, Sir Henry Bedingfield with Mistress Clarencieux,[44] Her Grace was brought into the garden unto a stair's foot that went into the queen's lodging, Her Grace's gentlewomen waiting upon her, her gentleman usher and her groom's going before with torches; where her gentlemen and gentlewomen, being commanded to stay all, saving one woman, Mistress Clarencieux conducted her to the queen's bedchamber, where Her Majesty was; at the sight of whom Her Grace kneeled down and desired God to preserve Her Majesty, not mistrusting but that she should try herself as true a subject towards Her Majesty as ever did any and desired Her Majesty even so to judge of her, and said that she should not find her to the contrary, whatsoever false report otherwise had gone of her; to whom the queen answered: "You will not confess your offense but stand stoutly in your truth. I pray God it may so fall out." "If it do not," quod she, "I request neither favor nor pardon at Your Majesty's hands." "Well," said the queen, "you stiffly still persevere in your truth. Belike you will not confess but that you have been wrongfully punished." "I must not say so, if it please Your Majesty, to you." "Why then," said the queen, "belike you will to other[s]." "No, if it please Your Majesty," quod she; "I have borne the burden and must bear it. I humbly beseech Your Majesty to have a good opinion in me and to think me to be your true subject, not only from the beginning hitherto, but forever, as long as life lasteth."

And so they departed with very few comfortable words of the queen in English. But what she said in Spanish God knoweth. It is thought that King Philip was there behind a cloth and not seen and that he showed himself a very friend in that matter, etc. Thus Her Grace, departing, went to her lodging again and the sennight after was released of Sir Henry Bedingfield, her jailer, as she termed him, and his soldiers; and so Her Grace, set at liberty from imprisonment, she went into the country[45] and had appointed to go with her Sir Thomas Pope,[46] one of Queen Mary's councilors, and one of her gentlemen ushers, Master Gage, and thus straitly was she looked to[47] all Queen Mary's time; and this is the discourse of Her Highness' imprisonment. . . .

But, God be praised, shortly after was fetched away Gardiner,[48] through the merciful providence of the Lord's goodness, by occasion of whose opportune decease, as is partly touched in this story before, the life of this so excellent prince, that is the wealth of all England, was preserved. For this is credibly to be supposed, that the said wicked Gardiner of Winchester had long labored his wits and to this only most principle mark bent all his devices: to bring our happy and dear sovereign out of the way, as both by words and doings might and did well appear. But such was the gracious and favorable providence of the Lord, not to the prosperous safeguard only of Her Royal Majesty, but to the miserable and woeful state rather of this poor island and subjects of the same, that the crafty practices of this wretched Achitophel[49] prevailed not; but contrary it fell that the snares and traps of pernicious counsel laid against another was turned to a net to catch himself, according to the proverb: "malum consilium consultori pessimum."[50]

After the death of this Gardiner followed the death also and dropping away of other her enemies; whereby by little and little her jeopardy decreased, fear diminished, hope of more comfort began to appear as out of a dark cloud; and though as yet Her Grace had no full assurance of perfect safety, yet more gentle entertainment daily did grow unto her; till at length in the month of November, and day above-written, three years after the death of Stephen Gardiner, followed the death of Queen Mary, as is before declared. After whose departure, the same day which took away the said Queen Mary brought in the same, her foresaid sister, Lady Elizabeth, into the right of the crown of England; who after so long restrainment, so great dangers escaped, such blusterous storms overblown, so many injuries digested and wrongs sustained, the mighty protection of our merciful God, to our no little safeguard, hath exalted and erected out of thrall to liberty, out of danger to peace and rule, from dread to dignity, from misery to majesty, from mourning to ruling: briefly, of a prisoner hath made her a prince and hath placed her in her throne royal, being placed and proclaimed queen, with as many glad hearts of her subjects as ever was any king or queen in this realm before her or ever shall be, I think, hereafter.

In whose advancement and this her princely governance, it cannot sufficiently be expressed what felicity and blessed happiness this realm hath received in receiving of her at the Lord's almighty and gracious hand. For as there have been diverse kings and rulers over this realm, and I have read of some, yet I could never find in English chronicle the like that may be written of this our noble and worthy queen; whose coming in not only was so calm, so joyful, so peaceable, without shedding of any blood, but also her reign hitherto, reigning now four years and more, hath been so quiet that yet —the Lord have all the glory—to this present day, her sword is a virgin, spotted and polluted with no drop of blood. In speaking whereof, I take not upon me the part here of the moral or of the divine philosopher, to judge of things done, but only hope me within the compass of an historiographer, declaring what hath been before and comparing things done with things now present, the like whereof, as I said, is not to be found lightly in chronicles before. And this, as I speak truly, so I would to be taken without flattery, to be left to our posterity, ad sempiternam clementiae illius memoriam.[51] In commendation of which her clemency, I might also here add how mildly Her Grace, after she was advanced to her kingdom, did forgive the foresaid Sir Henry Bedingfield without molestation, suffering him to enjoy goods, life, lands, and liberty. But I let this pass.

Thus hast thou, gentle reader, simply but truly described unto thee the time first of the sorrowful adversity of this our most sovereign queen that now is, also the miraculous protection of God, so graciously preserving her in so many straits and distresses; which I thought here briefly to notify, the rather for that the wondrous works of the Lord ought not to be suppressed and that also Her Majesty and we likewise, her poor subjects, having thereby a present matter always before our eyes, be admonished both how much we are bound to His Divine Majesty and also to render thanks to him condignly[52] for the same.

Notes

1. Earl of Derbyshire.
2. Rebellion.
3. He also plays an important role in 6.5.B.
4. Member of the Privy Council and comptroller of the queen's household.
5. Accused.
6. Leader of the rebellion in Devon.
7. In shame.
8. Eve.
9. Henry Radcliffe.
10. Nor.
11. Cruise under.
12. Descent.
13. Customarily.
14. Bible.
15. Matt. 7:24–27.

16. Leader of the rebellion along the Welsh border.

17. Outer.

18. Storage room for ewers (pitchers) and linen.

19. Broke.

20. John Bridges, first Baron Chandos and lieutenant of the Tower of London.

21. So long as.

22. A member of the Privy Council.

23. Position.

24. Site of the beheading of Lady Jane Grey.

25. One who modifies.

26. Insolent.

27. Scoundrels.

28. Edward Stanley, third Earl of Derby.

29. Roaming idly.

30. Kept from.

31. Foxe's gloss, "Like a sheep to the slaughter" (Isa. 53:7, Acts 8:32), likens her to Christ by reference to the first reading for Good Friday in the lectionary of the Church of England.

32. Permitted.

33. A medical practice.

34. Against.

35. Prince Philip of Spain, betrothed to Mary I.

36. A royal palace.

37. A tavern.

38. Ere.

39. First Baron Howard of Effingham, Lord High Admiral, member of the Privy Council, and a great granduncle of Princess Elizabeth.

40. Henry Fitzalan, 12th Earl of Arundel.

41. Francis Talbot, 5th Earl of Shrewsbury.

42. Sir William Petre, Secretary of State.

43. Gladly.

44. Susan Clarencieux, lady-in-waiting to Mary I.

45. I.e., to Hatfield.

46. Officer of the Court of Augmentations and member of the Privy Council, appointed to supervise Princess Elizabeth's household.

47. Observed.

48. He died on 12 November 1555.

49. Archetype for a traitorous counselor (2 Sam. 15–17).

50. "Ill council is worst to the counselor."

51. "to the eternal memory of her clemency."

52. Deservedly.

C. The Deliverance of Catherine Parr
from Court Intrigue (1570)

Catherine Parr (1512–1548), the sixth wife of Henry VIII, developed a legendary reputation for learning and piety. She patronized Protestant reformers such as Miles Coverdale, who completed Tyndale's project of translating the Bible into English (see 1.1), and Hugh Latimer (see 2.3) as her devotional advisors. She became queen at a time when a conservative faction that included Thomas Howard, Duke of Norfolk, and Thomas Wriothesley, Lord Chancellor, opposed evangelical ideas with which she was associated.

Not only does this romance-like fiction idealize Catherine Parr as an advocate of Bible interpretation by members of the laity, but it represents her as the victim of a plot organized by Stephen Gardiner, bishop of Winchester, as a means of destroying the evangelical faction at the royal court. It focuses as much or more on his inhumanity than on her religious conviction. He seized upon her willingness to debate with Henry VIII concerning the Bible in order to accuse her of studying prohibited Protestant books. He and his associates lodged related charges against Anne Askew, who was alleged to have received support from Parr's circle of pious women, who included Catherine Brandon, Duchess Dowager of Suffolk (see 6.1, 6.5.D). Henry VIII dissemblingly permitted Gardiner to proceed with his potentially lethal plot in order to test him. This story affirms that Parr undergoes providential deliverance when she conforms to patriarchal expectations and obediently submits to the king as her ruler, husband, and instructor in Bible interpretation.

SOURCE: *STC* 12223, pp. 1422–25.

EDITION: Foxe 2000.

REFERENCES: Hannay; Redworth.

About the same time above noted, which was about the year after the king returned from Boulogne,[1] he was informed that Queen Catherine Parr, at that time his wife, was very much given to the reading and study of the holy scriptures and that she for that purpose had retained divers well learned and godly persons to instruct her thoroughly in the same, with whom as at all times convenient she used to have private conference touching spiritual matters, so also of ordinary;[2] but especially in Lent, every day in the afternoon, for the space of one hour, one of her said chaplains in her Privy Chamber made some collation[3] to her and to her ladies and gentlewomen of her Privy Chamber or other that were disposed to hear, in which sermons they ofttimes touched such abuses as in the church then were rife. Which things, as they were not secretly done, so neither were their preachings unknown unto the king. Whereof at the first, and for a great time, he seemed very well to like. Which made her the more bold, being indeed become very zealous toward the Gospel and the professors thereof, frankly to debate with the king, touching religion and therein flatly to discover[4] herself, ofttimes wishing, exhorting, and persuading the king that, as he had to the glory of God and his eternal fame begun a good and godly work in banishing that monstrous idol of Rome, so he would thoroughly perfect and finish the same, cleansing and purging his Church of England clean from the dregs thereof, wherein as yet remained great superstition. . . .

Moreover, besides the virtues of the mind, she was endued with very rare gifts of nature, as singular beauty, favor, and comely personage, being things wherein the king was greatly delighted, and so enjoyed she the king's favor, to the great likelihood of the setting at large of the Gospel within this realm at that time, had not the malicious practice of certain enemies professed against the truth, which at that time also were very great, prevented the same, to the bitter alienating of the king's mind from religion, and almost to the extreme ruin of the queen and certain others with her, if God had not miraculously succored her in that distress. The conspirers and practicers[5] of her death were Gardiner, Bishop of Winchester; Wriothesley, then Lord Chancellor; and others more as well of the King's Privy Chamber, as of his Privy Council. These seeking, for the furtherance of their ungodly purpose, to revive, stir up, and kindle evil and pernicious humors in their prince and sovereign lord, to the intent to deprive her of this her great favor, which then she stood in with the king, which they not a little feared would turn to the utter ruin of their anti-Christian sect, if it should continue, and thereby to stop the passage of the Gospel; and consequently, having taken away her, who was the only patroness of the professors of the truth, openly without fear of check or controlment, with fire and sword after their accustomed manner, to invade the small remainder, as they hoped, of that poor flock, made their wicked entry unto their mischievous enterprise after this manner following.

The King's Majesty, as you have heard, misliked to be contended withal in any kind of argument. This humor of his, although not in smaller matters, yet in causes of religion, as occasion served, the queen would not stick[6] in reverent terms and humble talk, entering with him into discourse with sound reasons of Scripture, now and then too contrary.[7] . . .

[Bishop Gardiner then insinuated that Queen Catherine was a heretic.]

Thus then Winchester, with his flattering words seeking to frame the king's disposition after his own pleasure, so far crept into the king at that time, and with doubtful fears he with other [of] his fellows so filled the king's mistrustful mind, that before they departed the place the king, to see belike what they would do, had given commandment with warrant to certain of them made for that purpose to consult together about the drawing of certain articles against the queen wherein her life might be touched, which the King by their persuasions pretended to be fully resolved not to spare, having any rigor or color of law to countenance the matter. With this commission they departed for that time from the king, resolved to put their pernicious practice to as mischievous an execution.

During this time of deliberation about this matter, they failed not to use all kinds of policies and mischievous practices, as well to suborn accusers as otherwise to betray her in seeking to understand what books by law forbidden she had in her closet. And the better to bring their purpose to pass, because they would not upon the sudden but by means[8] deal with her, they thought it best at the first to begin with some of those ladies whom they knew to be great[9] with her and of her blood. The chiefest whereof, as most of estimation and privy to all her doings, were these: the Lady Herbert, afterward Countess of Pembroke and sister to the queen and chief of her privy chamber; the Lady Lane, being of her privy chamber and also her cousin-german;[10] the Lady Tyrwit of her privy chamber and for her virtuous disposition in very great favor and credit with her.

It was devised that these three above-named should first of all have been accused and brought to answer unto the Six Articles, and upon their apprehension in the court, their closet and coffers should have been searched, that somewhat might have been found whereby the queen might be charged. Which being found, the queen herself presently should have been taken and likewise carried by barge by night unto the Tower. This platform thus devised, but yet in the end coming to no effect, the king by those aforesaid was forthwith made privy unto the device by Winchester and Wriothesley and his consent thereunto demanded. Who, belike to prove the bishop's malice, how far it would presume, like a wise politic prince, was contented, dissemblingly, to give his consent and to allow of every circumstance, knowing notwithstanding in the end what he would do. And thus the day, the time, and the place of these apprehensions aforesaid was appointed, which device yet after was changed.

The king at that time lay at Whitehall[11] and used very seldom, being not well at ease, to stir out of his chamber or privy gallery, and few of his Council, but by special commandment, resorted unto him, these only except[ed], who by reason of this special practice used oftener than of ordinary to repair unto him. This purpose so finely was handled that it grew now within few days of the time appointed for the execution of the matter and the poor queen knew not nor suspected anything at all, and therefore used, after her accustomed manner when she came to visit the king, still to deal with him touching religion as before she did.

The king all this while gave her leave to utter her mind at the full without contradiction, not upon any evil mind or misliking, ye must conceive, to have her speedy dispatch, but rather closely dissembling with them to try out the uttermost of Winchester's fetches. Thus after her accustomed conference with the king, when she had taken her leave of him, the time and day of Winchester's final date approaching fast upon, it chanced that the king of himself upon a certain night after her being with him and her leave taken of him, in misliking her religion brake the whole practice unto one of his physicians, either Doctor Wendy or else Owen, but rather Wendy, as is supposed, pretending unto him as though he intended not any longer to be troubled with such a doctress[12] as she was and also declaring what trouble was in working against her by certain of her enemies, but yet charging him withal upon peril of his life not to utter it to any creature living, and thereupon declared unto him the parties above-named, with all circumstances and when and what the final resolution of the matter should be.

The queen all this while, compassed about with enemies and persecutors, perceived nothing of all this nor what was working against her and what traps were laid for her by Winchester and his fellows, so closely the matter was conveyed. But see what the Lord God, who from his eternal throne of wisdom seeth and dispatcheth all the inventions of Achitophel[13] and comprehendeth the wily beguily[14] themselves, did for his poor handmaiden in rescuing her from the pit of ruin whereunto she was ready to fall unawares.

For as the Lord would, so it came to pass, that the bill of articles[15] drawn up against the queen and subscribed with the king's own hand, although dissemblingly ye must understand, falling from the bosom of one of the foresaid counselors, was found and taken up of some godly person and brought immediately unto the queen. Who, reading there the articles comprised against her and perceiving the king's own hand unto the same, for the sudden fear thereof fell incontinent into a great melancholy and agony, bewailing and taking on in such sort as was lamentable to see, as certain of her ladies and gentlewomen being yet alive which were then present about her can testify.

The king, hearing what perplexity she was in, almost to the peril and danger of her life, sent his physicians unto her. Who, travailing about her and seeing what extremity she was in, did what they could for her recovery. Then Wendy, who knew the case better than the other and perceiving by her words what the matter was, according to that the king before had told him, for the comforting of her heavy mind began to break with her in secret manner touching the said articles devised against her, which he himself, he said, knew right well to be true, although he stood in danger of his life if ever he were known to utter the same to any living creature. Nevertheless, partly for the safety of her life and partly for the discharge of his own conscience, having remorse to consent to the shedding of innocent blood, he could not but give her warning of that mischief that hanged over her head, beseeching her most instantly to use all secrecy in that behalf, and exhorted her somewhat to frame and conform herself unto the king's mind, saying he did not doubt but if she would so do and show her humble submission unto him, she should find him gracious and favorable unto her.

It was not long after this but the king, hearing of the dangerous state wherein she yet still remained, came unto her himself. Unto whom, after that she had uttered her grief, fearing lest His Majesty, she said, had taken displeasure with her and had utterly forsaken her, he like a loving husband with sweet and comfortable words so refreshed and appeased her careful[16] mind that she upon the same began somewhat to recover, and so the king, after he had tarried there about the space of an hour, departed.

After this the queen, remembering with herself the words that Master Wendy had said unto her, devised how by some good opportunity she might repair to the king's presence. And so first commanding her ladies to convey away their books which were against the law, the next night following after supper, she, waited upon only by the Lady Herbert, her sister, and the Lady Lane, who carried the candle before her, went unto the king's bedchamber, whom she found sitting and talking with certain gentlemen of his chamber. Whom when the king did behold very courteously he welcomed her and, breaking off the talk which before her coming he had with the gentlemen aforesaid, began of himself, contrary to his manner before accustomed, to enter into talk of religion, seeming as it were desirous to be resolved by the queen of certain doubts which he propounded.

The queen, perceiving to what purpose this talk did tend, not being unprovided in what sort to behave herself towards the king, with such answers resolved his questions as the time and opportunity present did require, mildly and with a reverent countenance answering again after this manner:

"Your majesty," quoth she, "doth right well know neither I myself am ignorant what great imperfection and weakness by our first creation is allotted unto us women, to be ordained and appointed as inferior and subject unto man as our head, from which head all our direction ought to proceed; and that, as God made man to his own shape and likeness, whereby he, being endued with more special gifts of perfection, might rather be stirred to the contemplation of heavenly things and to the earnest endeavor to obey his commandments, even so also made he woman of man, of whom and by whom she is to be governed, commanded and directed. Whose womanly weakness and natural imperfection ought to be tolerated, aided and borne withal, so that by his wisdom such things as be lacking in her ought to be supplied.

"Sithence therefore that God hath appointed such a natural difference between man and woman, and your majesty being so excellent in gifts and ornaments of wisdom, and I a silly poor woman so much inferior in all respects of nature unto you, how then cometh it now to pass that your majesty in such diffuse causes of religion will feign to require my judgement, which when I have uttered and said what I can, yet must I and will I refer my judgment in this and all other cases to your majesty's wisdom, as my only anchor, supreme head, and governor here in earth, next under God, to lean unto."

"Not so, by Saint Mary," quoth the king. "You are become a doctor,[17] Kate, to instruct us, as we take it, and not to be instructed or directed by us."

"If your majesty take it so," quoth the queen, "then hath your majesty very much mistaken me, who have ever been of the opinion to think it very unseemly and preposterous for the woman to take upon her the office of an instructor or teacher to her lord and husband, but rather to learn of her husband and to be taught by him. And where I have with your majesty's leave heretofore been bold to hold talk with your majesty, wherein sometimes in opinions there hath seemed some difference, I have not done it so much to maintain opinion, as I did it rather to minister talk, not only to the end that your majesty might with less grief pass over this painful time of your infirmity, being intentive[18] to our talk, and hoping that your majesty should reap some ease thereby, but also that I, hearing your majesty's learned discourse, might receive to myself some profit thereof. Wherein I assure your majesty I have not missed any part of my desire in that behalf, always referring myself in all such matters unto your majesty, as by ordinance of nature it is convenient for me to do."

"And is it even so, sweetheart," quoth the king, "and tended your arguments to no worse an end? Then perfect friends we are now again as ever at any time heretofore," and as he sat in his chair, embracing in his arms and kissing her, he added this saying that it did him more good at that time to hear those words of her own mouth than if he had heard present news of an hundred thousand pounds in money fallen unto him. And with great signs and tokens of marvelous joy and liking, with promises and assurances never again in any sort more to mistake her, entering into other very pleasant discourses with the queen and the lords and gentlemen standing by, in the end, being very far on the night, he gave her leave to depart. Whom in her absence to the standers-by he gave as singular and as effectuous commendations as before time to the Bishop and the Chancellor, who then were neither of them present, he seemed to mislike of her.

Now then, God be thanked, the king's mind was clean altered, and he detested in his heart, as afterwards he plainly showed, this tragical practice of those cruel Caiaphases who, nothing understanding of the king's well-reformed mind and good disposition toward the queen, were busily occupied about thinking and providing for their next day's labor, which was the day [they] determined to have carried the queen to the Tower.

The day and almost the hour appointed being come, the king being disposed in the afternoon to take the air, waited upon with two gentlemen only of his bedchamber, went into the garden, whither the queen also came, being sent for by the king himself, the three ladies above-named alone waiting upon her. With whom the king at that time disposed himself to be as pleasant as ever he was in all his life before, when suddenly in the midst of their mirth the hour determined being come, in cometh the Lord Chancellor into the garden with a forty of the king's guard at his heels, with purpose indeed to have taken the queen, together with the three ladies aforesaid, whom they had before purposed to apprehend alone even then unto the Tower. Whom the king sternly beholding and breaking off his mirth with the queen, stepping a little aside, called the chancellor unto him. Who upon his knees spake certain words unto the king, but what they were, for that they were softly spoken, and the king a good pretty distance from the queen, it is not well known, but it is most certain that the king's replying unto him was, knave, for his answer; yea, arrant knave, beast, and fool, and with that the king commanded him presently to avaunt[19] out of presence. . . . Thus departed the Lord Chancellor out of the king's presence as he came, with all his train, the whole mold of all his device being utterly broken.

The king after his departure immediately returned to the queen. Whom she perceiving to be very much chafed, albeit, coming towards her, he enforced himself to put on a merry countenance, with as sweet words as she could utter, endeavored to qualify[20] the king his displeasure with request unto His Majesty in the behalf of the Lord Chancellor, [with] whom he seemed to be offended withal, saying for his excuse that albeit she knew not what just cause His Majesty had at that time to be offended with him, yet she thought that ignorance, not will, was the cause of his error, and so besought His Majesty, if the cause were not very heinous, at her humble suit to take it.

"Ah, poor soul," quoth he, "thou little knowest how evil he deserveth this grace at thy hands. Of my word, sweetheart, he hath been towards thee an arrant knave, and so let him go." To this the queen in charitable manner replying in few words ended that talk, having also by God's only blessing happily[21] for that time and ever escaped the dangerous snares of her bloody and cruel enemies for the Gospel's sake.

Notes

1. Circa October 1545. Henry VIII was in France from 14 July until 30 September 1544, where he joined an English military expedition that besieged Boulogne. Catherine Parr served as regent during this period.

2. Order of devotion.

3. Sermon.

4. Reveal.

5. Plotters.

6. Adhere.

7. Contradictory.

8. Through intermediaries.

9. Familiar.

10. First cousin.

11. Royal palace.

12. Learned woman.

13. See 7.5.B (n. 49).

14. Trapped by one's own guile.

15. Indictments

16. Sorrowful.

17. Learned person.

18. Heedful.

19. Depart.

20. Appease.

21. By chance (haply).

Appendix: List of
Notable Persons

John Bale (1495–1563), at one time a Carmelite friar, was an extraordinarily forceful and prolific Protestant propagandist who composed plays, led a troupe of itinerant actors who performed them, preached sermons, edited and translated texts, operated a bookshop in London, and compiled the earliest bibliographies of books written by English writers. He fled to continental Europe after the execution of his patron, Thomas Cromwell (see below), marked the conclusion of the first, cautious phase of the English Reformation. He returned to England under Edward VI, who appointed him to serve as a missionary bishop in Ireland. Having gone into exile for a second time during the reign of Mary I, he returned after the accession of Elizabeth I and spent his final years as a prebendary of Canterbury Cathedral. See 1.1.B, 3.1, 6.1–2, Figure 4.

Edmund Bonner (c. 1500–1569) was a protégé of Cardinal Thomas Wolsey who served as an ambassador during the period of time when Henry VIII sought a divorce from Catherine of Aragon. The king then appointed him Bishop of Hereford (1538) and London (1539). After he was imprisoned during the reign of Edward VI because of his resistance to Protestant reforms, Mary I restored him to episcopal office. Protestants vilified him as "Bloody Bonner" because of his uncompromising persecution of heretics, many of whom were burned alive during her reign. See 2.4.

William Cecil (1520–98) was employed during the reign of Edward VI by Edward Seymour, Protector Somerset, prior to appointment as secretary of state. Even though he remained in service to Mary I, at a time when he was also a Member of Parliament, he sponsored a secret press on which John Day printed Protestant propaganda. Resuming office as Secretary of State, he was the chief minister of Elizabeth I, who rewarded him through his creation as Baron Burghley (1571) and appointment as Lord Treasurer (1572). See 2.6–7, 4.3.

Thomas Cranmer (1489–1556) was Archbishop of Canterbury from 1533 until 1553. He was the architect of the English church service introduced during the reign of Edward VI and reintroduced, with some modifications, under

Elizabeth I. Deprived from office and imprisoned for treason under Mary I, he recanted his religious beliefs only to spurn his recantation. He was burned alive at Oxford in 1556. See 2.2, 6.5.B.

Thomas Cromwell (c. 1485–1540), a member of Parliament, rose under the patronage of Cardinal Wolsey before Henry VIII appointed him to the Privy Council. Not only did he revolutionize the bureaucracy and govern as the king's chief minister, but he also instituted royal control over the Church of England. As vicegerent for religious affairs, he presided over the dissolution of monastic houses. He advocated implementation of Protestant reforms, in company with Archbishop Cranmer, and patronized the publication of the Great Bible (1539). After his creation as Earl of Essex in 1540, he fell from royal favor prior to his execution as a traitor. See 3.1.

John Day (1522–84) received patronage from prominent Protestant aristocrats throughout his career as a printer and publisher. Very active as a publisher of Protestant propaganda during the reign of Edward VI, he went to prison after the accession of Mary I, during whose reign he operated a secret printing press under the protection of William Cecil. Arguably the most successful Elizabethan master printer and publisher, he is known chiefly as the publisher of Foxe's *Book of Martyrs*. See 2.3, 4.1, 6.5, 7.5, Figure 11.

Edward VI (1537–53) was the son of Henry VIII and his third wife, Jane Seymour. As Prince of Wales, he received a humanistic education under the charge of his stepmother, Catherine Parr (see 7.5.C). The elder royal uncle, Edward Seymour, Earl of Hertford and later Duke of Somerset, governed England in the manner of a king after Edward's accession as a minor in 1547. John Dudley, Earl of Warwick and later Duke of Northumberland, then deposed Protector Somerset. In collaboration with Archbishop Cranmer, these powerful lords attempted to introduce Protestant theology and devotional practices that were compatible with the king's religious zeal. See 2.2–3, 3.2–4, 4.1–2, 5.1–2, 6.2, Figures 3, 5.

Elizabeth I (1533–1603) underwent illegitimation after her father, Henry VIII, countenanced the execution of her mother, Anne Boleyn, on grounds of adultery. She received an outstanding humanistic education from Roger Ascham, the Cambridge scholar who tutored her under the charge of her stepmother, Queen Catherine Parr (see. 7.5.C). In danger of death when she was suspected of treason during the reign of her half-sister Mary I, she escaped the fate of Lady Jane Grey (see 7.1) by remaining steadfastly silent concerning her religious and political beliefs. She acceded to the throne at her sister's death in 1558. Her shrewd administrator William Cecil (see above) presided over the introduction of a modified form of the Edwardian religious settlement. Her favor of religious practices suggestive of Catholicism (e.g., clerical vestments, ritual practices, and kneeling during the communion service) incurred increasing opposition from Puritans and presbyterians. See 1.1.C–D, 1.2.C, 2.5–7, 4.3–5, 5.3, 6.5–8, 7.3–5, Figures 16–17.

John Foxe (1516–87) was educated at Magdalen College, Oxford, prior to his ordination in 1550. Going into exile during the reign of Mary I, he published two Latin precursors of his *Acts and Monuments* at printing houses in the Rhineland. His publisher and collaborator John Day (see above) printed four increasingly massive versions (1563–83) of it during the remainder of their lifetimes. From the beginning, this ecclesiastical history has been known as the *Book of Martyrs*. Foxe received patronage from John Parkhurst, Bishop of Norwich, and William Cecil (see above), who also patronized John Day. See 6.1, 6.5.A–D, 7.1, 7.5.A–C, Figures 3, 5, 8, 10–13, 17.

Stephen Gardiner (1490?–1555), a protégé of Cardinal Wolsey, was appointed Bishop of Winchester by Henry VIII, deprived of his see under Edward VI, and reinstated and appointed lord Chancellor by Mary I. He was a staunch conservative who opposed Protestant attacks on traditional religious practices. He diligently prosecuted Protestants as heretics and advocated their execution by burning during the 1540s and 1550s. See 6.1, 6.5.D, 7.5.B–C, Figure 14.

Henry VIII (1491–1547) was crowned King of England in 1509. Although he defended religious orthodoxy against attack by Martin Luther, he initiated England's schism from the Church of Rome as a result of the failure of Pope Clement VII to grant him a divorce from Catherine of Aragon. Under the guidance of Thomas Cromwell (see above), Parliament passed legislation that took the radical step of declaring the monarch supreme head of the Church of England. Despite this political change, he condoned retention of Catholic ritual and theology. The religious convictions of his offspring – Edward VI, Mary I, and Elizabeth I – had a profound impact on English politics and religion during the remainder of the sixteenth century and beyond. See 1.1.A, 1.2.A–B, 2.1, 3.1, 6.1, 6.5.A, 7.5.C, Figures 1 and 2.

Hugh Latimer (c. 1485–1555) was the spiritual father of many members of the first generation of English Protestant clergy and of aristocratic women.

Henry VIII appointed him Bishop of Worcester (1535–39), but he resigned when his style of evangelical episcopacy lost favor with the king. A vigorous opponent of clerical abuses and the selfishness of wealthy individuals, he was arguably the greatest English preacher of his time. A recipient of patronage from Catherine Parr and the Duchess of Suffolk, he had an obscure connection to Anne Askew. He was burned alive for heresy during the reign of Mary I. See 2.3, 6.1, 6.5.B, Figures 3, 13.

Mary I (1516–58) was the daughter of Henry VIII and Catherine of Aragon. She underwent illegitimation after her mother's failure to deliver a male heir triggered revolutionary changes in church and state consequent upon her father's insistence upon a divorce (see above). When she refused to conform to the Protestant religious settlement imposed during the reign of her half-brother Edward VI, her chaplains celebrated Mass in her private chapel. After her accession to the throne of England in 1553, she sought to restore Roman Catholic worship and reconcile England with the Church of Rome. The rebellion of Thomas Wyatt in opposition to her marriage to Prince Philip (later Philip II) of Spain led to the imprisonment of her half-sister Elizabeth; the decapitation of Lady Jane Grey; the burning of more than three hundred Protestants as heretics; and the exile of many of their coreligionists. For more than a century, Protestants celebrated the day of her death and the accession of Elizabeth I as a national holiday. They have continued to stigmatize her in modern times as "Bloody Mary." See 2.4, 3.5, 6.2–4, 6.5.B–D, 7.1–2, 7.5.B, Figure 15.

William Tyndale (c. 1495–1536), a humanistic scholar under the influence of Erasmus and Luther, earned the antipathy of members of the ecclesiastical hierarchy by advocating translation of the Bible into the vernacular. He went into exile in Germany and the Low Countries, where his translations of the New Testament and portions of the Old Testament, in addition to controversial religious treatises, were published for illicit exportation to England. John Foxe, his first biographer, recounts the story of his life and execution. See 1.1.A, 1.2.A, 2.1, 6.5.A, Figure 12.

Thomas Wriothesley (1505–50), Earl of Southampton and lord chancellor, collaborated with Stephen Gardiner (see above) in the persecution of Protestant heretics. He played a prominent role in the interrogation, torture, and subsequent burning of Anne Askew. See 6.1.

Glossary

assoil: absolve.

ay: an exclamation of regret.

Babylon: the city of the Antichrist identified with Rome and represented by the Whore of Babylon (see 1.1), whom Protestants identified with the Church of Rome (see 1.1.C–D, 1.2)

baggage: morally despicable person.

bairn: child.

bawdry: immorality.

beads: rosary.

beshrew: curse.

bewray: betray, disclose (esp. inadvertently).

Caiaphas: high priest before whom Christ was tried (Matt. 26), often applied by Protestants as prototype for Roman Catholic prelates.

cake: Mass wafer (derogatory).

certes: certainly.

compline: last of the daily canonical hours, periods set aside for prayer and devotion; office recited in the evening.

conscience: inward knowledge, consciousness, recognition of right and wrong, moral sense.

corse: body, living or dead.

curate: cleric in charge of a parish.

cure: parish; office of a curate.

dight: to appoint, manage, treat.

doctor: theologian.

eke: also.

evensong: evening service.

evil: badly, ill.

fantasy: imagination, imagined opinion, delusion.

frieze: coarse woolen cloth.

gear: absurdity, stuff, junk.

ghost(ly): spirit(ually).

gospeller: zealous Protestant (often derogatory).

gossip: friend.

groat: silver coin worth fourpence.

hight: signify, be named.

honesty: integrity, chastity.

incontinent: unrestrained, without an interval.

incontinently: immediately.

indite: write.

indifferent(ly): impartial(ly).

iwis: certainly.

leech: physician.

leman: lover.

let: hesitate.

lightly: easily.

list: desire, choose.

lust: pleasure, desire, wish.

mark: monetary unit equal to thirteen shillings and fourpence (two-thirds of a pound sterling).

marry: certainly; expression of agreement or surprise.

matins: in conjunction with *lauds*, the first of the canonical hours, periods set aside for prayer and devotion or the service for it; office recited late at night or in the morning.

mean: intermediary.

naughty: wicked.

new learning: humanism, often associated with the Protestant Reformation.

nonce: present or particular occasion.

nones: one of the canonical hours, periods set aside for prayer and devotion; office recited in mid-afternoon.

papist: Roman Catholic (derogatory).

pharisaical: self-righteous, hypocritical (see *Pharisees*).

Pharisees: members of a Jewish sect who had very strict beliefs concerning law and tradition; mentioned in the New Testament. Christians associated them with sanctimoniousness and hypocrisy (see *scribes*).

popery: Roman Catholicism (derogatory).

portas: portable breviary.

pretend: conceive of, carry out.

primer: prayer book.

quick: alive.

quod: said.

rede: counsel.

rehearse: tell.

rochet: surplice or vestment worn by abbots and bishop.

runagate: renegade.

scribes: learned men mentioned in the New Testament, whom Christians associated with traditionalism and hypocrisy (see Pharisees),

sennight: seven-night (i.e., a week),

shamefast: modest, shy, ashamed,

shaveling: tonsured monk or friar (derogatory),

silly: pitiable, helpless, innocent, weak,

Sir John: nickname for a priest (derogatory).

sithence: seeing that.

spital: (n.) hospital, hospice; (adj.) impoverished.

stomach: inclination, pride.

strait: strict, narrow

stones: testicles.

suffragan: priest who recites intercessory prayers.

synagogue: church, congregation.

terrene: worldly, secular.

trow: believe.

troth: faith.

trumpery: deceit, trickery, rubbish (applied contemptuously to allegedly superstitious religious practices and ceremonies).

unshamefast: immodest.

ware: aware.

weeds: clothing.

ween: think, know, believe.

wight: man, person.

wis: know (see *iwis*).

wise: manner.

withal: in addition, moreover.

wolves: members of the Roman Catholic clergy (slur based on Matt. 7:15).

wot, wottest: know(s), understand(s).

Select Bibliography

Askew, Anne. *The Examinations of Anne Askew*. Edited by Elaine V. Beilin. Oxford: Oxford University Press, 1996.

————. *Anne Askew* Edited by John N. King. Aldershot: Scolar Press, 1996.

Baldwin, William. *Beware the Cat by William Baldwin: The First English Novel*. Edited by William A. Ringler, Jr. and Michael Flachmann. San Marino, Calif.: Huntington Library, 1988.

————. *The Mirror for Magistrates*. Edited by Lily B. Campbell. Cambridge: Cambridge University Press, 1938.

Bale, John. *The Complete Plays of John Bale*. 2 vols. Edited by Peter Happé. Cambridge: D.S. Brewer, 1985–86.

————. *The Image of Bothe Churches*. The English Experience 498. Amsterdam: Theatrum Orbis Terrarum, 1973.

————. *The Select Works of John Bale, Bishop of Ossery*. Parker Society 36. Cambridge, 1849.

————. *The Vocacyon of Johan Bale*. Edited by Peter Happé and John N. King. Renaissance English Text Society 14. Binghamton, N.Y.: Medieval and Renaissance Texts and Studies, 1990.

Bauckham, Richard. *Tudor Apocalypse*. Appleford, Eng.: Sutton Courtney Press, 1978.

Beilin, Elaine V. *Redeeming Eve: Women Writers of the English Renaissance*. Princeton, N.J.: Princeton University Press, 1987.

Bentley, Thomas. *The Monument of Matrons Containing Seven Several Lamps of Virginity*. 1582.

Betteridge, Thomas. *Tudor Histories of the English Reformations, 1530–83*. Aldershot: Ashgate, 1999.

Bevington, David. *From Mankind to Marlowe: Growth and Structure in the Popular Drama of Tudor England*. Cambridge, Mass.: Harvard University Press, 1962.

The Bible in English. Subscription database. Cambridge: Chadwyk Healy, 1996. www. ohiolink.edu/db/bible.html.

Bond, Ronald B., ed. *Certain Sermons or Homilies (1547): and A Homily Against Disobedience and Willful Rebellion (1570): A Critical Edition*. Toronto: University of Toronto Press, 1987.

Booty, John, ed., with David Siegenthaler and John N. Wall, Jr. *The Godly Kingdom of Tudor England: Great Books of the English Reformation*. Wilton, Conn.: Morehouse-Barlow, 1981.

Bray, Gerald, ed. *Documents of the English Reformation*. Minneapolis: Fortress Press, 1994.

Brigden, Susan. *London and the Reformation*. Oxford: Clarendon Press, 1989.

Brownlow, F. W. *Robert Southwell*. New York: Twayne, 1996.

Cecil, William, and William Allen. *The Execution of Justice in England, by William Cecil; and A True, Sincere, and Modest Defense of English Catholics, by William*

Allen. Edited by Robert M. Kingdon. Ithaca, N.Y.: Cornell University Press for the Folger Shakespeare Library, 1965.

Chester, Allan. *Hugh Latimer, Apostle to the English.* Philadelphia: University of Pennsylvania Press, 1954.

Collinson, Patrick. *The Birthpangs of Protestant England: Religious and Cultural Change in the Sixteenth and Seventeenth Centuries.* London: Macmillan, 1988.

Cressy, David, and Lori Anne Ferrell, eds. *Religion and Society in Early Modern England: A Sourcebook.* London: Routledge, 1996.

Crowley, Robert. *Select Works.* Edited by J. M. Cowper. Early English Text Society e.s. 15. London: Trübner, 1872.

Daniell, David. *The Bible in English: Its History and Influence.* New Haven, Conn.: Yale University Press, 2003.

————. *William Tyndale: A Biography.* New Haven, Conn.: Yale University Press, 1994.

Duffy, Eamon. *The Stripping of the Altars: Traditional Religion in England 1400–1580.* New Haven: Yale University Press, 1992.

Elizabeth I. *Elizabeth I: Collected Works.* Ed. Leah S. Marcus, Janel Mueller, and Mary Beth Rose. Chicago: University of Chicago Press, 2000.

Fox, Alistair, and John Guy, eds. *Reassessing the Henrician Age: Humanism, Politics and Reform 1500–1550.* Oxford: Blackwell, 1986.

Foxe, John. *Acts and Monuments of These Latter and Perilous Days.* 1st through 4th eds. London: John Day, 1563, 1570, 1576, 1583.

————. *Acts and Monuments.* Variorum Edition. Online publication. hriOnline, Sheffield University (http://www.hrionline.ac.uk), 2004.

————. *Facsimile of John Foxe's "Book of Martyrs," 1583: Actes and Monuments of Matters Most Speciall and Memorable.* Edited by David G. Newcombe with Michael Pidd. Version 1.0.CD-ROM. Oxford: Oxford University Press for the British Academy, 2000.

Frye, Susan. *Elizabeth I: The Competition for Representation.* New York: Oxford University Press, 1993.

The Geneva Bible: A Facsimile of the 1560 Edition. Introduction by Lloyd E. Berry. Madison: University of Wisconsin Press, 1969.

Gilman, Ernest. *Iconoclasm and Poetry in the English Reformation: "Down Went Dagon".* Chicago: University of Chicago Press, 1986.

Greenblatt, Stephen. *Renaissance Self-Fashioning: From More to Shakespeare.* Chicago: University of Chicago Press, 1980.

Gregory, Brad S. *Salvation at Stake: Christian Martyrdom in Early Modern Europe.* Cambridge, Mass.: Harvard University Press, 1999.

Guy, John. *Tudor England.* New York: Oxford University Press, 1988.

Hadfield, Andrew. *Literature, Politics, and National Identity: Reformation to Renaissance.* Cambridge: Cambridge University Press, 1994.

Haigh, Christopher. *The English Reformations: Religion, Politics, and Society Under the Tudors.* Oxford: Clarendon Press, 1993.

Hannay, Margaret, ed. *Silent But for the Word: Tudor Women as Patrons, Translators, and Writers of Religious Works.* Kent, Ohio: Kent State University Press, 1985.

Happé, Peter. *John Bale.* New York: Twayne, 1996.

Helgerson, Richard. *Forms of Nationhood: The Elizabethan Writing of England.* Chicago: University of Chicago Press, 1992.

Highley, Christopher, and John N. King, eds. *John Foxe and His World*. Aldershot: Ashgate, 2002.

Hillerbrand, Hans J. et al., eds. *The Oxford Encyclopedia of the Reformation*. 4 vols. New York: Oxford University Press, 1996.

Kendall, Ritchie D. *The Drama of Dissent: The Radical Poetics of Nonconformity, 1380–1590*. Chapel Hill: University of North Carolina Press, 1986.

King, John N. *English Reformation Literature: The Tudor Origins of the Protestant Tradition*. Princeton, N.J.: Princeton University Press, 1982.

———. *Spenser's Poetry and the Reformation Tradition*. Princeton, N.J.: Princeton University Press, 1990.

———. *Tudor Royal Iconography: Literature and Art in an Age of Religious Crisis*. Princeton, N.J.: Princeton University Press, 1989.

Kipling, Gordon. *Enter the King: Theatre, Liturgy, and Ritual in the Medieval Civic Triumph*. Oxford: Clarendon Press, 1998.

Knott, John R. *Discourses of Martyrdom in English Literature, 1563–1694*. Cambridge: Cambridge University Press, 1993.

Loach, Jennifer. *Edward VI*. Edited by George Bernard and Penry Williams. New Haven, Conn.: Yale University Press, 1999.

Loades, David, ed. *John Foxe and the English Reformation*. Aldershot: Scolar Press, 1997.

———, ed. *John Foxe: An Historical Perspective*. Aldershot: Ashgate, 1999.

———. *The Reign of Mary Tudor*. London: Longman, 1991.

MacCaffrey, Wallace. *Elizabeth I*. London: Edward Arnold, 1993.

MacCulloch, Diarmaid. *Thomas Cranmer: A Life*. New Haven, Conn.: Yale University Press, 1996.

Marius, Richard. *Thomas More: A Biography*. New York: Random House, 1984.

Marotti, Arthur F., ed. *Catholicism and Anti-Catholicism in Early Modern English Texts*. London: Macmillan, 1999.

McGrath, Alister E. *Reformation Thought: An Introduction*. 2nd ed. Oxford: Blackwell, 1993.

More, Thomas. *The Complete Works of St. Thomas More*. Edited by Richard Sylvester et al. 15 vols. New Haven, Conn.: Yale University Press, 1963–85.

Mullaney, Steven. *The Place of the Stage: License, Play, and Power in Renaissance England*. Chicago: University of Chicago Press, 1988.

Norbrook, David G. *Poetry and Politics in the English Renaissance*. London: Routledge and Kegan Paul, 1984.

Norton, David. *A History of the English Bible as Literature*. 2nd ed. Cambridge: Cambridge University Press, 2000.

Redworth, Glyn. *In Defence of the Church Catholic: The Life of Stephen Gardiner*. Oxford: Blackwell, 1990.

Reynolds, E. E. *Campion and Parsons: The Jesuit Mission of 1580–81*. London: Sheed and Ward, 1980.

Scarisbrick, J. J. *Henry VIII*. Berkeley: University of California Press, 1968.

Shell, Alison. *Catholicism, Controversy, and the English Literary Imagination, 1558–1660*. Cambridge: Cambridge University Press, 1999.

Shepherd, Luke. *An Edition of Luke Shepherd's Satires*. Edited by Janice Devereux. Renaissance English Text Society 26. Tempe, Ariz.: Medieval and Renaissance Texts and Studies, 2001.

A Short-Title Catalogue of Books Printed in England, Scotland, and Ireland, and of English Books Printed Abroad, 1475–1640. Compiled by A. W. Pollard and G. R. Redgrave. 2nd ed., rev. and enlarged by W. A. Jackson, F. S. Ferguson, and Katharine F. Pantzer. 3 vols. London: Bibliographical Society, 1976–91. Cited as *STC*.

Spenser, Edmund. *The Faerie Queene*. Edited by A. C. Hamilton et al. 2nd ed. London: Longman, 2001. Cited as *FQ*.

Somerset, J. A. B., ed. *Four Tudor Interludes*. London: Athlone Press, 1974.

Tyndale, William. *The Obedience of a Christian Man*. Edited by David Daniell. London: Penguin, 2000.

———. *Tyndale's New Testament: Translated from the Greek by William Tyndale in 1534*. Edited by David Daniell. New Haven, Conn.: Yale University Press, 1989.

White, Helen C. *Tudor Books of Saints and Martyrs*. Madison: University of Wisconsin Press, 1963.

White, Paul Whitfield. *Theatre and Reformation: Protestantism, Patronage, and Playing in Tudor England*. Cambridge: Cambridge University Press, 1993.

Yates, Francis A. *Astraea: The Imperial Theme in the Sixteenth Century*. London: Routledge and Kegan Paul, 1975.

Index

Acknowledgments

The project dates from the time when I undertook the study of this field as a graduate student. I profited then from the advice of faculty members at the University of Chicago, including David Bevington, the late Arthur Heiserman, and especially the late William A. Ringler, Jr., to whom I am particularly indebted for his encouragement of my interest in these materials.

For many valuable suggestions, I am grateful to Christopher Highley and Peter Kaufman, who read the complete typescript at different stages. I am deeply indebted to Steven Galbraith, Justin Pepperney, Bryan Davis, Mark Bayer, Mark Rankin, Christopher Manion, Thomas G. Olsen, Robin Smith, Barbara Brumbaugh, and Joseph Grossi for their steadfast assistance in the compilation of the book. I thank Michael Curley and Christopher Manion for assistance with Latin. Steven Galbraith and Mark Rankin compiled the Index with diligence and grace. The project has profited greatly from comments by members of National Endowment for the Humanities Summer Seminars for College and University Teachers, which met at The Ohio State University in 1990, 1997, 1999, 2001, and 2003, in addition to students in different classes at The Ohio State University.

Many friends and colleagues at The Ohio State University have offered generous assistance, encouragement, and wise counsel. Among them I count Morris Beja, James Bracken, David Frantz, Nicholas Howe, Christopher Jones, Gregory Jusdanis, Valerie Lee, John Norman, James Phelan, Geoffrey Smith, Phoebe Spinrad, Harry Vredeveld, Luke Wilson, and Christian Zacher. Their extramural counterparts include David Daniell, Peter Happé, Arthur F. Kinney, Gordon Kipling, Charles Larkowski, Barbara Kiefer Lewalski, David Norbrook, Jennifer Summit, and Anne Lake Prescott. I thank Jerome Singerman, my gracious and scholarly editor at the University of Pennsylvania Press, and Jennifer Shenk, my inspired copyeditor, for furthering publication of this book. All remaining errors of fact, transcription, or interpretation are my own.

Completion of this project owes much to librarians and keepers at collections and archives that provided me with access to important holdings. They include the British Library, Bodleian Library, Department of Prints and Drawings at the British Museum, Folger Shakespeare Library, Henry E.

Huntington Library, Library of Congress, New York Bible Society Library, and The Ohio State University Libraries.

I gratefully acknowledge a Coca-Cola Grant for the Study of Women and Gender (administered by the Department of Women's Studies at The Ohio State University), which helped the project toward completion. For further support I am thankful to the College of Humanities, Department of English, and Center for Medieval and Renaissance Studies at The Ohio State University.

My greatest obligation is to Pauline and Jonathan, my wife and son, who have sustained this project for many years.